Wonderful to Relate

THE MIDDLE AGES SERIES

Ruth Mazo Karras, Series Editor
Edward Peters, Founding Editor

A complete list of books in the series
is available from the publisher.

Wonderful to Relate

Miracle Stories and Miracle Collecting
in High Medieval England

Rachel Koopmans

PENN

UNIVERSITY OF PENNSYLVANIA PRESS

PHILADELPHIA · OXFORD

Published by
University of Pennsylvania Press
Philadelphia, Pennsylvania 19104-4112

Printed in the United States of America on acid-free paper
10 9 8 7 6 5 4 3 2 1

Library of Congress Cataloging-in-Publication Data

Koopmans, Rachel.
    Wonderful to relate : miracle stories and miracle collecting in
high medieval England / Rachel Koopmans.
        p. cm. — (The Middle Ages series)
    Includes bibliographical references (p.   ) and index.
    ISBN 978-0-8122-4279-9 (hardcover : alk. paper)
    1. English literature—Middle English, 1100–1500—History
and criticism.   2. Literary form—History—To 1500.
3. Monastic and religious life—England—History   Middle
Ages, 600–1500.   4. Literature and society—England—
History—To 1500.   5. Christian saints—England—
Biography.   6. Miracles.   I. Title.
PR255.K66   2010
820.9—dc22   2010016970

To my parents, Sherwin and Karen Koopmans

CONTENTS

ILLUSTRATIONS

Whenever I read a medieval miracle collection, I am reminded of the appeal of looking at a collection of butterflies. Both kinds of collections are hard to resist, no matter how much one might disapprove, in theory, of killing butterflies, or of reveling in stories of miracles. The colors of the insects can be so startling, and their shapes so arresting, that it is easy to feel captured and chloroformed yourself, mesmerized by the variety of the display. There is a pleasure too in contemplating the ordering of the specimens: the straight rows, the squared and spread wings, the labels pasted under each one. The stories in medieval miracle collections line up like this as well. Caught in the nets of writers, spaced out and ordered, the stories neatly march along in chapter after chapter, some of them presenting such unexpected contours and coloring that you can feel your eyes widening in surprise.

The zeal of the writers who made such collections seems as wondrous today as the stories of miracles. Collections of saints' miracles fill the volumes of our editions of medieval sources in the same way butterfly collections of the early Victorian era clog the storerooms of our natural history museums. A few collections were highly formalized, the same stories reappearing in different guises again and again, but most collections of miracles contain no such plagiarism. Their narratives, often collected by a single enthusiastic writer, were derived not from other texts but from the swarm of stories in current oral circulation. Conversation about miracles sent writers to their desks when little else seemed worthy of written record. Some medieval collectors amassed hundreds of stories, creating textual giants that dwarfed even the longest of saints' lives.[1]

R. W. Southern considered the "writing of marvels," especially the English creation of the first versions of the "Miracles of the Virgin," to be one of the most significant achievements of the twelfth-century renaissance in England.[2] Other historians have noted in passing that twelfth-century writers in England and elsewhere made many miracle collections, but the extent of that production has not been quantified.[3] By my count, writers living in England between 1080 and 1220 compiled at least seventy-five collections of saints' posthumous miracles.[4] Anglo-Saxon writers were largely uninterested in miracle collecting. It was in the late eleventh century, some decades after the Norman Conquest, that a miracle-collecting mania began to spread. In the course of the twelfth century and into the early thirteenth century, writers collected the miracles of famous Anglo-Saxon saints such as Cuthbert, Edmund, Swithun, and Æthelthryth, of lesser-known Anglo-Saxons such as Oswine, Ithamar, Frideswide, and Wenefred, of new saints like William of Norwich, Thomas Becket, and Gilbert of Sempringham, and also of bits of foreign saints housed in England: the miracles of the finger of St. Germanus (at Selby), the altar of St. Bartholomew (in London), and the hand of St. James (at Reading) became the focus of collectors in this period. After this outpouring of texts concerning every manner of saint, the collecting mania evaporated almost as quickly as it had begun. By the mid-thirteenth century, miracle collecting had again become a sporadic and occasional pursuit.

In this book, I examine the miracle-collecting craze of high medieval England. I sketch out the parameters of the oral world from which the collectors drew their stories of divine intervention, chart the literary arc of miracle collecting from the late tenth to the early thirteenth century, and study the works of six influential collectors within this larger history. English miracle collections were written in the same monastic contexts and frequently by the same authors who produced the other Latin prose texts of the period. In terms of number of authors, miracle collecting was actually a more important and mainstream literary activity in England than the writing of chronicles.[5] The creation of miracle collections is usually thought to have been driven by the local pressures of cults and the immediate political needs of monastic communities.[6] Except in studies of pilgrims, disease, illness, and the like, it has been rare for miracle collections to be considered as a body.[7] But the stark rise and fall of miracle collecting in high medieval England demonstrates that we need to think in terms of broader patterns of production, to read individual collections within these broader patterns, to weigh the influence of specific authors, to formulate explanations for peaks and troughs in the popularity of miracle collecting, and to recognize the miracle collection for what it was: a defining genre and major literary phenomenon of the long twelfth century.

This book is set apart from other studies of medieval miracle collections in its attention to the creation and circulation of oral stories and in its construction of a detailed chronological account—in essence, a literary history—of English miracle collecting. A comprehensive survey of medieval miracle collecting would span the entire European continent and many centuries, and it remains to be seen how representative English miracle collecting might be.[8] When the whole story is told, it may well be that miracle collecting in England stands at the head of twelfth-century developments. During this period, English miracle collectors produced two texts of wide European influence: the "Miracles of the Virgin," a text that was hugely popular throughout the late medieval period, and Benedict of Peterborough's miracle collection for Thomas Becket, the most widely circulated shrine collection of the age. My account of the sweep of English miracle collecting in this book is intended to provide a basic framework for the study of these and other English miracle collections. My chief goal, however, is to demonstrate that miracle collections can tell us about more than saints, pilgrims, and local politics. They are also essential sources for our understanding of orality, literacy, and the much heightened concern for written record in the high medieval period; for genre formation, literary Latin, individual rhetorical ambitions, and transformations in learned monastic culture; and for a new and more intimate type of interaction between the religious and laity in the late twelfth century, interactions that foreshadowed major developments within medieval society.

In the course of the book, I isolate and discuss two main phases in the surge of popularity of miracle collecting in England, phases running roughly from c.1080–1140 and c.1140–1200. In the first phase, collectors tended to compose medium-sized texts, in the range of ten to thirty chapters, tell miracle stories with some pretensions at rhetorical prowess, and preserve stories that were being talked about in monastic circles. In many of the prologues of these texts, English miracle collectors mourn the loss of stories from the past and state their determination to save miracles known in their day in written record. The late eleventh and early twelfth centuries saw a pan-European movement to commit orally transmitted truths, customs, and stories to writing. English monks became markedly concerned with their past and with history-writing in this period, perhaps even more so than in other regions because of the great political rupture of the Norman Conquest. As the new thinking about written record worked its way through European culture, some English monks began to think the miracles of their saints ought to be written. It was an idea that spread from house to house, moving in much the same way that schemes for grand relic translation ceremonies and the rebuilding of churches and cathedrals spread through the small social world of English Benedictine monasticism in the late eleventh and early twelfth centuries.

In the second phase, roughly c.1140–1200, many of the same trends continue, and one can find collections that look much like their counterparts from the earlier period. But many collections began to take on a new form. Collectors now created longer texts, some of them running up past one hundred chapters; they wrote individual stories at less length and with fewer rhetorical frills; and, most strikingly, they drew many, sometimes most, of their stories from outside of their own conversational circles. They were seeking out the stories of lay strangers. Miracle stories concerning the laity had appeared in earlier collections, but they typically concerned the few dramatic healings witnessed by monks at the shrines of saints or stories told by close lay friends and relatives of monks. Now, though, collectors were listening to the stories of lay visitors to their relics and churches.

Giles Constable describes the last stage of the great monastic reforms of the twelfth century as "an intense concern with the nature of religious life and personal reform of all Christians," a stage he dates to 1130–60.[9] This is about the time that one starts to see miracle collectors focusing their attention on the stories of the laity. It is important to recognize what this involved: monks and canons listening patiently, for days, months, and sometimes years to stories about stomachaches, sexual misadventures, sick children, swollen legs, shipwrecks, and stolen coins, and then devoting resources of their scriptoria to committing these stories to parchment so that other religious men could hear and read these stories all over again. With this new attention to the stories of the laity also came new worries about truth, falsity, and the validity of the stories the monks were hearing. Many writers still took pride in the rhetorical flair they imparted to their collections, but the whole collecting enterprise became more taxing, more like a bureaucratic process than a warm conversation with friends. It could well be that the writers were willing to make the effort in part because they sought some sense of control—as well as record—of the stories being told outside of their religious communities. This is the same period in which the religious establishment began to think that the laity should make annual confession of their sins to a priest, an action that is strikingly similar to the telling of personal experiences of miracles. Moreover, this concerted effort to engage with the religious experiences of the laity came before canonization procedures were instituted, and almost certainly impacted their formation. One could imagine, for instance, the pope making the miracle stories of the religious the standard for canonization and excluding those of the laity, but this is not what happened.[10]

The close interface between the collectors' motivations and efforts and the oral telling of miracle stories unites these two phases of miracle collecting. The oral telling of miracle stories in this period is, of course, impossible to access directly, but it was likely an even more important historical phenomenon than the writing of the collections. The posthumous "fama" of saints was constituted by these oral stories, most of them, it appears, stories of personal and recent experience of a saint's actions. These narratives suggested ideas and behaviors that could lead to the perception of still more miracles. As new stories multiplied, they erased the old ones from conversations, and these in turn could be replaced by still more new creations: this, I believe, was the essential process driving the growth of cults. Since written records of the stories are all we have left, it is tempting to read the writing as making or sustaining cults, but a cult did not need a text, and a text could not make a cult. Cults were orchestras of voices that could not be conducted, swarms of stories that shrank and expanded according to their own internal and often mysterious rhythms. Monks in high medieval England turned to writing as a formaldehyde that could stabilize the oral stories they most liked in a secure and unchanging format. The procedure was a stiffening and deadening one, quite the opposite of a propagandistic effort; throughout the high medieval period, English writers were engaged in imprisoning and pinning down stories, not setting them free. In the same way that one must understand the butterflies in a natural history display to be only dead and inactive representatives of a much larger whole, so we must be careful not to read the miracle stories frozen in textual collections as having had more impact than they actually had.

Between the writing and the telling of miracle stories, the telling was the dominant and autonomous discourse, likely many magnitudes larger than what we now see preserved in the texts. How this telling may have been different in different eras and regions or for different saints is all but impossible to extricate from the surviving texts. But though we never will know particulars of this conversational world, it is not wholly unfathomable. The texts contain many references to the telling of miracle stories, and oral stories and their circulation have been the subject of many studies in contemporary contexts. In Chapter 1, I propose that most of these oral stories were of the type that researchers in the social sciences term "personal stories"—stories that people told about their own experiences—and discuss the volume, longevity, and emotional intensity of such stories. In Chapter 2, I consider the dynamics of this circulating body of stories in more depth, arguing that many of the repetitive similarities between stories in different collections were not the result of writers working to set models. Rather, these similarities were already a feature of the oral stories the collectors heard. Oral miracle stories had a tremendous capacity to spread, to replicate themselves, and to spring up around a new saint: understanding these dynamics helps make sense of the functioning of medieval cults and the secondary position of miracle collectors within those cults.

In Chapter 3, I start tracing the history of English miracle collecting. I begin in the late Saxon period, and examine its sole substantial miracle collection: Lantfred of Fleury's *Translation and Miracles of Swithun*, written in the 970s at Winchester. In Chapter 4, I study the early career and miracle collections written by a more famous foreign monk working in England, Goscelin of St.-Bertin, the only writer collecting miracle stories in England in the 1070s and 1080s. Both of these foreigners, I argue, thought more about their own careers and literary production in the making of these texts than local political concerns. But whereas Lantfred's work found few imitators, Goscelin's prolific and peripatetic labors helped spark off the new craze for miracle collecting in England. In Chapter 5, I examine the collection of the monk who appears to have been the first native English writer to imitate Goscelin: Osbern, a monk of Christ Church, Canterbury, who compiled a collection of the miracles of Dunstan in the early 1090s. In Chapter 6, I map out the Anglo-Norman collecting boom of the early decades of the twelfth century and focus on a writer whose prolific output is representative of the period: Eadmer of Canterbury, Osbern's younger colleague at Christ Church. In these chapters, I consider how oral stories of miracles may have been exchanged in the immediate aftermath of the Conquest. I argue that the work of convincing Normans of the validity and power of Anglo-Saxon saints had been completed before the burst of Anglo-Norman miracle collecting began. The collections of the period should be read within the context of the growing concern for preserving oral information in general and a fad for miracle collecting in particular. My close studies of the collections of Lantfred, Goscelin, Osbern, and Eadmer are designed to elucidate and flesh out the development of miracle collecting in this first phase of miracle collecting, to contrast the approaches of different collectors within the movement, and to demonstrate the advantages of reading miracle collections as a writer's dialogue with a much larger oral discourse.

I devote Chapter 7 to an appraisal and chronological analysis of the many miracle collections made in England between c.1140 and c.1200, the period in which collectors began to focus on stories told by the laity. I show that the new trends in miracle collecting were well underway before the murder of Thomas Becket in 1170, but that his cult and the circulation of Benedict of Peterborough's collection for Becket accelerated and solidified these trends among other English miracle collectors. In Chapters 8, 9, and 10, I focus on the story of miracle collecting for Becket at Christ Church. As Benedict was bringing his text to a conclusion, his colleague, William of Canterbury, was starting his own. William's collection would not see anything like the circulation of Benedict's, but it would be the longest compiled in medieval England. These two texts are the most impressive of all English miracle collections. In the three chapters dedicated to these texts, I situate them within their cultic and literary contexts and demonstrate how the personalities of Benedict and William shaped their strikingly different approaches to the stories they were hearing at Canterbury.

Collecting is comforting. As Susan Stewart has put it, collecting is an "objectification of desire."[11] The point and pleasure of collections is that they exist, that something has been saved and made visible, with luck, permanently, out of what would otherwise have vanished. By making miracle collections, English writers in the high medieval period could assuage their anxieties about the oral discourse and feel that they were saving it, improving on it, doing it good, in fact, even as it is obvious how self-promoting their efforts could be. But the more ambitious the writers were in their dreams of stabilization, the more defeating the oral world could become. Often, for example, the future, full of miracle stories of its own, forgot, ignored, or even lost the texts the writers had sent so lovingly from the past. Even what seem to be the simplest collecting goals, such as picking out the best stories and displaying them the best way, can reveal themselves to be impossible fantasies, pulling the collector into an endless round of joyless acquisition. And the more the collectors gathered in stories, the more the fissures and the problems within them—what do these stories *really* mean?—stood out.

In the conclusion to the book, I outline how miracle collecting fell in popularity among English writers in the thirteenth century. The telling of miracle stories appears to have continued full force in the thirteenth century and throughout the late medieval period. Chaucer's description of his pilgrims traveling to Canterbury to seek the saint "that hem hath holpen whan that they were seeke," is just one of the many indications that cults themselves did not change greatly in form from the high to the late medieval period. But however wonderful these new miracle stories might have been, few late medieval monks or canons were struck by a desire to relate them in writing. We are left with efforts of their high medieval brethren. Their collections have been praised and explored as "remarkably rich portrayals of English society in the twelfth century,"[12] but they testify most of all to a passion for collecting miracle stories that lasted well over a century, a passion that caught up both monks and miracle stories in ways not seen before or since.

CHAPTER ONE

Narrating the Saint's Works:
Conversations, Personal Stories,
and the Making of Cults

In the early 1170s, a judge in Bedford sentenced Eilward of Westoning to blinding and castration for petty thievery. Eilward, a pauper, was duly blinded—a jailor stabbed his eyes with a knife—and castrated. Some days later, however, after asking Thomas Becket for help, Eilward discovered that he could see again. Benedict of Peterborough, one of the two monks at Canterbury who recorded this story in a miracle collection, describes how people came to see Eilward in Bedford and hear his tale: "Word of this went out among the vicinity, and the new thing attracted no small multitude of people."[1] As Eilward traveled to Canterbury to give thanks at Becket's tomb, he told his story to crowds along the road, a scene later pictured in an early thirteenth-century glass panel in Canterbury Cathedral (Figure 1). The original inscription to this panel read, "The people stand by as he narrates the mighty works of the saint" (*ASTAT NARRANTI POPULUS MAGNALIA SANCTI*).[2] Eilward's story caused such a buzz and was picked up and retold so often that it beat him to Canterbury. The Christ Church monks, Benedict comments, had heard about Eilward's miracle from many others before he arrived.[3]

While the extent of the oral circulation of Eilward's story was clearly extraordinary, the references to conversation, speech, and oral storytelling in the written accounts of his miracle are not. Medieval miracle collections are full of such references: as John McNamara has pointed out, the analysis of hagiographic texts often "reveals surprising amounts of information about the tellings of these legends in their own contexts."[4] Simon Yarrow writes of

Figure 1. Eilward of Westoning tells his story. Canterbury Cathedral, Trinity Chapel Ambulatory Window n.III (16). Author's photograph used with the kind permission of the Dean and Chapter of Canterbury Cathedral.

how "miracle collections are packed with people in conversation," and he does not exaggerate.[5] For example, in a collection of the miracles of Modwenna, Geoffrey of Burton describes how Abbot Nigel brought a certain Godric, who had accidentally swallowed a pin-brooch and nearly died as a result, to Queen Matilda, "who loved to hear about the miracles of the saints. He showed the man to her and told the story of what had happened to him, also recounting many other occasions on which the virgin Modwenna had declared through miracles that she was in heaven with the Lord."[6] In his collection of the miracles of Edmund of Bury, Osbert of Clare recounts how a paralyzed man healed by Edmund told his story to Tolinus, the sacrist of Bury, who told Abbot Baldwin, who called all the monks together, along with some lay people, and had the healed man stand in the middle of them and retell his story.[7] An anonymous clerk of Beverley, whose collection of the miracles of John of Beverley is particularly rich with oral references, concludes a story about a deaf-mute by describing how "as a schoolboy I saw this elderly man . . . and I knew him very well . . . with the younger boys sitting or standing around, he used to tell how the Lord, through St. John, gave hearing and speech to him."[8] This same clerk recounts in another chapter how his parents "asked me if I knew the crippled girl who was accustomed to go begging from door to door. When I replied that I did not know her at all, they were amazed at this when she [and her miracle] were very well known by very many men and women."[9]

In this chapter and the next, I consider the dimensions and dynamics of what R. W. Southern dubbed the "chattering atmosphere" behind the texts of miracle collections.[10] Though questions about orality have engaged scholars of the medieval past for some time, little close attention has thus far been focused on the oral creation and circulation of miracle stories. As Catherine Cubitt has noted, "historians have tended to focus upon questions of orality and literacy in governmental administration and legal dealings, while amongst literary scholars, the most pressing questions have concerned the composition of Old English poetry and the nature of heroic verse."[11] Most studies of oral storytelling in a hagiographic context, including Cubitt's own, are focused on stories with folkloric motifs: a holy man throwing a key in a river only to recover it later in the stomach of a fish, for instance, or a wolf guarding the decapitated head of a holy king, rather than a story like that of Eilward of Westoning's healing.[12] Brian Patrick McGuire, who has examined the "oral sources" of Caesarius of Heisterbach's *Dialogus Miraculorum*, a mammoth early thirteenth-century miracle collection, is one of the few to attempt to say something specific about the speakers behind collections of posthumous miracles. McGuire catalogues the different types of people who told Caesarius miracle stories, finding that he heard stories from Cistercian monks from his own house, Cistercian monks from other houses, abbots, Benedictine monks, laybrothers, secular canons, priests, nuns, and the laity.[13] McGuire demonstrates in the course of this study, moreover, that Caesarius derived 95 percent of his stories from oral sources, as opposed to just 5 percent from written sources.[14] The two massive Christ Church collections for Thomas Becket, the closest comparative example to the *Dialogus* among the collections produced in high medieval England, show very similar proportions of oral vs. written sources, about 94 to 6 percent.[15] Most shorter collections show no evidence of the use of written sources whatsoever. The stories in the collections of Geoffrey of Burton, Osbert of Clare, and the anonymous clerk at Beverley mentioned above appear to have been derived 100 percent from oral sources.[16]

It is, of course, impossible to extract the original oral stories from the written collections, but this should not deter us from exploring and taking account of the many references to speech and conversation in the texts. Research concerning "conversational stories" and "conversational analysis" has burgeoned in recent years in sociology, linguistics, and other disciplines in the social sciences and humanities. This work provides a very valuable resource for historians interested in texts like miracle collections, and I draw on it frequently in this chapter and the next.[17] In the first part of this chapter, I suggest that the principal oral narrative form behind posthumous miracle collections was what researchers term the "personal story." This identification is important because it can help us block out basic answers to questions such as how many stories might have been available to collectors, who would have created and told such stories, and how long such stories likely remained in oral circulation. In the second part of the chapter, I take something of a social scientist approach myself, and focus my attention on one particularly illuminating story—the miracle of a knight of Thanet as retold by Osbern of Canterbury in a collection composed in the early 1090s. I use this narrative as a means to draw out the essential dynamics of personal miracle stories and to consider what kinds of things were likely lost in Osbern's textual rendering of his conversation with the knight. Though most particulars about the oral creation and exchange of the stories preserved in medieval miracle collections are forever beyond our grasp, it is vital to keep in mind the original complexity and emotional force of these stories—otherwise, we can never come to grips with what it meant to be a medieval miracle collector. At the close of the chapter, I argue that these conversational narratives were the lifeblood of cults.

The Volume, Tellers, and Longevity of Personal Miracle Stories

When reflecting on the oral exchange of miracle stories, medievalists tend to think first in terms of "oral tradition," that is, stories that were passed down and most akin to folktales. These are the kinds of miracle stories that fill saints' *vitae*—the story of otters drying a saint's feet with their fur, for example, or a saint hanging up his cloak on a sunbeam—and one can find examples of them in posthumous miracle collections as well. Collectors describing a history of a long-lasting cult would sometimes draw on legendary stories of vengeance or marvels. For instance, at the close of his life of the murdered Archbishop Ælfheah (d.1012), Osbern of Canterbury describes how a wooden oar, dipped in the dead archbishop's blood, sprouted and blossomed the next day.[18] A similar "flowering staff" motif can be found in other hagiographic texts.[19] To take another example, an anonymous early twelfth-century collector of the miracles of Swithun described how an elderly woman was dragged from her bed by a wolf. When she invoked Swithun's name, she was able to flee and outrun an entire pack of wolves.[20] On occasion, one can find such folkloric stories in the collections of miracles of saints recently dead. William of Canterbury tells a story about a pet starling caught in the talons of a hawk in his collection for Thomas Becket. When the starling squawked the name of the martyr, the hawk fell dead and released the starling unharmed.[21]

The vast majority of stories found in high medieval miracle collections, however, have quite a different ring. William of Canterbury made up his collection almost wholly from stories like that of Eilward of Westoning—stories that living people told about their own experiences. The miracles of the man who swallowed the pin-brooch, the paralyzed man healed by Edmund, the deaf-mute and the crippled girl healed by John of Beverley—these were all stories about the self. The anonymous collector of Swithun's miracles mainly focused on such stories too. He describes, for instance, how a priest's servant was extremely ill and in intense pain until he was brought to Swithun's shrine, where he recovered after thrashing about on the floor and having a terrible nosebleed, and how a deaf boy supported by the monks, so silent that he "possessed the habits and nature of a fish," recovered his hearing and began to speak.[22] In his study of the twelfth-century miracle collection of Our Lady of Rocamadour, Marcus Bull has suggested that "we should treat the majority of miracle stories as the end-product of genuine attempts to formulate explanations of real experiences."[23] Even very brief chapters from the collections, such as the following from Benedict of Peterborough's collection for Becket, appear to echo a story of personal experience: "In the same abbey another person was extremely swollen up. To say it shortly, after he drank the martyr's water his stomach returned to its former size."[24] As bare as it is, this account almost certainly originated in someone's telling of an experience of illness, of drinking, and of recovery of health—a story that likely meant a good deal to the teller.

Paging through miracle collections, one finds stories of personal illness and recovery, peril and rescue, oaths forgotten and remembered, injuries and punishments, and so on and on—there are thousands of such stories in the English miracle collections alone. Researchers in folklore studies and the social sciences term these stories "personal experience narratives," "conversational narratives," "memorates," or, simply, "personal stories."[25] As these researchers have shown, the borders between "memorates" and "fabulates" are porous. A personal experience narrative might evolve into a folktale-like story over time (might something like that have happened with the old woman and the wolf?), while a folktale-like story might inspire new miracle stories of personal experience (the starling story could encourage people in a dangerous situation to invoke Becket).[26] Yet most medieval miracle stories can be easily placed within one camp or the other, and it is crucial not to blur the distinctions between the two too much. Folktale-like stories tend to act in certain ways, conforming around certain structures and following certain dynamics of oral production and exchange; personal stories tend to act in quite different ways.

Most medieval miracle collectors were interested in hearing and preserving personal stories. As we read their texts, we need to orient our thinking to the dynamics and characteristics of such narratives. When miracle collectors exclaim at the sheer volume of stories available to them and complain that they can not possibly tell them all, for instance, we should believe them. To take just a few examples of such complaints, at the close of his account of a man recovered from a fever, the anonymous collector of the miracles of the Hand of St. James at Reading writes, "in a similar way and by a similar remedy another knight named Ralph Gilbuin was cured of a similar disease, as also were so many others, both men and women, that I cannot cover them all in this account."[27] A collector of the miracles of St. Bartholomew in London similarly despaired at the prospect of telling all the stories of the "men of the seaports": "very many of them are wont to visit his holy church every year with lamps and peace offerings of oblations and to tell joyfully of his many miracles worked among them."[28] The anonymous Beverley collector noted, "the passage of time would detain me for a very long time if I wished to write down every single release of prisoners through the merits of St. John."[29]

Such statements about the volume of miracle stories are so prevalent, particularly in prologues of miracle collections, that they are usually taken as a rhetorical device and pious propaganda.[30] But the oral form at issue here is the personal story, "the most common form of narrative the world over," in the words of Elinor Ochs and Lisa Capps.[31] Charles Keil has commented that "even if we calculate just one personal experience narrative per person, the planet's proven narrative reserves are staggering, and the folklore empire will never suffer a scarcity of resources."[32] It is quite believable that the collectors at Reading, London, and Beverley heard far too many stories about recoveries from fevers, peril at sea, and released prisoners to try to tell them all. A good comparative example is the experience of a sociologist interested in oral stories told about saints, Candace Slater, who did field research in Brazil and Spain in the 1980s. To keep her projects "manageable," Slater decided to eliminate all narratives based on personal experience from her source base, despite the fact that these were by far the easiest stories for her to elicit. In defense of this decision, Slater notes that in fifteen years 47,079 accounts of personal miracle stories were reported to those in charge of the canonization procedure of one of her saints.[33]

Folkloric stories are collective, communal creations. Personal stories are different. Individuals make them about themselves, all the time—it takes no special storytelling skill to make them, nor any special permission or expertise to claim that an experience is the result of divine intervention. Oral stories do not lend themselves to quantification, but there seems little question that there would have been many more personal miracle stories than folkloric miracle stories in circulation at any given time. Some cults would have been bigger than others, of course, but when collectors say in their prologues that there were many stories they were not recounting, most of them were likely telling the plain truth. The fact that compilers of miracle collections so rarely plagiarized from others is particularly suggestive. In her study of dozens of collections from France, Patricia Morison remarks, "of many hundreds of individual miracle-stories there is hardly a single duplication."[34] The same can be said about English miracle collections. Finding material, even for the laziest collectors, never seems to have been a problem.[35]

We need, then, to think in terms of large quantities. We also need to think of these stories as being exchanged in the same social circles where personal stories usually circulated. That is, *every* social circle, including the highest. In his study of Caesarius of Heisterbach's *Dialogus Miraculorum*, Brian Patrick McGuire writes that the General Chapter of the Cistercian order should be seen as "a great yearly exchange center for stories . . . it seems to have been a general practice for the assembled abbots to share with each other edifying stories concerning monks in their own houses."[36] A text that provides a particularly interesting glimpse into this high-level circulation is the *Dicta Anselmi et Quaedam Miracula*, a text written by the Christ Church monk Alexander of Canterbury between about 1109 and 1116.[37] In the *Dicta* section of the text, Alexander recounts some of the formal discourses he heard Anselm give. In the second section, *Quaedam Miracula*, Alexander retells miracle stories, most of which appear to derive from the time Anselm was exiled from Canterbury. Baldwin, a monk who accompanied Anselm into exile, tells a story about his illness and healing by St. Peter the apostle; Hugh, the abbot of Cluny who hosted Anselm and his exiled companions for a time, tells a story about St. James; Anselm himself tells a miracle story that he had heard as a boy about a judge in Rome; Tytso, a monk in the cell of Blangy in Normandy where Anselm stayed for a time, tells about a child living in the area who was afflicted with a demon; the archbishop of Lyon, another of Anselm's hosts, tells a story about a clerk in his church named Ademar, and so on.[38]

As the editors of Alexander's text point out, "the only connection that most of the thirty-two stories have with Anselm arises from the fact that the author heard them in Anselm's company."[39] Alexander's collection paints a picture of archbishops, abbots, and monks gathering together not just to hear Anselm's formal discourses but also to hear stories from each other's stock of personal miracles, to exchange news of what the divine had done in that region or in their past experience. The stories Alexander recounts were probably told over a space of some years, but the movement in Alexander's collection from story to unrelated story and speaker to speaker is probably quite a good portrait of the mishmash of subjects and voices in most conversations about miracles.

Interest in divine activity could and clearly often did form common ground across customary boundaries of social class, age, gender, and religious status, as one sees with the story of Godric, the pin-brooch swallower, standing before Queen Matilda. Catherine Cubitt writes that "oral stories of saintly exploits must have circulated within the intersections between lay and religious, in monastic ambits created not only by pastoral ministry but also by the ties of property ownership and tenurial relations."[40] Innumerable second-hand, many third- or even fourth-hand retellings of personal stories are visible in English miracle collections. Priests retell the stories of their parishioners, abbots of their monks, parents of their children, husbands of their wives, mistresses of their servants, innkeepers of their customers, neighbors of their neighbors, and many other permutations.[41] Benedict of Peterborough relates a story about a Becket miracle that he heard from a priest who heard it from a mother who heard it from her children, and also a story he heard from a "truthful man" who heard it from a certain Gilbert who heard it from a blind man.[42] One of the longest daisy chains visible in the English collections concerns a woman who worked as the governess of the children of the knight Herbert de Fourches. This woman, whose name is not recorded, had a vision of Æthelthryth in a church in the west country. Prior Osbert of Daventry heard about the vision from the woman's companions. He retold the story of the vision to Osbert of Clare. Osbert of Clare wrote a letter about the vision and sent it to the monks of Ely. At Ely, the compiler of the *Liber Eliensis* preserved Osbert's letter along with many other accounts of Æthelthryth's miracles: this compiler was at least three stages removed from the woman's oral description of her vision.[43]

Some stories were particularly volatile, reaching dozens or even hundreds of listeners besides the collectors. Eilward of Westoning's miracle is an example of a story that moved very rapidly, like an exploding firework, into many conversational circles. In addition to the crowds of ordinary people who came to hear his story, we know that the burgesses of Bedford, the bishop of Durham, and the monks of Christ Church—and likely many others of their religious status and social rank—came to know the story of this pauper.[44] We must envision many more listeners and retellings of stories than are spelled out in the miracle collections, in which stories are usually only moving toward the collectors themselves. If we could map it, the conversational web along which stories about Thomas Becket moved between Bedford and Canterbury, Canterbury and southern England, and England and the wider medieval world on the day Eilward arrived in Canterbury would probably look something similar to the lines of a telephone network. This map would be more bewildering in its complexity the closer we came to the reality of the conversational exchange of miracle stories in this period. Stories about Becket would not be the only ones moving through this network, and all the conversational lines connecting people would be in a constant state of flux.

The stories themselves would also be in a state of flux and constant turnover. In comparison to folkloric miracle stories, the elephants of the oral world—slow-moving, long-lasting, not very numerous—personal miracle stories were more like butterflies. They were everywhere; they fluttered and darted in and out of innumerable conversations; but they were also short-lived. An individual might tell some personal stories again and again throughout his or her life, but most are recounted a few times, or even just once.

Some personal stories may be retold after a person's death, but not as much, and not for long. Once those who knew the creator of the story are dead themselves, the few surviving stories usually die out too. In her study of the stories about Padre Cícero told in Brazil, Candace Slater notes that first person narratives "seldom find their way into a larger communal repertoire."[45]

Novelty accounted for a large part of the appeal and rapid dispersal of the personal miracle story. Fresh new stories crowded out the old and then were crowded out in turn. When one looks at which miracle stories from Becket's early cult were remembered and retold in later generations, one does not find Eilward of Westoning's story, or any of the other personal stories recounted by the first collectors. They were forgotten. Strikingly, though, there was one story that was remembered: the story of the starling and the hawk. This tale, so different from the others William of Canterbury recorded, is found again in Caesarius's *Dialogus*, in Jacobus de Voragine's *Golden Legend*, and in other texts.[46] It was a durable story—charmingly memorable—in a way that the personal stories were not.

Miracle collectors were well aware that stories had been lost, and that more stories would be lost if they did not write: preservation was, as I will discuss in the chapters below, the chief motivation for high medieval miracle collectors. In the next section, I will take a closer look at one personal story that a miracle collector decided ought to be written down and saved for future generations.

The Knight of Thanet's Miracle Story

Medieval miracle collectors usually retold personal stories in their collections in an omniscient third person voice, the most compact means of relaying a story. Occasionally, though, a collector tried a different rhetorical tack. One of the more interesting and suggestive of these rhetorical experiments is found in Osbern of Canterbury's collection of the miracles of Dunstan (written c. 1090).[47] Toward the end of this collection, Osbern recounted a story in the form of a conversational dialogue between himself and the man claiming to have experienced a miracle, a knight of Thanet. Perhaps the setting of the conversation stuck in Osbern's head—the knight and Osbern were walking together on a beach when the knight told him his story. Whatever the reason for the special treatment, Osbern's account of the knight's story provides a convenient springboard for a discussion of the complexities of the personal miracle story. Osbern did not have the benefit of the quotation mark (it had not yet been invented), but I will use it here for clarity. The chapter starts in Osbern's own voice:

When I was on the isle of Thanet, I went walking along the seashore with a knight who had asked me there for his edification. We considered those things that were marvels of God there and drew from them material for good conversation. From there the conversation turned to father Dunstan, as every time I find occasion for speaking about him I always obtain the greatest benefit. Recalling that name, the knight paled, and breathing deeply as if in pain he said, "Oh, how ungrateful I am, I who am forgetful of his great kindnesses."

"What is it that makes you breathe so heavily?" I said.

"Do you know," he said, "how much the abbot of St. Augustine's plagued me while he lived, as he wished to strip my inheritance from me?"

"I know."

"And do you know that not only was he unable to do anything intemperate, but that it all turned out for my greater glory?"

"Nor is this unknown," I said, "but I don't know why you are recounting these things."

"Know then," said the knight, "that the night before the day set for the suit between him and me, I recalled how when I was in my house (which is nearby), you frequently used to extol father Dunstan by your accounts. Now, I said to myself, I have the chance to know by experience what I have heard, such that he might be praised. Kneeling in prayer, I said, 'God of father Dunstan, favor my part today.' Then giving my body to rest, I saw in my dreams the city of Canterbury, the basilica of the Savior, and the memorial of the father, as if I were resting upon it. I saw a man standing next to it, of decorous form and beautiful garments, holding a lamp of light in his hand. Terrified by his image, I said 'Who are you, most glorious man?' He said, "I am the one to whom you prayed for help a short time ago.' 'Incredible!' I said, 'how quick you are to comfort the suffering! Do you know what the lord threatens?' He said, 'Do not fear any of his threats, or weigh them as of any consequence.'"

So the knight spoke. Afterward he turned to me again and said, "you already know the rest, how you and I consulted together, fought, and triumphed."

"On that day," I said, "the saint gave a grand sign: while there were many there with polished wit, they left conquered by those few with less polish." Then, seeing those who were present, I presented to them in words what I now produce in letters.[48]

The ubiquity and familiarity of personal stories can make them seem rather simple. The recitation of *Beowulf* by bards, the singing of ballads in the streets of medieval Paris, the *fama* or oral reputation that mattered so much in medieval law courts, the stories of sprouting oars and flowering staffs—this all feels exotic and complex, and has received substantial study from scholars.[49] In contrast, personal stories can seem so straightforward, so reflective of experience itself, that it can appear there is nothing that particularly needs analysis. Scholars have usually assumed that the oral stories miracle collectors heard reflected reality quite closely, and that what needs attention is how collectors would have twisted and shaped these accounts to their own ends. But researchers in the social sciences have found that personal narratives are quite complex constructions—that they are more difficult to analyze, in many respects, than folktales.[50] These researchers particularly stress the danger of failing to distinguish between a person's lived experience and an oral story of that experience. Rom Harré comments, for instance, that "the telling of tales is more readily researchable than the living of lives."[51]

Three contexts are essential for decoding the meaning of a personal story: the creator's own personality and sense of himself or herself; the circumstances in which the story is articulated—place, audience, timing, and so on; and the oral and physical dimensions of the story's telling.[52] This is the kind of data we gauge automatically, often unthinkingly, when we hear and evaluate personal stories from people we know well. But without it, personal stories become extremely hard to dissect, harder, in fact, than stories—like that of the blossoming oar—with less personal content.[53] Even with the richness of Osbern's retelling of the knight of Thanet's story, it is difficult to probe far into its meaning. We might be able to find out more about the abbot of St. Augustine's, or inheritance law, or the number of knights on the isle of Thanet, or the position of Dunstan's tomb in the cathedral, but this information is peripheral to the meaning of the knight's story. The essential problem with analyzing a narrative like the knight of Thanet's story at this distance is that we know so little about him. Osbern must have had a sense of what the knight's inheritance entailed. How much did he need it? Did he have any previous dealings, good or bad, with the abbot of St. Augustine's? Were other members of the family disputing the inheritance? A personal story is best grasped by someone who has known the teller for years, someone who can place a personal story in the context of others. Did the knight normally tell stories about his anxieties or his dreams? Had he told a story about a miracle before, or was this his first one? In the knight's personal history, would this story rank its own chapter, or just a footnote? What did the knight's wife, if he had one, think about all this?

One could multiply these questions, and ask them about any of the personal stories preserved in miracle collections. To catch the full resonance of the knight's story, we would need to know more than this, however—we would also need to know more about the knight's relationship with Osbern. The knight and Osbern appear to have been alone as the knight told his story. The two were well acquainted with each other. Not only had they had conversations before this particular walk on the beach, but Osbern had been personally involved in the knight's lawsuit with the abbot of St. Augustine's. It also appears that Osbern took the lead in this friendship. He came to talk with the knight at his special request and looks to have been directing the conversation where he wanted it to go. These kinds of things make an enormous difference in how a personal story is told, how it is received, and the meaning it conveys. So much eludes us, though. Did Osbern go to Thanet solely to meet with the knight, or did he have other business there? How did these two come to know each other? Who was the older? Trading personal stories is one of the chief ways people forge bonds with each other: as Sandra Dolby Stahl has commented, "the exchange of personal narratives [is] an emotionally satisfying experience for both the teller and audience. . . . This intimacy is more marked in the exchange of personal narratives than in other kinds of storytelling."[54] By telling Osbern his story, the knight exposed his anxieties, his dreams, his interpretations, and ultimately himself. Did the friendship between Osbern and the knight change after this story was told?

The specifics of how this all played out are beyond our reach. The complexities of oral performance present yet more difficulties. Personal stories are constructed through the voice, facial expressions, and body language of the teller as much as in the sense of the words. This is the case with the oral delivery of any kind of story, of course, but the stakes are heightened considerably with the personal narrative, stories of the self told by the self. Osbern gives us a few clues, writing that the knight "paled" and "breathed heavily" at the beginning of his story. But did the knight remain pale, or did he perk up? Did he speed up in certain places, slow down in others, speak more loudly, more softly? Did he pause, backtrack, misspeak? Personal stories root themselves in the self in ways even the teller might not grasp. We effortlessly absorb and process these nonverbal cues when we listen and see other people telling their stories, cues that may well contradict the meaning of the words being spoken. Though it is almost all gone now for the stories in miracle collections, we must try to imagine those flesh and blood speakers, to think of the expressions shifting across faces, eyes making contact or looking to the side, shrugging shoulders, sighs, gestures, hesitations—and how all of this invigorated and shaped the meaning of personal stories as they were being told.

To gain a full picture of the telling of these stories, we also have to account for the reaction of listeners. The relationship between teller and audience in the telling of a personal story is a particularly active one. An encouraging question, a comment, a grimace, or a glance away—all these can invigorate, redirect, or halt the telling of a personal story. Personal stories exist in the moment, rarely if ever told the same way twice. Tellers adjust them, sometimes radically, depending on who is listening and how they respond. Osbern gives us a taste of the kind of conversational give and take that most personal stories involve, but again there is so much that we don't know. Was Osbern rapt during the whole of the knight's story? How might the knight of Thanet have told his story later or to another companion? Since the meaning of personal stories is so deeply embedded in personalities, relationships, and oral performance, even the most carefully composed texts will fail to convey their complexity.[55] Osbern's textual rendering inevitably deadens and radically simplifies the knight's story. Still, the power of the personal story is such that even in this severely muted form the reader can feel its pull. Reading this story invites a sense of intimacy with the knight beyond what one would feel, for instance, from reading a charter issued by him.

It also invites a sense of intimacy with the saint at the center of the story. A triumph over an enemy is a common narrative trajectory for a personal story. What makes the knight's victory in his lawsuit a miracle story is the credit he gives to Dunstan for his success. The knight could have claimed that it was Osbern's help, or his own skill or luck, that achieved that result. Instead, he links his prayer, his dream, and his success together: Dunstan won the case for him. Dunstan, though dead, becomes the actor at the center of the story, as real a persona as the knight himself. Today, miracles tend to be envisioned in theoretical and nonfigurative terms: a miracle is a breaking of the laws of nature. Most stories in miracle collections have a much more particularized flavor. Dunstan was here. Dunstan helped me. That's why I won my lawsuit, why I felt better after being sick, why my daughter was saved after falling into the river. Saints might not always be seen or sensed, but they live out posthumous lives in which they continue to care about the people on earth. Rather than reading the knight's story expecting a law-breaking event, we should instead read it as a narrative, a story created by the knight to describe how his life and the posthumous life of Dunstan became intertwined.[56] It remains very much a personal story. In fact, if anything it is a double personal story, about the knight's *and* Dunstan's personal histories. The knight's story tells about them both; it packs a double punch. We can term the result a personal miracle story.[57]

Personal stories define and empower a teller's sense of identity; personal miracle stories do so as well, indeed even more so. At first, this may seem counterintuitive: the knight certainly now cannot claim the glory of triumph-ing over the abbot of St. Augustine's. But this story claims something even better: Dunstan acted for me. This saint, living in heaven, was willing to help *me*, to enter into *my* concerns, to respond to *my* prayer with amazing speed and efficacy. Miracle collectors used exceptionally emotive and powerful lan-guage to describe their subject matter. Strikes of lightning were a favorite analogy: saints were said to "flash," "gleam," or "shine out" in miracles after their death.[58] Somewhat similar effects are evident in modern personal stories recounting the visit of a celebrity—the touch of Princess Diana or an encoun-ter with Michael Jackson. The famed presence enlarges rather than diminishes the creator of the story in the striking blend of abject self-importance that such stories convey.

We cannot know now, of course, what the knight's story about Dun-stan's aid might have done for his self-image, or how many more times he told it or to whom. There was a reason besides his own self-image that the knight might well have decided to tell his story more than once. He pales and groans at the beginning with good reason. Dunstan would act, but he was not going to speak for himself. In this way, he was like any dead friend. If the knight did not tell the story, Dunstan's actions would not be known by others. The knight has to tell the story for the silent Dunstan as much as for himself. Osbern had probably heard stories, perhaps many stories, of the knight's personal experience before this walk on the beach. Listening to this particular story, Osbern gets a double benefit: he finds out not just about the knight's recent actions, but about Dunstan's too. Osbern knew the stories from Dunstan's lifetime long ago better than most. What the knight's story offered was a sense of Dunstan's current life, a glimpse of what Dunstan was doing and how he was acting in Osbern's own present. Precious, thrilling, joyous information, that, even if it was not always easy to interpret. Did Dunstan's speed in answering the knight's prayer have something to do with the way the knight worded his request? Did Dunstan's physical appearance in the dream—a handsome man holding a lamp—have deeper significance? Did Dunstan hold a grudge against the abbot of St. Augustine's?

Such uncertainties, typical of personal miracle stories, did not usually blunt listeners' desire for these stories. Unlike the well-worn miracles of a saint's life, these personal miracles were fresh and new, and their exchange offered an even greater emotional zing than did most personal stories. Knowing more about Dunstan, Osbern can feel more personally attached to him. In the discussion of a mutually beloved divine self, the knight and Osbern can delight in each other's company even more. Not only that, but the knight's story suggested possibilities in case Osbern were ever in need of divine aid himself. Personal miracle stories were full of clues for how to get a saint on one's side. Indeed, a miracle story like the knight's, though less sensational than a story of sunbeams acting as clotheslines or oars sprouting and flowering, had much more immediate relevance to those listeners hoping for divine help with their own personal problems.

Osbern found the knight's story so stirring that he immediately retold it himself to new listeners, "those who were present." Personal stories tend to be retold only among people who have an interest in the creator. Outside of the creator's familiar circle, interest in his or her stories usually drops dramatically. The difference with the personal miracle story is that there is a second, much wider circle in which the story can circulate: all those who desire news of the saint. Such mobility exacted a cost. When Osbern retold the knight's story, it lived in Osbern's face and gestures, in Osbern's breath and voice. Osbern chose when and where and to whom and at what length he wanted to tell the story. He decided how to introduce and conclude the story, how to mediate every aspect of it. The question is not whether the outlines of the knight's original story were blurred and deformed, but to what degree. The further a story traveled, the more these effects were compounded. Moreover, if "those present" on the beach did not know the knight, much of the resonance of the story would be lost. The personal miracle story would have been most potent and affecting when told by its creator to close friends, people who could fully appreciate both the personal and the divine ramifications of the story.

The personal miracle story, then, was generally more intense, more desirable, more mobile, and more long-lived than the ordinary personal story, but in its essential characteristics it remained a personal story. Though these stories interested people outside of personal circles and could travel through multiple tellers, they originated in stories people told about themselves. When reading miracle collections, we must keep those individuals before us. They were all as real as the knight of Thanet, and their stories all had a multiplicity of personal resonances and meanings that we will never recover.

Conversations and the Making of Cults

Medieval cults tend to be thought of in terms of their visible manifestations and remains: the relics, the churches, the rituals, the tombs, the pilgrims' badges, the stained glass, and the texts, the texts most especially.[59] Since texts tell us so much about the cults and largely define our own thinking about them, it is easy to slip into thinking that they define cults themselves. But what actually makes a medieval cult? What was its animating essence? In the high medieval period, we should not look to texts in languages most could not read in a scattering of handwritten manuscripts most did not own. We should not even look to liturgies, pilgrimages, or rituals, as these could be carried out when the saints themselves seemed dead and inactive. I believe that what most defined cult, what made people, literate and illiterate alike, think of a cult as living and active, were personal stories of a saint's intervention. These stories were the warm, pulsing evidence that a saint lived now, acted now, and was worthy of past and future veneration. The creation and circulation of these stories required no money, no pen or parchment, no building, not even the presence of a physical relic, but simply a person seeing a saint's actions in his or her own life and telling other people about it.

Cult is the knight of Thanet, Osbern, and "those present" talking on a beach about Dunstan's recent actions. Cult is Eilward of Westoning telling his story about Becket's healing powers to the crowds in Bedford and along the road to Canterbury. Cult is not, at least not so essentially, Osbern or Benedict writing accounts of these stories later in their cloister. What happened on the beach, what happened along that road, and what happened in far more conversations than these collectors could hear or hope to recount, were the important things. Compared to the tangible texts, these innumerable lost conversations can seem wispy, even untrustworthy, something we might term mere "rumor." But we should not be blinded to what the oral creation and circulation of personal miracle stories possessed: the easy, all but effortless ability to spread word, to leapfrog social barriers, to create a sense of warm camaraderie, and to energize the veneration of saints. When he created his story about Dunstan, the knight joined or strengthened his association with the larger group of people who saw Dunstan as a saint. Osbern, listening, added another story to his personal store and refreshed his own sense of belonging. Retelling the knight's story to "those present," Osbern may have created a sense of cultic association or interest in a group of people who had never heard of Dunstan before. Scholars have argued for the important role of the miracle as a social bond in the medieval period, but it was actually the telling of stories, and not miracles per se, that acted as the bonding device.[60] People felt part of the familiar circle of a saint in the way one feels part of anyone's familiar circle, by sharing, knowing, and especially creating stories about them. Becket became England's most famous saint through the exchange of stories: these conversations were the generators of cultic communities, groups of people feeling a strong attachment to a saint and believing in his or her power in the world.

Julia Smith has written that "oral traditions of posthumous miracles were more important than written accounts in sustaining a cult."[61] I would go further and say that written accounts were in fact not needed at all. Cults did not need texts or their writers to form, to function, or to be terrifyingly strong. Moreover, a miracle collection, no matter how long or carefully wrought, was itself no guarantee that a cult would grow or continue. Medieval miracle collections need to be viewed as secondary manifestations of the animating discourse: they fed off the oral world far more than they ever added to it.

The medieval cult of saints is often presented as being generated, led, and controlled by the religious aristocrats of the society. Bishops and abbots are envisioned as making cults at tombs for their own self-promotion and interest, with pilgrims responding to the call, experiencing miracles, and depositing their coins.[62] But while the religious elite could tell miracle stories and hope to create their own stories of divine intervention—as Osbern did—their exalted status availed them little in the midst of the ever-shifting body of voices and stories that made up a living cult. Working in an age before print and significant levels of literacy, much less television or other powerful communicative tools, the religious elite had extremely limited means of directing the spread of these stories or how they were told. Nor could they generate cults at will. Miracle collections often represent attempts to radically simplify the discourse, to make it sound as though a "we," the religious, have a "them," ordinary people, in harness, but while miracle collectors found these sorts of representations satisfying we must not mistake them for the whole reality. The powers inherent in moving miracle stories, some of the most forceful narratives people make, were multidimensional and directional. Moreover, much as we might envision medieval people making up miracles for themselves out of the contingency of their experience, those experiences were still as unpredictable as ours, with no way for them to presage what the divine would or would not do, no matter what they hoped or desired.

Before turning in earnest to the collectors who decided to take some of these oral stories and turn them into texts, in the next chapter I will examine another fundamental feature of this oral world: the ways in which personal miracle stories could be and often were patterned after each other. It would seem that the presence and knowledge of other people's stories would have little effect on anyone's own creation. Certainly, all these oral creations were unique: the knight of Thanet's story, as we have seen, was very much his own. Nevertheless, the production of personal miracle stories was not completely free-form. Those other stories mattered. The flow of conversation had direction, moving in certain channels and not others, constraining individual voices even as it was made up and directed by them.

To Experience What I Have Heard: Plotlines and Patterning of Oral Miracle Stories

Readers have long been struck by the similarities of stories preserved in miracle collections. The late Victorian editors of the miracle collection of William of Norwich, for instance, commented that "even in their nauseous details [William's miracles] all have a strong family likeness to one another."[1] Scholars today use less florid language but often make the same observation, describing medieval miracle collections as "extraordinarily repetitive," "stereotyped," "highly conventionalized," and "schematized and topoi-ridden."[2] The types or clusters of certain kinds of stories in miracle collections have especially attracted attention. It is a rare collection that does not include a story about a blind person gaining sight or a paralyzed person regaining movement. Nor can one read many collections without running across stories about liberated prisoners, sailors spared from shipwreck, lepers being healed, evil people being punished, and so on.[3]

Medievalists have formulated an explanation for this clustering, an explanation that itself seems to be repeated and rehearsed in analysis after analysis. The idea is that early Christian and early medieval miracle collections were normative for the genre. These early texts set up the *topoi* or types of stories that later collectors would work to include and imitate in their own creations. Hedwig Röckelien argues, for instance, that the miracle narratives in Augustine's *City of God* "already contain the most important of the motifs and types that are to be found in the later miracle stories in stereotypical repetition."[4] Marcus Bull speaks of an "unofficial but widely recognized typological 'canon'" that "governed the selection and presentation of mainstream miracles." He notes that "in addition to biblical precedents, early writers such as St. Augustine, Sulpicius Severus, Pope Gregory the Great, Gregory of Tours and Bede had cumulatively created a body of language and imagery that was highly influential."[5] The writing of miracle collections is often described as a kind of clash, with the accounts of pilgrims colliding with and being transformed by the typological preoccupations and didactic goals of the writers. Thomas Head speaks of two movements in the writing process: "from the folkloric culture of the layman to the clerical culture of the monk, and from the reality of the event to the topoi of the text."[6] Gabriella Signori expressively refers to this as a "cooking" process in a "miracle kitchen," in which the "raw" oral account is "cooked" to the clerical norms of the writer.[7]

In its extreme forms, this assumption that miracle collectors were working to topoi can lead to the suggestion that certain stories in collections were invented altogether. This argument has been applied to the cluster of stories concerning lawsuits in Osbern of Canterbury's collection of the miracles of Dunstan, written in the early 1090s. The knight of Thanet's story, discussed at length in Chapter 1, is one of three stories of legal disputes in Osbern's collection. The other two concern Archbishop Lanfranc's dispute with Odo of Bayeux (William the Conqueror's half-brother), and Osbern's own dispute with unnamed opponents.[8] In all three stories, the men pray to Dunstan to help, have an encouraging vision, and win their legal case. Jay Rubenstein uses the similarities between these stories to dismiss the one about Lanfranc. He argues that the stories about Osbern and about the knight of Thanet demonstrate that "the triumph of a saint in a legal proceeding is a topos of the Dunstan cult."[9] He then suggests that "Osbern knew of Dunstan's association with miraculous legal interventions and wished to connect the saint with the most famous legal victory in the life of the *incomparabilis* Lanfranc." So, then, Osbern had no "factual basis" for the story: it "most likely . . . originated in Osbern's imagination."[10]

It could be that Osbern imagined Lanfranc's resort to Dunstan. Shelving the story about Lanfranc as the repetition of a "topos," though, as if the fact that this story sounds similar to others automatically makes it less credible, is problematic. In general, *topoi* arguments have not served the study of miracle collections well. *Vitae* writers, particularly in the early medieval period, often did imitate each other's work very closely, and this has attuned scholars to be highly sensitive to the ways hagiographers could model their texts on others. Miracle collectors did, of course, "cook" their books, choosing the stories they wanted and writing them as they pleased, even inventing stories if they really thought it necessary. But the stories they heard were not raw. Narrative imitation occurs on an oral level, too, and the personal miracle stories the collectors heard were already modeled after and shaped by others in oral circulation.

In this chapter, I will suggest that most of the clustering of similar stories now to be seen in miracle collections resulted from oral rather than textual processes. People aimed, as Osbern's knight of Thanet put it, "to know by experience what I have heard": they wanted to live out for themselves the miracle stories they knew.[11] Circulating stories functioned as blueprints for the active creation and telling of new ones, a process that tended to create clusters of like-sounding narratives. While we cannot reenter that original oral world in any detail, thinking about oral patterning and the power of plotlines helps make sense of many of the similarities one sees in medieval miracle collections.[12] I will begin with the conception and communication of the miracle plotline itself.

The Miracle Plotline and Patterns of the Divine

One reason the stories in miracle collections sound so similar is that they constantly repeat a single plotline. The knight, Osbern, and Lanfranc all start off in trouble and end up victorious because of Dunstan's aid. Almost every story in medieval miracle collections follows the same problem to solution trajectory. The reason for the solution is always the same too: some form of divine intervention. The miracle plotline—problem, divine intervention, solution—can accommodate an enormous variety of human experience, and the range of stories in miracle collections is often broader than people realize, but still, these stories all have the same basic components lined up in the same general way.[13]

Explaining human experience by means of a miracle was not, of course, a medieval invention. The miracle is an extremely ancient story line, present in the earliest known texts. Somebody at some point must have first had the idea of reading past experience in this way—interpreting positive change as the result of divine intervention—but this happened such a long time ago that we may consider the idea to be, in human terms, timeless. Osbern and the religious elite did not have to work to communicate the elemental miracle plotline to people like the knight of Thanet. Any member of medieval society would have known it from a young age. Indeed, it is so ubiquitous in human conversation that, to this day, even in secular societies, it seems just to be known, not heard or learned.[14]

The miracle plotline is an extraordinarily powerful cultural concept. The knowledge of this plotline could shape not just how a knight of Thanet might interpret his past, but also what he did in the present and what he hoped for the future. It appears that the vast majority of the miracle stories recounted in medieval collections were created by people who consciously and proactively attempted to acquire miraculous solutions to their problems and make the miracle plotline their own. Osbern's account of the knight of Thanet's story suggests how this works. At the outset, the knight of Thanet has a problem: the abbot of St. Augustine's has seized his inheritance. The knight had a range of options for solving this problem, options suggested by what worked for others in similar situations. He could prepare a fine speech for his defense, bribe the abbot, hope for the best and trust in the workings of the law, and so on. As the knight tried to decide what to do, he remembered how Osbern "frequently used to extol father Dunstan. . . . Now, I said to myself, I have the chance to know by experience what I have heard." Because of Osbern's stories, the knight prayed for Dunstan's help. If the knight had then lost his case, if this course of action had failed to resolve his problem, there would have been no miracle. But since the knight was successful, he too had a story to tell of Dunstan's intervention. If others heard the knight's story and decided to try out its blueprint as well, still more analogous stories could be produced.[15]

One can begin to see how and why personal miracle stories took on the coloring of others in circulation. The knight's story, like those Osbern was telling him, named Dunstan as the intervening divine figure. The medieval Christian idea that dead humans of special qualities could act in the present world was conceived many centuries before the knight or Osbern was born, and it appears to have been patterned on other, earlier religious traditions.[16] Still, what one might call the Christian saint metanarrative was a specific cultural conception of the miracle plotline, one that had not always been present in western Europe, much less in other societies. Throughout the medieval period this metanarrative underwent some slow shifts, but remained relatively stable overall: the intervening divine figure at the center of most medieval personal miracle stories was a saint.

Underneath the umbrella of this defining metanarrative, the discourse was in constant flux, with specific saintly figures going in and out of conversational currency at different times and places. People seeking saintly help usually had many options to choose from. The knight of Thanet need not have selected Dunstan. How about Mildred, the saint associated with Thanet who had been translated to St. Augustine's in the early eleventh century? How about Cuthbert, Edmund, or Æthelthryth, the famed English saints? Or maybe a non-English saint, St. Denis or St. James? Or perhaps someone new, as yet untried? The strength of a saint's cult depended on the collective weight of such individual decisions. Sometimes, as with the many thousands of people appealing to Thomas Becket in the late twelfth century, a saint new on the scene could win big in the saintly sweepstakes, his or her stories sweeping through conversational networks and drowning out those of other saints. Local favorites might be appealed to for years, the successes generating a stream of stories for decades or centuries. In other cases, a spring of stories concerning a particular saint might well up for a year or two and then disappear entirely. Some saints might be favored only in the stories of a single region while others were talked about far and wide.

All this depended on which stories were in current circulation, which stories individuals heard and chose to imitate, and which of those narrative trials were successful. A single story might open up a fountainhead of narrative creation, while other stories with seemingly equal potential might never have any progeny at all. There must have been a few people willing to try out a new possibility before anyone else did, a few unwilling to experiment at all, and a lot in the middle, like the knight of Thanet, who turned to the narratives of friends and neighbors for possible solutions. Could the knight of Thanet have suffered a failure with another saint before he tried out Osbern's favorite? Had he ever appealed to a Christ Church saint before? Did Osbern's stories drown out those of someone else close to the knight? As we rarely know anything about the context of such individual decisions or the constellation of circulating narratives, it is often extremely difficult to understand, from any analytical perspective, why some saints were at the center of so many miracle stories and others, seemingly as attractive, were not.

We will never be able to reconstruct all the specific ways in which the stories the knight of Thanet had heard inspired his own course of action, or the stories he told about himself, or the actions others took—much less how this worked for all the hundreds of other stories in high medieval miracle collections. Nevertheless, what is clear is that though the knight's story was unique to him, it was blueprinted on others he had heard before. He did not invent the underlying plotline of his story or the culturally specific form of that plotline, the Christian saint metanarrative. He did not invent the idea of appealing to Dunstan as a divine figure. Nor did the blueprinting process stop there. Stories in circulation suggested not just who to ask for help, but also how that asking should be done.

Patterns of Invocations

Once the knight of Thanet decided that Dunstan was his saint of choice, he kneeled and prayed. Osbern writes that he said: "God of father Dunstan, favor my part today." Invocations form a part of nearly all stories in high medieval miracle collections, usually appearing in the point of the story after the problem is described and before the solution takes shape. In some stories a saint is unintentionally invoked, as when a person insults a saint and provokes divine punishment. In cases in which an individual is too ill or otherwise unable to ask for help, the invocation might be done by friends or relatives. Most of the stories, though, follow a predictable pattern: the saint acts after aid is specifically requested by the person in need.

The repetitiveness of this narrative arc and the similarity of many of the invocations are another reason why accounts of personal miracles can sound so much the same. The knight was obviously not the first to think of praying for help. A verbal request is the most ancient and most widespread mode of divine invocation. Osbern and Lanfranc also chose to pray for Dunstan's help, as did other people in the stories of Osbern's collection, as did many other people in many other societies with many other deities. Still, there was much that was culturally specific even about prayers designed to invoke the divine: how to arrange one's body, for example (the knight knelt), and especially what kinds of words should be said. The knight's prayer, carefully phrased to invoke God through Dunstan rather than Dunstan himself, looks suspiciously like Osbern's own tweaking. Was the knight really so aware that God, not Dunstan, should be considered the ultimate source for any help he received?

Perhaps he was. Perhaps those conversations with Osbern shaped the words the knight said in just this way. Whether or not, the knight must have known that he could try to get Dunstan's attention by other means. Prayers were just one option. The knight had almost certainly heard stories in which saints were stimulated to action by a person's contact with a relic, by entry into sanctified space, or by the presentation of a gift. These were also very old ideas, and they too took on a variety of culturally specific forms depending on the kinds of stories being exchanged in a particular time and place. Stories in the Becket collections, for instance, describe people invoking Becket's aid by bending a coin over an ill person or by taking measurements of a person's body and making a candle to the length. The Becket collectors mention these gift-giving practices without comment, as if they had always been used to invoke saintly aid in Canterbury, but coin bending is not mentioned in stories collected by Osbern or other Anglo-Norman collectors. It is possible that they were not part of their conversational milieu.[17]

Someone must have had the initial idea of bending a coin over an ill person, just as someone had to have been the first to think of asking the dead Dunstan for help. How a new cluster of stories started to coalesce is not usually easy to perceive in our sources, but Benedict of Peterborough's collection provides a remarkable glimpse into the first clustering of stories describing the use of the "Canterbury Water," or just the "Water": a mixture of water and Thomas Becket's blood people drank in hopes of healing.[18] When Becket was murdered in December 1170, he lay for some time on the floor of the cathedral in his own blood. People from Canterbury dipped bits of cloth and clothing into this blood. Later, when the monks came to tend to Becket's body, they gathered the remaining blood, apparently into some kind of vessel. Drinking water that had come in contact with a saint's relic or tomb was a time-honored practice.[19] But drinking blood was different. As Benedict later commented, the monks were fearful of endorsing this idea, "and with no wonder, for it was an unusual thing for people to drink human blood."[20] The monks later diluted the blood partly to prolong its use but also, in Benedict's words, "lest the taste or color of blood produce horror in the drinker."[21] A bigger problem than the disgust factor, though, was how drinking Becket's blood mirrored the Eucharistic ritual. When Christ's blood was drunk in liturgical celebrations, was it right to experiment with drinking Becket's blood?

A Canterbury citizen was probably the first person who decided that it was. At the close of his *vita* for Becket, William FitzStephen writes that some hours after the murder a Canterbury man, who had acquired a cloth stained with Becket's blood, washed the cloth, gave the water to his paralyzed wife to drink, and cured her.[22] Whether or not FitzStephen got this right, it does seem highly likely that it was a Canterbury citizen who took this first step rather than the Christ Church monks themselves. But though the monks did not start the practice, they did have to decide for themselves whether they would participate. When people like Atheldrida, a Canterbury woman suffering from fevers, "asked the custodian monk of the tomb if she might drink of the martyr's blood,"[23] what would they do? "This was not begun without great fear," Benedict writes after telling of William of London's cure, the blood miracle he claims to have been the first, "but seeing that it gave profit to the ill, our fear receded, little by little, and security came."[24] Later Benedict again comments on the nervous tension this "experiment" [*experimentum*] produced: "although many had already experienced the efficacy of this medication, yet it was not given without fear to those seeking it."[25]

What eventually overcame all objections was that drinking Becket's blood so often worked. "O marvelous water," Benedict exclaims, "that not only quenches the thirst of drinkers, but also extinguishes pain! O marvelous water, that not only extinguishes pain, but also reduces swellings!"[26] Set as the invocation in untold numbers of stories, stories told and repeated in many different places, the use of the water was solidly established. In fact, in the second miracle collection for Thomas Becket, started by William of Canterbury in 1172, drinking the water is already mentioned as casually as any other invocation method, such as bending a coin, with no discussion of its development. William's only comment concerns his awe at the fact that Thomas's blood was a safer option than the Eucharist: you could eat and drink the Eucharist to your damnation, but even Becket's enemies could seek healing through his blood.[27]

The success of the blood and water mixture appears to have drowned out other incipient invocation strategies. In the early days of Becket's cult in Exeter, a man had a vision in which he was told how to cure an outbreak of disease: boiled eggs were to be cut into quarters, Thomas's name written on them, and then eaten.[28] Perhaps this inventive and apparently effective invocation practice was continued in the region, but it is never heard of again. In another story, told by Benedict, a London priest named Roger became ill with a fever, but did not have the water, nor the means to travel to Canterbury. Roger came up with the idea of sleeping in a place where he heard Thomas had once slept, and after he woke up healed, he had another idea. He collected some of the dust from that place, mixed it with water, and when he gave this mixture to others to drink (no doubt with a telling of his story), "he gave happiness to many ill people."[29] Yet although Roger's idea was an initial success, nothing more is heard about drinking dust-laden water in the rest of the Becket collections. Benedict decided to recount Roger's narrative, he says, because it shows "how much virtue must be in his blood, when the dust from his bed is able to do such things."[30]

Once stories about drinking the water had ballooned to such a degree that they overrode all objections, what made them frightening at the beginning—their overtones of Eucharistic sacrifice—were their biggest asset, the blood overwhelming mere dust, and the narrative line linking into other strong currents at large in medieval culture.[31] The proactive experimenting process that initiated these stories continued. In addition to drinking the water, people found successful resolutions when they tried sprinkling it on swellings or bathing suffering limbs with it. One woman even poured some of the water into a beer mash in the hopes of making it ferment. From the story, it worked wonderfully well.[32]

In this manner, then, variations on the theme "I drank the water and Becket healed me" materialized and were repeated in many hundreds, even thousands, of personal stories circulating in the late twelfth century. New invocation strategies that appeared to work well could reproduce themselves in other stories as quickly as fruit flies, both within and across cults. Other new invocation strategies, such as quartering eggs, could die off entirely if conditions were not right for their increase. Invocation practices would have risen and fallen in conversational popularity in the same vacillating and often inexplicable manner as one sees with the figures of saints. Invocation strategies tied to specific saints, such as the Canterbury water and Becket, would rise and fall in rhythm with the saint's own popularity, but most strategies, such as coin bending, or drinking something that had come in contact with a saint's relics, did not depend for their continuance on a specific cult.

Success counted the most. Stories circulated, people based their attempts to resolve their own problems on what they had heard, successful experiments created new stories that reinvigorated the conversation, leading to more imitation and experimentation and still more new stories. This continuous process produced stories that could sound strikingly the same, even in terms of the types of problems being solved.

Patterns of Problems

In the abstract, one could ask a saint for help with anything. The variety of problems discussed in medieval miracle collections is often impressive. Unfermenting beer, a lost cheese, a dead goose, a cancerous toe: Becket helped with all these difficulties, and more. Still, when the stories in collections are totted up and categorized, it is clear that they do not represent the whole spectrum of human problems in equal proportions. In almost all rankings of the stories in medieval miracle collections, for instance, cures of blindness and of paralysis lead the lists.[33] Blindness and paralysis were no doubt more common then than they are today, but I doubt that these were the top two afflictions suffered by medieval people or that they appear in large numbers because the collectors were imitating exemplars. Rather, the high numbers are best understood as reflecting, though not with any precision, how often these particular problems were offered up for saintly aid and how frequently a solution was forthcoming.

Blindness and paralysis are problems very well suited for the miracle plotline. Both are severe and debilitating problems that, even for those not suffering them, induce a horrified awe: the lightless eyes, the groping hands, the useless limb, the frozen tongue. As appalling as they are, though, neither condition is usually fatal in itself, leaving a sufferer time to seek solutions. The causes of blindness and paralysis, as we now know, are manifold, including nutritional deficiencies, disease, shock, mental illness, and multiple kinds of trauma. We tend to think of them as permanent, lifelong conditions, but the experience can often be temporary, leaving room for hopeful experiments and dramatic recoveries.[34] For those who did experience a recovery from blindness or paralysis after invoking a saint, it must have been an exhilarating event. From darkness to light, from powerlessness to movement—the restoration of light and life would have been as amazing as the loss was terrifying. Here are stories to tell and to celebrate! Notably, too, blindness and paralysis are perhaps the easiest ailments to fake.[35] This potential for fakery must have driven up the numbers of these stories, but cannot alone account for such persistent clustering of blindness and paralysis stories in miracle collections. I suspect that most of the blindness and paralysis stories the collectors heard were heartfelt accounts of recoveries from frightening and incapacitating difficulties.

Looking closely at the other types of stories that cluster in miracle collections, it is striking how many of them are severe problems that have the potential for abrupt reversal. Drownings, for instance, are very well represented. The limp body drawn from the water: here again is a spectacular problem and, here again, if water is expelled from the lungs soon enough, there is a chance for quick and total recovery. What a great story. In fact, if you forgot to say a prayer or promise a gift in all the excitement, you might well think a saint must have helped anyway, so dramatic is that experience. It is also instructive to note what one does not find in collections. Some medieval people must have suffered serious burns, for example. There are numerous stories in miracle collections about fires dying out or fires moving in a different direction or fires not injuring a particular object, but I have seen none about burned people recovering from their injuries. Quick and total recovery from a bad burn does not happen today, and it apparently did not happen then either.

Ships about to sink, people chained and languishing in prison, the mad raving and thrashing, the sick in awful pain or delirious from fever: these are more of the daunting scenarios that are frequently described in miracle collections. The chief reason we see so many of these types of stories is that certain problems lent themselves to the perception of divine aid. Only a percentage of those asking for help would have recovered, of course, but these processes worked to create large clusters of like stories.

Once these clusters reached a certain density, moreover, another self-reinforcing cycle would have been activated. Large numbers of stories gave a reassuring cultural sanction to the appeal to divine aid for particular problems. If a woman who had heard many stories of blind people being miraculously healed became blind herself, she might well seek divine aid as her first course of action. She might even find it difficult to envision any another solution for her problem. As Elaine Showalter has noted in a similar context, "the human imagination is not infinite . . . we all live out the social stories of our time."[36] In a conversational culture saturated with stories of blind people healed by saints, the majority of people becoming blind will seek such healing themselves, making it likely that a significant number of new stories will be produced along the same lines.[37]

The numbers of stories concerning certain types of problems would have waxed and waned in different cultural circumstances and in different conversational circles. Not every society exploits all the possibilities afforded by the miracle plotline. One scenario likely to result in abrupt reversals but rarely encountered in medieval miracle collections is the person in desperate need of money or material help. Contemporary American religious culture produces masses of stories involving this scenario, and masses of books and speakers encouraging the creation of more. The bestseller *The Prayer of Jabez*, for instance, urges its readers to pray daily for God to "bless me indeed, and enlarge my territory."[38] While there are clusters of stories concerning money in the Becket collections, they have a very different flavor. Benedict, for instance, tells a story about a shoemaker named Curbaran who finds a precious gold coin with Becket's help. Curbaran, though, had not been praying for money. He had been praying daily for Becket's soul (a mistake, Benedict comments, but never mind), and as a reward for his devotion Becket appeared to him in a vision and directed him to the hidden coin.[39] Even this is unusual: in most of the money miracles in the Becket collections, money is given *to* Thomas, not received from him.[40] There is simply not the proactive seeking after money or material objects familiar from today's miracle stories. Medieval saints cure blindness, divert fires, revive the drowned, punish enemies, and so on. They rarely provide windfalls, apparently because they were not often asked for them.

Large clusters of stories about particular problems formed in part because certain problems were more likely to result in satisfying narratives than others, in part because people tend to imitate rather than innovate, and in part because of what people think to ask for at particular times. Nevertheless, in any categorization of stories in miracle collections, there is inevitably a sizable "other" category. If enough people kept knocking at the door of miraculous aid, even the most unlikely and difficult problems might be solved. In the early years of the Becket cult, it would appear that a significant proportion of *all* the many problems people experienced in England and in France were offered up to Becket for help. In these circumstances, numerous stories appeared of blind eyes seeing again, swellings reducing, scaly skin clearing, pregnant women surviving difficult childbirths—all the usual problems that suit the miracle plotline. But there were a few other highly unusual, lucky strikes too. There was the man digging into a hill who was buried alive, called for Becket's aid, and survived in an air pocket until others heard him calling and dug him out; the man shot through the neck with an arrow who asked for Becket's aid and recovered; and the man who had his eyes sliced by the judge's knife, and yet, some days later after committing himself to Becket's care, found he could see with one of them again.[41] The collectors and people at the time were well aware that these stories were out of the ordinary run of miracles, and they were greatly celebrated.[42]

Becket, invoked by thousands, got credit for more outlying stories than most, but in every collection there are stories that do not fit any of the usual clusters. Even stories concerning the most typical problems, moreover, were told by individuals who experienced unique circumstances and created stories that, for all their similar strands, were still unique. No matter how many stories of the blind seeing you might have heard, if your closest friend became blind and then could see again after a pilgrimage, the story would have a deep impact. The sameness that can be wearying when reading many miracle collections with their flattened and abbreviated accounts would have been much less pronounced in the oral climate in which each story was told by an individual and grew out of a unique personality. Osbern, the knight of Thanet, and Lanfranc all told stories about lawsuits, prayers, and Dunstan's aid, but if we could hear them tell their stories, there surely would be no mistaking whose story was whose. What we might notice, though, was that the kinds of stories to be heard from men of such high status tended to be different, generally speaking, from those told by people lower in the social scale. An important kind of patterning and grouping of oral miracle stories was caused by social stratification. Status influenced how a person told a story, how listeners reacted to it, and what kind of story he or she was likely to produce.

Social Status and Patterns of Story Creation

Scholars have often pointed out that issues of social status must have come into play as wealthy monastic writers listened to the stories of illiterate peasants and decided how or whether to recount their stories, but few have considered how extensively social status could impact the making of stories in the first place.[43] Certain kinds of people tend to be associated with certain kinds of stories in medieval miracle collections. In his analysis of over 150 French collections from the eleventh and twelfth centuries, Pierre-André Sigal uncovered some striking correlations. Women of the "popular classes" almost all told healing miracles: 90.1 percent of their stories concerned their bodies. Men of the popular classes told fewer healing miracles: 70.7 percent of their stories concerned healings, still a majority, but notably less than women of their same status. The percentage of healing miracles falls precipitously with the stories of the religious. Only 22.8 percent of their stories concerned their bodies. What they were talking about instead were their dreams: a whopping 44.6 percent, nearly half of their stories, concerned visions. In contrast, a tiny percentage, just 1.2 percent, of the popular classes told vision narratives.[44] What Sigal found is not unusual: similar proportions to these are evident in other categorizations of stories in medieval miracle collections.[45]

Chances were, if you heard a poor woman tell a miracle story about herself, it would be about a healing; if you heard a wealthy religious man, it would not. It may well be that poor women became ill more frequently than wealthy and well-fed religious men, but that does not account for such a stark skewing of the percentages. To explain these differences, it is best to think first about issues of storytelling and authority. A healing almost always involves visual signs. Other people are aware when you get sick and when you get well: even if you want to, it is not easy to hide the evidence of illness. A vision, on the other hand, usually leaves no visible traces, nor is it a shared experience. You could have a vision every night and no one would be the wiser. Convincing listeners that you had a vision is significantly more difficult than convincing them you've been sick and healed. In the case of the knight of Thanet's story, a listener would simply have to trust that the knight was not lying about his state of mind, his prayer, or his dream: there is nothing that he can point to in order to buttress his story. Fortunately for the knight, he was not in great need of a buttress. The knight's social position as a high status male spoke for him, filling in and overriding any doubtful gaps.

Because of famous female visionaries like Hildegard of Bingen, Julian of Norwich, and Catherine of Siena, it can be hard to imagine that women had more difficulty than men telling personal stories of visions in the medieval climate, but miracle collections strongly suggest that this was so. Hildegard, Julian, and Catherine were exceptional. Poor women probably had as many dreams or experiences that they took as visions as anyone else in medieval society, but the general rule was they would have a harder time getting their stories of visions believed, particularly if they were talking to an elite man. Rules could be bent. William of Canterbury, for instance, tells a story about a young woman named Adelicia whose dreams he interpreted as visions even though her own parents viewed them as mere illusions.[46] For some, stories of visions could work to subvert and even overturn normal social and religious hierarchies: a laywoman named Godelief, for instance, claimed to have had visions from Thomas Becket that directed her to expose the faults of other people in her village.[47] But, in general, one's gender, social status, and religious status had an influence on what one could or could not easily say. Even though he retold Godelief's stories in his collection, William expressed hesitancy about them.[48] For every Adelicia who kept telling her stories despite her parents' disapproval, there must have been other women who kept silent, lacking the brazenness needed to break free of the heavy crust of social expectations.

Self-censorship probably had as large a role as any external reproof in the social stratification of stories. Benedict writes about a layman named Adam who twice saw and heard a man speaking to him in his sleep but twice dismissed it all as a mere dream. It was only when a priest gave him the go-ahead that Adam felt comfortable interpreting his dreams as a vision.[49] Self-censorship could work for those higher up as well. Osbern tells a story about a rich man named Ceowulf who, although he was very ill, did not want to go to Dunstan's memorial because he felt embarrassed at the prospect of the "company of the poor." Finally Ceowulf swallows his pride, goes, and is healed, but afterward, when his friends comment how wonderful it is that God helps the powerful as well as the poor, Ceowulf replies: "Do you count me among the poor, since you say I was healed among them? It is not so, since although Dunstan was not there, he touched me."[50]

At the end of the story Ceowulf is punished for his pride. Still, this story helps to explain why the stories in miracle collections connected to high status men are less likely to be stories of healing. Recoveries from desperate illness always made good stories, and one certainly finds such stories about elite men in miracle collections—Osbern describes, for instance, how Archbishop Lanfranc was saved from a serious illness by Dunstan.[51] But social factors pressed people into the creation of certain types of stories. It is not just that the elites, unlike the poor, were able to afford medical care and did not resort to the saints as soon or as often. This mattered, but running parallel was also an aversion to the "company of the poor," a desire to have a story to tell with more cachet, more suited to one's class, more like those one heard one's fellows telling: stories of lawsuits won, enemies punished, visions seen, even hawks recovered.

The precise factors acting on individuals shifted depending on particular social constellations, circumstances, personalities, and audiences. It is now extremely difficult to see how this operated in all but the most general terms.[52] Nevertheless, such factors must have worked not just in the types of stories people created but also in how they told their stories. There were all sorts of ways to make a story a little more flashy, to claim a bit more or tell it at more length, or to downgrade it, claiming less or leaving out parts that were more risky. The kind of adjustments people might make to their stories is suggested by an emendation Benedict made to the story of John, a servant, who fell into the Tweed River. Benedict writes that John, as he made for the shore, "thought that he was walking" on the water, but, in actuality, he was just swimming" [*ambulare se aestimans, super aquas natabat*].[53] How many other lower-class laymen might have saved Benedict the trouble of such a narrative demotion—and saved themselves from sneering or incredulous looks and questions—by toning and cutting down their stories themselves? How often did the collectors reject stories altogether that did not seem to them to befit the social position of their tellers?

Medieval miracle stories are often seen as the particular province of "the people," especially peasants or the poor. Sometimes this sense of miracles being the religious expression of the lowest classes is taken to such an extent it seems as if being literate or wealthy must have put one at a disadvantage for creating miracle stories. But while the literate and the wealthy tended to tell different kinds of miracle stories about themselves than the poor, they certainly told them, and when they told them to a collector, they probably got to talk at more length than the poor. Of course, there could be exceptions. Benedict decided to give the story told by Eilward, the pauper who could see again after his judicial blinding, the longest treatment in his collection. In Eilward's case, a fantastic story that excited Benedict and the other monks at Christ Church to no end, the normal rules were reversed. But, in general, those with more social authority were freer to tell lengthy, detailed, and vision-filled stories about themselves.

Conversational Currents and Cautions

The patterning processes discussed here are some of the key ways in which stories already in circulation and social conditions could shape the creation of new personal stories. When these factors worked together, they could create sets of strikingly similar narratives. The knight, Osbern, and Lanfranc all think to ask for help with their legal dispute from Dunstan and to invoke his aid with a prayer. Who did this first is now impossible to tell, but the conversational links between these three men almost certainly had an impact on the types of stories they individually produced. No doubt, too, it was not just the content of these stories but in the ways that they were told that the connections between these three men had an effect. In the same way that different peer groups, regions, or families have distinct ways of telling stories, so there must have been distinct patterns of vocabulary, speech rhythms, and imagery in the telling of miracle stories in different medieval communities, patterns also in a constant state of change as small innovations were picked up and imitated by others. The interaction likely between the knight, Osbern, and Lanfranc was at work on many different levels and between many different people in the oral world as a whole. Taken together, these currents of conversation made up a vast, dynamic, and multifaceted sea of narrative exchange that, though now essentially unmappable, deeply shaped how people created their own stories of divine intervention. Each person told his or her own story, but they all were patterned, some more, some less, on the stories already in circulation.

The oral realm of story creation and circulation must, then, constantly be considered when miracle collections are subjected to analysis. In this chapter I have surveyed how the stories in current circulation shaped how people created new ones: we must also consider, of course, what was likely to happen to a story as it was picked up and retold by new speakers. As they moved away from their creators, the sharp individual edges of stories were likely to be smoothed away, making stories sound even more similar to each other.[54] As memories became fuzzy, stories might well morph together or become more fantastic creations. The longer stories were in circulation, the more they were reshaped and reinvented in all the ways familiar to anyone who has played the game of whispering a story around a circle and hearing what the last person in line has to say. People could also, of course, simply invent stories about other people along the lines of old ones. The best storytellers were likely more guilty of this than anyone else. Miracle collectors, well aware of these problems, were often careful to get stories from their creators whenever possible.

Considering the power of these shaping processes from the moment of story creation on, we need to be cautious about drawing conclusions from miracle collections about the kinds of threats faced by medieval people. Miracle collections do not mirror all of the dangers or diseases of the medieval world, just the ones that the saints were thought to help with. Counting up the numbers of stories in collections in an attempt to rank the relative importance of this hazard or that illness invites serious miscalculation. At best, such counting across collections provides us with a very rough sense of how many miracle stories of a certain type were in circulation, quite different from what people found to be most or least troublesome in their lives.

We must also be careful when evaluating the ways in which types of miracle stories are connected with types of people or social groupings. These connections do not allow us to tap into raw human experience. A poor woman, for example, did not necessarily voice the most significant aspects of her life in a miracle story. Nor did a rich monk. Even before a collector determined how to shape the stories he heard, those stories were *already* shaped by the kinds of problems preferred by the miracle plotline, by other stories in circulation, by social expectations about the types of stories individuals should create, and by the motivations and personalities of the tellers and retellers of the stories.

Equally perilous is the temptation to use written miracle collections as a means to rank the relative strength of cults. One must always keep in mind that only a tiny percentage of the many stories created and exchanged in the oral world in the medieval period were ever collected in texts. These written texts give us only a snapshot of the kinds of stories being told about a certain saint at a certain time, and they are blurry snapshots at that. It would be nice to assume that most collections were compiled when a cult was at its all-time height, but we cannot. Cults went through short-and long-term fluctuations, and where a collection was compiled along a cult's trajectory is often difficult to gauge. Moreover, while there must have been differences in the relative numbers of stories about particular saints at any given time, we cannot suppose that these differences are clearly reflected in our texts. Because one collection has twenty-five chapters and another has fifty, for instance, does not necessarily or even probably mean that the second saint's cult was twice as big. The scale of production of stories in the oral world outrun the handwriting speed of the most energetic collectors. Twenty-five, fifty, one hundred—the number of chapters in a collection was determined by the collector, not the absolute scale of cults, in which a hundred stories in circulation was no great feat. We cannot assume that the surviving texts provide us with anything like an even sample.

Nor can we assume that the most important stories or the most important cults at a given time found a collector. When utilizing the miracle collection as a historical source, it is important to recognize that miracle collecting *itself* was a faddish activity. Whether a story was redacted in text depended more on the popularity of miracle collecting at the time and the willingness of a well-placed individual to work than the significance of a story or the power of a cult. Miracle collecting waxed and waned in tune to its own rhythms and the enthusiasms of individuals. In the same way that there was nothing raw or impersonal about the stories the collectors used to make their texts, so the collectors were not raw or impersonal instruments. In the chapters to follow we will see just how distinct the individual collecting motivations and methods of collectors could be, even when the collectors in question were working at the same time and collecting the stories of the same saint.

Still, what other people were doing mattered too. Just as the knight of

Thanet's decision to appeal to Dunstan was almost certainly influenced by his conversations with Osbern, so Osbern's decision to write a miracle collection was almost certainly influenced by the fact that a man named Goscelin of St.-Bertin was collecting miracle stories at the monastery of St. Augustine's less than a mile away. It is to the miracle collectors of England, and the reasons why they wanted to "produce in letters" what had already been produced in speech, that we will now turn.

A Drop from the Ocean's Waters: Lantfred of Fleury and the Cult of Swithun at Winchester

No hagiography of any kind was written in England between 800 and 950. Bede had composed numerous hagiographical texts in the early eighth century, including a particularly influential account of the life and posthumous miracles of Cuthbert (d. 689), but the Viking invasions destroyed many monasteries in England and brought this literary tradition to a standstill. When the political situation had finally stabilized somewhat in the second half of the tenth century, there was a renewal and reform of monastic life in England. With this came a "mini-revival," in Rosalind Love's words, of hagiographic composition.[1] In the late tenth and early eleventh century, new and often quite substantial Latin *vitae* were composed for Wilfrid, Ouen, Edmund, Dunstan, Oswald, Æthelwold, Ecgwine, and others; *vitae* were also written in Old English in this period.[2] Late Saxon monks translated saints' relics, built special apses, crypts, and chapels to house these relics, and lavished precious metals on saints' shrines. They compiled lists of the resting places of saints—lists that were necessary because they had moved so many of them. They celebrated saints in liturgies and litanies and cherished their presence in their monasteries and churches.[3] What late Saxon monks rarely did, however, was to collect stories of saints' miracles.

Anglo-Normans would scold their forbearers for negligence on just this point. They looked in vain at the close of late Saxon *vitae* for stories of miracles and complained about the lacunae they found there: the first miracle collections for Wilfrid, Ouen, Edmund, Oswald, and Dunstan would be written by Anglo-Normans, not Anglo-Saxons. The modern scholar searching for evidence of late Saxon miracle collecting is also in for a frustrating time. Antonia Gransden has identified two stories about the miracles of Edmund that appear to have been written by an author named Ælfwine in the early eleventh century: these stories are known only from their incorporation in a larger Anglo-Norman collection.[4] Rosalind Love, too, has found evidence of pre-Conquest miracle stories being utilized by a post-Conquest author. In this case, a cleric named Ælfhelm seems to have written a collection of Æthelthryth's miracles that was rewritten by an anonymous early twelfth-century author.[5] Neither of these pre-Conquest collections appears to have been very substantial in their original form. In terms of surviving texts, we have a little *vita* about Neot, likely composed in the mid-eleventh century, that includes a couple stories of healing as part of the text's account of the building of a church for Neot in Cambridgeshire.[6] Wulfstan of Winchester's *Life of Æthelwold*, composed at the end of the tenth century, closes with five stories of recent miracles, while Byrhtferth of Ramsey's *Life of Ecgwine*, composed in the early eleventh century, ends with four posthumous miracle stories of a distinctively folkloric flavor.[7] There is also the *Historia de Sancto Cuthberto*, a curious text of anonymous authorship. The composition of the *Historia* has been placed anywhere from the tenth to the early twelfth century. The *Historia* appears to have been compiled mostly or even wholly out of previously written texts: it reads principally as a list of donations granted to or stolen from Cuthbert's community by a procession of early Anglo-Saxon nobles who are rewarded or punished by Cuthbert accordingly.[8]

Evidence of miracle collecting in Old English is even more faint. One surviving composition that could perhaps be thought of as a collection is the little text known as the *Vision of Leofric*. Though it does not concern any specific saint, it contains stories such as earl Leofric's experience of seeing a marvelous light shine out in Canterbury cathedral. The *Vision of Leofric* is probably a post-Conquest composition, but there may have been pre-Conquest texts like it.[9] Goscelin of St.-Bertin says he used an account in Old English as the source for a miracle concerning St. Edith of Wilton.[10] Osbern of Canterbury, too, mentions sermons about Dunstan in Old English.[11] An anonymous twelfth-century writer of a short *passio* and miracle collection for St. Indract at Glastonbury claims to have used an Old English exemplar.[12] Most intriguingly, a late eleventh-century text refers to sheets of parchment attached to the walls near the shrine of St. Leofwynn in Sussex. Accounts of Leofwynn's virtues were written on these sheets in Old English, a language the Flemish writer could not read.[13] From such a sprinkling of references to texts now lost, it is difficult to judge what might once have been. Still, it seems safe to conclude that late Saxon hagiographers composing in Old English, like those writing in Latin, concentrated their efforts on *vitae*.

There is only one miracle collection surviving from late Saxon England that fully justifies the term: the *Translation and Miracles of St. Swithun* by Lantfred, a monk of Fleury.[14] Michael Lapidge, whose monumental volume on the cult of Swithun has put the study of Lantfred's text on a firm footing for the first time, terms the collection "one of the most substantial Latin prose texts which has survived from Anglo-Saxon England."[15] Lantfred wrote the *Miracles* sometime after July 971, the year that Bishop Æthelwold, the chief leader of the monastic reform movement in England, translated Swithun's relics from an outside grave into the Old Minster at Winchester.[16] The *Miracles* has little to say about the translation: its forty chapters are almost all concerned with Swithun's contemporary miracles.[17] The collection makes it clear that Lantfred was present at Winchester in the 970s and was thrilled by what he witnessed there: "I myself saw more than two hundred sick people cured through the saint's merit in ten days, and in the course of a year, the healings were countless! I also saw the precincts around the minster . . . so packed on either side with crowds of sick persons, that any traveler would find difficulty in gaining access to it."[18] In the collection, Lantfred tells story after story of healings and liberations and states that there were many more miracles he could have recounted. "I . . . have come trembling to the mighty vastness of this sea," he writes in the letter prefacing the collection, "and, as if it were a drop from the ocean's waters, thus have I collected together a very few from the many miracles of our saint."[19]

As it would turn out, Lantfred's collection now serves not just as a "drop from the waters" of Swithun's cult of the 970s, but of late Saxon cults more generally. While we can assume that the late Saxon religious landscape was, in Diana Webb's words, "honeycombed with local cults,"[20] Lantfred's text stands alone in giving us a wealth of specifics about individual supplicants and their miracles. Webb has noted the "inestimable value" of Lantfred's collection, "for it shows that . . . the practice of pilgrimage and the conventions of miracle stories were familiar to the English in the late tenth century."[21] Indeed, Lantfred's text is like a spotlight on a stage that otherwise remains dark or barely illuminated. Why was miracle collecting so rare in late Saxon England? It is not that Lantfred's text was not admired: Wulfstan of Winchester versified the entire collection around 996, while Ælfric, the famed Old English homilist, made a Latin abbreviation of Lantfred's collection and

translated it into Old English.[22] Wulfstan concluded his versification by noting that Swithun's miracles continued "up to the present day," and Ælfric
stated at the end of his vernacular translation that "as long as I have lived,
there have been abundant miracles [of Swithun]."[23] While both Wulfstan
and Ælfric added a couple of miracle stories in the course of their writings,
neither thought to make a collection of new stories, not even with Lantfred's
splendid example before them.[24] It would be left to a post-Conquest collector
to start where Lantfred had left off.

In this chapter, I read the composition of Lantfred's collection in the
context of the lack of miracle collecting in late Saxon England and seek
explanations for both collection and context. Lantfred's collection is usually
thought to have been written at the instigation of Bishop Æthelwold and the
monks of the Old Minster with the aim of promoting Swithun's cult and the
monastic reform movement. I see little evidence for this. I argue that Lantfred's collection is better viewed within a literary framework and as a largely
self-instigated work. The collection, in my reading, is the result of a conjunction of highly unusual circumstances. There were many cults, but very few
writers of Lantfred's west Frankish background and interests in England in
the tenth and eleventh centuries. Late Saxon monks who could have collected
miracle stories, someone like Ælfric, for instance, did not share Lantfred's
sense that it was important to do so. To take an analogous example, late
Saxons also did not think it was important to build the kind of enormous
churches that Normans would begin to construct soon after their arrival in
England.[25] The lack of large churches in the late Saxon landscape does not
indicate disrespect for Christian worship. So too, the lack of late Saxon miracle collections should not be read as disrespectful: cults, as argued in the
chapters above, did not need collections to thrive. Lantfred's composition of
this one collection, this foreign monk's sense that he should write about
Swithun's miracles "so that such great favours may not lie hidden from succeeding generations,"[26] was a happy chance. His text gives us, in Lapidge's
words, an "astonishingly detailed picture . . . of life in late tenth-century
England."[27] It also gives us a base from which to explore the early history of
English miracle collecting.

Lantfred begins his collection with a prefatory letter addressed to the
monks of the Old Minster and then a preface that describes Christ's incarna-
tion, the Anglo-Saxons' conversion to Christianity, and Christ's decision "to
grant to His Anglo-Saxons a heavenly gift [i.e., Swithun]."[28] Lantfred complains in the letter that "very little" was known of Swithun's life and quotes

Priscan's lament about "the shortage of writers." Lantfred would not attempt to describe Swithun's life either: "let us come to those things which without any doubt took place posthumously at the man of God's tomb."[29]

The ensuing collection divides into two sharply distinct sections. In the first three chapters of the text, Lantfred constructs a tidy origin myth or "inventio" for the beginnings of Swithun's cult. In 968, the dead Swithun announces himself in a vision to a blacksmith (chapter 1); in 969, Swithun performs his first miracle (chapter 2); in 971, Swithun performs a miracle that convinces everyone of his sanctity (chapter 3).[30] At the close of chapter 3, Lantfred states briefly that Swithun's relics, which were situated by a cross in a graveyard outside of the Old Minster, were exhumed and placed inside the church by "the venerable lord bishop Æthelwold and by the distinguished abbots Ælfstan and Æthelgar." These three chapters are the longest in the collection, together comprising over one-third of the entire length of the text. The fourth chapter is transitional: here Lantfred discusses the many miracles in the days and months after the translation and writes about his own eyewitness of the great crowds at Winchester.

Chapters 5 through 39 of the collection all concern post-translation miracles. In this, the longer section of his text, Lantfred does not bother with dates or attempt to tell an overall story.[31] The cult is just there, hugely there. In the first story of this section (chapter 5), ill people on the Isle of Wight already know that "the holy bishop was prevailing with his marvelous miracles" at the Old Minster in Winchester, and when they get there, the monks already have a "usual manner" for celebrating Swithun's miracles.[32] Lantfred alludes to the size of Swithun's cult in many other chapters as well: he describes how a sick man in Rome heard from other English pilgrims that "the Lord was healing countless illnesses of sick persons through the merit of St. Swithun," and so hurried home to try his luck at Winchester; in another chapter, he tells how throngs of pilgrims were streaming by a blind man frustrated by his young guide's desire to stop and eat lunch before entering Winchester.[33] Over three-quarters of Lantfred's stories concern healings: the blind, the paralyzed, the crippled, the mute, and those suffering from accidents or simply "serious" or "manifold" illnesses all make appearances.[34] Lantfred also liked what one might term "liberation" miracles, such as stories about slaves in fetters.[35] In almost the last lines of the collection, Lantfred excuses his interest in these liberation stories—at the same time restating his primary interest in Swithun's healing miracles—by writing, "this is highly remarkable: that this holy servant of God . . . should not only have healed

the sufferings of the diseased . . . but that he even released many who were
shackled from powerful bindings."[36] Lantfred concludes the text with a very
brief chapter in which he urges his readers to rejoice that "Christ . . . in
our days deigned to bestow so many benefits on suffering men through the
restorative intercession of St. Swithun."[37]

In assessing why Lantfred created this collection, it is especially important to consider what the text reveals about Lantfred's own engagement with
Swithun's cult. Lantfred appears to have been genuinely amazed by the magnitude of the cult he witnessed at the Old Minster. "No one person could
see with his own eyes, nor learn by reading aloud the holy parchment letter
by letter, nor comprehend as rumour struck his stinging ears, that so many
had been cured at the tomb of one saint," he exclaims in the collection's
preface.[38] To give his readers a sense of the cult's breathtaking scale, Lantfred
dedicates some chapters to describing how large groups of people were cured:
25 people healed in one day, 124 cured in two weeks, and so on.[39] Notably,
less than a quarter of Lantfred's stories are about Winchester citizens.[40] His
focus on the stories of nonresidents—people coming from Essex, Wiltshire,
London, Bedfordshire, Rochester, Abingdon, Collingbourne, the Isle of
Wight, "the west," Rome, and France—demonstrated that Swithun's cult
was not just local. These nonresidents, moreover, were like Lantfred himself:
they too were outsiders who had a conceived a strong devotion to this saint
of Winchester.

Lantfred's foreign origins did not prevent him from developing a personal zeal for Swithun. If anything, the cultural difference seems to have
piqued Lantfred's interest. He speaks a lot about "the English" in this text
and formulates an extraordinary explanation for the strength of English
saints' cults. Lantfred explains in the preface that the miracles of Swithun
and other English saints were heavenly rewards for a much earlier event, what
he considered to be England's quick conversion to Christianity. It was because the early Anglo-Saxons did not slaughter their missionaries and were
devoted to the faith that "[Christ] bestowed an immense bounty on the
aforesaid nation, such that it would have from its own peoples a nearly incal-
culable number of saints who . . . would be able to heal the sick people,
afflicted with various illnesses, of the whole island."[41] Here and elsewhere in
the text it is clear that Lantfred envisioned non-English readers of his collection. He describes, for instance, how the king had an enormous retinue with
him when he traveled to an estate "as is the custom among the Anglo-
Saxons,"[42] and he also makes explanatory statements about English geogra-

phy: "a certain powerful lady was living in another region of England which in their language is called Bedfordshire," he writes, as well as stating that a paralyzed man "was living in a province of the English which is called Ham in their language."[43]

In addition to writing this collection so that his brethren at Fleury would understand it, Lantfred told other people about Swithun's cult in his homeland of Frankia. He devotes one of the later chapters of the collection to the story of a "priest from England named Lantfred," who was traveling in France when a nobleman sent him messengers asking for advice. It was not unusual for writers of the time to speak of themselves in the third person in this manner—this traveling priest was clearly Lantfred himself. The messenger explained to Lantfred that his friend's wife was very ill. Lantfred writes that he replied, "'As you well know, I have not studied the practice of medicine from an early age. Nevertheless, I shall give you some excellent advice . . . arrange for [a candle] to burn this coming night . . . in honour of the kindly bishop through whom God is performing many miracles among the English."[44] The friend had a wax candle made, and Lantfred carved a supplicating poem to Swithun onto it, a poem he includes in his account of this miracle. It worked: the noblewoman was well again the next day.

This story illuminates the depth of Lantfred's enthusiasm for Swithun; it is also interesting for its biographical detail about Lantfred's study of "the practice of medicine." Unusually in a collection of this size and date, Lantfred does not tell a single story about monastic property, lawsuits, battles, shipwrecks, fires, or lost objects: his unwavering focus is on healing and liberation miracles, most especially healings. His keen interest in Swithun's "medication to ailing bodies,"[45] and descriptions of how the saint "confers the benefit of health on the bodies of the sick, innumerable because of their multitude,"[46] may well be tied to this early personal appetite for medical learning.

When Lantfred first came to Winchester is unknown. Lapidge believes that the New Minster Foundation charter, dated to 966, may show Lantfred's influence. Part of the document is composed in rhyming prose, a trademark of Lantfred's *Miracles* and otherwise extremely unusual in tenth-century Anglo-Latin prose.[47] It seems likely, as Lapidge suggests, that Lantfred was initially invited to England to help Æthelwold with his reform program.[48] Fleury was a powerful and flourishing monastic center in the tenth century, and it had ties with England: Æthelwold, we know, wanted to study there, and saw it as a model for the refoundation and reformation of monastic life in England.[49] In the introduction to the *Regularis Concordia*, Æthelwold states that he had summoned advisors from Fleury and Ghent to help him develop the monastic observances outlined in the text.[50] An Englishman sent to Fleury by Æthelwold—Abbot Osgar—was known to Lantfred, and Lantfred must have known Æthelwold: toward the end of his collection, he includes a miracle story that he heard recounted by the bishop.[51] Lantfred wrote the *Miracles* sometime after July 971. From internal evidence, it is clear that he had to have finished the text by the early 980s at the latest.[52] Lantfred was also likely the author of mass-sets for the liturgical celebration of Swithun's cult.[53] We have one other piece of evidence about Lantfred's residence in England: Lapidge has identified a letter that Lantfred wrote to Archbishop Dunstan at Canterbury thanking him for his kindness while he was England and requesting the return of books. Lantfred sent the letter from Fleury; it is dated 974 x 984.[54] Lantfred's name is found on a list commemorating the monks of the Old Minster in Winchester, but where or when he died are unknown.[55]

Scholars have always read Swithun's cult within the framework of Æthelwold's monastic reforms. Lapidge writes of Æthelwold "conceiving" the idea of Swithun's cult and sees it as beginning on the day Æthelwold translated the relics: "the cult of St. Swithun began, at a stroke, on Saturday 15 July 971."[56] Mechthild Gretsch is more doubtful about whether Swithun's cult was created ex nihilo, but writes, "There is little doubt, however, about what, for Æthelwold, would have mattered most in the cult of Swithun . . . Swithun's 'revelation' confirmed to Winchester and to all England that these recent political and ecclesiastical developments had indeed been pleasing to God."[57] Robert Deshman's reading is very similar: "Æthelwold began to promote Swithun's previously obscure cult so that the saint's unexpected rise to prominence and his subsequent flurry of miracles would appear as signs of heavenly approval for the bishop's policy of monastic reform."[58]

While Lantfred must have supported Æthelwold's reform efforts, he never once suggests in the collection that Swithun's miracles were signs of approval of Æthelwold's policies. Lantfred addressed the collection's prefatory letter to the monks of the Old Minster, not to Æthelwold. In the letter, he says nothing about reform. In the preface of the collection, Lantfred presents Swithun's cult as a reward for the Anglo-Saxons' bloodless conversion to Christianity centuries earlier; again, he says nothing about reform.[59] Lantfred has so little to say about the translation performed by Æthelwold that Lapidge suspects he might not have been present for it.[60] The miracle stories themselves are about healings and liberations, not reform. The overall moral Lantfred saw in Swithun's miracles was a general one: he thought that they were meant so that "the kindly love of our Lord may be manifest to all peoples," and "so that the stony hearts of evil men may become gentle and recover their senses, and so hasten toward heavenly joys with their good works."[61] The conclusion to the collection would seem to be an ideal place to press home a reforming message, but here again Lantfred simply tells his readers to rejoice that "Christ . . . in our days deigned to bestow so many benefits on suffering men through the restorative intercession of St. Swithun."[62]

As desirable as it might be, then, to read Lantfred's collection as a text written in the service of Æthelwold and reformed monasticism, Swithun was clearly the figure who was uppermost in Lantfred's mind. He seems to have been thinking of Æthelwold little or not at all. Lantfred certainly did not view Æthelwold as the creator of Swithun's cult. For Lantfred, Swithun's cult was both bigger than and separate from Æthelwold's monastic reform—it was created by Christ himself. Historians will, of course, take a more detached view of this question, but we too should be careful not to give a prelate like Æthelwold more credit than he is due. It appears that Swithun's cult was active, possibly quite active, before Æthelwold translated his relics.[63] The rash of relic translations undertaken at reformed monasteries in the late tenth and early eleventh centuries by Æthelwold and others were most likely done not with the thought of initiating cults, but of hitching on to them.[64] A prelate could help the visibility of a cult by a translation, but could not force a cult into existence: Swithun's cult subsisted and grew because of the enthusiastic creation and exchange of miracle stories among many scores of people, most of whom never spoke with or even laid eyes on Æthelwold. Would the blind man seeing again, or the slave-girl freed from her unkind master, credit their experiences to Æthelwold's actions or think of them as advancing Æthelwold's monastic reforms? Would Æthelwold, for that matter?

Æthelwold himself does not mention Swithun in any of his writings. From the few instances in which Æthelwold and Swithun are connected in contemporary texts, it appears that Æthelwold may have viewed Swithun's cult as helping his pastoral efforts: the reformation of hearts, in other words, more than the reformation of monasteries. Wulfstan of Winchester devoted a brief chapter to Swithun's cult in his *Life of Æthelwold*. In it, he writes: "two lamps blazed in the house of God, placed on golden candlesticks; for what Æthelwold preached by the saving encouragement of his words, Swithun wonderfully ornamented by display of miracles."[65] In one of the closing chap-

ters in his collection, Lantfred retells a story about the vision of an ill nobleman that he says Æthelwold told him. In Lantfred's description of the man's
vision, Swithun is unusually full of moral guidance. Swithun exhorts the
nobleman to "follow in Christ's footsteps," "do no evil to anyone," "imitate
Christ," "love your enemies; do good to them that hate you," "if thy enemy
be hungry, give him to eat," and so on. Might we hear Æthelwold's voice
here?[66]

Æthelwold appears in only a few other passages of Lantfred's collection.
The key human player in Lantfred's collection is not Æthelwold, but Eadsige,
the sacrist of the Old Minster. Eadsige had been a canon of the Old Minster
before Æthelwold reformed the house in 964. He was expelled along with
the rest of the canons when Æthelwold installed monks from Abingdon at
the Old Minster, but he later rejoined the community as a monk.[67] This
extraordinary figure appears to have been Lantfred's chief conversational partner in the making of the collection.[68] He appears in five chapters spaced
throughout the collection (cc. 1, 5, 16, 20, 36), including the story about the
blacksmith's vision that begins the collection. In the vision, Swithun tells the
blacksmith to send word to Eadsige, then expelled and living at Winchcombe, that he was to tell Æthelwold it was time to translate Swithun's relics.
Eadsige, Lantfred writes, was at that time full of disgust "not only with the
bishop of Winchester cathedral but also with all the monks dwelling there,"
and refused to speak with the bishop.[69] This is just the first example in the
collection of Lantfred writing from Eadsige's perspective. Lantfred concludes
the chapter by rejoicing that two years after the message came from the
blacksmith, Eadsige was finally able to overcome his anger, rejoin the community at Winchester, and "become a devout monk much beloved by
God."[70] Strikingly, Lantfred forgets to tell us whether Eadsige ever discussed
the translation with Æthelwold: the point of the story becomes Eadsige's
return to the Old Minster.

No other monk of the Old Minster appears like this in Lantfred's collection—in fact, no other monk is even named. Lantfred describes how Eadsige
held the keys to the enclosure surrounding Swithun's tomb and how he
would ring a bell to alert the community that Swithun had performed a
miracle. In one chapter, Eadsige carries on a lengthy discussion with a slave-
girl and a young cleric; in another, Eadsige comforts a crippled young man
and returns later to find him cured; in a third, Eadsige questions a man about
his state of health before his miracle.[71] Perhaps the most telling story, though,
has to do with the ringing of the bell. Some monks "bore it ill that they

were so frequently awakened from their night-time sleep" to give thanks for miracles, Lantfred writes, and "they perversely persuaded others" to ignore Eadsige's bell-ringing.[72] After nearly two weeks of this—Eadsige must have been very upset—Swithun appeared in a vision to a noblewoman, telling her to tell Æthelwold that the monks of the Old Minster were not being properly grateful. Æthelwold sent a reprimand to the monks, and things improved: "From that time on . . . no matter how often a miracle was performed at the body of the blessed saint, whether during the day or in the middle of the night, and the sacrist rang the bell even lightly, the monks went to the monastery in order to praise the omnipotent Lord."[73]

The detail about "ringing the bell lightly" certainly sounds like it would have come from Eadsige. When Lantfred writes that 25 people were cured on the day of the Feast of the Assumption or that 36 people were cured in three days, it likely that such information came to him from the man who rang the bell for all those miracles.[74] Indeed, Eadsige may well be behind more chapters of Lantfred's collection than those in which he is named. If Lantfred did not speak Old English, or spoke it haltingly, it would have been difficult for him to get details about many of the miracles in his collection for himself. Lantfred claims to have spoken with the blacksmith whose vision was relayed to Eadsige—"I learned from the smith himself that these things had happened exactly as the present little book describes"[75]—but otherwise does not present himself as listening to the lay English men and women featured throughout his collection. In two chapters, Lantfred mentions how people came and "reported to the monks of that place" about their miracles—it seems likely that Lantfred then heard the story from the monks, rather than the original tellers.[76] Lantfred many well have heard many of the stories he recounts in the comfortable company of Eadsige and other Old Minster monks enthusiastic about Swithun's cult.

In the collection's prefatory letter, Lantfred addresses the monks of the Old Minster: "I, the most worthless of all men . . . sustained by no prerogative of divine learning nor by any authority accruing from my good conduct, but obeying your commands, trusting in your prayers—have come trembling to the mighty vastness of this sea." In the next sentence, Lantfred speaks of "the good will of you who are requesting the work."[77] Lapidge reads this passage as indicating that after Swithun's translation, "the monks of the Old Minster soon felt the need to have these abundant miracles recorded, and the task fell to Lantfred."[78] However, Lantfred's presentation of his composition as the result of a "request" seems more like a considerate genuflection than

an indication that it was the Old Minster monks who had first felt a need for
such a text. It had been over 150 years since an English monk had produced
a miracle collection. Lantfred, in contrast, came from a monastery and a
region in which miracle collections were actively being made. Fleury, Lantfred's own monastery, had a distinguished tradition of miracle collecting. It
was home to one of the most well-known collections of the early medieval
period, Adrevald's collection of the miracles of St. Benedict written in the
860s.[79] While Adrevald's collection was not so focused on contemporary healing miracles as Lantfred's would be, this collection must have been known to
Lantfred and impressed on him how a text could keep the memory of past
miracles alive. Lantfred was also likely aware of the translations of relics and
miracle collections compiled at Trier in the 960s, at Metz around the same
time, in Picardy after 964, at Gorze in 965, and other contemporary examples, as Lapidge has outlined.[80]

It seems likely that Lantfred was the one who thought it was important
to write a miracle collection. Writing was something Lantfred clearly enjoyed;
in his collection for Swithun, he employs grecisms, rhyme, and other rhetorical pyrotechnics. Lantfred was such a fine writer, in fact, that Lapidge terms
him "the most accomplished prose stylist active in England since the days of
Aldhelm and Bede."[81] A different monk from Fleury might have been impressed by the goings-on at Winchester, told his friends about Swithun's
miracles, and enjoyed mulling over miracles with Eadsige, but written nothing. Lantfred, though, wanted to write—and, as noted above, he was thinking about Frankish readers as well as English ones. Four manuscripts of
Lantfred's collection survive. There are two early copies written at Winchester, one dated to the late tenth century, perhaps 996, the other to c.1000;
there is one copy with a Fleury origin, dated c.1000–1050; and there is a copy
made at Worcester between about 1050 and 1075.[82] Without Lantfred's text,
it would be hard to guess at the full vibrancy of Swithun's cult in the 970s.
Apart from his collection, all we have concerning Swithun from this ten-
year period is an enigmatic and unlabeled image in the *Benedictional of St.
Æthelwold*, a set of benedictions that briefly mention Swithun's abundant
miracles in the same manuscript, and recently discovered archaeological evidence indicating a rebuilding of the Old Minster around this time.[83]

"It was in no small measure a result of Lantfred's eloquent advocacy of
St. Swithun," Lapidge writes, "that he quickly became established in the
vanguard of Anglo-Saxon saints."[84] Surely, though, it was not Lantfred's elo-
quence that placed Swithun in this vanguard, but the volatile oral spread of

stories of his miracles and the making of more and more. By the time Lantfred began collecting miracle stories, Swithun's cult had already reached far
more locales outside of Winchester than his text ever would. Lantfred's essential motive for miracle collecting—I want this cult and these stories to be
remembered, "so that such great favours may not lie hidden from succeeding
generations"—would be articulated again and again by later miracle collectors in England. It is a less ambitious and less political motive than scholars
tend to want to read into miracle collections, but it is precisely what Lantfred's text accomplished, both in the medieval period and up to the present
day.

Lantfred's collection, in sum, appears to be the result of a fortunate and
unusual conjunction of circumstances. Here was a Frankish visitor whose
home monastery was a traditional center for miracle collecting, a gifted writer
coming upon a cult that astounded him, a foreigner who developed a friendship with and appreciated the stories of the prickly sacrist at Winchester.
Lantfred's initial trip to England likely had nothing to do with Swithun. We
should not imagine that Lantfred's sole business in England was miracle
collecting, nor that he came to England with the intent of creating such a
text. Instead, he seems to have been inspired to write by the contemporary
cult, whenever he first came upon it. It was an extremely unusual project
for someone residing in late tenth-century England. Lantfred's efforts were
respected, considering Wulfstan's pains to versify the collection and Ælfric's
to abbreviate and to translate it, but his example seems to have done little to
inspire more miracle collecting in England. After Lantfred finished his collection, new English cults appeared (Dunstan's at Canterbury seems to have
been particularly strong), other cults faded, and still others, including
Swithun's, rolled on, all with minimal or no written record of the miracle
stories being created and exchanged.[85] It would be a full century before another writer—a foreigner, again—would think it important to preserve miracle stories about English saints in texts.

Fruitful in the House of the Lord: The Early Miracle Collections of Goscelin of St.-Bertin

Though they lived a century apart, the careers and interests of Goscelin of St.-Bertin (d. after 1107) and Lantfred of Fleury (fl. 970s) bear close comparison. Both were born and spent their childhoods outside of England—Lantfred in west Frankia, Goscelin in Flanders. Both were members of large and influential Benedictine abbeys in their home regions. After coming to England, both spent their time visiting and living among Benedictine monks. Both were highly accomplished writers with a particular interest in miracle stories and miracle collecting. Both wrote about English saints for whom there was little or no previous written commemoration, and both filled their miracle collections principally with in-house stories told by their Benedictine hosts. But whereas Lantfred appears to have written just one collection, Goscelin wrote many. He never seems to have gone home again after leaving St.-Bertin as an adolescent in the early 1060s. After the death of his patron in 1078, he spent much of his life moving from monastery to monastery. In the course of these travels, Goscelin produced so much hagiography that his contemporary, William of Malmesbury, wrote:"in the celebration of the English saints he was second to none since Bede."[1]

Unlike Lantfred, Goscelin was determined to write accounts of the lives of saints, even in the face of a severe paucity of information. But he almost always gave equal or more room in his texts to stories of saints' actions after their deaths. Miracle stories most captured his imagination: as Rosalind Love writes, Goscelin "is at his best and most lively as a narrator of the miraculous in the lives of ordinary mortals, of little vignettes full of circumstantial detail."[2] Hagiographic works securely attributed to Goscelin include texts about Wulfsige at Sherborne, Edith at Wilton, Kenelm at Winchcombe, Ivo at Ramsey, Hildelitha, Ethelburga, and Wulfhilda at Barking, Seaxburg, Eormenhild, and Withburh at Ely, Wærburh at Chester, and Augustine, Mildreth, and numerous early bishops (Laurence, Mellitus, Justus, etc.) at St. Augustine's.[3] Excepting only the minor saints connected to Ely and some of the lesser early bishops at St. Augustine's, Goscelin collected posthumous miracles for all of these saints. These were not short texts. Goscelin's account of Ivo's miracles runs over thirty chapters. His miracle collection for Augustine stretches over fifty chapters, so long that he himself made an abbreviation of the text for easier circulation.[4] In the case of Kenelm and Wulfsige, Goscelin devotes more space to the saints' posthumous histories than their lives. Some of Goscelin's most ambitious works were those concerning the translations of Edith, Augustine, and Mildreth; these texts too are largely made up of stories of posthumous miracles.

In the early part of his career, Goscelin was quite alone in his interest in preserving miracle stories. The few other hagiographers active in England in the first decades after the Norman Conquest cared little for miracle collecting: the anonymous authors of the *Life of Edward the Confessor*, the *Life of Rumwold*, and the *Life of Erkenwald* mention that their saints were performing posthumous miracles but describe none in detail.[5] The lack of interest in miracle collecting is especially striking in the case of Folcard, who, like Goscelin, was a monk of St.-Bertin resident in England. Folcard wrote a *Life of John of Beverley* sometime in the 1060s. He states at the conclusion of the *Life* that "through [John's] merits, cripples were cured, demons were banished, the blind were made to see, the deaf were made to hear," but he did not make the effort to tell a single story.[6] Miracle collecting only began to gain in popularity in England in the 1090s—in large part, as I will argue in the next chapter, because of Goscelin's own example, reputation, and peripatetic labors.

In this chapter, I will examine Goscelin's first three compositions concerning the lives and miracles of English saints: the *Life of Wulfsige*, the *Life and Translation of Edith*, and the *Life and Miracles of Kenelm*. These texts all appear to be products of the late 1070s and early 1080s.[7] This early corpus is particularly revealing of Goscelin's approach to miracle collecting, an approach that would serve as a model for the first native English collectors in addition to Goscelin's own prolific later work. In making these texts, Goscelin listened to the same sorts of people, selected the same sorts of stories, and organized his material in very similar ways. Goscelin's hagiographies are almost always read as serving the political interests of local monastic houses, but while the monks and nuns who told Goscelin stories about Wulfsige, Edith, and Kenelm no doubt valued his writings, these texts appear to have been stimulated and guided much more by Goscelin's own interests, needs, and literary ambitions than by theirs. Though these texts were compiled just a decade or so after the Norman Conquest, Goscelin says nothing about this event and exhibits no concern about Norman skepticism about English saints. What worried him more, it seems, was Norman skepticism about *him*. The late 1070s and early 1080s were a trying time for Goscelin. His long-term patron died in 1078, he was frustrated with his own lack of literary output, he was deeply grieved by the departure of a young nun of Wilton whom he loved dearly, and he was being forced out of the west country—likely because of his overly intense relationship with said young nun. Goscelin wrote his early corpus under a cloud of personal disappointment if not downright disgrace. But though this time must have been a low point, it was also the launching point of his career as "the busiest of all Anglo-Latin hagiographers."[8] He was fascinated by the stories told about the saints in his adopted homeland. He possessed the desire and the ability to convert oral stories into graceful written histories that both Saxons and Normans could appreciate. An analysis of this remarkable monk's work and career is essential for an understanding of the beginning of the miracle collecting craze in England.

Goscelin came to England as a protégé of Herman, a distinguished Lotharingian whom Edward the Confessor had made the bishop of Wiltshire in 1045. In 1055, Herman resigned this post, left England, and stayed some years at St.-Bertin. Around 1062, Herman was appointed bishop of Sherborne and went back to England to take up this new position. At this point or shortly thereafter, Goscelin joined him there.[9] Goscelin would speak of himself as being a "youth" [*adolescentulus*] when he arrived in England. Since he appears to have lived past 1107, he may have been in his late teens when he left St.-Bertin.[10] He had already experimented with hagiographic composition by this time. His first known text is his *Life and Translation of Amelberga*, a text about a nun some three hundred years dead whose relics were housed in Ghent. In the preface, Goscelin terms himself a "boy" [*puer*] who has never attempted such a project before. Rosalind Love describes the text as "truly the work of youth."[11] Perhaps Herman wished to secure Goscelin's nascent talents as a hagiographer when he invited him to join his retinue, or perhaps he simply thought of him as a promising young man. Goscelin would later comment that his lodgings on arrival in England were shocking to him, "more like a pigsty than a human habitation," though later, "what I had first abhorred I now loved."[12] Nowhere in his works does he say why he decided to leave home.

After he arrived in England, Goscelin appears to have spent at least a decade in Herman's company without producing much, if any hagiography.[13] In the silent period between the early 1060s and late 1070s, it appears that Goscelin identified Sherborne, the initial seat of Herman's bishopric, as his home monastery. In the prologue of his *Life of Wulfsige*, Goscelin describes a monk of Sherborne as "a fellow monk [*confrater*] I knew, saw and heard," and speaks of how he learned about Wulfsige's life and death "from the brothers' most truthful testimony."[14] As a member of Herman's retinue, Goscelin made many trips to London and undoubtedly other places as well. In his *Translation of Edith*, Goscelin mentions being at Salisbury during Herman's lifetime, a stay that was probably connected with Herman's transfer of the see from Sherborne to Salisbury in 1074–75.[15] Wilton looks to have been Goscelin's most frequent stopover. Located not many miles from Sherborne, Wilton was an ancient and prosperous nunnery patronized by the royal house of Wessex. It was used as something of a safehouse for princesses, widows, and other noblewomen. Goscelin is frequently termed a "chaplain" of Wilton, but he does not describe himself as such and did not necessarily have a formal connection with the nunnery.

Under whatever terms he visited Wilton, Goscelin came to know its inhabitants well. The *Life and Translation of Edith* is shot through with references to sisters and senior nuns at Wilton telling stories about Edith and their other saints.[16] It could be too that the *Life and Miracles of Kenelm* was inspired, at least in part, by conversations he had at Wilton. In the prologue to the work, Goscelin names Queen Eadgyth, widow of King Edward the Confessor, as a "most learned" informant, someone who told him about what she had read concerning Kenelm. Eadgyth probably went to Wilton after Edward's death in 1066; in a charter dated 1072 she is said to be at Wilton.[17] At some point in the 1070s, Goscelin became emotionally involved with his "most dear," "most sweet," and "most beloved" Eve, a young woman at Wilton probably ten years or so younger than himself.[18] We know of this relationship from Goscelin's most well-known work: the *Book of Consolation*, an extended treatise intended for Eve's eyes.[19] In the *Book*, Goscelin describes how he annoyed Eve with his attentions, received books from her, taught her to revere St. Bertin, wept at her consecration ceremony, accompanied her to church dedications presided over by Herman, and grieved with her over Herman's death in 1078. Sometime after this death, Goscelin came to Wilton with plans of visiting Eve as usual, and was devastated to find that she had left, forever, to take up life as a recluse in Normandy. She had not told him she was going.[20]

Goscelin's charged friendship with Eve may not have lasted long, but her departure (exact date unknown, but assumed to have been c.1080) coincided with other major changes in his life. Herman's death in 1078 left Goscelin without a patron. Osmund, the Norman chancellor of King William, was appointed as Herman's replacement in 1078. Goscelin seems to have finished his *Life of Wulfsige* shortly after Herman's death, as he dedicates the text to Osmund, speaks of Herman's death, and describes at the text's close how Osmund translated Wulfsige and the relics of another saint, Juthwara, to silver reliquaries.[21] But if the text was read by the new bishop, it did not persuade him to retain the Flemish monk in his service. Bishop Osmund seems to have been the one who, in Goscelin's words in the *Book of Consolation*, "forced [me] to wander far" because of "the envy of vipers and the cruelty of a stepfather."[22] The date of Goscelin's departure from the region of Sherborne and Wilton is not known, but scholars have speculated that Goscelin's passion for Eve incurred Osmund's condemnation, and that Eve herself may have been ordered to leave Wilton rather than setting out for Normandy voluntarily.

Whatever happened, after some fifteen years in England in Herman's service, and now probably in his early thirties, Goscelin lost his standing in the bishop's household as well as his dear Eve, "the sweetest child of my soul." It was at this point that texts began to pour out of him. Goscelin wrote the *Book of Consolation* c.1080–82. The *Life and Miracles of Kenelm* could not have been written before 1066: it is likely a composition of the late 1070s or early 1080s.[23] Goscelin states that he began both the *Life of Wulfsige* and the *Life and Translation of Edith* while Herman was alive and with his encouragement, but he did not finish either of them until after his death: they are usually dated c.1080. In the prologue to the *Life and Translation of Edith*, the most ambitious work of this early hagiographic corpus, Goscelin dedicates the work to Archbishop Lanfranc and declares that "it is your part to accept the votive offerings of all those bringing gifts to the tabernacle of the Lord . . . I seek to offer a previous jewel."[24] By the jewel, Goscelin meant Edith herself, "famous throughout the whole land," but Goscelin's texts themselves bear comparisons to gems. In early Norman England, miracle collections like these were actually a good deal rarer than precious stones, and it is to those texts that I now turn.

Wulfsige, Edith, and Kenelm died in different centuries and would seem to be quite different saints, but in the 1070s all three were lodged in Benedictine monastic houses and were viewed as active miracle-working saints. Wulfsige, the most recently dead, was a bishop at Sherborne. Within a decade after his death in 1002—from what Goscelin tells us—Wulfsige had been translated to a shrine near an altar.[25] Edith, an illegitimate daughter of King Edgar, was probably born in the 960s. She was enclosed at Wilton from the time she was a young girl. Wulfthryth, Edith's mother, became abbess at Wilton, but though Edith was appointed the abbess of three nunneries, she refused these posts. She died a virgin in 984 or 987.[26] Kenelm, possibly a wholly fictitious figure, was supposedly a young Mercian prince killed through the machinations of an evil sister in the early ninth century. At some unknown point, his relics were translated to Winchcombe. The place of his supposed martyrdom also served as a cult site. Kenelm was widely celebrated in Anglo-Saxon litanies by the eleventh century.[27]

Swithun's healings were what fascinated Lantfred and impelled him to write his collection at Winchester. In the years he spent at Sherborne and Wilton, Goscelin probably did not see a cult of the magnitude of Swithun's in the 970s, but Wulfsige and Edith were certainly both revered as healers. Goscelin describes how the water used to wash the relics of Wulfsige and Juthwara was "a source of healing for many sick people."[28] Monks of Sherborne, servants of the monks, and relatives of the monks were all claiming healing from this drink at the time he wrote his miracle collection.[29] Edith, too, was busily curing cripples and striking off the chains of lay supplicants at her tomb.[30] But, strikingly, these recent healing and liberation miracles among the laity, of such fascination for Lantfred, held little appeal for Goscelin. He tells few of these stories, and what he does tell he tends to compress.[31] The more recent the story, in fact, the less Goscelin seemed to feel it needed elaboration or record. After describing, rapidly, a set of Edith's recent miracles among the laity, he writes, "why should more of these miracles be recounted which are so well-known and frequently perceived by the eyes, that they may be known more certainly by eyewitness experience than by written testimony? There is no need to relate more of these revelations which are so frequent."[32]

What Goscelin saw a need for, instead, was a written reconstruction of the whole history of a saint and his or her cult. For Goscelin, contemporary miracles were an endpoint, a way to wrap up the overall narrative rather than the center of attention. The *Life and Miracles of Kenelm*, the *Life of Wulfsige*, and the *Life and Translation of Edith* are balanced, carefully conceived surveys that encompass the saints' lives, deaths, burials, translations, and past and present miracles.[33] The three texts have a remarkably similar structure despite their differing titles and subjects. Of the thirty chapters in the *Life and Miracles of Kenelm*, Goscelin devotes six to Kenelm's life (cc. 1–6), two to Kenelm's death (cc. 7–8), eight to the discovery and translation of Kenelm's relics to Winchcombe and accompanying miracles (cc. 9–17), nine to miracles "from modern times" (cc. 18–26), and the final four (short) chapters to "recent miracles" (cc. 27–30). He applied equal weight to posthumous miracles in the *Life of Wulfsige*. After six chapters about Wulfsige's life (cc. 1–6), he devoted three to his death and burial (cc. 6–9), five to miracles that started twelve years after Wulfsige's death (cc. 10–14), six to miracles from "modern times" (cc. 15–20), and then four to contemporary miracles (cc. 21–24). Though the *Life and Translation of Edith* is a much longer and more prettified text, Goscelin measures out Edith's story in roughly similar proportions. After twenty-seven lengthy chapters concerning Edith's life, death, and burial and immediate post-burial miracles, Goscelin dedicates a second book entirely to posthumous events, starting with Edith's translation in the late tenth century (cc. 1–2), then digressing into a mini-*vita* and miracle collection for Wulfthryth, Edith's mother (cc. 3–7, life and death; cc. 8–11, miracles), and finally eleven chapters concerning Edith's miracles from the age of Cnut to the present day (cc. 12–22).[34]

Goscelin seems to have been quite conscientious about listing the written sources he was able to find concerning these saints—if any—in the preface or in the course of his text. These references to written sources were apparently meant to enhance the credibility of his texts, but he did not have much to report. He apparently found nothing from or about Wulfsige's life except for two foundation charters issued in Wulfsige's name.[35] At the end the *Life of Wulfsige*, he mentions an account of Juthwara's miracles that described a miracle during the time of Bishop Ælfwold (bishop of Sherborne after 1045 and until at least 1062), a text unfortunately otherwise unknown.[36] For Edith, he seems to have had very little in writing. All he claimed to have was an Old English account of a miracle from the time of Abbess Brihtgifu (c.1040–65).[37] The sources were a little richer for Kenelm, at least for his *vita*: he claims to have had a letter about Kenelm's martyrdom (supposedly sent from heaven), some writings from a certain Wulfwine, and a song and other material in Old English.[38]

This fluky little handful of written sources could not have been much help in constructing the broad histories Goscelin aimed to write. His material came instead from long soaking in the conversations of the communities of Sherborne, Wilton, and Winchcombe. Goscelin writes in the preface that he had learned about Wulfsige "long ago . . . from the present brothers, who like thirsty sucklings eagerly drank in these stories from their predecessors."[39] Goscelin, aptly described as a thirsty suckling himself, could have been listening to stories from the Sherborne monks for fifteen or more years before he completed this text. At Wilton, Goscelin heard stories about Edith from the abbess and the nuns, both "the things which they saw with their own eyes," and "those things which they heard from the venerable senior nuns, who both saw the holy virgin herself and devotedly obeyed her."[40] Goscelin does not provide such a direct statement about hearing stories from the brothers at Winchcombe, but many of the stories he tells about Kenelm show clear signs of having come from them: in a chapter about Kenelm healing a mute man, for instance, Goscelin describes how the man was "restored to speech in the sight of the aforenamed abbot and the brothers and the assembled crowds."[41]

Thus, though Goscelin did not dig into contemporary cults the way Lantfred had, his texts are still almost wholly comprised of stories being told at the time. No single informant stands out in any of Goscelin's texts the way Eadsige does in Lantfred's, but there was a type of conversation partner he sought out: elderly monks and nuns, people who could explain why things looked the way they did in their churches and tell stories about the miracles that had happened in their youth, people who were in a chain of testimony stretching back, in the case of Wulfsige and Edith, even to the living presence of the saints themselves. Goscelin talks about hearing the stories of Ælfmær, for instance, a monk who he says "was with [Wulfsige] himself not only during his life but also as he lay dying."[42] Counting from the time Wulfsige died and when Goscelin arrived in England, Ælfmær must have been in his seventies, at least, when the young Goscelin first met him. Bishop Herman, Goscelin's own elderly patron, was a source for a story about one of Edith's miracles.[43] In the *Translation of Edith*, Goscelin describes a miracle of Wulfthryth experienced by "a sister, who is still alive under the nursing of the younger nuns"; he also discusses the story of a nun who was healed by Edith in her infancy and was "still surviving" in Goscelin's day.[44] Queen Eadgyth, one of Goscelin's conversation partners for the composition of the *Life and Miracles of Kenelm*, must also have been elderly by the time he spoke to her. She died in 1075.[45] Goscelin did interact with younger people. In his *Translation of Edith*, for instance, he writes about a nun named Ealdgyth, "still in the springtime of her youth," who was "grumbling to us" about the loss of some possessions of the nunnery.[46] There was also, of course, Eve, though with her Goscelin seems to have done more talking than listening. In general, though, Goscelin seems to have sought out old stories from older informants when he was collecting stories for his texts.

From his conversation partners at Sherborne, Wilton, and Winchcombe, Goscelin heard hand-me-down stories about the saints' lives, deaths, and burials. He heard and recorded stories of all sorts of miracles—about fetters bursting and the healing of many kinds of illnesses, but also stories about lawsuits, property, and punishments for those who failed to observe feast days; stories about translations, kingly gifts, and patronage; stories that explained how certain objects came to be hanging up near shrines; stories about former abbots, recently dead monks, fellow nuns, relatives outside of the monastery, and lay visitors from near at hand and far away. Notably, Goscelin does not appear to have tried to track down or speak to any lay supplicants. Almost all of the miracles involving the laity in Goscelin's texts closely involve someone in the monastic house, such as the affecting story of how Abbot Godwin of Winchcombe rubbed wax into the sores of a man whose stomach had been tightly bound in chains, a story that was still remembered twenty-odd years later when Goscelin came to Winchcombe.[47] Some of the miracles about lay people in these three texts concern blood relatives of the monks and nuns, such as the story of the evildoings of a certain Brihtric, the kinsman of a nun at Wilton; the cure of crippled man "connected by kinship" to the abbess of Wilton; and the mother of a monk at Sherborne cured by the water of Wulfsige and Juthwara.[48]

To all appearances, Goscelin did his story collecting in-house. That, and Goscelin's decision not to bother much with the swirl of current cults, made his collecting task easier, in certain ways, than Lantfred's. But Goscelin was determined, in a way Lantfred was not, to arrange the stories he heard into a chronology. Whereas Lantfred had not worried about chronology after the first three chapters of his collection, Goscelin wanted to put the stories remembered and treasured by the monks or nuns about their saints in their proper order. This was difficult. Goscelin might ask, for instance, whether anyone knew the story behind the distaff and spindles hanging up over Wulfsige's shrine.[49] Even if a monk said he knew what had happened—that an obstinate woman had refused to stop her work on Wulfsige's feast day and found that she was frozen to those very objects—that did not necessarily mean he knew or remembered *when* this happened. How could Goscelin know where to insert such a story into his overall narrative of Wulfsige's life and afterlife?

Often, it is clear, he did not know. Stories about the life, death, and burial of a saint should obviously go in that order, but things were much more free-floating when it came to posthumous miracles. Goscelin's strategy was to place stories within the succession of religious leaders at the local house in question or (sometimes and) within the succession of Anglo-Saxon kings. In his *Life and Miracles of Kenelm*, for instance, he ties posthumous miracles to the time of King Cnut, Abbot Godwin, Abbot Godric, and then to the present living abbot, whom he does not name. Goscelin structures the *Translation of Edith* around the regimes of Archbishop Dunstan, Abbess Wulfthryth, King Cnut, then abbesses Brihtgifu, Ælfgifu, and finally Godiva, the living abbess. The succession of bishops forms the skeletal structure of the *Life of Wulfsige*, although past priors and kings—Cnut again—also make appearances. Quite a few of the miracles Goscelin tells directly concern these religious leaders: Abbess Ælfgifu's eye is healed, Bishop Ælfwold and Prior Ælfweard have visions about translating Wulfsige, the present abbot of Winchcombe takes Kenelm's relics on a tour to Clent, Kenelm's martyrdom site, and so on.[50] Goscelin never provides dates for these abbots, abbesses, kings, or bishops, but he uses a considerable amount of parchment moving the narrative from one leader to another. Many transitions between chapters concern the death of one and the succession of the next.

Goscelin sweated over these chronological frameworks, but, as we can see now, they are riddled with error. Goscelin starts his *Translation of Edith*, for instance, by announcing that "thirteen years" after her death, Edith appeared in a vision to Archbishop Dunstan, "then still living," and demanded to be translated.[51] Edith died in 984 or 987. Add thirteen and that makes 997 or 1000. At this point, Dunstan had been dead himself for at least nine years: there is no way to make these numbers work. In the *Life and Miracles of Kenelm*, Goscelin places a miracle story in the reign of Cnut (1016–35) *and* the regime of Abbot Godwin (1042–53).[52] In the *Life of Wulfsige*, Goscelin refers to a bishop of Sherborne succeeding Wulfsige that we now know not to have existed.[53] Editions of Goscelin's texts bristle with footnotes noting and attempting to rectify his blunders. "Goscelin here seems to have got into

confusion over his kings of England," writes Rosalind Love in a typical editorial comment.[54]

Frustrating as they are, these mistakes are some of our best clues to
Goscelin's working process. He appears to have learned about these leaders
the same way he learned about the miracles: by steeping himself in house
conversation, listening and asking questions. The further back he tried to go,
the more he struggled and stumbled. One can imagine the nuns of Wilton
telling stories in which Dunstan played a role in Edith's translation and not
realizing themselves that this was chronologically impossible. It must have
been equally difficult for the monks of Winchcombe to recall whether Abbot
Godwin's tenure overlapped with Cnut's reign or not. Old Ælfmær's memory seems to have failed him when it came to the names of Wulfsige's immediate successors, or maybe Goscelin did not to think to ask him about this
until it was too late, or got confused about what he had said. In sum, these
are the kinds of mistakes one would expect to find if someone was attempting
to put chronologies together working only with passed-down oral stories and
very few written texts.[55]

Goscelin himself saw limits to what he could do in this situation. In his
Life and Miracles of Kenelm, he skips over two centuries of Kenelm's posthumous history, leaping from the story of Kenelm's translation to Winchcombe
(which Goscelin presents as occurring very soon after Kenelm's death in the
early ninth century) to a story placed in the time of Cnut, saying, "Having
recounted afresh these things of old sent from heaven, let us describe a few
of the many miracles of modern times and of our own time" [*ex multis
moderni et nostri temporis*].[56] Goscelin uses the term "modern times" again in
his *Life of Wulfsige*, here as a transition after a story about Cnut: "of his very
many miracles, we here faithfully report in addition to the above those which
have been wrought in modern times."[57] Though Goscelin does not explicitly
mark out a transition to "modern times" in the *Translation of Edith*, here
again, strikingly, he launches his account with three stories about Cnut and
Emma.[58] The reign of Cnut, about fifty years earlier, seems to have been the
dividing line for Goscelin, what he considered to be the limit of living memory and after which he could start to write with confidence.

It is hard to say now whether the monks and nuns who told stories to
Goscelin would also have viewed Cnut's reign as the starting gate of the
"modern," or whether this was Goscelin's own working shorthand. In any
case, "modern" stories, the ones from about a generation ago, were his favorites. Goscelin's texts bulge with stories from about twenty to thirty years

before his time. Most of the posthumous miracle stories Goscelin tells in the *Life and Miracles of Kenelm* derive from the time of Abbot Godwin (1042–53).[59] In the *Translation of Edith*, Goscelin highlights the abbacy of Brihtgifu (c.1040–65).[60] In the *Life of Wulfsige*, Bishop Ælfwold, who held the bishopric sometime after 1045 until c.1062, is mentioned more than Goscelin's own mentor Bishop Herman.[61] The closer Goscelin got to the present, the more cursory he became. After story upon story from the time of Abbot Godwin in the *Life and Miracles of Kenelm*, Goscelin makes an explicit transition to "miracles recently brought about" [*nuper patrata*], and describes a miracle connected to Godric, abbot of Winchcombe from 1054 to 1066.[62] It is a short chapter, followed by three even shorter chapters about events "last year" (likely sometime in the 1070s or early 1080s) and so the text comes to a swift close. In the *Translation of Edith*, Goscelin labels a miracle that happened "in the time of bishop Herman"—probably dead when Goscelin was writing—a "recent" miracle, and with that story, he ends the text.[63]

Stories the older monks and nuns remembered from their youth were clearly the most to Goscelin's liking in terms of time period. In terms of type, he tells a wide range in all three of these texts—healings, releases, property disputes, feast day punishments, and so forth—but he seems to have especially liked stories that explained the existence of shrines and cultic objects. Goscelin has much more to say about relic translations than Lantfred did, even though most of the translations he describes happened before he was born.[64] Structuring his texts by abbacies made tracking and inserting multiple translation stories easier, and may well have determined his decision to organize his texts this way in the first place. Goscelin was also eager to tell the stories behind objects like the distaff and spindle at Wulfsige's shrine, the blood-stained psalter at Winchcombe, the little white pallium at Wilton, the broken chains hanging up at Edith's shrine, Wulfsige's staff, Edith's pastoral ring, and where the gold came from for the shrines.[65] The difficulty was knowing where to put these stories. Goscelin terms the distaff and spindle story a "modern" miracle, for instance, but does not connect it to any bishop or prior.[66]

Miracle stories about other local saints were also difficult to place. The standard format of a text focused unwaveringly on a single saint did not seem to reflect the conversational realities Goscelin encountered at many houses. At Wilton, Goscelin was hearing a significant number of miracle stories about Wulfthryth, Edith's mother. At Sherborne, Wulfsige and Juthwara also seem to have been quite tightly linked together by the 1070s—

Goscelin said that they shone "with twin brightness."[67] A century earlier,
Lantfred may well have been hearing about miracles performed by St. Iudoc
or other Winchester saints, but kept his text's focus unwaveringly on
Swithun.[68] Goscelin, with his stronger interest in translations, objects, and
the development of cults at these houses, found ways to slip in a few stories
about Wulfthryth and Juthwara even though they fit neither the organization
nor the titles of his works. He made excuses for the insertion of a mini-vita
and miracle collection for Wulfthryth in his *Translation of Edith*: "it is right
that the same page should celebrate them both together since the same church
embraces them."[69] Juthwara's story appears rather abruptly toward the end
of the *Life of Wulfsige*, where Goscelin jumps back a bishop in order to
explain when Juthwara was translated, reaches further back to describe how
she had died by being beheaded by her brother, and then leaps forward to
the present to relate how bishop Osmund had put Wulfsige and Juthwara
into "reliquaries splendidly adorned with gold."[70] He concludes his text overall by stating "we have added to [Wulfsige's] noble train the martyred virgin
Juthwara, and have woven roses among lilies . . . [so that] by being blended
they might give a more splendid display."[71]

In all three texts, Goscelin will also ignore chronology and link stories
together by type rather than by time. For instance, he describes how Edith
saved Cnut from shipwreck at sea, and, in the same chapter, he describes
how "later on," Ealdred, the archbishop of York, was also saved at sea by
Edith.[72] Just a few chapters afterward, Goscelin describes how Edith defended
the property of Wilton during the reign of Queen Emma, and then writes
"we also add an event which has recently taken place, very similar to this
one," going on to tell a story about Brihtric in the next chapter.[73] Similar
pairings are evident in Goscelin's work for Kenelm: he matches together two
stories about feast day punishments (cc. 20–21), two stories about mute men
speaking (cc. 23–24), and two stories about fetters bursting (c. 26). These are
all in a section ostensibly dedicated to stories from abbot Godwin's tenure.
Matching stories together like this held rhetorical as well as practical value,
beautifying Goscelin's texts in ways that later miracle collectors would also
emulate.

Perhaps the most intriguing aspect of Goscelin's work to slot miracle
stories into chronologies is his treatment—or, rather, lack of treatment—of
the Norman Conquest. In Goscelin's histories, William the Conqueror and
Norman prelates appear briefly at the end of the story simply as the next in
the line of succession of leaders, with no mention of Harold's brief reign and

no suggestion that a watershed event had occurred. Goscelin describes the abbacy of Ælfgifu at Wilton, for instance, as "partly under [King Edward] and partly under the present king, William."[74] In his three early works, the closest Goscelin comes to mentioning the consequences of the Conquest is at the end of the *Translation of Edith*, where he describes how a young Wilton nun felt upset about Edith's failure to prevent the "erosion of the possessions of the monastery." Yet even here, Goscelin does not name or blame any Norman for this erosion—it is the nun who is chided for disbelieving in Edith's powers.[75]

Goscelin's silence about the Conquest and reluctance to tell stories about the very recent past invite a range of readings. Paul Antony Hayward reads parts of the *Life and Translation of Edith* as "a direct command to Lanfranc to support [Edith's] cult" with the "veiled aggression that typifies his work."[76] In general, Hayward sees the English hagiography of the 1070s and 1080s, nearly all of it written by Goscelin, as intended "to assert the righteousness of these English communities": "These saints' cults may well . . . have been the most formidable weapon left to the English in their resistance to Norman attempts to deprive them of their offices."[77] Stephanie Hollis views Abbess Godiva at Wilton as the woman behind the *Life and Translation of Edith*, suggesting that Godiva sought "to employ Edith again in the service of the convent by commissioning a Legend from Goscelin, with a view to attracting powerful patronage in defense of the monastery's lands."[78] Susan Ridyard, who does not believe that Norman prelates were generally hostile to English saints' cults, nevertheless suggests that Goscelin's *Life and Translation of Edith*, along with other texts of the period, could be read as "defensive hagiography," that is, "an attempt to vindicate not only the status of a saint but also the history, the traditions and the political status of the religious community with which that saint was associated: it was an act of monastic propaganda on a grand scale."[79]

One difficulty with reading Goscelin's early corpus as monastic propaganda is the very limited circulation of these works. This fact makes it difficult to view these texts as winning patronage or propagandizing for Wilton or Sherborne even within religious circles. One complete and two abridged manuscript copies of Goscelin's *Life of Wulfsige* survive; all of them date from the fourteenth century.[80] There are also only three extant copies of the *Life and Translation of Edith*. The earliest of these, from the early twelfth century, lacks the dedicatory letter to Lanfranc and the *Translation*.[81] The *Life and Miracles of Kenelm* appears to have been the most widely circulated of these three texts, with nine extant manuscript witnesses, but unfortunately Goscelin does not name his (likely Norman) dedicatee.[82] Rosalind Love, the editor of the *Life and Miracles of Kenelm*, remains undecided whether or not the text should be read in the context of "the sweeping of the new broom" at Winchcombe.[83]

Two Normans we know Goscelin thought of as readers of his early texts were Bishop Osmund, to whom he sent the *Life of Wulfsige*, and Archbishop Lanfranc, who received the *Life and Translation of Edith*. Osmund had been in England for less time than Goscelin and probably did not know many of the stories Goscelin recounts in the *Life*. If Osmund read the text, he likely did come away with a clearer understanding of Wulfsige's history at Sherborne. But, importantly, he does not seem to have needed the text to respect Wulfsige. Osmund had honored Wulfsige and Juthwara with a translation to new silver reliquaries *before* Goscelin completed the text.[84] Archbishop Lanfranc, too, probably knew few of the stories Goscelin recounts in the *Life and Translation of Edith* and would have learned something if he read it. However, it is highly unlikely that Goscelin thought of him as a man hostile to English saints in general or Edith in particular.[85]

It is much easier to make an argument that Goscelin's west country hagiography was designed to gain Norman respect and patronage for *Goscelin* than for the saints and houses he wrote about. Goscelin's dedicatory letters beseech his readers for their good favor. He begins his letter to Lanfranc, for instance, by reminding the archbishop that it is his responsibility to accept all gifts and to see "for what uses of the Church the work of each individual is fit."[86] At a point when Goscelin had likely been driven out of the west country, he rather poignantly declares to the archbishop that "no person is shut out, we are all invited to the supper of the Lamb . . . the gifts of all are demanded."[87] Goscelin plays up the humility game in these letters, requesting, for instance, that Osmund see in the *Life of Wulfsige* "not so much the clumsiness of the workman as the evidence of truth, so that under your bright gaze the night and gloom of bombastic incredulity might not mar the bright radiance of sanctity."[88] If we did not know that Osmund already celebrated Wulfsige's cult, it would be easy to read this passage as expressing a fear of Norman "incredulity," but it seems rather to reflect Goscelin's anxieties about Osmund accepting his work. Goscelin's care to name his chief oral and written sources in his texts also seems designed to enhance the credibility of his own writing. Although Goscelin implores Lanfranc to accept the *Life and Translation of Edith* despite the fact so much of it was based on stories told by women—"nor will their sex be a reason for detracting from the truth of their testimony . . . the handmaids of the Lord prophesy as well as the men-servants"—he never expresses any fears that *English* testimony per se would be doubted by his Norman readers.[89]

Goscelin's longing, as he states in the *Book of Consolation*, for a "little refuge similar to yours . . . where I might pray, read a little, write a little, compose a little; where I might have my own little table . . . where I might revive the dying, tiny spark of my little intellect, so that, unable to be fruitful in good deeds, I might yet be just a little bit fruitful by writing in the house of the Lord," suggests that Goscelin's composition of hagiography had a lot to do with his own sense of fulfillment.[90] Goscelin also complains to Eve of lethargy: "I wish I could point to my successes and say . . . 'with the pen of a scrivener that writes swiftly.' I have become more sluggish than a snail."[91] When he wrote this, he may well have been thinking specifically of the *Life of Wulfsige* and *Life and Translation of Edith*, texts that appear to have loitered long in the planning and gathering stage. Goscelin attributes his failure to complete the *Life of Wulfsige* before Herman's death to "day-dreaming," and writes of delaying the completion of the *Life and Translation of Edith* as a result of "bashfulness or negligence."[92] He speaks of "the requests of the senior nuns" at Wilton and the requests of the brothers at Sherborne in the prologues of these hagiographies, but Goscelin seems to have completed these texts on his own timetable and in response to his own pressing needs—his precarious position after the loss of Herman and of Eve—rather than any of theirs.

Rather than reading Goscelin's early corpus as "commissioned" works, then, they are better read as textual offerings—novelties, in the late eleventh-century context—that he could give to his hosts at Wilton and Sherborne and use as calling cards for himself. The *Life and Miracles of Kenelm* could well be the first work Goscelin composed as a visiting resident rather than as an integral part of the community, as he was at Sherborne and Wilton. But even at Winchcombe and the other houses he would visit, it is unlikely that "commission" or "employment" is the right word to describe his efforts. He likely did not receive any formal remuneration for his writings. He lived off Herman's patronage for many years without producing hagiographies, and even once he was on the move, we should probably think of him less earning his keep by writing hagiographies than making himself a desirable guest with his ability to work the sprawling conversational life of a monastery into polished prose narratives.

Goscelin's reluctance to address the recent past or sensitive political topics is a frustrating aspect of his texts today, but his ability to create elegant,
lively, and yet inoffensive histories of the saints posed obvious advantages to
both himself and his hosts. It is possible that Goscelin, who was after all a
foreigner himself, did not see a great deal of difference with the Conquest,
particularly because he was insulated by Herman's patronage for more than
a decade after the event. Whatever tension he experienced in the aftermath
of the Conquest, he kept himself and his textual creations out of the fray.
Reginald of Canterbury would later say of him: "You, O Goscelin, overflow
with the arts as the sea flows over with water and sand. Kindly, cheerful,
and well-stocked with honest qualities, you keep clear of the disputes and
dissensions that occur among us. You are the glory, grace, and adornment of
our monks, a comfort to the sorrowful, the sweet solace of the troubled."[93]

Our best evidence for how Goscelin viewed his position as a foreign
monk working as a hagiographer in England is found in a text he composed
about St. Mildreth in the 1090s. In the text, the *Libellus contra inanes S.
Mildrethae usurpatores*, Goscelin describes an ongoing dispute about Mildreth: her relics were being claimed by both the monks of St. Augustine's
and the canons of St. Gregory's in Canterbury. He then explains how a "very
learned and upright man called Bertrann, a foreigner said to be an archdeacon
in his own country, arrived upon this scene . . . Certain whisperers of vain
assertions approached him and asked, with much pleading, that he immortal-
ize their imaginings in letters [*ut sua figmenta litteris perpetuet multis precibus
fatigant*]." Bertrann turns them down, saying that he did not come in order
to "affirm your deliriums in writing." Whatever penalty they received for
speaking lies, "I would suffer more ruinous punishment by perpetuating
them in writings [*ego perniciosius luam scriptis perpetuando*]."[94]

Goscelin presents the hagiographer in a powerful position in this story.
Bertrann's writings will perpetuate the stories he chooses to record. He carries
a heavy responsibility to sort out truth from fiction, to affirm only what
should be affirmed and remembered. The learned and unbiased foreigner
realizes immediately that the stories he is hearing are lies. The dispute concerns not Anglo-Saxon versus Norman, but right versus wrong.

By the time Goscelin wrote this passage, he was by far the most experienced hagiographer on English soil. The sluggishness he had complained of
in his early thirties was long gone. The hagiographies Goscelin composed for
Wulfsige, Edith, and Kenelm were just the beginning: he became the talented
foreigner coming on the scene at house after house, the one who listened to

stories of the saints, selected the ones he thought best, and composed texts that stand at the beginning of written record for many of the houses he visited (see Figure 2: boxes marked with a "G" are collections composed by Goscelin). William of Malmesbury would say of Goscelin that "in his religious life learning was matched with integrity" [*in eius conuersatione certaret honestas doctrinae*].[95] Whatever disgrace he had experienced as a result of his intimacy with Eve and explusion from the west country had been forgotten. Goscelin had been more than "a little bit fruitful by writing in the house of the Lord."

In the prologue of the *Life and Translation of Edith*, Goscelin exclaims about the newness of things, how "the whole earth sings a new song; harmonies and choirs and psalteries and every kind of music resounds everywhere. New histories, new written works are dedicated to divine praise."[96] A decade or so after Goscelin sent this text to Lanfranc at Canterbury, a famed musician there, a monk of Christ Church named Osbern, would decide to try his hand at a "new song" and "new written work" himself. His collection of the miracles of Dunstan would be the first major miracle collecting effort undertaken by a native English monk in many generations.

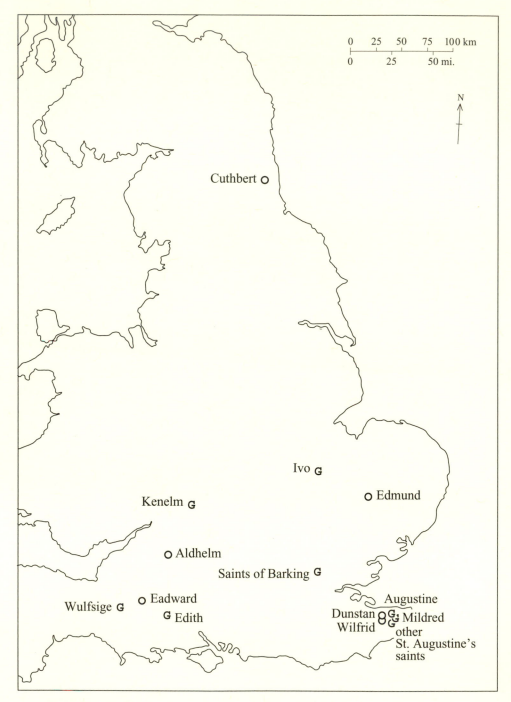

Figure 2. Miracle collecting in England c.1075–c.1100. Goscelin of St.-Bertin and the First English Miracle Collectors.

CHAPTER FIVE

They Ought to be Written:
Osbern of Canterbury
and the First English Miracle Collectors

In the early 1090s, Osbern of Canterbury described the miracles of Dunstan as "those things that ought to be written" [*eorum quae scribenda sunt*].[1] It was a novel sentiment for an English monk. For centuries, English literati had not felt it necessary to turn spoken stories into text. Miracle collections compiled in tenth-and eleventh-century England were almost all the work of foreign monks. The most prolific was Goscelin of St.-Bertin, a Flemish monk who arrived in England in the early 1060s and began writing hagiographic texts for a wide range of English saints in the late 1070s and early 1080s. A portrait of the mature Goscelin at work is found in a chapter of the *Liber Eliensis*, the late twelfth-century compilation of an anonymous author at Ely. The *Liber Eliensis* author describes how the abbot and monks of Ely experienced a healing miracle of Æthelthryth, the major saint of their house. The author terms it another miracle that the "most clever" Goscelin, "who all over England was rewriting the lives, miracles, and deeds of saints," happened to be visiting the monastery at the time and could write it down for them.[2]

In the 1090s, Goscelin was resident at St. Augustine's Abbey, located less than a mile from Christ Church, and was producing the masterworks of his large corpus.[3] In this same decade, Bertrann, a French monk from the region of Paris, wrote *Of the Miracles of St. Edmund*. This long and highly sophisticated text, completed c.1100, was the first significant collection of the miracles of Edmund of Bury (d. 869), a famed English saint.[4] At Malmesbury, an Italian named Faricius wrote a *Life of St. Aldhelm* between 1093 and 1099, a text that actually has more to say about Aldhelm's posthumous miracles than about his life.[5] But there are also the first glimmerings of a native tradition (see Figure 2). Sometime between 1083 and 1104, an anonymous writer at Durham picked out four stories about Cuthbert's miracles from the *Historia de Sancto Cuthberto* and added three new stories of his own.[6] At Shaftesbury, an anonymous writer—possibly a nun—wrote the *Passion of St. Edward* sometime before 1090. The text is short, but it appears to have been closely modeled on the structure of Goscelin's hagiographies. The writer includes a few contemporary posthumous miracle stories at the close of the text.[7] At Christ Church, Canterbury, two monks were writing hagiography in the 1090s. Eadmer, fifteen to twenty years Osbern's junior, was working on his first known composition: a rewriting of a difficult tenth-century *vita* into a more readable text. At the close of this *Life of St. Wilfrid*, Eadmer included two stories about recent miracles experienced by Christ Church monks.[8] Osbern, in contrast, devoted a whole book of his *Life and Miracles of Dunstan*—some twenty-six chapters—to Dunstan's posthumous miracles.[9] Osbern had access to at least two previous *vitae* of Dunstan.[10] He may also have had an Old English *vita* that is now lost.[11] But Osbern appears to have had little to draw on when he compiled his collection of Dunstan's miracles. It is the most original part of his work, and by far the most ambitious of the first English-authored miracle collections.

Osbern's *Miracles of Dunstan* holds a vanguard position in the remarkable upsurge of hagiographical writing at English monasteries in the post-Conquest period. Such texts are often read as defensive works meant to contest the Norman takeover of the English Church and Norman discomfort with Anglo-Saxon saints.[12] Read with such arguments in mind, though, Osbern's collection is a disappointing and even rather confusing text. Osbern makes no mention of Norman skepticism about English saints. Moreover, as Jay Rubenstein has noted, "Osbern offers us no commentary, negative or positive, on the difference between Saxon and Norman monastic customs. . . . [he is] frustratingly silent on the points which most relate to the effects of the Conquest on monastic life at Canterbury."[13] Osbern also would seem to have missed his moment if his plan was to establish Dunstan's credentials with the new Norman leadership. Osbern had grown up in Christ Church and had reached adulthood at the time of the Conquest. He was present when Lanfranc, the Italian abbot of Bec, arrived at Canterbury in 1070 to take charge of the English Church. He could conceivably have written a collection then. But Osbern did not write his *Miracles* until sometime after Archbishop Lanfranc's death in 1089. Furthermore, it becomes clear on reading the *Miracles* that Osbern considered Lanfranc to be something of a saint himself.

Rosalind Love writes that "there must also be a better explanation than skepticism for the undeniable link between the arrival of the Normans and the large-scale production of Anglo-Latin saints' Lives. It may be safer to think in terms of cultural assimilation."[14] Cultural assimilation is indeed reflected in post-Conquest literary production, but in this chapter I will focus on a factor thus far overlooked: the literary context. Osbern's sense that he should write down Dunstan's miracles seems to have been more keyed to the arrival of *Goscelin* than the arrival of the Normans. The timing, structure, and contents of his collection make the most sense when read alongside Goscelin's work. William of Malmesbury would mention the Christ Church monk and the Flemish visitor in the same breath, saying that Goscelin was "second only to Osbern in music," and it is quite likely that the two men knew each other personally.[15] Like Goscelin, Osbern placed stories of Dunstan's miracles in a rough chronological framework, told few stories of the recent past, did not bother to collect stories from the laity, steered away from speaking of the Conquest, and focused his attention on stories that were years old by the time he compiled his collection. But whereas Goscelin had the detachment of an outsider, Osbern wrote because, as he explains, he had seen Dunstan's miracles in others and felt them in himself [*cum in alios me vidente, tum in meipsum me sentient*].[16] His collection is marked by its bombastic style, sensitivity to music, reverence of Lanfranc, and numerous personal reference points. Eadmer would later find Osbern's collection so sloppy and overly personal that he rewrote the entire text. "Verbose and contorted" is a modern scholar's verdict on Osbern's prose.[17] Taken as a whole, Osbern's collection reads as a rather clumsy imitation of Goscelin's work. Still, Osbern's collection holds considerable charm as well as significance. It was written by a man who wanted his memories of Dunstan's miracles to be remembered as much as the miracles of Augustine, or Æthelthryth, or Mildred, or any of the other saints Goscelin was commemorating in writing. Osbern's collection, the first of the major English-authored texts, would also be one of the more cheerfully self-absorbed to be composed in England.

Osbern entered Christ Church as an oblate and grew up in the community. When he first appears in our sources, though, he is at Bec, in Normandy. Osbern is discussed in four letters written in the mid- to late 1070s by Anselm, the philosopher who was then abbot of Bec and would later become archbishop of Canterbury.[18] From the letters, we learn that Osbern is at Bec to repent of his faults. Anselm addresses two of the letters to Henry, the Italian prior of Christ Church who had come to Canterbury with Lanfranc. In the first letter, he writes "insofar as you suffer with me in your righteous heart over his affliction, forgive Osbern if he sinned against you." In the second, written when Osbern was about to return to Canterbury, Anselm tells Henry that Osbern "freely accuses and curses the perversity of his former life," and asks that Henry "nourish the infancy of his resolutions toward improvement with the milk of pure affection."[19]

Osbern's fault has been described as "a rebellious attitude towards the Norman hierarchy,"[20] but while Osbern clearly had troubles with Henry, these letters read to me as if there were more at issue than disobedience. Rubenstein has suggested that Osbern may have had close personal involvement with Ægelward, a monk of Christ Church whose homosexual proclivities threw the house into uproar during Lanfranc's tenure and whose miracle forms the longest story in Osbern's collection.[21] Whatever the reason Osbern was sent away, he seems to have used his time in Bec well. In his letters to Lanfranc, Anselm states that Osbern "daily develops admirably," and speaks of his great personal affection for Osbern: "as long as I live I should never wish to be separated from him." He asks Lanfranc to "treat him kindly unless you perceive that his way of life has earned him something else." As an addendum to one of these letters, Anselm tells Lanfranc that he had "heard that Saint Dunstan drew up a 'Rule of Monastic Life'" and that he "would very much like to see the famous *Life* and *Institutes* of so great a father."[22] Osbern must have been telling Anselm stories about Dunstan.

How long Osbern remained repenting at Bec is unclear—Anselm's letters cannot be dated any more precisely than to the mid- or later 1070s—but Osbern appears to have been back in Canterbury c.1080.[23] Just around the time that Osbern returned home, Goscelin ran into trouble in the west country, began writing a great deal of hagiography, and started his travels from monastery to monastery. Goscelin dedicated his first major hagiographical work, the *Life and Translation of Edith*, to Archbishop Lanfranc c.1080.[24] Osbern may well have seen this text. It seems to have been sometime in the 1080s that Osbern wrote a brief *Life and Translation* for Ælfheah, an archbishop of Canterbury who was killed by the Danes in 1012.[25] Osbern says little about posthumous miracles in this text. Eadmer would later tell a story about a conversation between Lanfranc and Anselm concerning the sanctity of Ælfheah, but Osbern does not mention this conversation in the preface of his work.[26] What he says is that he had written music for Ælfheah at Lanfranc's instigation, and then he complains about the "idleness" of those who did not write in the past. It is necessary to write a *Life of Ælfheah* now, he writes, "otherwise we may blame our predecessors in this matter, yet seem far more blameworthy for that same fault to our successors."[27] This same attitude would drive Osbern's later work as well as much of the miracle collecting of the early twelfth century.

Thanks to Eadmer, we have a vivid picture of Osbern from around the time he was writing the *Miracles of Dunstan*. In a passage in his text *Of the Relics of Ouen*, Eadmer describes how he was writing in the cloister when Osbern came to him with a proposition. Osbern reminded Eadmer how Lanfranc, then dead, had delegated them to look through all the cathedral's chests containing relics, and how they had found an especially magnificent one full of bones. "Now," Osbern said, "I think I know what is in it, but lest we never know for sure . . . let us go, you and I, with the sacrists, and inspect it." And so they did, but, Eadmer says, without confessing first, and without letting the prior—still Henry at this point—know anything about it [*inconsulto priore*]. To their delight, Osbern and Eadmer found what they were hoping for: a slip of parchment among the bones that proved they were those of St. Ouen.[28]

This relic search happened after Lanfranc's death in 1089 and (it appears) before Anselm's accession to the archbishopric in 1093. These were fractious years in Canterbury. Four years before his death, Lanfranc had established St. Gregory's, a new secular college of canons. These canons, meant to help the archbishop and to manage pastoral duties in the city of Canterbury, almost immediately got themselves entangled in a dispute with the monks of St. Augustine's over the possession of the relics of St. Mildred. The canons claimed they had translated Mildred from Lyminge to their own church, a claim Lanfranc supported.[29] The monks angrily argued that they had the true relics of Mildred, which they had translated from Thanet to St. Augustine's some fifty years earlier. This dispute set the stage for serious tumult when Abbot Scotland of St. Augustine's died in 1087 and Lanfranc appointed his successor, Abbot Guy. The monks and prior refused to accept the new abbot. Peace was restored when Lanfranc sent some monks to live in other monasteries and put others in fetters, but the tension continued: sometime later, Lanfranc found out that a monk was plotting to kill Abbot Guy. After Lanfranc's death in May 1089, open revolt broke out, and Abbot Guy fled to Christ Church for safety. The bishops of Rochester and Winchester suppressed the revolt and dispersed some of the monks of St. Augustine's, replacing them with monks from Christ Church. Abbot Guy, reinstalled in late 1089, now needed, in Richard Sharpe's words, "to make clear that all was well again at St. Augustine's."[30]

It was around this time, in the early 1090s, that Goscelin began writing at St. Augustine's, possibly at Abbot Guy's invitation. His first projects were about Mildred. He compiled a *Life, Translation, and Miracles of St. Mildred* and he also wrote a text titled *A Little Book Against the Wrongful Usurpers of St. Mildred the Virgin*, a work as polemic and as pro-St. Augustine's as its title suggests.[31] Abbot Guy also began preparing for a grand translation ceremony.[32] Over the course of a week in September 1091, Guy opened tombs and translated saints' relics to new resting places in the church. Goscelin was there. William of Malmesbury would later comment that Goscelin wrote "the story of St. Augustine's translation so vividly that he seemed to point a finger at every detail for his contemporaries and make future ages see it with their own eyes."[33] While Goscelin did not finish his *Translation of St. Augustine* until after 1099, his intention to write such a work and others about Augustine was no doubt well known among all the monks of Canterbury, both at St. Augustine's and at Christ Church.[34]

These are the specific circumstances in which we should read Osbern's decision to compose a *Life and Miracles* of Dunstan. Osbern and Eadmer's search of the relic chests very likely came on the heels of the impressive translation ceremonies at St. Augustine's. This search is usually read as another sign of Osbern's "rebellious" nature, but it probably should be read at least as much as a sign of envy. Just down the road, the monks of St. Augustine's—many of them Osbern and Eadmer's former colleagues at Christ Church—were getting to open and inspect all the tombs of their saints. These new monks had also gotten Goscelin to agree to write for them. The translation ceremonies were obviously a thrilling public event, but Goscelin's writing projects must have been thrilling too, perhaps even more so. He was going to or had already started writing a series of hagiographical texts the likes of which had never been seen in Canterbury before. Goscelin was asking questions, plumbing memories, and writing down miracle stories told about Mildred and Augustine and other saints housed in the monastery for the first time. This is when Osbern decided that Dunstan's miracles "ought to be written," so that "in future times all English people might know what honor and reverence they owe to the name of such a man."[35]

Those future readers were much on Osbern's mind as he composed the prologue to his collection. Osbern's goal was to preserve stories for those readers, but he worries about whether they will believe what he has to say: "we invite all those who read this to believe for this reason: if they might desire to write other things which happened in their time and wish to be believed themselves, so they should believe us."[36] Of the stories he was going to tell, "most of them, nearly all, we know to have been done in our own times, but we have received a few from other times, presented to us by the most true telling of most true men."[37] Osbern also informs his readers that he intends to tell the miracles "in the order in which each thing happened" [*quo ordine quaeque res acta sit*].[38] His collection breaks into four rough chronological blocks: stories from before his time (cc. 2–10); stories from Osbern's youth (cc. 11–16); stories from the time of Lanfranc's tenure as archbishop (cc. 17–22); and three additional stories, some of them, perhaps, from the period after Lanfranc's death (cc. 23–25).

Goscelin, too, organized his collections chronologically, but he did so much more systematically than Osbern. Whereas Goscelin placed miracle stories within a framework of a succession of abbots, archbishops or kings, the only archbishop Osbern talks about in the collection is Lanfranc. Osbern's ordering of the nine stories from "before his times" is particularly fuzzy. Dunstan was clearly considered to be a powerful miracle-working saint soon after his death in 988. To take just one example, in a benedictional written in 1023 for use at Canterbury, Dunstan is praised as one who "restored health to innumerable ailing ones," and who was "associated with the company of angels by the flashing of miracles"—this is the same language that one finds in benedictions honoring Swithun.[39] Osbern might have had a written source for some of these early stories. In the prologue to the *vita*, he stated that he would "excerpt some stories from his books of miracles, of which very little now remain."[40] But he mostly seems to have been working with stories that he remembered hearing as a youth. He begins this section with a couple of miracles that ostensibly happened soon after Dunstan's death, and closes soon after telling a story about the healing of a musician at Christ Church named Elward whom Osbern seems to have known himself.[41] Except in the case of the last miracle of this section, which Osbern says he heard from "a venerable old man," Osbern does not provide any information about who he heard these stories from.[42]

Osbern carefully marks the transition in his collection from old stories to his stories: "We will now speak of those things that happened in our own age," he says at the close of the tenth chapter, and so introduces a set of seven stories from the period of Osbern's boyhood and the years before Lanfranc arrived at Canterbury. Osbern frequently highlights his own personal experience or witness in these miracles, beginning with a story of a young woman who recovered her sight in Canterbury cathedral. He describes how he, along with the other boys, saw the signs of this miracle, and realized that "our good father had done something good." The boys were going to be whipped that day, but their masters decided that it was not fitting to do so since a miracle had occurred.[43] He then tells about the day when "I was attending at the altar along with another boy," and a woman approached them with her crippled daughter. The daughter was later healed by Dunstan.[44] Osbern tells how a crippled man was cured on Easter, describes the miracle of a contracted boy in a slapdash chapter consisting of a single sentence, and then completes the section with yet another long story about boys being under threat of a whipping (Osbern again identifying himself as one of their number) and a chapter about the burning of Canterbury cathedral in 1067.

If Goscelin had been the one to compose a *Life and Miracles of Dunstan*, he would likely have been very interested in Osbern's memories of pre-Conquest miracles: he liked hearing stories from people of Osbern's generation. But Goscelin's approach to such stories was more scholarly, impersonal, and discriminating.[45] Osbern does not seem to have taken much care with the ordering of the stories within this section. Eadmer later thought that at least one story was markedly out of place.[46] Osbern's failure to complete his story of the contracted boy—Eadmer would later write it out for him—is also a kind of shoddy workmanship that Goscelin would not have tolerated. It is hard to imagine, moreover, that Goscelin would have written about this period in the history of Christ Church without any mention of the archbishops of Canterbury, as Osbern does, nor that he would have included two very long and fairly similar stories revolving around impending whippings.

Osbern, though, could fill his collection as he liked: these were the miracles he "felt in himself" and wanted others to remember too. There is also something more politically pointed about the last two stories in this section than one usually finds in Goscelin's collections. In the first story, one of the boys of Christ Church sees Dunstan in a vision. Dunstan tells the boy that they would escape a whipping that day, but also that he should tell the prior that the unbaptized corpse of the "infant son of the earl Harold" should be removed from the church. The boy tells his superior about this vision, but is ignored.[47] In the following chapter, Osbern describes how Dunstan continued to warn the brothers in visions that he could not remain in a place with "the fetus of the pagan boy," but nothing was done. This, Osbern says, is what precipitated the terrible fire of 1067 that destroyed a great deal of Canterbury cathedral and the Christ Church cloister buildings.[48] What are these stories supposed to mean? Could stories about Harold's son, Dunstan's warnings, and the awful fire that came in 1067 be some kind of cloaked commentary about Canterbury's role in the Conquest?[49] As enigmatic as these stories are, they are closer than Goscelin would get in his hagiographies to talking about the Conquest. It seems possible that these stories held political resonances that would have been obvious to Osbern and his contemporaries but are now (intentionally) hard to decode.[50]

Osbern transitions out of this delicate territory into a discussion of the arrival of Lanfranc, the man who, Osbern proclaims, "turned the hour of our ruin into good," and was "of all those who were on earth in our age the most holy and the most wise."[51] The stories concerning Lanfranc (cc. 17–22), form the longest section of Osbern's collection by a considerable margin. These six chapters take up as much of the text as the early miracles and Osbern's boyhood memories combined. Osbern describes Lanfranc's rebuilding of the cathedral and translation of Dunstan, with an associated miracle concerning Abbot Scotland (c. 17), Lanfranc's victory over Odo of Bayeux through Dunstan's aid (c. 18), the miracle concerning the "mad" Ægelward (c. 19), Lanfranc's illness and healing by Dunstan (c. 20), the healing of Lanfranc's chaplain at the same time (c. 21), and two miracles that Lanfranc told Osbern to preach to the people (c. 22). Lanfranc's attitude toward Anglo-Saxon saints has been much debated. H. E. J. Cowdrey's assessment, following on that of Susan Ridyard, is that the evidence "points to no racial hostility or even skepticism on [Lanfranc's] part."[52] Jay Rubenstein and Paul Antony Hayward, however, both argue that Lanfranc took a much more hostile stance.[53] In a far-reaching discussion of Norman and English relationships after the Conquest, Hugh Thomas suggests that "any Norman hostility to English saints (and, despite the problematic nature of the sources, I suspect that there was some) would in practice have been muted, and generally directed at obscure cults," and that "Ridyard was quite right in claiming that the Normans as a group sooner or later embraced English cults."[54]

I agree with Thomas's appraisal, and think that we can sharpen our understanding of this issue by envisioning what was likely happening on an oral level as Norman appointees first took up leadership positions in the English church. When Lanfranc came to Canterbury, it could not have been long before he heard stories about Dunstan's miraculous powers. The same must have been the case elsewhere. Indeed, one would assume that even before Norman appointees arrived at places like Canterbury, Ely, Bury, Winchester, and Durham, they knew the names and reputations of the major saints of those establishments. They had good reasons, both personal and political, to want powerful miracle workers on their side. The key moment would have been when Norman leaders started requesting aid from English saints for themselves and seeing themselves as their beneficiaries. It is clear from Osbern's collection that Lanfranc made the transition from hearing stories to asking Dunstan for help. What the collection does not tell us, though, is when he first did so. Was it months after coming to Canterbury? Years? A decade? Could the Ægelward miracle, which Osbern terms the "most admirable" of them all, have been the turning point?[55]

Unfortunately, our evidence is not good enough to chart this process for Lanfranc. Osbern provides no dates in these stories, and his ordering of the miracles should not be trusted as a reliable chronology. However, William of Malmesbury provides a narrative of such an assimilation process in his account of the miracles of Aldhelm, the major saint of Malmesbury. Abbot Warin arrived in Malmesbury in 1070, the same year Lanfranc came to Canterbury. He was, William says, "at first doubtful of Aldhelm's sanctity, as the saint was not responding to his prayers with any display of miracles."[56] But then a blind man regained his sight in the church in a very dramatic fashion: blood gushed from his eyes as he was lying prostrate before a crucifix. "This event," William writes, "which was witnessed by the townspeople and all the monks alike, was instrumental in increasing Aldhelm's prestige among the Normans."[57] After this, Warin "put his mind to honouring the precious confessor," and prepared for a translation of Aldhelm's relics. In 1078, with Bishop Osmund of Salisbury in attendance, "the bones were decently placed in the shrine, and the people gave vent to their joy."[58]

Once a new Norman leader, in Osbern's phrase, "saw in others or felt in himself" the miracles of a major local saint, it must have been a powerful force in welding him to his new community. English monks may have initially resisted the idea of their major saints giving aid to the new Norman leadership (an important side of the equation that is rarely considered). However, once English monks accepted a story of their saint helping or healing their Norman prelate, it must have been a central factor in their acceptance of him as well. Thomas writes that there is "a surprising amount of evidence for co-operation and close emotional bonds between native and Continental monks, beginning at a very early date after the conquest," and argues that "many in the church were pioneers in creating harmonious relationships across ethnic lines."[59] Instead of reading Anglo-Saxon saints as flashpoints for English/Norman hostility, we should look to them as loci of integration. The initial period of trial, experimentation, and adjustment does not seem to have lasted long. Abbot Warin was one of the most doubtful of the new Norman leaders, and it took him just eight years to go from skepticism to relic translation ceremonies. Even Abbot Walter of Evesham (1077–1104), who tested relics by fire, was convinced of the sanctity of St. Credan and sent the relics of the major saint of the house, Ecgwine, on a fund-raising tour.[60] Sharing in the miracles of the major saints bonded Norman churchmen to communities of English monks, and vice versa.[61]

By the time Osbern wrote his *Miracles of Dunstan*, such an oral assimilation process seems to have run its course at Canterbury. Lanfranc became a devotee of Dunstan, and Osbern had become a devotee of Lanfranc. In the central part of his collection, Osbern does not discuss miracles among the laity, his own absence in Bec, or anything else except Lanfranc. The last chapter of this section, in fact, has nothing to do even with Dunstan: in the chapter, Osbern retells two miracle stories (not about Dunstan) that Lanfranc had told him. In her study of Bertrann's collection for Edmund, Antonia Gransden speaks of Bertrann acting as the "apologist" of Baldwin, the abbot of Bury, but Osbern goes even further.[62] He makes Lanfranc into a proto-saint. When Lanfranc has a vision of Dunstan, he tries to kiss his foot. Dunstan pulls his foot away, "as if to show honor to Lanfranc," Osbern explains.[63] When Lanfranc is ill and healed by Dunstan, so is his chaplain. The chaplain had been lying on a cot made out of the wood of Lanfranc's cot, and Osbern reports that the chaplain believed he was granted healing on account of Lanfranc's grace.[64] In the miracle concerning Ægelward, Lanfranc binds the madman with "holy hands" and tells him to confess his guilt.[65] Lanfranc leads a procession to Dunstan's tomb where he exorcises Ægelward's evil spirit, and Osbern writes that he and the other monks rejoiced greatly that they had an archbishop who could quiet the fury of demons.[66] When Lanfranc seems to be dying, the Christ Church monks wail and mourn because "they knew they would never find the likes of him again."[67]

Osbern seems to have thought the Christ Church monks had a new Dunstan on their hands. This section of his collection could serve a dual purpose for future readers, making them aware not just of Dunstan's merits, but of Lanfranc's as well. In the story of a certain Edward who wanted to leave the monastic life and was struck dead by Dunstan, Lanfranc appears yet again: Edward decided to became a monk "under the regime of the glorious

Archbishop Lanfranc," and when he tried to leave the church, he saw
Dunstan with a "terrible visage"—this was not, Osbern comments, the way
Lanfranc had seen him in his vision.[68] Goscelin only wrote hagiography for
long-established saints. The "youngest" saint he commemorated in his oeu-
vre was Wulfsige of Sherborne, who had died in 1002. Osbern's focus on
Lanfranc hints at the more rooted attitude of homegrown hagiographers.
They were on the lookout for saints in their midst, and quite ready to feel
the actions of established saints in their own lives as well.

The last two stories in Osbern's collection are the most personal accounts
in the entire text. They do not fit into the overall chronological framework
of the collection. Osbern introduces the first by writing that it happened
"before these days"—that is, before the story of the discontented monk Edward. "Before those days" was when Osbern was walking along the beach
with his friend, a knight of Thanet, who had asked him for help in a lawsuit.[69] Osbern writes the chapter in the form of a personal dialogue between
himself and the knight. Osbern frequently injects life into his *Miracles* by
means of prayers and speeches he puts into the mouths of the actors, but his
experimentation with conversational dialogue in this chapter is particularly
notable.[70] The final story in the collection is about Osbern's own victory in
a lawsuit by means of Dunstan's aid. Osbern is circumspect about the problems that brought him into court, but he describes the facets of the vision he
had at Dunstan's tomb in considerable detail, including the fact that at the
wonderful moment he had been invited to play an instrument with a choir
of angels, he woke up.[71]

Osbern concludes his collection by comparing himself to a singer stop-
ping in the midst of a beautiful song, thus leaving his listeners eager for more.
"I think this is enough," he writes, "to commend to the faithful of the
universal church [Dunstan's] eternal glory."[72] He had completed the first
significant narrative composition ever composed by a Christ Church monk,
and one of the very first texts of any kind to be written by an Englishman
after the Norman Conquest.[73] The text is a textual ark designed to carry the
stories Osbern treasured into the future. He does not appear to have spent
much time talking to lay visitors to Christ Church or even to his own monastic colleagues about Dunstan's miracles. He certainly did not bother to search
archives for material, as the foreign hagiographers did.[74] Instead, he transformed his own memories and experiences into textual collectibles.

What we cannot know is which stories Osbern decided not to tell, nor
how different the collection's tone would have been if he had written it in

1067, after the fire at Canterbury, or in 1071, shortly after Lanfranc's arrival. In the years around the Conquest, what miracle stories might have been circulating about Dunstan, Archbishop Stigand, and other Anglo-Saxon prelates? When was the story about the corpse of Harold's baby created, and by whom? If Lanfranc heard the story of the corpse, what did he think of it? From the perspective of gaining evidence about the initial impact of the Norman Conquest, Osbern's is not a very helpful collection. This, the earliest of the significant English-authored collections, was written too late. By the time Osbern wrote his collection, the first exchange of miracle stories between the Normans and the English was already well in the past, and the Norman leadership was enthusiastic in their support of the major Anglo-Saxon saints. What drove Osbern's efforts was a desire to preserve a comfortable set of stories—*his* stories—of Dunstan's miracles for later readers. Though Eadmer would not be happy with the results, others were: Osbern's *Miracles of St. Dunstan* survives in at least six manuscripts, more than many other collections of the period.[75]

Osbern was just the first English monk to follow Goscelin's lead. Richard Sharpe has argued that Abbot Guy's translation of Augustine's relics in 1091 "set a model—it almost became a fashion—for such events in England," and shows how translations at Winchester, Bury, London, Durham, and Ely followed similar patterns.[76] Goscelin's work at St. Augustine's, Ely, Wilton, Barking, and other monasteries equally set a model and created a fashion for miracle collecting in England. The Benedictine establishment in England was a small social world. Almost all the miracle collectors at work in the late eleventh century seem to have been acquainted with each other. Goscelin writes about Bertrann, the collector of Edmund's miracles, being in Canterbury at one point.[77] Eadmer knew Osbern; he knew Goscelin; and he knew or came to know Faricius, the miracle collector at Malmesbury, as well.[78] In such a tight-knit social sphere, the vogue for miracle collecting spread quickly. Eadmer's work typifies the new variety and quantity of miracle collecting in the early twelfth century. He was far more sophisticated, ambitious, and prolific than Osbern, and yet more ambivalent and conscious of the limitations of his writing than Osbern would ever be.

CHAPTER SIX

Obvious Material for Writing:
Eadmer of Canterbury
and the Miracle Collecting Boom

Eadmer of Canterbury was likely in his forties when he decided to rewrite Osbern's *Life and Miracles of Dunstan*. He declared that his aim was to correct the style and the faults in Osbern's work such that "all ambiguity [will be] set aside both to those living and to those who will follow later." Although some might accuse him of being inspired by arrogance or envy, he knew of no such motive in himself. He wrote out of "the love of truth alone."[1] In his reworking of the *Miracles*, Eadmer left no story or even phrase handed down by Osbern untouched. He got rid of most of Osbern's nattering about "my times" and "their times," switched the order of some chapters, abbreviated most of them, and downgraded Lanfranc from a proto-saint, as he is in Osbern's collection, to an admirable, but mere human archbishop.[2] Most strikingly, anywhere Osbern had mentioned his own experience or eyewitness, Eadmer rewrote the story to erase Osbern's presence. For instance, when Eadmer retells the story about a woman being healed by Dunstan and Osbern and other boys of Christ Church escaping a whipping as a result, there is nothing about the boys. Eadmer reduces the story to a single, tepid paragraph, less than one-quarter the length of Osbern's enthusiastic version.[3] He cut out the most personal stories of Osbern's collection completely. The stories Lanfranc told to Osbern, the knight of Thanet's story, and Osbern's own victory in a lawsuit found no place in Eadmer's collection.[4] He also gave the miracle concerning Ægelward, the longest in Osbern's collection, a new and backstabbing interpretation. For Osbern, the moral of Ægelward's story was to confess one's sins. Eadmer says that the miracle was meant to shock the lordly Christ Church monks out of their worldly ways, to induce them to give up and scorn as dung their gold and silver, fancy clothes, horses and dogs—and musical instruments.[5]

Looking at what Eadmer did with Osbern's collection, one has to wonder whether Eadmer had always some difficulties with his older colleague. When Eadmer heard Osbern proudly telling his stories or reading out his finished text, was he thinking dark thoughts about how miracle stories ought to be told or how a collection ought to be written? Eadmer was perhaps fifteen to twenty years younger than Osbern. He, like Osbern, had entered Christ Church as a child, but he was very young at the time of the Conquest—just six or seven years old.[6] He wrote his first known composition, a *Life of Wilfrid*, in the early 1090s, the same time that Osbern was composing his *Life and Miracles of Dunstan*. He may have written his next work, a *Life of Oda*, while Osbern was still alive, but Osbern had almost certainly died by the time Eadmer rewrote the *Life and Miracles of Dunstan* c.1103–6.[7] On completing this text, he had already written more than Osbern ever had, but much more was to come. Eadmer's later oeuvre includes sermons, letters, hymns, and a major chronicle, the *Historia Novorum*, as well as hagiography for more saints, including accounts of the lives and miracles of Oswald of Worcester and Bregwine, Ouen, and Anselm of Canterbury.[8] He wrote up to the very end of his life, until his "white hairs and trembling fingers" forced him to halt.[9]

In the early twelfth century, few English writers equaled the quantity or variety of Eadmer's output.[10] But Eadmer was not alone in his frustration with the faults of his predecessors, nor in his sense that miracle stories were "obvious material for writing," as he puts it in his collection of Anselm's miracles. In the first four decades of the twelfth century, Benedictine monks composed over two dozen miracle collections for a wide variety of English saints (Figure 3). Many of these saints had never been commemorated in writing before. In this period, English monks also created the first versions of the *Miracles of the Virgin* and recounted numerous miracle stories in their chronicles. This surge of hagiographic writing is, in E. Gordon Whatley's words, "an important aspect of English intellectual and literary history."[11] I devote the first part of this chapter to a survey of these miracle collections and their underlying contexts: the growth of English monastic libraries, a new drive to preserve oral stories and information in written record, and a general blossoming of Latin prose composition, particularly in the form of letters and chronicles.[12]

In the second and third parts of the chapter, I turn back to Eadmer's work, concentrating on the texts he wrote at Christ Church in the last years of his life. Eadmer was a fretful man. His warning to the readers of the *Life and Miracles of Dunstan* exemplifies his manner: he writes "not for those who are anxious to criticize . . . if anyone is not sympathetic to what I am seeking to do, may he not waste his time with the things I am writing."[13] In his old age, Eadmer found much to fume about at Christ Church. He had spent most of his forties and fifties away from Canterbury. When Anselm was forced into exile, he had gone with him. After Anselm's death, Eadmer left Christ Church again to travel with Archbishop Ralph. In 1120, Eadmer was chosen to become the bishop of St. Andrews. He went to Scotland to take up the post but never received consecration, probably because of his uncompromising views on the primacy of Canterbury. When he returned to Canterbury, he spent his last years writing hagiography. These final writings highlight Eadmer's nostalgia for the Anglo-Saxon past, his concern for minor saints in post-Conquest devotion, and the purposes and limitations of preserving oral miracle stories in texts.

Miracle Collecting in England c.1100–c.1140

In early twelfth-century England, established Benedictine monasteries became more wealthy. Their populations swelled—some monasteries had close to one hundred members—and their monks took up pen and ink like never before.[14] In his discussion of the manuscripts of early Norman England, Richard Gameson has noted that the growth of monastic libraries was "fairly limited" after the Norman Conquest, but that "around the turn of the century, there was a substantial increase in the rate at which libraries were growing. The growth rate climbed further at the beginning of the twelfth century; and then rose even more dramatically in the early twelfth century."[15] Nearly all of these new books were copies of old texts. Monks worked to stock monastic shelves with the works of the Church Fathers and post-patristic theologians, though some hagiographical and historical texts (especially the works of Bede) were being copied too, as well as small corpus of Latin Classics.[16] It is striking how exactly the making of miracle collections in England tracks the overall trajectory of book production outlined by Gameson. Miracle collecting, too, was very limited after the Conquest, gained traction at the close of the eleventh century, and then spread dramatically in the early decades of the twelfth century.

In the first twenty-five years of the century, many of the major preexisting miracle collections for English saints were rewritten and expanded. At Winchester and Sherborne, an anonymous writer working c.1100 compiled a long collection of the miracles of Swithun. For the first part of his text, he reworked Wulfstan of Winchester's versification of Lantfred of Fleury's miracle collection. The last fifteen chapters of the collection are his own, including five final stories that appear to be contemporary.[17] In this same period, an anonymous monk at Bury abbreviated Bertrann's miracle collection for Edmund and added on three new stories. Though this was not a long text, it was written with considerable rhetorical pretensions.[18] At Durham, a seven-story collection formed between 1083 and 1104 received an addition of eleven stories between 1100 and 1115. Someone added three more around 1124.[19] At Ely, an anonymous early twelfth-century writer wrote a collection of Æthelthryth miracles in an ornate and garrulous style, declaring, "I have toiled at committing to the page in a new style the noble and extraordinary miracles, recorded on ancient scrolls, of . . . the venerable and glorious Æthelthryth."[20] Rosalind Love has proposed that the writer was reworking a tenth-century collection.[21] In this same period, Gregory of Ely composed a metrical poem of Æthelthryth's life and miracles, a text now known only in an incomplete state.[22] Still more evidence of miracle collecting at Ely is found in the *Liber Eliensis,* a late twelfth-century compilation of historical and hagiographical materials. The *Liber* contains numerous miracle narratives that seem to be of early twelfth-century manufacture.[23] Eadmer, as noted above, thoroughly revised Osbern's collection for Dunstan c.1103–6, and William of Malmesbury, the finest English historian of his generation, rewrote and expanded Faricius of Arezzo's late eleventh-century account of Aldhelm's life and posthumous miracles c.1125.[24] "There still survives much that Faricius either did not know or omitted to put down," William explains, "Faricius, though not altogether without style, lacked exact knowledge . . . for he was a native of Tuscany, and did not know the language."[25]

Collections already existed for Swithun, Edmund, Cuthbert, Æthelthryth, Dunstan and Aldhelm by the early twelfth century, however short, unsatisfactory or ripe for revision and expansion they were seen by monks of the period.[26] For other Anglo-Saxon saints, early twelfth-century monks found only *vitae.* Eadmer rewrote Byrhtferth's *Life of Oswald* between 1095 and 1116 (likely more toward 1116), and added on the first collection of Os-

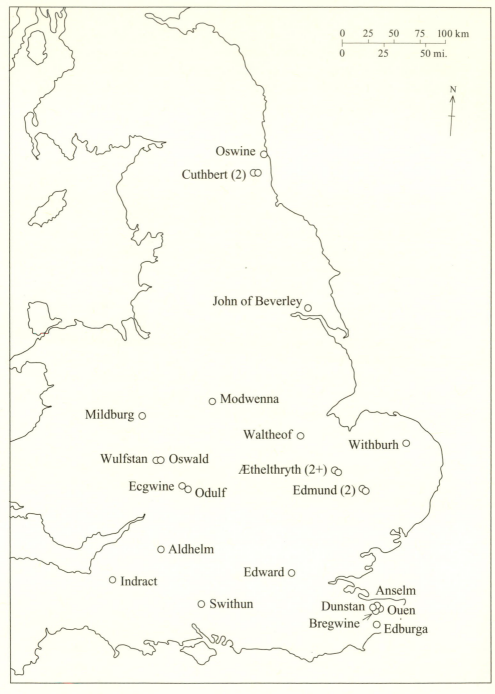

Figure 3. Miracle collecting in England c.1100–c.1140: the Anglo-Norman collecting boom.

wald's miracles.[27] "If I wanted to set down in writing for posterity all the marvelous things which happened through the intervention of this glorious father and which people talk about," he writes, "then I have set my hand to work on something which can never be brought to proper conclusion."[28] His collection is a carefully selected set of eleven stories. Sometime after 1104, Dominic of Evesham rewrote Byrhtferth's *Life of Ecgwine* and added to it a "second book" of miracles, an impressive text concerning twenty-five miracles of Ecgwine from before and after the Conquest.[29] In the prologue to the text, Dominic justifies this new work: "because we know that many of the miracles which God deigned to perform through our blessed father, St. Ecgwine, have been assigned to oblivion because of the negligence and carelessness of writers, it seems fitting for us to hand down a written account."[30] Around this same time in Beverley, William Kellet added a ten-chapter collection to Folcard's earlier *Life of John*: "for a long time," he explains, "I had wanted to commit to posterity certain miracles of St. John which I saw personally, or I knew had been proved by truthful witnesses, . . . [so] that they should not lie hidden concealed under a bushel, or should become completely forgotten through the lapse of time."[31] In a little later period, between 1118 and 1135, Geoffrey of Burton reworked a preexisting *vita* for St. Modwenna and then moved into fresh territory: "a large number of [Modwenna's miracles] have been forgotten through negligence," he writes, "but I append an account of some few of them which happened more recently in our own times."[32]

English miracle collectors strike these same chords repeatedly: they condemn the "negligence" of their predecessors and declare their intentions to do better "for posterity." Scholars have long assumed that Anglo-Normans wrote so much hagiography because written records were necessary for a cult to be firmly established and a saint to be accepted in the post-Conquest climate. R. W. Southern argued, for instance, that "after the Conquest, important questions of cult and the proofs of the efficacy of saints and relics *required* a record to be made of past and present miracles" (my emphasis).[33] But twelfth-century collectors express little anxiety about what their contemporaries think of the saintly status or miraculous power of their saints. They worry volubly about forgotten stories and what posterity will remember in the future. What they were seeking to defend themselves against with these texts, it appears, was the weight of time and the fragility of human memory.

Frustration with the workings of oral processes was becoming widespread in the twelfth century. Michael Clanchy discusses monastic writing briefly in

his magisterial account of the formation of an increasingly literate and docu-
ment-oriented culture in high medieval England, stating that "monasticism
gave writers the humility or the arrogance, depending on one's point of view,
to care about posterity. Their acute awareness of the passage of time is expressed in numerous chronicles. . . . for monks the primary purpose of writing was to inform, or misinform, posterity."[34] Though this is a broad-brushed
treatment, it nevertheless well describes the outlook of English miracle collectors in this period. They were distressed by the loss of stories about their
saints' miracles. They thought—accurately—that many stories from the past
had been forgotten. As the Conquest receded beyond living memory, this
regret for lost stories seems to have been, if anything, sharpened: who could
now remember all the marvelous things their saints had done before the
Normans came? Why hadn't anyone taken the trouble to write down those
stories? "It is splendid to fill the ears of the people with a series of the miracles
of the saints," writes Osbert of Clare in a collection of the miracles of Edmund, "and it is more splendid to commend them by setting them down in
reliable writings" [*scriptis authenticis*].[35] This new attitude was one of the
fundamental forces driving the collecting craze. Speaking was good, but writing was better. Posterity would not have to mourn the disappearance of stories or try to sort out what happened in the past from vague memories, as
early twelfth-century monks did. They would have "reliable writings."[36]

The collections of Osbert of Clare, monk and prior of Westminster (d.
after 1139), contain good illustrations of the type of stories early twelfth-
century collectors wanted to hand down to posterity. Osbert's collection of
Edmund's miracles is now known only from a later twelfth-century compilation, but it appears to have been a collection of some thirteen stories, a typical
size for this period. Antonia Gransden thinks this "booklet" of miracles was
written "perhaps as a thank-offering for hospitality in the abbey [of Bury]
during [Osbert's] exile from Westminster" between c.1125–34.[37] Osbert seems
to have heard the stories in his collection either when he was at Bury himself
or from friends among the monks there. Ralph, the *custos* of the shrine at
Bury, certainly supplied Osbert with some stories.[38] Most of the miracles
concern monks, clerics, or wealthy men and women, and it has a markedly
in-house feel. Osbert's collection of the miracles of Edward the Confessor,
appended to his *Life of Edward*, is very similar. The collection is a set of
eleven carefully chosen stories derived, again, from Osbert's own conversational circles. The first six stories describe miracles from before Osbert's time,
including stories concerning King Harold, Wulfstan of Worcester, and Gil-

bert Crispin's translation of Edward's relics in 1102. In the last five stories, Osbert describes how a girl was punished for not keeping Edward's feast day, how he himself was cured of a fever by Edward, how he told the story of his healing to the crowds in Westminster and a similarly feverish man was cured, how a nun at Barking was healed by Edward (Osbert had close ties to Barking), and finally how a monk of Westminster was cured of three diseases.[39]

Osbert's *Life of Edward the Confessor* would be the first English composition used in the context of a canonization bid. In 1139, Osbert brought this text to Rome and attempted to persuade Innocent II that Edward should be canonized.[40] He appears to have been the sole proponent of Edward's canonization at this point. In a letter to the abbot and convent of Westminster, Innocent II wrote that while he was impressed with Osbert's pleas, a request for Edward's canonization should properly come from representatives of the whole kingdom of England [*totius regni*].[41] Osbert's death date is unknown, but he certainly did not live to see the bid for Edward the Confessor's canonization revived and his text utilized again in the early 1160s. Osbert's collection, it bears noting, has none of the bulk or notarialese that would come to characterize later canonization dossiers. Its rhetorical style is closer to Osbert's letters. Overall, the highly polished, affective, and episodic nature of the miracle collections of the early twelfth century has much in common with the art of letter-writing and making of letter collections so fashionable among monks of the period.[42]

Osbert's collection for Edward the Confessor (d. 1066) was among the few early-twelfth century English collections written for a recently dead saint. Eadmer added on a booklet of miracle stories to his *Life of Anselm* (d. 1109) in the 1120s, to be discussed in more detail later in the chapter. Around this same time, an anonymous author at Crowland compiled a collection of the miracles of Earl Waltheof (d. 1076). After Waltheof was executed for rebelling against William the Conqueror, his body was taken to Crowland and buried in the monks' chapter-house. In 1093, Waltheof's relics were translated into the church. The early twelfth-century miracle collection for Waltheof is unfortunately incomplete in the sole surviving manuscript. Eleven chapters of miracle stories appear in this manuscript, but the collection was likely longer than this.[43] Coleman, a Worcester monk, wrote a life of Bishop Wulfstan of Worcester soon after his death in 1095. This text, composed in Old English, does not survive, but William of Malmesbury made a Latin translation and expansion of the text in the 1120s.[44] William's *Life* includes a few stories of posthumous miracles at its close, including some that were probably not in Coleman's original text.[45]

The collections of the period written in the context of doubt or dispute over the possession of saint's relics carry the most political electricity. The most wrathful text Eadmer ever composed concerned a counterclaim to a relic. In the 1120s, monks at Glastonbury were spreading what Eadmer (and modern historians, too) considered a cock-and-bull story about how Dunstan's body was translated from Canterbury to Glastonbury during the Viking invasions of the early eleventh century. In a letter to the Glastonbury monks, Eadmer furiously implored the elders to "bridle the wanton violence of your foolish young men who open their mouths only in order to seem to know how to speak. . . . I once knew such youths, and perhaps I was one, so I do not doubt that young men are the same these days."[46] Around this same time, William of Malmesbury wrote a *Life of Dunstan* for the monks at Glastonbury. Writing this *Life*, as its editors have noted, "put [William] in a most embarrassing position: he had to satisfy Glastonbury, and yet he surely had no desire to attack Eadmer or his community."[47] In the course of the *Life*, William promises to add a book about Dunstan's posthumous miracles, but he never did.[48] There would have been no way to gloss over the question of where Dunstan's relics actually were in such a text.[49]

Paul Antony Hayward discusses the tensions between the monasteries of St. Albans and Durham that led to the composition of a series of *Lives, Inventions and Miracles of Oswine*, a murdered early Anglo-Saxon Northumbrian king. The first of these texts appeared in the early twelfth century.[50] An unpublished miracle collection concerning Edburga of Lyminge, an eighth-century abbess, ignores the fact that her relics were supposedly translated to St. Gregory's in Canterbury, along with Mildred's, in 1085. This collection may, in Michael Lapidge and Rosalind Love's words, "reflect a continuing counter-claim to possession of Eadburgh's relics at Lyminge."[51] An early twelfth-century miracle collection concerning Withburh, sister of St. Æthelthryth, has recently been edited by Rosalind Love. The anonymous author never mentions Ely in his collection, though that is where Withburh's relics supposedly were in the early twelfth century: instead, the miracles concern Dereham, where Withburh had originally been buried and where there was a healing well.[52] Dominic of Evesham, in addition to his extensive collection for Ecgwine, wrote a short *Translation and Miracles* concerning Odulf, a Frisian missionary whose relics were supposedly brought to England and sold by Viking pirates. A Norman abbot tried to translate Odulf from Evesham to Winchcombe, Dominic writes, but was thwarted.[53]

In his letter to the Glastonbury monks, Eadmer makes a pointed dig at foreign hagiographers as well as the monks themselves. "I am confounded by [your] patent stupidity," he writes, "especially because it is said that these tales were made up by Englishmen. Alas, why did you not look overseas, where they have more experience, more learning, and know better how to make up such stories? You could even have paid someone to make up a plausible lie for you on a matter of such importance. Oh, poor pitiable you, and men of my nation, to be blackened with such stupidity."[54] Monks like Goscelin, Bertrann, and Folcard had certainly taken the lead in hagiographic composition in Eadmer's youth, but by the 1120s the situation had changed radically. Eadmer seems to have been expressing some leftover bitterness from his youth here rather than the current reality. Hardly any collections of the period were written by foreigners. At Much Wenlock, a recently transplanted Cluniac community, a Milanese author wrote an *inventio* for Mildburg explaining how the community acquired the saint's relics; the text includes miracle stories.[55] On two separate occasions in the early twelfth century, canons of Laon took their relics on a tour of southern England, gathering both donations and miracle stories on their way.[56] The only other foreigner writing down miracle stories in England was Archbishop Anselm's nephew, also named Anselm, who was educated at Chiusa and came to England later in life. This Anselm, known as "Anselm of Bury" because he was appointed abbot of Bury St. Edmund's, was the author of one of the first collections of *Miracles of the Virgin*.[57]

Dominic of Evesham and William of Malmesbury also made collections of the *Miracles of the Virgin*: R. W. Southern remarks on "the astonishing rapidity with which, within a space of about thirty years, three collections of miracle stories of type little known before this time were compiled, disseminated, conflated and launched on a career of almost boundless popularity."[58] Alexander of Canterbury, from the circle of Anselm, wrote a similarly placeless collection called *Dicta Anselmi et Quaedam Miraculi* between 1109 and 1116. The first part of this text describes Anselm's "sayings," discourses, or anecdotes from sermons or formal discussions in the chapter house; the second part relates miracle stories told either by Anselm or by people in his familiar circle. Only two of the miracles are attributed to Anselm himself; otherwise these are miracles performed by various saints, the Virgin, and God Himself.[59] Posthumous miracle stories would also find a home in chronicles written by English monks of the period. The *Liber Eliensis*, as noted above, is a remarkable instance of intertwined miracle stories and documentary material, but even writers of national histories, such as Henry of Huntingdon, dedicated space in their chronicles to miracle stories.[60] In forty years, in sum, English monks preserved many times more miracle stories in text than they had in the previous four centuries.

"Just as We Said": Eadmer's Concerns for Minor Saints

When Eadmer returned to Christ Church in the early 1120s after failing to become the bishop of St. Andrews, he was an old man, and he felt it. In the last works Eadmer added into his personal manuscript, now Cambridge, Corpus Christi College MS 371, he would reminisce often about his youth and refer to his "now white hair."[61] In his final years, one of Eadmer's chief worries was the devotion paid to the minor saints of Christ Church. Christ Church possessed many relics imported, or reputed to have been imported, from other locales, as well as many bodies of former archbishops. One of these was Bregwine, a name now (and then) little known. Bregwine was an archbishop of Canterbury who had died in the eighth century. After he was put to rest in the cathedral, he had not done much since. But in the early 1120s, as Eadmer recounts in the longest chapter of his *Life of Bregwine*, a visitor to Canterbury, a German monk named Lambert, took a sudden liking to Bregwine and asked to take his relics to Germany. Archbishop Ralph gave Lambert's idea his blessing. Many of the monks at Christ Church at this point had no problems with the plan either, as Eadmer recounts. Eadmer was clearly horrified, though, and it seems possible that he was the one who mobilized the Christ Church monks to oppose Lambert. When Lambert came to take the body, the monks would only agree to give him Bregwine's left arm. Frustrated, Lambert left to take his case to the king, but before he could do so he became ill and died, probably in 1123. No one took up Lambert's case, and Eadmer wrote in part to make sure no one ever would.[62]

Eadmer's *Life of Bregwine* is more a miracle collection than a *vita*, with more than half the short text devoted to posthumous miracle stories. It is a text characterized by a remarkable blend of spleen and wistful personal reminiscence. Eadmer knew almost nothing about how Bregwine had led his life at Canterbury over three centuries earlier. He dedicates just six short chapters to Bregwine's life, and one of them is a lengthy discussion of the fact that Bregwine did not seem to have performed any miracles during his lifetime. The "voice of the father," Eadmer believed, was enough to inspire and strengthen faith. No miracles were necessary for the people of those days, but, Eadmer wearily remarks, "These good things did not remain for long."[63] He points out that Gregory the Great had said that miracles were for the unfaithful, not the faithful; Eadmer was clearly thinking about Christ Church monks in the "unfaithful" category. Bregwine's few contemporary miracles, in Eadmer's presentation, were less occasions for rejoicing than for guilty remembrance of unfulfilled duties: in addition to telling about Lambert's untimely death, he describes how two Christ Church monks, on separate occasions, felt hard, invisible blows when they were working in the region of Bregwine's tomb.[64] Eadmer was clearly frustrated—and rather worried, too—that Bregwine himself so often had to take matters into his own hands to get the respect he deserved. At the end of one of his stories, Eadmer states that the Saxons were more habituated to showing reverence.[65]

Whether the Saxons actually had been more reverent toward their Bregwines is questionable. Eadmer himself could hardly have known, being such a young boy at the time of the Conquest, but he certainly thought he remembered something different.[66] His *Life of Bregwine* is principally made up of stories he remembered from long ago, including a mournful description of the fire of 1067 that had taken place over forty years earlier (c. 11). There is no miracle narrative at all in this chapter, just an accounting for posterity of how many books and papal bulls had been lost and where Bregwine's body had been before and where it was put after the fire.[67] Eadmer concludes the *Life* by telling a story with a more positive outlook: a monk named William made a new shrine for Bregwine and was cured of an illness by the invocation of Bregwine and Plegmund (yet another early archbishop).[68]

Eadmer may have seen his composition of *Life of Bregwine* as a companion to William's construction of a new shrine. The text was meant to preserve what little he knew about Bregwine in order to stabilize Bregwine's position, to keep the community from eternally backsliding in their devotion or forgetting altogether that this saint, even if only barely active, still deserved proper reverence. Around this same time, Eadmer wrote a little work titled *Sententia de memoria sanctorum quos veneraris*, in which he makes this point with even more force. In the text, he discusses the importance of veneration of all the saints in the church, declaring firmly, "the devout supplication will not be useless, will not be in vain, will not be empty of grace."[69] But in the long run, Eadmer's own devout supplication appears to have been largely in vain.

Bregwine does not ever seemed to have gained a solid foothold in the veneration of the community or city. There is only one known copy of the *Life of
Bregwine*, that preserved in Eadmer's personal manuscript, and little more is
ever heard about Bregwine at Canterbury.

Bregwine's fate must have been a common one. The numbers of saints
that fell into obscurity or never rose above it must have been far higher than
those who maintained a high level of popularity for decades or centuries.
Scholars have been much interested in the Norman "housecleaning" of the
liturgical calendar, that is, in Richard Pfaff's words, "the removal of numerous saints, whether Anglo-Saxon or not, who in the age of Early Scholasticism
(Lanfranc's period and after) must have seemed hopelessly obscure or confused."[70] In Jay Rubenstein's phrasing, Anglo-Norman churchmen removed
these saints because of "liturgical or historical-critical concerns."[71] We can
define major and minor saints in a more helpful way, though, and better
understand Eadmer's attitude toward them, if we think first in terms of the
telling of miracle stories. It seems that Dunstan was considered a major
Anglo-Saxon saint not so much because of a particular holiness of his life or
message (in fact, many of the lesser and discarded saints had better claims to
sanctity, in this abstract sense, than he did), but because at the time of the
Norman Conquest he was the subject of many miracle stories. He was seen
to be acting, alive, in the near past and present. A minor saint is best defined
as a saint who was not the subject of many, or any, contemporary miracle
stories. Such saints must have seemed lifeless. They may have worked miracles in the past, or may never have seemed to wake up after their deaths at
all, but the chances of them reviving again were not good. Nearly all of them
would eventually drift off into permanent oblivion, left to molder as active
saints gained adherents.

One effect of the integration of Normans into Anglo-Saxon monastic
communities must have been to highlight and accelerate this process. "Who
is in that tomb?" or "Who is this saint on your calendar?" must have been
common questions posed by the Normans, and it could be that no one
currently living in the community had worried much about that question
before. If no one could quite remember, or think of a case in which the body
or name on the calendar had shown any signs of posthumous life, it is not
surprising that such a relic would not receive much, if any, veneration from
the newcomers. We know that Abbot Warin at Malmesbury (1070–c.1091)
and Abbot Paul at St. Alban's (1077–93) questioned the propriety of keeping
the faintly saintly relics of their predecessors in places of honor in their

churches. Abbot Warin, in William of Malmesbury's account, took "the bones of Meildulf . . . together with others, once abbots of Malmesbury and later bishops in various sees" that had been kept "in two stone bowls, one on each side of the altar," and had them "hidden away and blocked off with stones."[72] At St. Alban's, Abbot Paul did not preserve the tombs of his predecessors and refused to translate the supposed relics of the founder of St. Alban's into his new church.[73]

It seems that the Anglo-Saxons themselves did not much mourn the downgrading or loss of such minor saints, especially as the major ones received so much loving attention from these same Norman abbots—Abbot Warin translated Aldhelm's relics and Abbot Paul appears to have had no doubts about the power of Alban.[74] But Eadmer's attitude to minor saints was different, and difficult. In his view, *all* of the saints of Christ Church needed to be properly and publicly venerated. His fellows may have been happy to devote themselves to Dunstan, running to him "daily" when they needed help and more or less ignoring the somnolent ones, but Eadmer was not.[75] He showed signs of this unrealistically egalitarian position at the very beginnings of his writing career, as one sees with the chastising tenor of an early sermon about Wilfrid and his early composition of a *Life of Oda*, another lesser archbishop.[76] He also remembered with resentment a conversation between Lanfranc and Anselm over the status of Ælfheah, the archbishop of Canterbury killed by the Danes. This famous conversation took place c.1080, when Eadmer would have been just out of his teens. In Eadmer's account in his *Life of Anselm*, Lanfranc tells Anselm that he doubts whether Ælfheah should be venerated as a saint. Anselm explains, at some length, how Ælfheah was a true martyr, and Lanfranc, appreciative of this "solid argument," says he will now "venerate Saint Elphege with all my heart."[77]

Ælfheah's is the only known case in which a kind of "scholastic" argument was made over an English saint in the wake of the Norman Conquest, and in this case, such argument *saved* a saint from oblivion, propelling him to a position of honor in the church despite his apparent lack of activity. Lanfranc appears to have translated Ælfheah's relics alongside Dunstan's, and he instituted the celebration of Ælfheah's death as a national feast.[78] Were it not for Eadmer's account in the *Life of Anselm*, we would not know why Lanfranc was taken with this minor saint to such a degree. But despite the fact that Lanfranc gave Ælfheah so much attention, Eadmer clearly found his questioning quite irritating. He describes Lanfranc as a "still a somewhat unformed Englishman" [*adhuc quasi rudis Anglus*] because he did not give

Ælfheah the benefit of the doubt, and he interrupts his story of the conversation between Lanfranc and Anselm to recount, at length, an important point in Ælfheah's favor that Anselm had overlooked.[79]

The older Eadmer got, the more irritated he felt. Even after it seemed that he had demonstrated clearly how and why minor saints deserved respect, Christ Church monks would keep forgetting or ignoring the lessons he thought they had learned.[80] The most best-known passage from Eadmer's *Of the Relics of Ouen* is his description of searching through relic chests with Osbern and finding written proof that the relics were those of Ouen. Perhaps the most revealing passage, though, is what comes next. After Osbern was dead, and Eadmer himself was away from Christ Church in exile with Anselm, the new prior did not believe what he had heard about Ouen. He tested the relics all over again. He found them to be, Eadmer grimly writes, "just as we had said."[81] Nor was this the end of it. Eadmer begins his text by stating that many still thought that the claims of Canterbury to Ouen's body were "frivolous" and "far from the truth" [*nonnullis hoc friuolum atque a ueritate uidetur esse alienum*].[82] The things that Eadmer had no doubt said time and again, the stories about Ouen he had heard from his elders and what he had seen and experienced himself, he now decided had to be put into written form.

Eadmer appears to have had somewhat more success with his attempt to preserve devotion to Ouen. There is a (now mutilated) continuation of his text that was written before 1137, and in 1180, when there was a fire in the city of Canterbury, the monks successfully used Ouen's relics to protect their monastic buildings.[83] Both Ouen and Bregwine were eclipsed, though, not just by Dunstan, but by a newly dead archbishop—Anselm, Eadmer's beloved superior.

"I Have Here Made an End": Eadmer and the Miracles of Anselm

When Eadmer completed his *Life of Anselm* a few years after Anselm's death in 1109, he concluded the work by referring to the "many visions" that had been seen concerning Anselm's sanctity. He had decided not to describe any of them, "choosing by our silence to put on an equality [on] all who in their sleep have seen these things."[84] Some years later Eadmer revised the entire text, probably in 1114, and at this point he awkwardly added two posthumous miracle stories to the tail-end of the *Life*. Later still, in the 1120s, Eadmer decided that he needed to make a collection of miracles after all.[85] He added on yet another section to the text, introducing it thus:

> I had already finished the task of writing the life of the venerable Father Anselm, and had said that I would not set down therein any account of the visions which appeared to various people about the time of his death. I did this because I considered it to be an endless business to write down everything worthy of notice which was revealed concerning him, nor did I wish to write of one incident and reject another, as if I judged one more worthy of credence or dignified by a more glorious revelation than another. But the just Judge weighing (to put it plainly) my folly in this matter condescended to give tokens not in dreams but in deeds done for our Father at the time of his death and afterward, which provided obvious material for writing. . . . Thus I was compelled to write down a few of the many things I had passed over previously—things so well known not only to myself but to many others that the whole world knows of them and I am considered a simpleton for having omitted them."[86]

Here is the same Eadmer one encounters in his earlier writings: the determined Truth teller, the writer hesitant to get pulled into the business of writing contemporary stories, a job that so easily could become "endless," and the man worried about his reputation and the criticism his work could elicit. But the pressure had become too great. What Anselm was doing now seemed to him "obvious material for writing."

Eadmer titled his collection "A Brief Description of Some of the Miracles of the Glorious Father Anselm of Canterbury."[87] It certainly is brief, not even a sixth as long as the *Life*. The collection fills about twelve pages of a new quire in Eadmer's personal manuscript and contains accounts of some fourteen individuals. Most of the fourteen were religious men. Six of them were Christ Church monks. Only three of fourteen were lay, and two of these, Humphrey the knight and a noblewoman in Scotland, were well known to Eadmer. The collection as a whole has a choppy feel, with one story juxtaposed against the next with little or no transition between them. He appears to have been writing with no clear plan in mind besides recording those stories he thought interesting or important. The few transitional links he does put in the collection are self-referential ones, such as "after this I went to Scotland" or "what I say now I heard many days later."

For all of Eadmer's dislike of the personal nature of Osbern's miracle collection for Dunstan, at the end of his life he too, in his own way, put himself at the center of this little collection. Eadmer never indulged himself to the extent of presenting a story of Anselm's intervention for his own benefit, but nearly all of the stories he chose to write were those to which he had an obvious personal connection. In many of the stories, Eadmer describes how he had talked in person with the recipient of the miracle, detailing what he had asked and what the person had said—and, frequently, Eadmer describes how he himself had first suggested that the ill person call on Anselm for help.[88] He explains his own thinking process for the interpretation of a vision, including how he had gotten it wrong at first, and focuses in particular on the wonders performed by his own personal possession, a belt worn by Anselm.[89] The stories in this little collection are considerably longer and much more lovingly told than any of those in his other collections. Eadmer even recounts how one cured knight, Humphrey, threatened not to give back Anselm's belt if Eadmer did not quickly take it back from him, and how Eadmer decided to give him a narrow strip of the belt as a keepsake—just the kind of extraneous detail that Eadmer had long ago cut out of Osbern's collection.[90]

As Osbern had done with his *Miracles of Dunstan*, Eadmer filled this collection with stories he held dear, the ones that were already in his mind and memory. The collection does not appear to have been completed in one sustained session. The quire in which the collection is found in Eadmer's manuscript is noticeably worn front and back, probably because it had been lying on Eadmer's desk for some time. Yet if Eadmer did work in fits and starts on this collection, it was not because he was waiting for fresh material or new stories. On the contrary, he states flatly that although the use of Anselm's belt was a "common practice" among sick people and especially among women in labor, he would not collect these stories: "If I should describe one by one the marvels wrought by this single belt alone, I should without doubt become burdensome to all my audience."[91] Earlier, when rewriting the *Miracles of Dunstan*, Eadmer had mentioned but refused to tell stories in any detail about miracles worked by the water in which Dunstan's staff had been dipped.[92] Like other Anglo-Norman collectors, Eadmer concentrated on the stories circulating within his familiar circle, not those of unknown lay strangers—their stories, it appears, automatically registered in the category of "popular rumor" for him.

Eadmer wanted to create a collection of those stories most well-known and important to him—and by that standard, too, it appears, the most "truthful." But even with these limited goals, the collection appears to be even more brief than Eadmer had initially intended. The last miracle story in the collection, the story about a fire at Bury St. Edmunds, is written in a different hand than the rest of the quire. Eadmer apparently could no longer write for himself. The different hand also adds a concluding paragraph to the collection in which Eadmer addresses Anselm directly: "I have written these things as best I could, O reverend father Anselm . . . Now my white hairs and trembling fingers constrain me to lay down my pen, both persuading and compelling me to turn myself wholly to prayer. . . . Farewell therefore, my dearest Father and advocate; assist me, thy pupil Eadmer."[93] The very last words of the concluding paragraph read: "If anyone after my death shall add to what I have written anything which God may do through thee, let it be ascribed to him who wrote it, not to me. I for my part have here made an end."[94] Was Eadmer worried about what the younger man, now transcribing his words onto the parchment for him, might write in the same manuscript after his death? Was he thinking, at the very end, of what he had done to Osbern's collection?

Eadmer and other Anglo-Norman collectors in England were chiefly concerned to save their knowledge of miracle stories for future reading audiences. But the fantastic success of Eadmer's writings in the case of the present writer and readers of this text, a future reading audience he never imagined, should not blind us to the general problems of writing for the future. The problem Eadmer points to at the end of his miracles for Anselm is an obvious one. Without Eadmer's warning, it would be easy enough to mistake a few more miracle stories jotted into his manuscript as his composition. He could not guarantee that manuscripts of his texts would be preserved or recopied after his death. Nor could he do anything to protect his textual voice from corruption—or correction from a brash younger colleague—in the future.

Yet even if a manuscript found its way intact into the hands of a future reader, there were other problems. Eadmer was asking future readers to care about the past, to listen to and invest themselves in the flattened echoes of past voices. Given the nature of the oral world, this was asking a lot. Readers have their own present to enjoy. With fresh stories to hear, why go back to the dead voice of the text, a wearying burden to read almost as much as it is

Figure 4. Insane man cured at Becket's tomb. Canterbury Cathedral, Trinity Chapel Ambulatory Window n.IV (15). Author's photograph used with the kind permission of the Dean and Chapter of Canterbury cathedral.

a wearying burden to write? The difficulty is represented in a panel in the stained glass windows of Canterbury cathedral (Figure 4). A book rests on a pedestal beside Thomas Becket's tomb. It is a time capsule, the words from the past fixed and stored and waiting—but it has no reader. All eyes are pulled instead to the other end of the image, to the excitement of the miracle of the man suddenly cured at Becket's tomb. Eadmer and other collectors worked hard to make their textual voices appealing, but they were in a losing battle when competing with animate lives and voices. The irony of his work is that he was asking the future to care more than he did himself about collections from the past. He was merciless, as we have seen, in his treatment of Osbern's collection.

The immediate future appears to have responded in kind. Eadmer's *Life of Bregwine* is found only in his personal manuscript and may never have been recopied at all. Eadmer's *Life of Anselm* spread widely, but the miracle collection for Anselm was often only partially copied or dropped altogether.[95] Before the twelfth century was out, moreover, it would be severely abbreviated.[96] Miracle collections were often treated in such cavalier fashion. While scribes seem to have seen copying *vitae* as a must, copying miracle collections was a maybe.[97] The making of miracle collections, however careful, elegant, or controlled, guaranteed nothing for the future. Writing fixed something of the present oral world, but could not ensure the continuance of that present cult into the future, just as the making of a time capsule does not stop time from passing. Cults went where they would, text or no text. They grew and developed, appeared and disappeared according to the interests of the living and their own oral rhythms.

Miracle collecting itself was to change, too, as time went on. The form, length, and content of late twelfth-century collections would be very different from those written by Eadmer and his contemporaries. Later English collectors would no longer focus on saving the stories of their own inner circles. They would instead turn their gaze outward, to the stories brought into their churches by layfolk. Someone like Eadmer, who thought it unnecessary to burden his readers with accounts of the people cured by the water touched by Dunstan's staff or the many marvels performed among the laity by Anselm's belt, would have found the collections compiled by later generations at Christ Church and elsewhere all but unrecognizable.

CHAPTER SEVEN

What the People Bring:
Miracle Collecting
in the Mid- to Late Twelfth Century

Near the close of his fifth book of the miracles of Thomas Becket, about two-thirds of the way through a collection that would become the longest ever created in medieval England, William of Canterbury began a chapter with a short but striking reference to his own collecting project. "Brother William returns to hear what novelty the people will bring," he wrote, perhaps trying to encourage himself to keep going, before recounting yet another miracle story.[1] In the early twelfth century, hardly any collections hit the forty-chapter mark. By the end of the century, a collection of forty chapters seems almost short (see Figure 5). These collectors valued volume, variety, and a new kind of secretarial precision in the recording of names and places.[2] They were less interested in retelling folkloric stories than in analyzing facets of contemporary miracle stories largely ignored before, such as the medical aspects of healing miracles and the "causes" of odd or distressing miracles.[3] The most consequential change in miracle collecting, though, was the collectors' new attitude to "what the people bring." Earlier miracle collectors had usually included a few stories about lay visitors in their collections, but collectors working between c.1140 and c.1200 increasingly concentrated on such stories. By the end of the century, English collectors were filling their collections all but exclusively with stories told to them by the laity.

Though the thirty-odd collections made in England in the mid- to late twelfth century have received less attention than those created in the Anglo-Norman period, this is arguably the most interesting phase in the history of English miracle collecting. In terms of the numbers of stories committed to

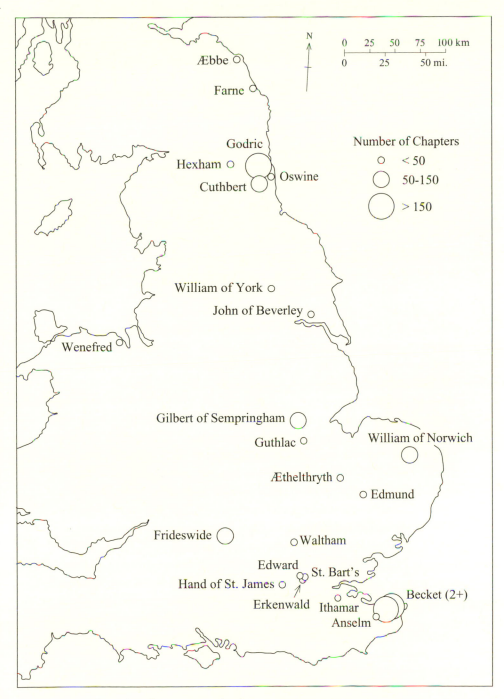

Figure 5. Miracle collecting in England c.1140–c.1200.

parchment, it was certainly the most productive. Collectors of the period—
whose numbers now included Augustinian canons and a Cistercian abbot as
well as Benedictine monks—were willing to spend many more hours working
on their collections than their predecessors.[4] As their attention shifted from
the tales told within their own conversational circles to those told by lay
strangers, the content of their collections transformed. The stories preserved
in early twelfth-century collections tend to reflect the experiences and difficulties of cloister monks: ill abbots, ill monks, ill friends and relatives, lawsuits, aggressive nobles, troubled young monks, thieves, property disputes,
lost books, cruel schoolmasters, and so on. Stories in later twelfth-century
collections tend to reflect the problems of lay men and women. Collectors
now amassed stories about sick children (enormous numbers of sick children), ill husbands, ill wives, work accidents, shipwrecks, drownings, troubled young women, difficult pregnancies, lost coins, even diseased animals.[5]

In the first part of this chapter, I survey the collections composed in
England from c.1140 to c.1170, a transitional period in which some collectors
were interested in collecting lay stories and others were not. I show how
collectors were starting to save vengeance stories with a new flavor, animal
stories and women's stories, as well as taking a more ambitious, medical and
technical approach to miracle collecting. I also briefly examine the canonization bids for Edward the Confessor and Anselm of Canterbury in the 1160s.
The miracle collections created in the context of these bids did *not*, notably,
participate in the new trends. In the second part of the chapter, I survey the
multiple miracle collections created for Thomas Becket after his violent death
in 1170. I examine the manuscript circulation of the two massive collections
for Becket created by Christ Church monks, and establish that the first of
these texts, written by Benedict of Peterborough, had the widest circulation
of any shrine collection of the age. I then assess how these manuscripts were
used. Though Benedict's collection was filled mainly with stories he heard
from the laity, there is little evidence that these stories were ever communi-
cated back to the laity. Like the other collections of the period, Benedict's
text was meant for the consumption of religious men and posterity. In the
third part of the chapter, I survey collections created in England from c.1170
to c.1200. One result of the Becket cult and collections was a very marked
increase in miracle collecting outside Canterbury. But the Becket cult did
not just inspire more collecting. It also accelerated the new trends, pushing
collectors toward laity-centered and longer collections. I conclude with a
discussion of two further developments at the close of the century: the trans-

lation of some collections into Anglo-Norman French and the shaping of a miracle collection for an English saint by the demands of a canonization process for the first time.

Later twelfth-century collections were formed in the vortices of specific cultic situations, individual inspirations, innumerable conversations, and many kinds of cultural change. The winds that blew in these cultural changes were powerful and felt by more than by miracle collectors. One sees the same blend of sincere pastoral impulses and desire for more control—both a fascination and a frustration with lay religious experience—in other late twelfth-century religious enterprises. This was the time of the creation of the Cistercian laybrotherhood, the extension of confraternities between monks and layfolk, the rapid accretion of indulgences designed to increase lay attendance at specific churches and religious festivals, and growing attention to the confession of sins among the laity.[6] What ultimately drove the new concern with the laity is hard to discern. Perhaps, with the new wealth and improved social conditions of the later twelfth century, lay people were able make their presence known at shrines in new and more insistent ways; perhaps the building of so many parish churches in this period made the pastoral needs of the laity more visible; perhaps the answer lies in the complex set of impulses and movements that we group under the label the "Reformation of the Twelfth Century."[7] What is clear is that religious men were waking up to the fact that there were a lot of souls and stories out there, a realization that would have major implications not just for miracle collecting but for medieval culture as a whole.

Miracle Collecting in England, c.1140–c.1170

While there is no sharp divide between miracle collecting of the 1130s and the 1140s, a good place to begin tracing the new interest in lay stories is in London, where, in the early 1140s, a canon of St. Paul's named Arcoid composed an ambitious collection of miracle stories for Erkenwald.[8] Erkenwald (d. c. 693) was termed "London's great saint" by William of Malmesbury.[9] Arcoid, lamenting that his predecessors were content to rejoice and remember Erkenwald's miracles, "neglecting, alas, to bind them with letters," declares his intention to "set forth his acts for the generations after ours" in the prologue to his collection.[10] Arcoid addresses his fellow canons at St. Paul's more than once in the text (e.g., "Let us therefore fear God, brothers, for there are few impieties [Erkenwald] ignores"), but few of the collection's stories, strikingly, are about the canons.[11] Instead, overseas visitors and local citizens take the star roles in most of the stories. Arcoid writes often of "the enormous crowd of people" at Erkenwald's shrine, "a few of whom," he comments, "desired him to heal their souls, while most wanted their bodies healed."[12] Arcoid became so familiar with the perspective of the ordinary lay supplicant that in one story he even has a citizen complain at length about the softness of the canons' lifestyle: "You can sing without care both day and night, for no necessity compels you to work. Your life should be thought of as more a game or stage play than a real occupation."[13]

The form of Arcoid's collection is rather more traditional than its content. He concerned himself more with quality than with bulk. Names and places are occasionally but not systematically included in the nineteen chapters of his collection. Like most Anglo-Norman collectors, Arcoid's aim was to retell a limited selection of stories with style and care; many of the chapters in his collection are quite lengthy and make for good reading. A particularly notable feature of Arcoid's collection, as Eamon Duffy has pointed out, is its number of "savage little stories" about saintly punishments.[14] Anglo-Norman collectors tended to tell vengeance stories about rapacious nobles being slapped down by saints or peasants being injured for refusing to honor a feast day. Arcoid's punishment stories are about London craftsmen. He describes the frightening experiences of a silversmith, a pelterer, a painter, and so on, stories he likely heard from the people themselves or people of similar status.[15] In other later twelfth-century collections, one finds numerous punishment stories about ordinary people aping holy rituals or mocking the saints, pilgrims refusing to help others in need, people misusing or stealing relics, women being overly vain, and so on.[16]

In the early 1140s, a monk of Rochester composed a collection of the miracles of Ithamar, an early bishop of Rochester (d. c. 660).[17] This anonymous collector could find out very little about Ithamar's life, as he states in his prologue, and did not try to compose a *vita*: he focused instead on the contemporary miracles of his ancient saint. His collection is shorter and considerably more clipped in style than Arcoid's composition, but he too was more interested in lay stories than was typical for Anglo-Norman collectors. In his fifteen-chapter collection, he gave over four chapters to miracles concerning Rochester monks and three to the stories of a priest, a clerk, and a knight. The rest describe miracles of ordinary layfolk. In earlier collections, the "crowd" often functions just as an applauding body; in the Rochester monk's collection, though, and in many collections of the time, people emerge from the crowd to tell their stories. In one story, for instance, a man speaks up from the crowd [*de turba exclamans*] to describe his healing from fever; in two other chapters, the Rochester monk describes how women among the crowds at the tomb were cured.[18]

The most notable element of the Ithamar collection is the first appearance of an animal healing in an English miracle collection. About halfway through the text, the collector describes the experiences of a man "of the vicinity" who had lost all but two of his cows to a pestilence. After petitioning Ithamar for the remaining animals' lives, the man returned home to find the once sickened cows in perfect health.[19] Animal stories in which living saints tend to animals or animals tend to saints are a familiar feature from early medieval saints' lives.[20] But before the Rochester monk compiled his collection, no English collector had preserved a story of a sick animal being healed by a dead saint. The idea that saints would extend their posthumous powers to heal animals was clearly a troubling one to many religious. The Rochester collector himself introduces his story guardedly, noting that Christ came "not for brute beasts, but for humans."[21] Late twelfth-century collectors at Norwich, Beverley, London, Canterbury, and Finchale would sound similar notes of caution, but would also choose to include stories of healings of animals such as pigs, sheep, cattle, horses, and falcons in their collections.[22] Such stories were probably quite common in a lay population that depended heavily on its animals for subsistence: the Rochester monk concludes his story by noting that "many of the poor" asked Ithamar to free their beasts from sickness. The inclusion of such stories in later miracle collections is one of the hallmarks of the new attitude toward lay informants.[23]

The differences between earlier and later collections are particularly clear when new collections were compiled for saints whose miracles had already found written record. At Beverley, an anonymous clerk added seventeen new stories to the collection of John of Beverley's miracles written by William Kellet some decades earlier. Sometime later, someone else—or possibly the same person—appended nine more stories, including one about John of Beverley's cure of animals.[24] These additions are difficult to date precisely (a range from 1154 to 1180 has been suggested),[25] but the author(s) certainly created collections of a different tenor than William Kellet's. One particularly notable difference is a shift in the gender of the subjects. Anglo-Norman collections are overwhelmingly tipped toward miracles experienced by men.[26] William Kellet did not include a single story about a woman or girl in his collection. The first anonymous compiler at Beverley, in contrast, gave over five of his seventeen chapters to stories of women or girls; the second compiler, four of nine chapters. In collections of any period, stories about women's miracles tend to be more tersely told than those of men. When one finds extremely short chapters in a collection, the odds are good that they concern women.[27] Nevertheless, as collectors started listening to more stories from outside of their communities, they found more women's stories they wanted to collect, and the ratio of male to female stories in their collections becomes less skewed. Three miracle collections of the period, those for Godric of Finchale, Frideswide of Oxford, and Æbbe of Coldingham, even include more stories about women than about men.[28]

Another noticeable change is with miracle stories involving sexuality. Miracle stories about religious men struggling to keep chaste make occasional appearances in Anglo-Norman collections.[29] Later twelfth-century collectors were willing to listen to and retell stories involving female sexuality. William of Canterbury, for instance, told a long story about a woman who was tempted to have sex with a knight and was vomiting up her menstrual blood; Philip of Oxford told the story of a woman who had sex with a pilgrim and was unable to approach Frideswide's shrine as a result.[30] The appearance of stories involving menstruation and pregnancies is another sign of the collectors' new attention to stories told by women.[31]

The anonymous collector of miracles connected to Wenefred's well at Holywell, dated roughly to the mid- to late twelfth century, did not exhibit any special interest in women's miracles, despite his female subject. What is most notable about this collection is the collector's approach to Wenefred's healing miracles. Wenefred's relics had been translated to Shrewsbury in 1138, and in 1140, the prior of Shrewsbury, Robert, wrote a *Life and Translation of Wenefred*.[32] It was some years later that the anonymous collector wrote a brief new *vita* and a collection of Wenefred's miracles at Holywell, a spring in north Wales.[33] He subdivided his collection into two sections concerning "miracles against the perverse" (punishment miracles) and miracles of healing. In the healing section, he works meticulously through stories of Wenefred's healing of contracted limbs (c. 16), bound arms (c. 17), dropsy (c. 18), epilepsy (c. 19), muteness (c. 20), lameness (c. 21), paralysis (c. 22), blindness (c. 23), and the stone (c. 24). It is unusual to see these ailments parceled into separate chapters and lined up so deliberately: the collector seems to have decided to make something of a catalogue of Wenefred's healing abilities. In chapter twenty-five, the author describes Wenefred's healing of worms, madness, and fevers. Then, with the sharpened medical vocabulary that would become a common feature of late twelfth-century collections, he writes that Wenefred "equally removes sciatica, roots out cancer, tones down madness, and removes hemorrhoids. She cures persistent coughs, expels stomach aches and discharges, dissolves obstructed menstruation which causes sterility, and blocks excessive and immoderate blood." In sum, "she quickly helps . . . all those who are suffering from any weakness."[34]

The Holywell writer caps off his collection with a type of healing miracle that would gain a new foothold in late twelfth-century texts: resurrections from the dead. As is often the case for such stories, the miracle concerns a young child. The collector describes how a little girl was being prepared for burial in the "shelter of the martyr [Wenefred]." Her cold and rigid body was wrapped in a cloth and she was left there overnight for burial the next day. The following morning, the priest found her alive.[35] Overjoyed parents telling stories about dead children and impending burials were, if not an everyday sight at late twelfth-century shrines, not unusual either: the Becket collections in particular contain many such stories.[36] As electrifying as they were, though, such stories could be suspect. Whereas animal healings were dubious because they were too trivial, resurrection stories were too extraordinary and resonant with meaning. Collectors often took care to justify their inclusion.[37] The Holywell collector prefaces his story with a defensive comment—"in no way should one despise what this virgin did on behalf of a little girl"—and closes defensively too: "what wonder if she calls the dead back to life with her prayer, when she herself once dead had come back to life?"[38]

At Norwich, a dead boy who did not come back to life became the subject of a very long miracle collection, by far the longest created in England up to that point. The boy was an apprentice tanner by the name of William. He was found dead in a wood near Norwich in 1144, supposedly the victim of a ritual killing by the Jews of Norwich.[39] In 1150, his remains were translated to Norwich; from 1154–56, Thomas of Monmouth, a monk of Norwich, composed *The Life and Miracles of William of Norwich*.[40] Thomas devoted two of the seven books of this text to the story of William's life and death; in the remaining five, he tells stories of the translations of William's relics and, most especially, of William's posthumous miracles.[41] All told, there are over one hundred stories of miracles in the text, most of them concerning Norwich locals. In one of the vision stories in the collection, William speaks of Thomas as "my secretary" [*secretarium meum*],[42] and Thomas was indeed acting more like a secretary than earlier collectors—not just in the size of this collection, but also in his concern to record the names and origins of his informants. Thomas's collection was the first that Ronald Finucane considered to be substantial enough for his 1977 statistical analysis of pilgrims and popular beliefs in England.[43]

One reason that Thomas went on so long and took care to identify his informants was because he felt William's miracles proved his sanctity in the face of some fierce protest. The murdered boy was not readily accepted as a saint by other religious, as Thomas acknowledges: "with their idle barking they weary the air . . . they try . . . under the garb of religion to make little or nothing of divine mysteries, or, at least, to turn them to ridicule."[44] Thomas styled himself as a David attacking these Philistines, and put heavy emphasis on the evidence of the miracles: "that [William] deserved to be called a saint and that he truly is one, the grace of God makes manifest by the daily miracles that are occurring round about his sepulcher."[45] Whether Thomas's extensive collection convinced many or even any of the "idle barkers," though, seems unlikely. The collection survives in a single late twelfth-century manuscript and saw very little circulation in the medieval period.[46] Thomas was more successful in his desire to save William's contemporary miracles for posterity. "Lest oblivion should avail to blot [St. William's miracles] out," he wrote, "I have been careful to hand them down to future times."[47] Thomas's desire to get William's miracles into text may have been goaded on by the example of Norwich's close neighbors, Ely and Bury. In comparison to these famed houses, Norwich was a very young community; it was not founded until after the Norman Conquest and had no saint before William. By writing such a long text, Thomas may have hoped to put his new saint on something of a par with Æthelthryth and Edmund, both of whom had been commemorated in *vitae* and multiple miracle collections by the mid-1150s.[48]

Thomas wrote so many stories that he got sick of it. In the prologue to the seventh book he complains of being "worn out by literary toil," but being "plunged once more into the labyrinth of labor" by the appearance of yet more miracles.[49] Other large-scale collectors would make similar complaints.[50] Still, they wrote on. Late twelfth-century collectors were no more literate, in an absolute sense, than their predecessors, but their inkpots seem more full and their pens more fluid. The age of bishops' registers, account books, rental rolls, and other such written memoranda was still in the future, but in the second half of the twelfth century monks were becoming far more accustomed to and concerned with the making of documents than they ever had before. They were beginning, moreover, to see the benefits of the accumulation and bulk preservation of documents. Charters recording monastic transactions were one focus. Every graph of charter production from this period shows skyrocketing increases; most of them were being produced by or for monks. Monks were becoming anxious to preserve these charters, too: four times more cartularies survive from the period after 1150 than from the first half of the century.[51] Letters received the same treatment. The production of letter collections increased sharply in the second half of the twelfth century, and these collections often contain large numbers of prosaic, businesslike letters. Well over three hundred letters sent by or to Thomas Becket, for instance, were preserved in a variety of collections.[52]

For later collectors, just working through a short selection of stories and calling it quits, as early twelfth-century collectors had done, no longer seemed like enough. Soon after Thomas completed the *Life and Miracles of William*, another English Benedictine monk would embark on a large-scale miracle collecting project, this time for an old Anglo-Saxon saint whose sanctity was not in doubt and whose miracles had already found written record. Reginald, a monk of Durham, began his *Little book of the admirable miracles of blessed Cuthbert which were performed in recent times* in the early 1160s.[53] At the beginning of the text, Reginald explains that he had often heard Aelred of Rievaulx tell stories about Cuthbert's miracles, but on inspection, Reginald could not find these stories written in books.[54] This was no doubt true. At least three different Durham monks of the late eleventh and early twelfth centuries had put Cuthbert's miracles in writing, but none of them had written at great length—the first monk had composed a collection of seven stories, to which another added eleven stories, and another three more. Reginald's enormous "little book" of 141 chapters would dwarf these earlier collections. Reginald begins with the Danish invasions and proceeds somewhat chronologically for part of his text. Most of his stories appear to date from the reign of King Stephen (1135–54) and from Reginald's own day. Reginald dedicated the collection to Aelred, who died in 1167, yet toward the collection's close Reginald mentions Becket's martyrdom and miracles, so he appears to have taken up his pen again after 1170. This addition consists of the last thirty-four chapters or so; Reginald did not mark this break of composition himself.[55]

Though Reginald's collection for Cuthbert is longer than Thomas's for William of Norwich, Ronald Finucane did not find it suitable for his statisti-

cal analyses. Lapidge and Love term Reginald's collection "rather hectic."[56]
It is indeed an extraordinarily rich and exuberant text, as yet barely plumbed
by scholars. Reginald tells stories about translations, punishments, cultic objects, fires, feasts, famines, healings, visions, gifts, thefts, bells, and songs. The
chapters stretch on and on as Reginald delights in describing architecture,
places, people, and even the wildlife on Farne Island. Reginald's text has been
read as an attempt to attract more pilgrims, enhance the community's position, and whip up new enthusiasm for Cuthbert in the face of threats from
Becket and others; most recently, Sally Crumplin has read the text as an
attempt "to maintain [Cuthbert's] popularity built since the seventh century
and to ensure the continuation of this devotion."[57] Like Thomas of Monmouth's collection, though, Reginald's text found few readers. It survives in
four manuscripts, one of these an abbreviation, and could have had little
influence on the shape of Cuthbert's cult itself.[58] It seems better to read the
text as Reginald presents it—as an effort designed to get more stories of
Cuthbert's miracles into a secure, written form. Reginald took this need to
get oral information into writing so seriously that even when there was a
written source he could have drawn on—as in the case of the story of Cuthbert's translation in 1104—he bypassed it, creating his own account instead.[59]
Reginald was an avid and seemingly inexhaustible writer, as demonstrated
not just by his huge and enthusiastically detailed collection of Cuthbert miracles but also by his compositions for Oswald, Godric of Finchale, and possibly Æbbe as well.

A third massive text of the period, the *Liber Eliensis*, is even harder to
categorize than Reginald's miracle collection for Cuthbert. In making the
Liber, the compiler, possibly Subprior Richard of Ely (d.1189), knit together
charters, *vitae*, miracle narratives, and other historical material related to
Æthelthryth and the religious foundations at Ely from the seventh to the
twelfth centuries. It appears likely that the compiler created this text in the
late 1160s and early 1170s: the third and largest book of the work concerns
the bishoprics of Hervey (d. 1131) and Nigel (d. 1169).[60] The compiler em-
ployed miracle stories in all three books of the *Liber*. They usually appear in
clusters—three here, ten there, eight later on, and so on. Overall, he devoted
some 55 of the 250 chapters in the *Liber* to miracles.[61] It is clear from the
stylistic differences between the stories that the majority of them were drawn
from preexisting collections. From the approximate dates of the stories the
compiler seems to have had collections dating from the tenth, late eleventh,
early twelfth, and mid-twelfth centuries.[62] Miracle stories toward the end of

the text, such as those concerning a poor women's vision relating to Bishop Nigel's death and other illnesses and deaths suffered around that same time, were probably the compiler's own contributions.[63]

For the most part, the compiler of the *Liber Eliensis* collected miracles out of collections. He was not interested in listening to lay pilgrims who had made their way to Ely, but rather with making a case for the longevity of Æthelthryth's miraculous powers and her protection of the monastery's best interests. Another collector of this period who spent little time listening to the laity was Aelred of Rievaulx, the Cistercian abbot and prolific writer whose storytelling inspired Reginald of Durham's collection of Cuthbert's miracles. One of Aelred's hagiographical works, *Of the Saints of the Church of Hexham* (composed after 1155), is a text focused, unusually, on a church's full collection of saints: Aelred discusses the translations and miracles of no less than five early Anglo-Saxon bishops of Hexham. The text is not long and says little about contemporary healing miracles among the laity.[64]

Aelred's longest and most widely read hagiographical text was his re-working of Osbert of Clare's *vita* and miracle collection for Edward the Confessor, a text he wrote after Edward had been canonized in 1161.[65] In the late 1130s, Osbert had been more or less alone in his attempts to get Edward canonized. In the late 1150s, the idea was revived, but this time Edward's promoters included some of the most powerful men in England. Lawrence, the abbot of Westminster, played a large role in reinitiating the bid. He presented Edward's case to the papal legates and also seems to have instigated a letter-writing campaign on behalf of Edward.[66] In 1160, Henry II, the archbishop of York, the bishops of Norwich, London, Ely, Winchester, and Salisbury, and others wrote to Pope Alexander III urging him canonize Edward. Some of these letter-writers broadly hinted at Henry II's desire to have his ancestor honored and the gratitude the pope should feel to England for its support during the papal schism. Without calling a council, and without asking for any further written materials or investigation into Edward's miracles, Alexander III did indeed issue bulls of canonization for Edward very shortly after receiving these letters. The first canonization of an English saint was quite clearly a quid pro quo, and a hasty one at that.[67] In his reworking of Osbert's text, Aelred recasts Edward as a model king, someone other kings—most immediately Henry II—should work to imitate.[68] It was clearly Edward's life that gripped Aelred, not his posthumous miracles. He duly retold the miracle stories he found in Osbert's text, but did not add on even a single new story of Edward's posthumous powers.[69]

Just a couple of years after Edward's canonization, Alexander III was asked to canonize another English saint. This time the saint was Anselm of Canterbury, and the petitioner was Thomas Becket. Becket had been archbishop for less than a year at the time of the petition. His dispute with Henry II was not yet hot. Still, Becket's idea seems to have been to counterbalance the canonization of an English king with the canonization of an archbishop of Canterbury and champion of the English church.[70] He had one of his clerks, John of Salisbury, rewrite Eadmer's *Life of Anselm* for the occasion, and he presented this text to the pope at the Council of Tours in early 1163. Alexander III was cautious: such a canonization could sour his relationship with King Henry.[71] In a letter dated June 9, 1163, Alexander told Becket that there were so many candidates for canonization brought forward at the Council of Tours that he had decided to postpone his decisions on them all. But his idea was not to take up the issue at a later date or ask for more investigation into Anselm's life or miracles. Instead, rather startlingly, Alexander states that he would "entrust the matter to your care." Becket was to convene an assembly of his ecclesiastics, "solemnly [read] the life of that holy man and publicly [proclaim] his miracles in their presence," and let him know "whatever you and the fore-named brethren decide in this matter." The pope promised to "ratify and confirm" whatever they decided.[72]

Canonization was beginning to carry political weight in the late twelfth century, but popes made their decisions in a remarkably ad hoc manner, even deferring the decision to others if that was more politically expedient.[73] Most importantly in this context, there were as yet no requirements or standards for texts presented to the pope about a candidate's life or posthumous miracles. This is quite clear from a reading of the text Becket gave to the pope—John of Salisbury's *Life of Anselm*, which fortuitously survives in an early sixteenth-century manuscript.[74] The work is little more than an abbreviation of Eadmer's *Life and Miracles of Anselm*. For his account of Anselm's posthumous miracles, John retold most of the stories Eadmer had collected, abbreviated the stories ruthlessly—many of them down to a sentence or two—and rearranged them into a more sensible chronological order. John added on just a single new miracle story, the healing of a certain Elphege who had been blind, deaf, mute, and crippled from birth. He told this story in just three sentences. Overall, John condensed his relation of Anselm's posthumous miracles into a shorter span than Eadmer's already "brief description."[75]

John of Salisbury, for all of his deserved fame as a writer and philosopher, was not much of a hagiographer. Nevertheless, his casual approach to Anselm's miracles in this text is striking. If Alexander III were demanding depositions of witnesses and detail-ridden accounts of contemporary miracles for candidates for canonization, presumably John would have compiled such a text. What John actually served up has very little in common with the dossiers that would be compiled in the early thirteenth century and beyond. It is more in the spirit of Aelred's rewriting of Osbert's *Life and Miracles of Edward,* a text Aelred was likely working on at exactly this time.

It does not appear that Becket ever convened an assembly to discuss Anselm's canonization. The dispute between Henry II and Becket intensified soon after Becket returned from the Council of Tours and left little room for such a discussion. In 1164, Becket fled England. When he returned, he survived barely a month before being killed in Canterbury cathedral late in the afternoon of December 29, 1170.

The Miracles of Thomas Becket: The Collections and Their Clientele

Robert Bartlett has termed the year 1170 "the 1066 of English saintly cult."[76] Within fifteen years of Becket's murder, an enormous flood of literature had been composed in his honor, including ten *vitae* (the earliest and shortest was written by John of Salisbury), a massive letter collection, and dozens of hymns and liturgies.[77] No English saint came close to Thomas Becket in either international fame or regional enthusiasm. A good indicator of Becket's permeation of the cultic conversation is the remarkable number of stories about him in the miracle collections of other English saints. Becket appears in the collections written for Godric of Finchale, William of York, Frideswide, Oswine, Cuthbert, William of Norwich, the Hand of St. James, Æbbe of Coldingham, and others.[78] In a typical storyline, a lay man or woman first appeals to Becket for help but eventually finds healing from the collector's local saint. There seems little reason to doubt that these stories reflect a new reality: Becket had become a saint of first resort.

There were at least five distinct miracle collections made for Becket in the late twelfth century (three surviving intact) as well as a number of short independent accounts of Becket's miracles composed by *vitae* writers.[79] Of the collections, the one that may have circulated the earliest is an anonymous text of twelve chapters that has been edited as "Quaedam miracula gloriosi martyris Thomae archiepiscopi Cantuariae."[80] This little collection describes stories from the early months of Becket's cult and is found in at least eight manuscripts.[81] In the early 1170s, Peter of Celle wrote a letter to the Christ Church monks in which he referred to a "letter of miracles" [*carta miraculorum*] circulating in his region. While the "Quaedam miracula" is not necessarily Peter's *carta*, it is the right size and of early date.[82] Two other considerably longer Becket collections survive only in part. The lost *Life and Miracles of Becket* composed by 1174 by Robert of Cricklade, the prior of St. Frideswide's, apparently had a substantial set of chapters devoted to Becket's miracles, but this is known only because the writer of an Icelandic saga drew some of his stories from Cricklade's text.[83] No manuscript of Cricklade's composition survives. A lengthy collection of Becket miracles was compiled in the late twelfth century at Dommartin, a Praemonstratensian monastery in northern France that claimed to have a rochet worn by Thomas Becket, but this collection too has been largely lost.[84]

By far the largest and most widely read collections of Becket's miracles were the two written by Christ Church monks at Canterbury cathedral in the 1170s. Benedict of Peterborough's collection, composed 1171–73, was the longest produced in England up to that date. William of Canterbury's collection, composed 1172–77, was an independent collection some 40 percent longer than Benedict's already massive text. It claims the prize as the longest English miracle collection.[85] Benedict, a man with a steady, administrative mind, told his readers early on that each miracle would be "doubted by us, lest it be doubted by others."[86] In practice, this meant that Benedict felt most confident retelling stories of miracles that happened under the eye of the Christ Church monks or stories told to him by visiting religious men. He saved most of his suspicion for stories brought to the cathedral by the people he termed "the cured," layfolk who had experienced Becket's miraculous powers outside of the cathedral. Benedict saw himself as a gatekeeper and was keen to demonstrate to his readers that he took that role seriously. He also liked enthusing about the ways Becket's miracles led the laity to confess their sins and "renounce their old life and the darkness of their faults."[87] William, like Benedict, made up nearly all of his enormous collection from stories of the laity, but that is where the similarities stop. The role of investigator held little appeal for him. William took pleasure in saturating his stories with technical medical vocabulary and in lining up long strings of stories concerning resurrections, cures of leprosy, cures of madness, and so on. He also liked animal miracles (Benedict had not), and infused his colossal text with colorful stories, sermonlike digressions, and playful rhetoric of a type Benedict never permitted in his collection.

In their size, themes, rhetorical ambitions, and striking individuality, the Christ Church collections exemplify the late twelfth-century cultural climate. Becket died and Benedict and William took up their pens at a point when large collections were already being written, when collectors were increasingly intrigued by and willing to listen to the stories of the laity visiting their churches, when a more technical, testing, and medical approach to miracle stories was becoming common, and when miracle collecting was still an individual and unprofessionalized pursuit. Had a similarly explosive cult begun at Canterbury seventy-five years earlier or seventy-five years later, it is most doubtful that similar collections would have been produced.

These two remarkable collections will be the subject of detailed analysis and comparison in the next three chapters. Here I am concerned with the impact of the Christ Church collections on later miracle collecting in England. For at least six years, starting in mid-1171, either Benedict or William—and, for a brief time, both—were asking lay visitors about their stories. Thomas of Monmouth had done a similar kind of bulk processing and collection of stories at Norwich in the 1150s, but the Canterbury projects affected more people from a much wider region. The Christ Church collections created a large lay population that knew about miracle collecting and may have been primed to expect it when they visited other churches and shrines. The religious came to Canterbury in large numbers too. While visiting Christ Church, such elite guests could have heard Benedict's collection read aloud in a formal setting. At the close of his *vita* for Becket, written in 1173–74, William FitzStephen states that Becket's miracles were written in a great book [*magnus codex*] and "were publicly recited in the chapter of the church of Canterbury."[88] FitzStephen probably attended such readings himself: he complains that while the English miracles were being recorded, "the writer fails to commend to memory" the miracles that Becket was performing in France, Spain, and elsewhere.[89] Brief mention is also made of chapterhouse readings of Benedict's collection in the letter prefacing William of Canterbury's collection.[90] It may be that these readings were ongoing as Benedict completed his collection stage by stage. Perhaps they were meant as a way to formalize communication about Becket's bewildering number of miracles within the community and among their many elite guests. Monks and canons would occasionally invite laymen of status into their chapterhouse to tell their miracle stories, as we know from other contemporary texts, but there is no indication that collections were read aloud in a similar manner elsewhere.[91]

Whether these readings were unusual or not, they would have given visitors of high status and Latin learning familiarity with the text of Benedict's collection, and possibly William's too, though we do not know for sure whether his text was read aloud in a similar fashion. Visitors party to these readings would have taken home a sense of the content of Benedict's collection. Some probably went further and brought home a copy of the collection itself. We know of a case in which a monk from Barcelona visited Compestela in the late twelfth century, made a copy of the Codex Calixtus while he was there, and carried it back with him.[92] Anne Duggan's work on the manuscripts of Benedict's *Miracles* has made it possible to track how one manuscript leaving Canterbury in the late twelfth century became at least four more. In two early manuscripts of Benedict's collection that were kept at Aulne and Signy, Cistercian houses in France, a letter from Odo, the former prior of Christ Church, prefaces the collection.[93] Odo, then the abbot of Battle, addresses the letter to two kinsmen, Adam and Ralph, who were monks at the Cistercian monastery of Igny (in the same region as Aulne and Signy). Odo writes that he was delivering to them "the book of miracles of the blessed martyr Thomas, miracles that, as you may be confident, have been tried and examined, such that there is nothing mixed in them that may appear false." Odo adds that he had "already sent to you a book of these miracles, a much better one, but because of the fraud of the messenger it did not reach you."[94] No copy of Benedict's collection is now known to exist from Igny, but in the late seventeenth century Caismir Ouidin, a traveling bibliophile, mentions seeing a manuscript of Becket's miracles there. Ouidin also saw a manuscript of Becket's miracles (now lost) at Foigny, yet another Cistercian monastery in the region.[95] The text that Odo took from Canterbury, then, was transmitted from Battle to Igny and then to at least three neighboring monasteries: Aulne, Signy, and Foigny.[96]

In the late 1170s, the anonymous author of the Lansdowne tracts wrote that Becket's miracles had been written in great volume, and "are extant among many" [*exstant apud plurimos*].[97] This author seems to have been a Christ Church monk. If so, he would have witnessed manuscripts leaving Canterbury. Whoever he was, he was not exaggerating about the wide circulation of the Becket collections. Appendix 1 is a listing of all the known medieval manuscripts of the two collections, many of them located by Anne Duggan.[98] Three lengthy copies of William's collection survive along with two other manuscripts containing selections from his text.[99] While this number of manuscripts indicates more circulation of William's text than most late twelfth-century collections, Benedict's collection—the first to be completed—outstrips it by a wide margin. There are seventeen more or less complete manuscript copies of Benedict's collection, eight more manuscripts with extensive selections from his text, and others with short selections. This list will no doubt grow as more libraries are searched and manuscripts catalogued.[100] Benedict's collection found a greater readership than the Codex Calixtus (which survives in some thirteen manuscripts), or the miracle collection of St. Foy (seven manuscripts).[101]

The geographical extent of this circulation is startling as well. The earliest known manuscript of Benedict's collection, dated to 1185, was made not at Canterbury, in England, or even in northern France, but in Portugal, at the Benedictine monastery of San Mamès de Lorvão. The maker of this manuscript wrote an inscription in which blessed "he who brought the text of this book to this land," evidently a foreign traveler. The Lorvão copy then rapidly became the exemplar for others.[102] Just around a third of the surviving manuscripts currently have an identifiable provenance. They thus can give us only a very partial glimpse of the circulation of Benedict's collection, but a mapping of these manuscripts nevertheless shows how far his text could move (see Figure 6).[103]

Only five of the surviving manuscripts have been tagged with an English provenance, and of these only one has been tied to a specific locale (St. Augustine's, Canterbury).[104] For a sense of the circulation of Benedict's collection in England, medieval library catalogues and other documentary references, such as the letter from Odo to his kinsmen in France, are more revealing than the surviving manuscripts. I have mapped references to *Miracula* of Thomas Becket in such catalogues and texts, with the date of the reference, on Figure 7.[105] These references almost never specify who the author of the *Miracula* was, but given the pattern of surviving manuscripts, it is best to assume that most of these were copies of Benedict's collection. Becket miracle collections were available to readers at large and at small English institutions, in East Anglia and further north as well as throughout the south, at Augustinian and Cistercian as well as Benedictine houses and at colleges as well as monasteries. This mapping should be taken as just a fraction of the circulation of Becket *miracula* in England, as medieval library catalogues are a notoriously fragmentary source base.[106]

How these manuscripts were used by their owners is an important ques-

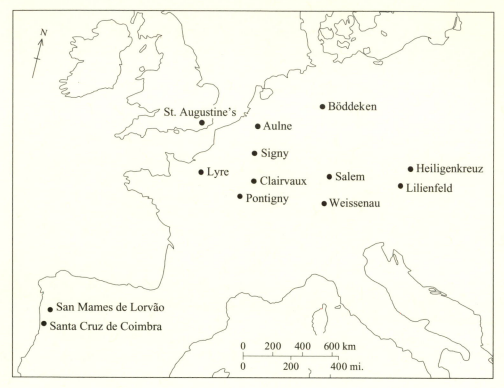

Figure 6. Manuscripts of Benedict of Peterborough's *Miracula S Thomae* with established provenance.

tion. A persistent thesis in the historiography of miracle collections holds that they were propagandistic texts aimed at the laity. With its wide circulation and many dozens of stories about lay recipients of Becket's miracles, Benedict's collection would seem to present an ideal test case for such a thesis, but there is strikingly little evidence that it was ever oralized to lay listeners. There is no known translation of any part of Benedict's or William's collection into Anglo-Norman French or Middle English.[107] In the early and mid-1170s, pilgrims who knew French could have heard an account of Becket's life being read in the crypt: the author of a *Vie de Saint Thomas*, Guernes (or Garnier), writes in its conclusion that he had "read it many times" at Becket's tomb.[108] Guernes's *Vie* is extraordinarily detailed; he says in the text that he spent two years at Canterbury gathering information and revising his account. Guernes must have known about the miracle collecting projects and may even have

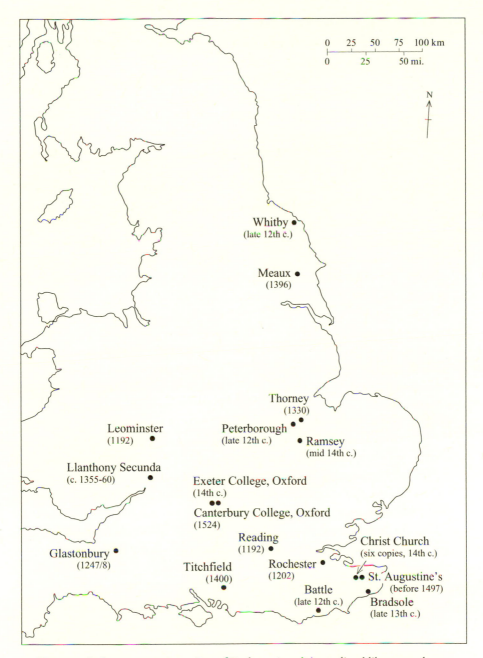

Whitby
(late 12th c.)

Meaux
(1396)

Thorney
(1330)

Leominster
(1192)

Peterborough
(late 12th c.)

Ramsey
(mid 14th c.)

Llanthony Secunda
(c. 1355-60)

Exeter College, Oxford
(14th c.)

Canterbury College, Oxford
(1524)

Reading
(1192)

Christ Church
(six copies, 14th c.)

Glastonbury
(1247/8)

Titchfield
(1400)

Rochester
(1202)

St. Augustine's
(before 1497)

Battle
(late 12th c.)

Bradsole
(late 13th c.)

0   25   50   75   100 km
0   25   50 mi.

N

Figure 7. References to manuscripts of Becket *miracula* in medieval library catalogues and other documents.

shared the scriptorium with Benedict or William. Yet, Guernes told only a single miracle story at the close of his *Vie*, and he did not derive even that one story from either Benedict's or William's collections.[109] A second Anglo-Norman French account of Becket's life in verse was composed by Beneit, a monk of St. Albans, about a decade later in 1184. Like Guernes, Beneit seems to have seen no reason to translate stories of Becket's miracles into French. He based his translation on Robert of Cricklade's *Life and Miracles of Becket*, but retold none of the miracle stories in Cricklade's text.[110] The only medieval account of Becket's miracles in the vernacular is the thirteenth-century Icelandic saga mentioned above. It is derived from selections from Benedict's collection as well as parts of Robert of Cricklade's *Life and Miracles*. This saga is known from a single manuscript. It is possible that we have lost a translation or that a new text will come to light, but there is a clear contrast between the very early efforts to get Becket's life into the vernacular and the subsequent circulation of these texts (Guernes's *Vie* is known from eight manuscripts, Beneit's from seven) and no apparent translation activity with the miracle stories.[111]

The men who could read the Latin of Benedict's and William's collections also do not appear to have used them as source texts for sermons. There are occasional references in high medieval miracle collections to monks or canons telling miracle stories to crowds of people. Osbern of Canterbury and Osbert of Clare, as noted in the chapters above, both speak of preaching miracles to the people in their miracle collections.[112] So does the anonymous author of the *Miracles of Ithamar*, who introduces a chapter by writing, "The virtues of the saint were preached to the people," and then describes how a man in the crowd told his own miracle story in response.[113] But miracle collections were not needed for such preaching to occur. Religious men knew stories of saints' miracles by personal experience and oral report. The most effective sermons were likely created impromptu out of recent stories. Indeed, almost all the references we have to preaching of saints' miracles occurred *before* a miracle collection was composed.[114]

Texts of medieval sermons preserved in manuscript hardly ever include descriptions of miracle stories.[115] Nearly two hundred sermons about Becket dating from the late twelfth to the late fourteenth century have been inventoried by Phyllis Roberts. These sermon-writers sometimes throw in glowing generalities about Becket's marvelous miracles, but they very rarely tell any story in detail. One fourteenth-century sermon writer recounts a vision of a youth who saw a seat among the apostles designated for Thomas Becket. A similar story is found in the first book of Benedict's collection, but the sermon-writer's account is so different that it seems likely that he heard or read the narrative elsewhere.[116] This is the only case of possible overlap between the Becket collections and the many sermons Roberts has inventoried. It should also be noted that no manuscript is known that contains both Becket miracle stories and Becket sermons. The separate circulation of these texts strongly suggests different uses.

While it is possible, then, that preachers sometimes turned to completed miracle collections for inspiration or material, there is no evidence in the manuscript record of collections being put to such use, not even in Becket's case. Another oral exit that scholars have envisioned for miracle collections is liturgical commemoration. Many liturgies composed for Becket refer to his miracles, but, again, Benedict's and William's collections did not serve as sources for these compositions (with the exception of Benedict's own *Historia*).[117] There is one manuscript in which miracle stories from Benedict's collection were marked out for lection readings: Rome, Vallicelliana MS Tomus III, a late twelfth/early thirteenth century manuscript of unknown provenance. In the Vallicelliana manuscript, a *vita* for Thomas is divided into eight lections, and then four more lections are formed out of the prologue to Benedict's miracle collection and three (nonconsecutive) chapters plucked out of the fourth book.[118] This manuscript can help us see one reason why was unusual for the Becket collections to be read as lections: they were far too long.[119]

The one place one does see medieval authors and copyists using material from Benedict's collection is at the close of *vitae* composed in Latin. Edward Grim drew stories from the collection to round out the end of his *vita* for Becket, as did an anonymous compiler of an early *passio* partially printed by Robertson.[120] The Cistercian Thomas of Froidmont, who wrote a *vita* for Becket in the early thirteenth century, drew stories from Benedict's collection as well.[121] John Grandisson, bishop of Exeter (d.1369), may also have included stories from both Benedict's and William's collection at the close of the *vita* he composed for Becket—if he did not, then an anonymous copyist did.[122] This use of Benedict's collection reinforces the impression that it was understood as a record for posterity and as reading material to be shared among the elite.

Benedict's collection circulated among a fraternity of literate men bound by religious affiliation, friendship, kinship, proximity, and a common interest in Becket's cult. They were eager to read about lay miracles, but made no effort to communicate those stories back to their subjects.[123] For these religious men, reading a miracle collection was analogous to modern university professors reading an anthropological or sociological study that its subjects will never see. There was only one truly propagandistic miracle collection created in high medieval England: the early thirteenth-century "miracle windows" of Canterbury cathedral.[124] The windows' numerous narratives of Becket's miracles, designed to be viewed by every pilgrim visiting Becket's shrine, are unfortunately too large and too late a subject to be treated in this book. Still, when one compares the animated figures of these panels, open to view and admired by thousands of tourists, with the texts of the Becket collections, even now locked away in specialist libraries, untranslated and inaccessible to those who cannot read Latin, it seems that some things have not greatly changed.

Miracle Collecting in England, c.1170–c.1200

In the first decade and a half after Becket's death, during the years so many lay and religious visitors were bringing home knowledge of the Canterbury miracle collections, there was a marked surge in miracle collecting in England.[125] In the 1170s, Reginald of Durham made a lengthy addition of stories to his collection for Cuthbert; Thomas of Monmouth added at least one new story to his collection for William of Norwich; and the compiler of the *Liber Eliensis* decided that a fitting conclusion to his enormous compendium would be an account of Thomas Becket's life and death.[126] Writers set to work creating collections for Godric at Finchale (compiled after 1172),[127] for Germanus at Selby (finished in 1174),[128] for Bartholomew in London (written between 1174 and 1189),[129] for William of York (c. 1177),[130] for the cross of Waltham (after 1177),[131] and for Frideswide at Oxford (after 1180).[132] Another collection that may belong to this same period is William de Vere's (now lost) collection for Osith, at Chich,[133] and possibly, too, Jocelin of Brakelond's collection of the miracles of Robert of Bury (d.1181), also lost.[134] When one tallies in the "Quaedam miracula," Robert of Cricklade's collection for Becket and the Christ Church collections themselves, there is no question that the fifteen years after 1170 were the most productive in the entire history of English miracle collecting.[135]

The Becket cult concentrated collectors' minds on healing miracles among lay pilgrims. This is particularly noticeable in Reginald of Durham's addition to his "little book" of Cuthbert miracles, a text he began in the 1160s and first completed before Aelred of Rievaulx's death in 1167. The addition, made sometime after Becket's death, consists of about thirty-four chapters. While Reginald's accounts in this addition still bubble over with extraneous detail, he changed his emphasis so radically that Victoria Tudor wondered "if the shrine had become a centre for faith-healing in a way [it was not] before."[136] In the pre-1170 collection, about a quarter of the stories concern healings and only two of these happened in the cathedral; in the post-1170 addition, over two-thirds of the stories are about healings, and over half of these healings are said to occur in the cathedral grounds. Cuthbert's cult could possibly have changed, but it is more likely that Reginald turned his attention to what was happening in his own cathedral after Becket's murder in a way he had not before.

The two largest collections of the post-Becket period were written for Godric at Finchale and Frideswide at Oxford. Ronald Finucane found these texts to be excellent fodder for his statistical analyses. The collection for Godric, with 263 chapters, is usually assumed to have been of Reginald of Durham's workmanship, but it has not been the subject of close research.[137] Many of Godric's miracles are described in terse, one- or two-sentence accounts, quite unlike Reginald's other work: in Benedicta Ward's words, the text "read[s] more like a collection of *scedulae*, bluntly transcribed, than a literary work."[138] It could be that someone from Durham was deputized to take notes at Finchale and, for some unknown reason, these notes were merely transcribed into a manuscript and not reworked into a finished text. Almost all stories of the stories concern healings of local pilgrims, many of them women. At Oxford, Philip, the prior who succeeded Robert Cricklade, composed a carefully rendered collection of some 110 chapters after a translation of Frideswide's relics in 1180. Philip, too, concentrated his attention on local healing miracles, many of them concerning women. Philip told a story of his own miracle of Frideswide toward the end of the text. He recounts how he became ill with a fever, consulted doctors, and then "called to mind the miracles I had seen and lamented the extinction of the light of faith in me that I had seen to shine in others. I remembered that the rich and poor, the little and the great had evaded the yoke of illness by the intervention of the blessed virgin, and I grieved to be denied the thing from heaven that I had seen to be granted to the small and poor of both sexes."[139] Philip then asked for help from Frideswide himself. This passage epitomizes the reversal of attitude one sees in miracle collecting from the Anglo-Norman period to the late twelfth century. Instead of ignoring the stories of the poor and of women, Philip is motivated and half-humbled by them.

After 1185 or so it is less likely that miracle collectors were as directly inspired by the example at Canterbury. Three or possibly four more collections were compiled in the north of England at this point. Another addition was made to the collection of the miracles of Oswine at Tynemouth in the late 1180s and early 1190s.[140] Around 1190, an anonymous monk of Coldingham composed a *Life and Miracles* for Æbbe, a seventh-century Anglo-Saxon abbess. The monk devoted much more attention to Æbbe's contemporary miracles than to her life: his collection of forty-three chapters concerns Æbbe's healing powers at Coldingham and at St. Æbbe's head in the late twelfth century.[141] At the priory of St. Bee's, in Cumbria, an anonymous author composed a short collection of miracles concerning Begu's bracelet sometime in the late twelfth or early thirteenth century.[142] At the turn of the century, an anonymous author created a collection of thirteen stories concerning miracles on Farne Island, stories supposedly once told by Bartholomew, a hermit of Farne who died in 1193.[143] In southern England, a monk of Reading wrote a collection for the Hand of St. James in the late 1180s or early 1190s. The Hand was supposedly acquired by Reading Abbey in the early twelfth century, stolen by the bishop of Winchester in 1136, and restored to Reading again in 1155.[144] The twenty-eight stories in the collection, nearly all of them stories of healing, date from the reign of Henry II.[145] At Bury, the writer of a new compilation of Edmund's miracles was one of the few post-Becket collectors to eschew the new emphasis on contemporary healing miracles among pilgrims. Like the compiler of the *Liber Eliensis*, the Bury writer collected his stories out of preexisting collections for Edmund rather than turning to new stories told at the shrine. The only story that this author added to his compilation concerns a man who attempted to take away a manor possessed by Bury St. Edmunds.[146]

Four Anglo-Norman French versifications of preexisting Latin collections were composed in the last decades of the twelfth century. None of these translators and versifiers did any new miracle collecting, and their texts, which survive in just one or two manuscripts, saw little circulation, yet their efforts put miracle stories in a written vernacular for the first time in England since Ælfric's composition of the *Life of Swithun* in Old English in the late tenth century. At Bury, an author named Denis Piramus composed a lengthy verse life of Edmund. The second part of the work includes accounts of posthumous miracles drawn from Hermann's *De miraculis* (composed c.1100). The two manuscripts that preserve Piramus's *Vie Seint Edmund le Rei* are both incomplete, halting in the midst of miracle stories from the early eleventh century.[147] The *Vie Seinte Osith*, written in the later twelfth century by an anonymous author, possibly a canon of Chich, also describes some of Osith's posthumous miracles. This text too appears to have been closely based on an existing Latin *vita* and miracle collection.[148] Between 1163 and 1189, a nun of Barking versified Aelred of Rievaulx's *Life and Miracles* of Edward the Confessor as the *Vie d'Edouard*. She too did not add any new miracle stories, but she did lavish special attention on a miracle concerning a Barking nun she found in Aelred's collection.[149] The *Vie Seinte Audrée*, a versification of Æthelthryth's life and miracles by an author who names herself in its last lines as "Marie," is again derivative of preexisting Latin texts. This *Vie*, the best known of the four discussed here, is dated to the late twelfth or early thirteenth century.[150] Its author, possibly Marie de France, included an extraordinary number of Æthelthryth's miracles in the text—nearly fifty stories altogether. The author's keen interest in miracle stories has occasioned far less comment than her identity, but this text deserves more study as one of the most concerted efforts to translate Latin accounts of miracle stories of an English saint into a vernacular.

The little spurt of translations made at the close of the twelfth century did not presage a later flood. Though *vitae* were frequently translated, the number of known translations of miracle collections into Middle English are small, and in the late medieval centuries miracle collectors very rarely worked in the vernacular itself.[151] A clearer sign of things to come was the compilation of the miracle collections of the *Book of St. Gilbert*, a text put into its final form between 1202 and 1205.[152] The anonymous canon who compiled the *Book* included a detailed account of Gilbert's canonization process.[153] He describes how Archbishop Hubert Walter ordered abbots in the region of Sempringham to investigate Gilbert's miracles and send a report to Pope Innocent III. They did so in January 1201, but Innocent was not satisfied with their account. He sent back word that they were to "seek confirmation of . . . [Gilbert's] deeds and miracles, relying not only upon statements of evidence but also upon witnesses . . . and when they had faithfully written an account of all these things, authenticated by their seals, they were to send it to the pope by suitable messengers, who, after taking an oath in the pope's presence, would also submit sworn evidence on these points."[154] In September 1201, Gilbert's miracles were duly investigated again, this time by a group led by the archbishop himself: "they most carefully questioned the sworn witnesses," and sent this report (with seals attached) to the pope. People who had experienced miracles of Gilbert were also sent to Rome "so that the statements made earlier to the pope by letter might now, through the live witness of those present before him, become certainties."[155] Once this entourage reached Rome, more examination took place, and finally, in a public session of the curia, "the evidence was received, the witnesses admitted, many causes were adduced and a host of compelling reasons put forward; and so [Innocent III] canonized him with the common assent of the whole church" on January 11, 1202.[156]

That Innocent III would be the first pope to demand a text and require a process like this is no surprise: his pontificate was the defining moment in the development of canonization procedures (and, of course, for much else).[157] The first miracle collection preserved in the *Book* is that created by Archbishop Hubert and sent to the pope in the fall of 1201. Its account of thirty of Gilbert's miracles is so full of statements about people swearing oaths and witnesses swearing oaths to the oaths that there is hardly any room for the stories themselves.[158] This is unlike any miracle collection compiled in England before. The second collection preserved in the *Book* has none of this excessive attention to witnesses or oaths, and possibly is the initial collection rejected by Innocent in early 1201.[159]

The Book of Saint Gilbert was compiled at the beginning of a sea change in miracle collecting, when the process of making a collection of miracle stories became more rigid and formalized—and much less common—in medieval England. It would be a very different environment from that of the late twelfth century. At Canterbury, Benedict and William did not have to worry about the expectations of a canon lawyer like Innocent III as they compiled their collections for Thomas Becket in the 1170s. But in the awful days immediately following Becket's murder, they were likely not thinking of canonization or miracle collecting at all. It must have seemed to the Christ Church monks that nothing good could ever come of the slaughter that had occurred in their cathedral. "After the most blessed martyr of Christ, Thomas, rested from his labors," the first sentence of Benedict's collection reads, "our choir was turned to mourning and our organ into the voice of the weeping." "I speak in Christ before God," he declares, "the sons of the church were not able to restrain their tears at table, but eating they silently mourned, and mixed their drink with tears."[160] It is to those weeping monks, and the miracle collections that two of them eventually wrote for Becket, that I now turn.

CHAPTER EIGHT

Most Blessed Martyr:
Thomas Becket's Murder
and the Christ Church Collections

The miracle collections for Thomas Becket written by Benedict of Peterborough and William of Canterbury at Christ Church are easily the most spectacular productions in the history of English miracle collecting. Despite their significance, though, the Christ Church collections have received less careful scrutiny than many shorter collections.[1] There is much that needs untangling before it is possible to look closely at the texts themselves.[2] In this chapter, I examine the creation of these two enormous texts and place their composition within the timeline of Becket's early cult and canonization. My conclusions concerning the dating and additions to the collections are summarized in Figure 8. Though they are often thought to have worked at more or less the same time, Benedict and William did not share the scriptorium for long. Benedict started first, in mid-1171, and finished his text by 1173, while William, starting in mid-1172, kept on collecting into the late 1170s. Careful analysis of the so-called "parallel miracles," the eighteen stories that both monks included in their collections, makes it possible to establish that Benedict handed notes over to William at some point, but the way William used those notes demonstrates that he did not view his collection as piggybacking onto Benedict's. His collection is far longer than Benedict's, no doubt intentionally so, and quite different in both form and content. The two collectors worked in tandem rather than in parallel, and they conceived of their collections as fully independent, freestanding texts.

Both Benedict and William were monks at Christ Church when Becket was murdered on December 29, 1170, but neither saw him die. In his *vita* for

Figure 8. Dating and relative size of Benedict of Peterborough's and William of Canterbury's miracle collections for Thomas Becket.

Becket, William describes how he fled when he heard the knights yell "Strike, strike!" At the moment of crisis, he felt "unworthy of martyrdom."[3] He was not the only one. When the knights caught up to Becket inside of Canterbury cathedral, everyone but Edward Grim, one of Becket's clerks, ran away.[4] After the knights had gone, the monks and clerks emerged from their hiding places to find Becket's body sprawled, butchered, and soaked in its own blood on the floor of their cathedral. The shock was tremendous. In those first traumatic hours, while the religious men at Canterbury did little, many townspeople came into the cathedral, viewed the corpse, and dipped fingers and clothing in Becket's blood: "there was no-one who did not carry away some portion of that precious treasure," Benedict would later write.[5] William Fitz-Stephen would say that Becket's first miracle happened later that same evening when a Canterbury citizen poured water over a cloth stained with Becket's blood and his ill wife drank the blood-tinged water.[6] Whether the story FitzStephen tells was truly the first miracle attributed to Becket or not, it does seem highly likely that people immediately experimented with their gory souvenirs and that Becket's first miracles were a consequence of their use.[7]

The monks of Christ Church had an unhappy relationship with the living Becket. They are sometimes thought to have hesitated in their approval of Becket's cult, or even to have actively opposed it, in its early months and years.[8] As Anne Duggan has pointed out, though, the truth is that "[their] delay and hesitation . . . lasted short of twelve hours" after Becket's death.[9] The night of the murder, the monks recovered themselves and tended to Becket's corpse. They moved it from the martyrdom site to a position before the high altar, the holiest place in their church, for the rest of that first night.[10] The next morning, the king's men threatened to dump Becket into a cesspool if he were not buried immediately.[11] Hurrying to get Becket in the ground, the monks were undressing him when, unexpectedly, they found a hairshirt next to his skin. The sight of this monastic instrument of torture provoked bitter tears of remorse: how could they have failed to recognize the holiness of this man?[12] It may have been after this discovery that the monks returned to the site of Becket's murder and collected the blood and brains still on the pavement in a container for safekeeping.[13]

The burial itself proceeded with haste. There happened to be a new and empty tomb in the easternmost chapel in the crypt. It was perhaps the most secure part of the entire cathedral—where, in fact, Becket might have found safety if he had fled from his killers as he had been urged to do. That was where they now put him. Because the cathedral had been desecrated by the murder, the monks could not grace Becket's burial with any religious service: after placing him in the tomb, they simply left, barring the doors to the crypt behind them (Figure 9).[14]

The next chapter of the story is more difficult to follow. After describing the burial, most medieval writers go on to celebrate the beginning of Becket's miracles in glowing but general terms, and, with that, bring their texts to a conclusion. In an influential article, Emmanuel Walberg argued that Benedict started composing his miracle collection immediately, starting "almost the day after the murder": Benedict begins his collection with early visions and what he terms Becket's "first five" miracles in late December and early January.[15] The first three books of Benedict's collection have been praised, in Raymonde Foreville's words, as forming "an accurate chronology of the greatest advantage,"[16] and scholars have felt free to use the first books of Benedict's collection as a more or less transparent source tracking the events after the murder.[17]

As attractive as the image of Benedict scribbling down miracle stories in the days immediately after Becket's murder may be, however, there are numerous indications in the collection that he could not have started writing it until after Pentecost (May 1171) at the earliest. Benedict did not hear of many of Becket's earliest miracles until weeks or months later. For instance, Benedict states that Becket's very first miracle was experienced by a woman in Sussex the third day after Becket's murder, or December 31. But, Benedict writes, this woman did not come to Canterbury after her healing. She delayed her pilgrimage "through negligence or forgetfulness" and did not appear at Canterbury "for a long time" [diutius].[18] When describing the early vision and healing of a certain William Patrick, Benedict is quite explicit about the gap between the time of the miracle and the time the news reached Canterbury: "This miracle happened around Lent and was revealed to us around the holy day of Pentecost."[19] The story that follows William Patrick's was also one that Benedict heard "in those same days," that is, around Pentecost. Robert, a young cleric, had been cured by Becket in Lent but, Benedict writes, was fearful of "the wind of persecution" and delayed his pilgrimage until "a less dangerous time."[20] Benedict's written composition of Robert's story, moreover, must have occurred at some distance from the conversation: at the end of his account, Benedict says that the name of Robert's village had slipped from his memory.[21]

Such examples can be multiplied.[22] The sporadic chronological refer-

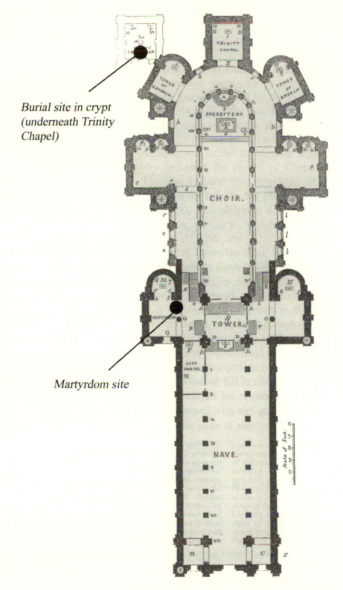

Burial site in crypt
(underneath Trinity
Chapel)

Martyrdom site

Figure 9. Canterbury cathedral and the murder of Thomas Becket. Plan of
Canterbury cathedral in 1174 from Robert Willis, *The Architectural History of
Canterbury Cathedral* (London, 1845), 38, with additions by Rachel Koopmans.

ences in Benedict's collection are not the results of journalistic, day-to-day recording, but rather Benedict's own studied and subjective attempts at historical reconstruction.[23] The closer one looks at Benedict's collection, in fact, the more it is clear that those early weeks and months after Becket's murder were bleak days for the Christ Church monks, largely devoid of miracles or good news of any kind. Benedict repeatedly describes the period between Becket's murder and Pentecost as "the first days of miracles."[24] By this, he meant the days *without* many miracles, contrasting it to what came later. William of Canterbury, too, would speak of "the early light of miracles" [*primitiva luce miraculorum*],[25] while Gervase, who lived through these months at Canterbury as well, refers to a period of "prelude" in Becket's miracles.[26] In those early weeks, the political wheels were turning very slowly, indeed, all but imperceptibly. For some months, it could not have been clear to anyone, lay or religious, how things would turn out. Benedict, William FitzStephen, John of Salisbury, and the anonymous Lansdowne writer note the danger of speaking of Becket as a saint in this period.[27] Alexander III was hesitant to censure Henry II. His first instruction to the king did not come until late April, four months after the murder, and even then, he requested only that the king not enter churches until he met with the papal legates, hardly a stinging rebuke.[28] Henry himself was unrepentant. Even at the reconciliation of Avaranches, a full year later, he scarcely seemed sorry for Becket's death.[29] For the monks and members of Becket's retinue at Canterbury, in a church recently terrorized, devoid of song and activity, and on a knife's edge for news, Becket seemed frustratingly dormant.[30] The very first story Benedict relates in his collection concerns his own vision in which he asks the dead Becket why he is not doing anything.[31]

Things changed at Canterbury, it appears, because of what the monks themselves decided to do: first, to open up their crypt to all visitors, which they did the week after Easter (early April in 1171), and second, to distribute their supply of Becket's blood (much diluted) to all visitors.[32] We do not know how long the monks debated these actions; they certainly could not have foreseen all their consequences. Before this, it appears that the monks had, on occasion, secretly introduced a visitor or two into the crypt and handed out samples of the blood.[33] "Many people" had been pressuring them to open up the crypt, Benedict says, and had accused the monks of sinning and of "hiding away their talent."[34] In April, the monks decided to allow visitors free access to Becket's relics, and with this, miracles started to happen in their cathedral "every single day," in Benedict's words.[35] In political terms, though, the monks had made these decisions too soon. Benedict describes how the monks got word that a large armed group of Becket's enemies was planning to attack the cathedral and steal away Becket's body. The anonymous Lansdowne writer also mentions threats against Becket's body that may well be linked to these events.[36] The plot was foiled, but afterward, for security's sake, the monks covered Becket's tomb in the crypt in a heavy marble structure.[37] It was after this that pilgrims began to come in large numbers to Canterbury cathedral, some of them with stories to tell of miracles they had experienced weeks or months earlier.

Benedict does not reveal much about the circumstances in which he began his project. In the collection's prologue, he says only that "by the will and precept of the brothers, I am compelled to commend [Becket's miracles] to the memory of letters."[38] Later, in the introduction to a miracle story, Benedict writes that it was around the time of Pentecost "when the church of Canterbury already shone forth with many miracles, and I was directing my attention to the ill people suffering throughout the entire church, according to the task assigned to me" [*juxta commissam mihi curam*].[39] By this "task," Benedict may not have meant the miracle collection: there was much to do simply looking after the ill people in the cathedral. But it does seem that Benedict began his collection sometime after Pentecost, in the summer months of 1171 when the cult was taking on a much more sunny and exciting cast. John of Salisbury's letter to the bishop of Poitiers describing Becket's murder, a letter he later expanded into a *vita*, is the only candidate among the Becket materials for earlier composition.[40] When he began collecting Becket's miracles, Benedict was unknown outside of the community, and may not yet have been prominent within it. In mid-1171, he had composed nothing that we know of, held no known monastic office, and had not yet begun the administrative career that led to his appointments as prior of Christ Church in 1175 and abbot of Peterborough in 1177.[41]

Around the time Benedict began working on his collection, the Christ Church monks sent a delegation to Alexander III asking for Becket's canonization. This early delegation and their failed petition is not well known because the chief text that mentions it, a letter from Alexander III to his legates Albert of San Lorenzo and Theodwin of San Vitale, was not included in Robertson's *Materials for the History of Thomas Becket*.[42] Written in the late summer or early autumn of 1171, Alexander's letter informs Albert and Theodwin that the monks of Christ Church had sent one of their brothers and "letters" to him to request a canonization.[43] He charges the legates to "seek to know the truth of this more fully from bishops and other secular persons concerning those miracles that are said to happen in the church. Write to us about the miracles and make known to us the certainty of the thing with all diligence . . . such that we are able to give assent to the petition of the aforesaid brothers securely and confidently, if it ought to be approved."[44] Alexander's wary doubtfulness—*if it ought to be approved*—seems surprising now, but gives a good sense of the murdered archbishop's wobbly status in 1171.[45]

Not much, if any, of Benedict's collection could have existed at the time this first delegation set out from Canterbury. The prologue of Benedict's collection mentions a miracle that likely occurred in late 1171 or early 1172.[46] The prologue was clearly a later addition, likely made when the bulk of the collection was complete. In general, Benedict's collection is so tightly constructed through its initial books that it seems a fruitless exercise to look for an early section that may have been sent to the curia. The "letters" that the pope refers to were probably just that: letters from the prior of Christ Church and other supporters of Becket, something in the manner of the letter-writing campaign conducted for Edward the Confessor a decade earlier. Albert and Theodwin appear to have made their way to Canterbury soon after receiving Alexander's letter, because sometime before December 1171 they sent the Christ Church monks a warm letter discussing Becket's remarkable miracle-working and instructing them to go ahead with the reconsecration of the cathedral "as you requested."[47] It is possible that Albert and Theodwin compiled a report about Becket's miracles in the autumn of 1171. That they did compile a report for the pope at some point is certain: Alexander specifically referred to their account of Becket's miracles in all of the letters he sent announcing Becket's canonization.[48] Unfortunately, unless the legates' account is to be identified with the anonymous and early little collection edited as "Quaedam miracula," their report has not survived.

By the time the Christ Church monks received the legates' letter and reconsecrated Canterbury cathedral in December 1171, Benedict was likely working full bore on his collection. Benedict does not mention taking notes, but William would later speak of rough notes [*schedulae*] he had to work up into a collection, and of "tablets" [*tabulae*], likely wax tablets, on which he had noted stories of resurrections that some other writer would have to compose.[49] As he transformed notes, letters, and his memories of conversations or events into sections of full-fledged chapters, Benedict never seems to have considered anything as dully unimaginative or impractically systematic as writing down stories in the order he had heard them. From beginning to end, Benedict's collection is full of pairs of miracles, sets of miracles, and other kinds of deliberately planned rhetorical series.[50] Benedict's literary sensibility, with its strong emphasis on doublings, harmonies, and resonances, is an aesthetic hard for a modern reader to appreciate, but it permeates his entire collection, including the passages modern readers have seen as the most chronological.[51] Benedict sometimes apologizes for not having included a story earlier, suggesting that he did little revision to completed parts of the text.[52] Once a section was completed, he kept moving forward, planning out a new section and "placing [stories] in the sequence" [*seriis interserere*], as he puts it one passage.[53] It is not clear when Benedict's collection was first read aloud in the chapterhouse of Christ Church to his brethren and visitors, but such readings must have been taking place by mid-1172, at the point William started working on his collection.[54]

In his *vita* for Becket, William describes how he was ordained as deacon and received as a monk of Christ Church just days before Becket's murder.[55] He was probably younger and certainly more of a newcomer to Christ Church than Benedict. As far as we know, William never held monastic office. From other sources, we know of a William from Christ Church who was named prior of Dover in 1187 and died the following year, and also, most tantalizingly, of a William from Christ Church who was sent to Henry II to plead the community's case in 1188 in a dispute with archbishop Baldwin.[56] William was a common name, and we will probably never know if William the collector was also William the short-lived prior of Dover or the William whose life was tied into knots by the great dispute with Baldwin.

A letter now prefacing William's collection provides a rich account of how William came to write his text. The letter, composed c.1175/76 after the bulk of the collection was complete, prefaced a presentation copy of William's collection that Henry II himself had requested.[57] In the letter, the king is told that William did not begin miracle collecting "in haste" or "precipitously." Starting soon after the martyrdom, William had visions in which he saw Becket thrusting a book "with beautiful but illegible letters" at him as he lay on a bench before the chapterhouse door, but he did not grasp the meaning of this. Then, seventeen months after the martyrdom (i.e., June 1172), William became "the co-worker and helper [*cooperator et coadjutor*] of the brother who had given himself to this work from the beginning," when "the matter seemed to exceed his powers and that brother alone did not suffice to hear and write the emerging miracles."[58] William had a third vision in which he was urged to "take up the work," and the next morning, when the assembled brethren asked "why the miracles were produced for the hearers with less diligence and care . . . from common decree it was ordered that this one put in his share."[59] Benedict's complaints in his collection indicate that he did indeed start to feel overwhelmed by his task. At the beginning of the fourth book, a part of the text he might well have reached by the middle of 1172, he wrote: "if I were given hands that could write not just speedily like a scribe, but annotate most rapidly like a notary, nevertheless my talent would be overcome, my tongue would fail, my fingers become senseless."[60] By the end of the fourth book and the close of his collection, Benedict was cutting corners and frequently mentioning the "tedium" of too many miracles of the same kind.

Benedict never mentions William by name nor refers to his project in his collection. Outside of the prefatory letter, William, in turn, never mentions him. Our best evidence for the working relationship between Benedict and William are the eighteen "parallel" miracles. On Figure 10, I have marked the position of these stories within Benedict's and William's collections.[61] In Benedict's collection, they are tightly clustered in the second half of the fourth book and in the short additions he made to his collection; in William's, they are more spread out, but are mostly found in the first, second, and beginning of his third books. Looking closely at the stories themselves, one finds that almost all the miracles that Benedict thought of as particularly significant and described at length toward the close of his collection show up again somewhere in the first half of William's collection. The parallel miracles include the stories of Eilward of Westoning, the sons of Jordan Fitz-Eisulf, the son of Yngelrann, Cecilia of Plumstock, the foundling of Abingdon abbey, Hugh Scot, Geoffrey of Winchester, the son of the earl of Clare, Salerna of Ifield, William of Gloucester, and John of Roxburgh: unfamiliar names now, but these were famed miracles. Many of these same stories were later chosen for inclusion in the "miracle windows" surrounding Becket's shrine. If William had thought of himself as merely working as Benedict's assistant, there would be no reason to tell these stories over again. William's decision to write these stories in his own way made his collection a freestanding alternative: if a reader had a copy of William's collection, there would be no need to consult Benedict's for these celebrated stories. In two of the three lengthy manuscript copies of William's collection, the text is introduced by the incipit, possibly penned by William himself, "Here begins the second work [*secundum opus*] of the miracles of the glorious martyr."[62] It was indeed a "second work," a wholly autonomous text, rather than an addition or supplement to Benedict's collection.

The parallel miracles also give us a sense of the kind of written notes and materials that Benedict shared with William. Letters were certainly changing hands. Benedict and William wrote their own independent versions of the stories of Eilward of Westoning and William of Gloucester, but they both copied in the same letters as supporting testimony.[63] They also both included the same letter from the bishop of Norwich at the close of their accounts of Cecilia of Plumstock's miracle.[64] On another occasion, Benedict silently paraphrased a letter that William decided to copy into his collection in full.[65] Rough notes may have been behind the three stories concerning sea rescues found in close sequence in both collections. There is very little verbal correspondence between these sea stories, so the collectors were clearly not using the same letters or some other lengthy written source: notes seem likely.[66] Perhaps the most interesting overlap is with the stories of Cecilia of Plumstock and Hugh Scot.[67] These are the only two of the eighteen parallel stories that show any syntactic parallels. Benedict's and William's accounts of these two miracles are so similar that they had to have been working off the same text. These common sources were, very likely, letters written by the priests involved in Cecilia's and Hugh's miracles.[68] It seems possible that letters or notes concerning the sons of Jordan Fitz-Eisulf, Cecilia, and Hugh were written together on a roll or tablet, or otherwise bound together in the order that Benedict recounts them. William tells the stories of the Fitz-Eisulf sons many chapters before getting to Cecilia's miracle, but he (most unusually) mentions the Fitz-Eisulfs again in the introduction to Cecilia's story, and then tells Hugh's story just a few chapters later.[69] William explains in the introduction to his *vita* how he was "asked by the brothers to set forth [Becket's] miracles worthy of transcription," which were then in "incorrect and imperfect" notes [*schedulis*].[70] The parallel miracles reveal that William did indeed inherit copies of letters and notes from Benedict.[71]

Strikingly, though, William does not seem to have used or consulted a copy of Benedict's collection as he composed his own. He never paraphrases material from Benedict's collection.[72] In addition, if William had been working through Benedict's collection in order to decide which stories to include in his, one would expect the parallel miracles to have been arranged in a similar order in the two collections. Instead, when one maps the position of the parallel miracles, what one gets is a messy conglomeration of intersecting lines (see Figure 10). William could only have been working with the com-

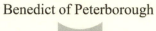

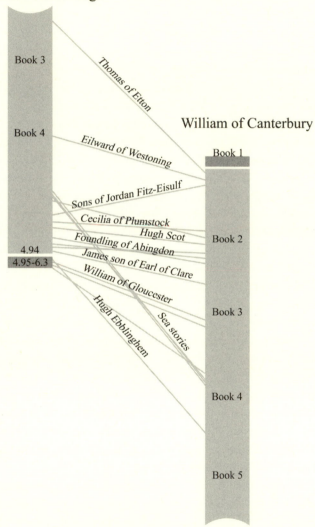

Figure 10. The "parallel miracles" in the Christ Church collections.

mon sources, the loose letters and notes on parchment that he sorted through, selected, arranged, and retold as he wished.[73] Miracle collectors frequently rewrote the texts of their predecessors, as we have seen, but William was not doing a rewrite: this was a wholly autonomous project.

William's retellings of the parallel miracles are often noticeably drier and shorter than Benedict's, suggesting that he was writing his accounts second.[74] Incidental details in his stories also suggest that he was writing later than Benedict. For instance, in his story of the foundling of Abingdon abbey, William states that a bishop involved in the story made a pilgrimage to Canterbury. Benedict does not mention this pilgrimage; it probably had not yet occurred.[75] In his account of Eilward of Westoning's miracle, William states that Eilward "stayed many days" at Canterbury and that he received a stipend for support. Again, Benedict does not mention this lengthy stay or financial aid.[76] It is only with the very last parallel miracles, the last four stories in Benedict's collection in an addition he made after the text began to circulate (unhelpfully numbered as 5.4 and 6.1–3 in Robertson's edition), that there are suggestions that the two collectors were vying with each other for oral accounts of the same stories. William tells these stories at as much length—or more—than Benedict does. Both collectors make claims for personal investigation in these stories. For instance, Benedict says that he made his own investigation of the depth of a well involved in one story, while William appears to have considerable knowledge of what the farm laborers were saying about this same miracle.[77] In another case, the story of a buried man named William of Gloucester, William claims to have spoken to the buried man personally, in one part of his story stating that he was reporting "not what the man could have said, but what he actually said."[78]

According to the dating of the Christ Church collections proposed by E. Walberg in 1920 and largely accepted by later scholars, Benedict worked on the first three books of his collection until 1173 or 1174, at which point he supposedly halted, not adding on the fourth book of his collection until 1179.[79] Walberg argued that William worked on the first five books of his collection until 1173 or 1174, at which point he too supposedly halted, not adding on the sixth and last book of his collection until 1178 or 1179.[80] Walberg seemed determined to paint a picture of Benedict and William working side by side—constructing the first books of their collections at the same time, pausing at the same time, adding on concluding books at the same time. But the parallel miracles suggest a very different timeline, as does the manuscript tradition of the two collections. Benedict was bringing his collection to a conclusion as William began his work. Miracle collectors could complete long collections in short periods when they put their mind to it, and Benedict was likely getting into his fourth book of stories by the time William had his "take up the work!" vision in mid-1172.[81] There is no evidence that Benedict paused between the composition of his third and fourth books nor, as will be addressed further below, that William halted between his fifth and sixth books. In all of the surviving manuscripts of Benedict's collection, the four books of Benedict's collection, plus or minus a few chapters at the end, appear together as a single entity. No manuscript contains just the first three books, nor is the fourth book ever found independent of the first three.[82] Walberg did not base any of his dating arguments on the manuscript tradition, of which he seems to have known little. In dating Benedict's fourth book to 1179, Walberg was following the suggestion of the Rolls Series editor of the Icelandic *Thomas Saga*, Eiríkr Magnússon, who thought that an event Benedict mentions at the beginning of his fourth book—a fire in Rochester—had to have happened in the late 1170s.[83] Both Magnússon and Walberg ignored the fact that everything else in Benedict's fourth book appears to date to late 1171, 1172, or, at the outside, 1173.[84]

One of the best clues to the time Benedict completed his collection is his prologue, a part of the text he likely composed shortly before the first versions of the collection began to circulate.[85] In the prologue, Benedict mentions the vacancy of the archbishopric.[86] Richard of Dover was elected archbishop by the monks and bishops in June 1173 and received his pallium in April 1174, so Benedict had to have composed the prologue before this. Benedict also names Alexander III twice in the prologue and carefully spells out the support Becket's posthumous miracles gave to Alexander's cause in the papal schism.[87] Could this have been meant specifically for the pope's eyes? In one of the later chapters of his collection, William tells a story about a clerk going to Rome to petition the pope for Becket's canonization in the name of the brethren of Christ Church. He arrived there to find that Becket was already canonized. Alexander III canonized Becket in February 1173.[88] If the clerk set out from Canterbury in the spring of 1173, he could conceivably have carried along a more or less finished text of Benedict's collection to present to the pope. Whether this was the case or not, Alexander obviously did not see the Christ Church monks' input or writings as necessary for his decision to canonize Becket in 1173. The previous year, 1172, had been an important turning point in Becket's cult: the strength and size of his cult was becoming apparent to all observers and demanded awe and attention.

Alexander had the legates' report about Becket's miracles in hand by early 1173, and that, along with many oral reports, convinced him of the truth of Becket's miracles. Even in his letter announcing Becket's canonization to the Christ Church monks (dated March 10, 1173), the pope stresses the importance of the legates' report rather than anything the Christ Church monks had provided for him.[89]

All the evidence points to Benedict bringing his collection to an end sometime in 1173, possibly even early 1173, as William was writing the first part of his collection and plowing through old notes and letters that Benedict had left behind.[90] All three of Benedict's compositions for Becket—*Miracula, Passio,* and *Historia*—were likely finished in 1173. Anne Duggan believes Benedict wrote the *Historia* before December 29, 1173, the third anniversary of Becket's death and the first since his canonization was announced.[91] Benedict's *Passio* is not a long text, and he was working on it—indeed, likely finished it—before the miracle collection was completed.[92] The last narrative compositions we have from Benedict are probably the two minor additions he made to his text. Duggan has identified three manuscript recensions of Benedict's collection. The first, represented by three manuscripts, ends at 4.94. A second recension, with two more chapters (4.95–96), is represented by three manuscripts, and a third recension, with seven additional chapters (5.1–6.3), is found in at least six manuscripts.[93] The brevity of these additions and the way in which the stories overlap with those in William's collection suggest that Benedict made them soon after the main text of his collection was complete. In 1174, Benedict began a busy administrative career. He became the chancellor of Archbishop Richard in 1174, and by the middle of the following year, 1175, he was the prior of Christ Church.[94] Letters about Becket's miracles arrived at Canterbury addressed to Prior Benedict, but it would be William, not Benedict, who put these letters in the last part of his miracle collection.[95]

For most of the time William was writing his collection, he worked alone. He compiled the bulk of his collection in three years or so, working from about mid-1172 to the end of 1175. William appears to have compiled his collection in much the same way Benedict did, by taking notes, organizing sections of chapters, writing in stages, and moving steadily forward. William sometimes arranged stories in couplets the way Benedict had, but what he liked better were longer runs of stories: five, six, seven, or even more of a similar kind of story in a row.[96] William starts his second book, for instance, with thirteen straight stories of resurrections and then twelve stories concern-

ing leprosy. William explicitly rejected the idea of putting stories into chronological order: "what happened first, or what happened later, is not
important and little is lost by not attending to such things."[97] Instead of
starting off books with a chronological marker, as Benedict had done with
three out of his four books, William began with stories that he judged particularly important. The first miracle story in William's book one, for instance,
is Eilward of Westoning's miracle, which William certainly knew was not
Becket's "first." Ironically, because William made no attempts at chronological reconstruction, the course of his collecting is rather easier to chart than
Benedict's. As one moves through his collection, one finds stories with dates
such as "eighteen months after the martyrdom" (July 1172),[98] "two years since
the passion" (1173),[99] the story of the clerk arriving in Rome to find Becket
canonized (1173),[100] the "fourth year after Thomas' passion" (1175),[101] a miracle dated in a letter to November 18, 1174,[102] another illness in the "fourth
year after Thomas' passion" (1175),[103] and, well into the sixth book, a recovery
from illness nine months after the siege of Huntingdon (the siege was May–
July 1174, putting the recovery in the spring of 1175, and William's composition of the story at least a few months later).[104] The picture these rough dates
project is of a collector working steadily, collecting and composing in turns,
through late 1172, 1173, 1174, and 1175.

There is no evidence to support Walberg's suggestion that William came
to a halt between books five and six. No manuscript contains a break here,
nor is there any internal evidence suggesting William stopped at this point.
But when he was well into his sixth book, probably sometime in late 1175, he
did call a temporary halt. At the end of the ninetieth chapter of his sixth
book, in a passage Walberg does not seem to have noticed, William describes
how he had a number of stories about miraculous resurrections "already
noted down in our tablets." These stories, though, would have "to wait for
another pen than mine . . . because of the evil times, we have neither the
necessities nor the time to write" [*nam malitia temporis impediti nec necessaria
nec tempus habemus ad scribendum*].[105] That William did halt at this point is
very clear from the manuscript tradition. The Montpellier copy of William's
collection ends at 6.88; a manuscript now in Évreux ends at 6.89; and a
fifteenth-century selection of miracles drawn from William's sixth book also
ends at 6.89.[106] Only one manuscript, Winchester College MS 4—the basis
for Robertson's edition—continues beyond this point. The Winchester
manuscript is also the only one with the first five chapters of William's first
book: these five chapters were clearly a later addition as well.[107]

Whatever the problem was that made William stop writing, he does not seem to have paused for long. The lengthy addition he made to his collection (numbered 6.91–6.168 in Robertson's edition) appears to have been composed c.1176–77. The first eight chapters of the addition (6.91–6.98) need to be treated with particular care. These chapters do not describe Becket's miracles—instead, they provide a lengthy account of the young Henry's rebellion, Henry II's penance in 1174, the end of the rebellion, and the king's decision to grant a charter of liberties to Christ Church. These historical chapters circulated separately and almost certainly were not written by William.[108] The rest of the addition, though, is very much in William's style. Stephan Langenbahn has pinpointed the date of the composition of a letter rewritten as seven chapters in the addition (6.128–34) to late 1175–early 1176.[109] These chapters all appear to have been drawn from a letter addressed to Prior Benedict. Just before this set of chapters, one finds four more copies of letters addressed to Prior Benedict, letters that were likely received at Canterbury in 1176 or 1177.[110] It is difficult to say when William brought the collection to a final close because none of the last chapters in the collection provides any firm dates. It is possible that the Winchester manuscript, the sole "complete" manuscript of William's collection, is missing material at the end.[111] From the evidence we have now, it is best to think of the addition as dating to c.1176–77.

Over the period William composed his collection, remarkable changes took place at Canterbury and in Becket's cult. Becket was canonized in 1173; Benedict completed his collection; and Richard of Dover became the new archbishop of Canterbury. John of Salisbury, Guernes, Edward Grim, and William FitzStephen had all completed their *vitae* for Becket by 1174. Alan of Tewkesbury, a Christ Church monk, completed the archetypes for his collection of Becket's letters by 1174. In July 1174, Henry II, weakened and frightened by his son's rebellion, performed penance for Thomas's murder at Canterbury. Just a few months later, in September 1174, a fire seriously damaged the eastern end of Canterbury cathedral, causing such consternation among the Christ Church monks that, in Gervase's words, they "howled" rather than sang their offices.[112] In July of the following year, 1175, Odo left Canterbury to become abbot of Battle. Benedict became prior. The rebuilding of the cathedral commenced. Henry II made another pilgrimage to Canterbury in 1175, would make another in 1177, and made still more, almost annually, until the end of his life. In mid-1177, Benedict left Christ Church for Peterborough. He sequestered impressive Becket relics for Peterborough, including, according to a thirteenth-century chronicler, a large quantity of Becket's blood in two crystal vases and the paving stones on which Becket had bled and died.[113] A new prior, Herlewin, took Benedict's place. In August 1179, by which point William had almost certainly stopped collecting, Herlewin resigned, Alan of Tewkesbury took his place as prior, and King Louis VII of France came on pilgrimage to Canterbury.[114]

William did not view his collection as a chronicle and mentioned few of these events in his text.[115] Something one can track over the course of William's composition, though, is an about-face in his attitude toward Henry II. In the initial books of his collection, William adopts something of the gloating tone Benedict used when speaking about miracles that mortified Becket's "enemies."[116] In the first book of the collection, William writes about the son of a friend of one of Becket's murderers being healed;[117] in the second, he rejoices in Bishop Gilbert Foliot's healing by Becket (Foliot had been one of Becket's most ardent detractors);[118] in the third, he states that the real miracle of a prisoner's escape was not the softening of a prisoner's irons, but the softening of the heart of the king, who decided to let the man stay free.[119] Starting in the first book, William devotes chapters to miracles relating to Henry II's military campaign in Ireland, a campaign he explicitly disparages.[120] But in the later parts of the collection, William's attitude noticeably relaxes. In his fourth book, William comments that a recovered leper who stayed at the tomb for many days was seen by "kings, counts, natives and foreigners coming to pray."[121] In his sixth book, William introduces a story by declaring, "Let my loving brethren hear what the English king, when a pilgrim at the martyr's tomb, heard from brother Robert, minister of the Temple at Jerusalem."[122] It was likely shortly after this, when William halted and his collection began to circulate, that the prefatory letter to Henry II was written. The warmth of this letter toward the king is remarkable. It is clear not only that William traveled to see Henry II to give him a copy of his collection in person, but that Henry II had himself requested such a gift: "we send to your clemency our beloved brother William with the little book to which he devoted some time, just as you asked."[123] William's later additions to the collection show that his visit with Henry II did nothing to dim his respect. In one of the five chapters he added to the beginning of the collection, William speaks of Henry II's name being written in "the book of life" along with that of Thomas Becket himself (!).[124] In one of the chapters in the addition to book six, just twenty chapters from the end of the collection, William describes the miraculous recovery of a falcon belonging to Henry

II. He says that the story "was told to the king, who gave thanks to the martyr."[125]

When William finished his collection, there were probably few people in England who had not given thanks to the most blessed martyr of Canterbury for one reason or another. The Christ Church monks hosted no more important guest than Henry II over the period of William's collecting project, but there were other distinguished persons arriving, more of them, quite clearly, than in Benedict's day. Benedict had collected stories from visiting abbots; William spoke with bishops.[126] Benedict had rejoiced over a miracle with the wife of the Earl of Clare; now the Earl of Albemarle and the count of Boulogne came in person.[127] Letters from other notables were flooding in. Messengers arrived at Canterbury with letters from Corbie, Poitiers, Durham, Bayeux, Derby, Lisieux, Gloucester, Cluny, Taunton, Exeter, Shrewsbury, Sawtry, Oseney, Berkeley, Pontigny, Welford, St. Omer, Reading, and more.[128] Some pilgrims made repeat visits over the course of William's project. In his third book, for example, William tells a story about the healing of Gerard, a Flemish knight. The same Gerard reappears in William's sixth book—he was cursing the saint for falling ill again.[129] More foreigners were arriving at the tomb, which caused problems, as William noted: "many came to us to tell what miraculous things had happened to them in languages we could not understand."[130]

The tremendous expansion of Becket's cult is also shown by changes in its physical infrastructure. Benedict focused considerable attention on miracles at Newington, the place where a cross had been set up to commemorate Becket's confirmation of children in the days before his murder.[131] William twice mentions miracles there,[132] but there were now more permanent and imposing structures along the road to Canterbury. In one of William's chapters, a nun rejoices that she has recovered the money that she had planned to donate "at the chapels [*aediculae*] built in the martyr's honor along the way."[133] Toward the end of his collection, William mentions the building of chapels dedicated to Becket in Germany, in Ireland, and in Devizes, as well as a hospital dedicated to Becket in London.[134] Another sign of the maturation of Becket's cult is William's discussion of the varied and abundant offerings brought to Canterbury by pilgrims. Robert, a knight, vowed an annual sum,[135] while another man promised an oblation of a hundred pounds of wax for every successful business voyage, a vow being performed, William writes, "to the present."[136] Most of the oblations seem to have been in coin, and William felt he knew why there were so many. He explains that the martyr wished to pay off the debts that he could not in life: "on this account there are kings, archbishops, pontiffs and princes, priests, knights, monks, nuns, people of all conditions and ages, who, by divine inspiration and excited by innumerable miracles in various regions . . . obligate themselves to pilgrimages, pensions and payments."[137]

Benedict's and William's collections are different in part because of their slightly staggered time of composition. Writing second and when Becket's cult was more solidly established, William could afford to be more free in his treatment of Becket's miracles than Benedict, and he was. But this time difference does not account for all the many striking contrasts between the two collections. Though they were members of the same community, Benedict and William took very different approaches to collecting the stories of the "people of all conditions and ages" who came to Canterbury, as we will see in the chapters to follow.

CHAPTER NINE

I Take Up the Burden:
Benedict of Peterborough's
Examination of Becket's Miracles

"We have not read that any saint in earlier times flashed out in so many and such great miracles so quickly after his death," Benedict of Peterborough explains in the prologue to his collection of Thomas Becket's miracles. "Therefore, by the will and precept of the brothers, I am compelled to commend them to the memory of letters. Although my wisdom does not suffice nor my faculties be plentiful, I take up the burden freely and devotedly, trusting in him who says 'Open your mouth and I will fill it.'"[1] Benedict took up his burden in mid-1171, when Becket's cult was in its first full blossom. From mid-1171 to 1173, Benedict listened to the stories of hundreds of visitors and created a huge collection of four books and some 282 chapters. Benedict's was not the first large English miracle collection, but it was the largest undertaken in England up to that point, its size no doubt intended to help drive home Benedict's point about the unprecedented outpouring of miracles after Becket's death.

Canterbury cathedral was a thrilling place to be in these years. Benedict writes that after Easter 1171, "the Lord conferred such grace of healing to the sick that every single day we were able to say with the evangelist, 'We have seen wonderful things today!'"[2] Benedict proclaimed early on in his collection that the "coming of the people" was the greatest of Becket's miracles [*inter maxima miracula . . . maximum*].[3] But in the midst of all this excitement was the need to create a trustworthy miracle collection. Hardly anyone had thought of Becket as saintly before his death. Peter of Celle had written to the Christ Church monks with this advice: "I implore both you and all those of you who will transmit to posterity the memory of the miracles of your and our martyr that nothing be written in most faithful truth about him or his miracles except what has been examined, purified, and sieved seven times."[4] Benedict himself tells his readers that "because of the disparagements of the wicked, it is not inexpedient to doubt each one. It is doubted by us, lest it be doubted by others: we have shown ourselves hard and as if unbelieving in the examination of the truth, so that the adversaries of the truth may be ground down into believing."[5]

How Benedict went about this vast "trying and examining" project and decided whose stories would appear in his collection is the subject of this chapter. Large late twelfth-century collections are often viewed as listings of miracles that are suitable for statistical analyses and not a great deal more.[6] But Benedict saw himself as much more than a mere recorder. He wanted his readers to think that his criteria for selecting and testing stories were good ones, and he often comments on why he or "we" (many other Christ Church monks were involved in Becket's cult), felt someone's story was to be trusted. Benedict portrays himself looking for proofs, demanding witnesses, questioning people, sending and receiving letters about miracles, getting upset when people failed to tell him their stories, and even making trips outside of Canterbury to investigate certain miracles. His collection is a benchmark for what a conscientious monk thought examining miracles meant in the period before canonization procedures were instituted.

Benedict describes the essential logistics of his collecting project early on in his first book. He tells his readers that his collection is created from three categories of stories: "the miracles of which we weave this history are these: those which we saw with our own eyes, or we heard from those ill people already healed and their witnesses, or those things we learned from the testimony of religious men, who had seen them with their own eyes."[7] Benedict devotes roughly equal proportions of his collection to stories from these categories. Stories "we saw with our own eyes," or, more generally, miracles occurring in Canterbury cathedral, take up almost 30 percent of the collection's chapters overall. Stories from "ill people already healed," or miracles occurring outside of the cathedral and told by laypeople, make up not quite 45 percent of the chapters; and stories from "the testimony of religious men," plus those told by the secular elite, account for the remaining 25 percent of the collection.[8]

In this chapter, I study Benedict's examination of stories through the lens of his own categories. Benedict did not respond to or "doubt each mira-

cle" equally. He found cathedral miracles to be the most emotionally resonant and exciting, and included long runs of these miracles at the beginning
of his second and third books.[9] Nearly all these stories involve healings of the
laity. He wanted his readers to know that he and his brothers watched people,
questioned witnesses, made them demonstrate their healings, and in general
took the responsibility of examining miracles in the cathedral seriously—the
legwork involved in this category of stories was considerable. Benedict was
the least comfortable with the second category of stories, those he heard from
"ill people already healed." He attached the most doubtful and suspicious
comments in the collection to their stories. In striking contrast, Benedict
seems to have done almost no examination of the miracles he "learned from
the testimony of religious men" or secular elites. Their eyes were like his eyes,
as he says in one passage, and for the most part he was comfortable accepting
their stories—even their hearsay stories—as if they were his own.

Like many other religious men of his generation, Benedict was curious
about and engaged by lay religious experience. He and his brothers often
gave advice and help to people seeking a cure in the cathedral. Benedict
became quite close to some lay visitors to the cathedral, including some who
failed in their hopes of healing—people on whom he is remarkably hesitant
to lay any blame. But Benedict never thought of lay pilgrims as being on the
same plane as himself or his colleagues. His sense was that for religious men,
Becket's miracles were to be more examined than experienced. They were the
watchers, judgers, helpers, advisors, interpreters, and writers. By investigating
the "truth" of what was happening, Benedict and his readers could feel that
he was in the act of stabilizing and confining the enormous lay discourse
about Becket's miracles. That sense was fictitious, and miracle collecting on
this scale was full of challenges and frustrations, but Benedict took up his
burden with cool determination. It may well have been Benedict's work on
the miracle collection that led to his election as prior just a year or two after
he finished the text.

We Have Seen Wonderful Things:
Benedict's Collection of Cathedral Miracles

Benedict found the sights on offer in Canterbury cathedral deeply gratifying.
After describing how extinguished candles on Becket's tomb miraculously
relit, for example, he writes, "It is difficult to relate how much everyone

rejoiced, how many floods of tears were shed, and the extent to which thanks
were rendered unto God."[10] The miracles, he thought, were consolation and
recompense for the horrors the monks had lived through. "Let the sons of
the church of Canterbury rejoice to be given the consolation of such miracles!" Benedict exclaims in his prologue.[11] Again and again in his collection,
Benedict describes cathedral miracles as those he and his brethren "saw."[12]
This insistent rhetoric reflects the emotional intensity of Benedict's engagement with Becket's miracles within his own church, but it also reflects his
perception of a division between the seers—the religious—and the seen—the
laity.

The main place Benedict and his brethren watched for miracles was in
the crypt chapel where Becket had been buried the day after his death. When
Becket was buried there in 1170 and throughout Benedict's (and William's)
collecting efforts, the chapel was not the bright, semicircular, airy space that
it is today. It was then a small dark box of a room, one-fifth its current floor
space (Figure 9). Becket had been buried in this privileged but rather awk-
ward spot for security concerns, and early fears that Becket's body would be
stolen were the reason Becket's gravesite was covered with a low structure
made of heavy marble slabs cemented together. This structure, with its openings in the side, is frequently pictured in the "miracle windows" (Figures 4,
11, 12). Benedict writes of monks "sitting" by this tomb.[13] These monks do
not seem to have spotted what they took to be a miracle in progress very
often, but if they did, the incidents appear to have been prime candidates for
inclusion in Benedict's collection. In one chapter, he describes how a men-
tally disturbed man somehow wedged himself inside the slabs covering Becket's tomb. The monks worried the slabs would have to be broken in order to
get him out, but the man eventually emerged and was in his right mind.
"Later, we ordered the healed man to do it again," Benedict writes, but he
could not even get his shoulders into the opening, and when they asked a
skinny adolescent to try it, "we saw him unable to do so."[14] In another
chapter, he tells how a Londoner blind in one eye approached the tomb,
stuck his head in one of the openings, withdrew it, and shouted, "What is
this? I see!": "Those of us who were there marveled, and examined the event
and the truth of the thing diligently," Benedict writes.[15] Most often, what
the monks saw was less instantaneous: they would observe someone obviously
ill or mad at the tomb who later appeared to them healed or sane. "We were
horrified," Benedict says, by the madness of Matilda of Cologne, who nearly
choked a young boy to death in her insane rage. After being chained "near

Figure 11. A monk swabs a blind woman's eyes. Canterbury Cathedral, Trinity Chapel Ambulatory Window n.II (71). Author's photograph used with the kind permission of the Dean and Chapter of Canterbury Cathedral.

the martyr" for four or five hours, little by little she began to get better, until by the next morning she was well. At that point, "we sought from her," Benedict writes, "what sent her into insanity."[16]

The monks often actively worked to help or advise people at the tomb. If they found healing, their stories were also first-rate fodder for Benedict's collection, at least as much as the few, rare "I can see!" incidents witnessed by the monks. Many of Benedict's cathedral stories involve water or relics provided or even personally applied by the monks. In one story, Benedict describes how an unnamed brother was distributing the blood and water mixture "at that hour," implying that it was a rotating duty.[17] In another, Benedict describes how the sacrist of Christ Church, Robert, was at the tomb

Figure 12. An ill boy kisses Becket's tomb. Canterbury Cathedral, Trinity Chapel Ambulatory Window n.II (57).

when he wrapped Becket's bloodied belt around the stiff neck of a certain Brian, who soon felt better.[18] Benedict also describes how a brother Roger, "deputized to the care of the holy body," ordered an ill woman who had requested some of the water to get up and get it herself in the name of the martyr.[19] In a rare use of his first person voice, Benedict describes how he himself saw a crippled man fall and then stand at the tomb, and how "I led [him] away from the crowd" to a place where he could rest.[20] Scenes like the monk swabbing the eyes of a blind woman pictured in the miracle windows must have been common (Figure 11). If healings resulted from such help, Benedict clearly felt confident that they were legitimate miracles and good material for his collection. He even started noticing patterns in healings and made note of them for readers. For instance, after describing how a young man's eyes swelled up and emitted an amazing amount of bloody matter after Becket's blood had been applied to them, he comments that "we saw this happen to many others."[21] The monks also encouraged people to keep trying if they did not finding healing right away. In three different stories, Benedict describes how an individual's "time" for healing had arrived [e.g., *Quum ergo venisset tempus ut misereretur ejus Dominus*], which may have been something they talked about at the tomb.[22] In other stories, he speaks of the monks "urging" people to courses of action. These urgings were not always effective. In a pair of chapters, Benedict describes how two boys, on separate occasions, slept overnight in the cathedral with their heads resting on Becket's tomb. One boy woke to say that Becket told him that he would not be cured. The other boy had a similar experience. Benedict writes, "we urged [the first boy] to nevertheless press on with his prayers, and he agreed, but time passed without any profit of healing."[23] The second boy died. Benedict states that it was definitely not the parents' sin that caused his death and concludes with the sympathetic statement, "I confess that we mourned a great deal for this boy, and the other's lack of healing saddened us, but the martyr gladdened us with others."[24]

This is not the only time that Benedict relates incidents in the cathedral that are hard to define as miracles. He also recounts the story of a knight, Robert, who came to the cathedral hoping for healing but instead died a most pious death, and of Ermenburga, a Londoner who prayed that Becket either kill her or heal her: "We who were there marveled at the presumptuous origins of [her] prayer," Benedict comments, "and we marveled nonetheless that there was such an immediate response to her devotion with a reward worthy of faith."[25] For Benedict, the displays of faith made their cases suitable for preservation in his collection, trumping the ambiguity (at best) of these stories. Benedict seems to have been particularly impressed by the devotion of a leper, Ralph of Langton. When Ralph first came to the tomb, Benedict writes, "he prostrated himself, completely dissolved in tears, and was heard to obligate himself with wonderful devotion to amazing vows conceived from his pain."[26] After nine days in the cathedral, Ralph was considerably improved, but the monks hoped for a better conclusion, and strongly urged him to return [*plurimum instantes postulavimus*]: "And it happened that as he went, he was cleansed . . . in the course of a month, we received a young man of most elegant form. Therefore from Pentecost almost to Advent he stayed with us, most whole, clean, handsome, and without a mark."[27] The fact that Ralph had a horrible relapse after he left the cathedral a second time—"by some hidden judgment of God unknown to me . . . no one ever existed more fouled by the contagion of leprosy"—did not dissuade Benedict from including his story in his collection. He even compares Ralph favorably to Eilward of Westoning, probably the most famous of all those cured by Becket.[28]

Did Benedict's brethren agree that he should include the stories of a dead boy, a dead knight, a presumptuous woman, and a horribly relapsed leper in his collection? Benedict almost always uses the term "we," or even more specifically, "we who were there" when he describes the monks' eyewitness at the tomb,[29] but that does not mean that the monks all saw or valued the same incidents, nor that the brothers collectively agreed with decisions Benedict made as he compiled his collection. William would make very different choices. There must have been politics behind collecting cathedral miracles that we will never now retrieve: things that other monks saw that Benedict decided not to include, things that Benedict saw that others would not have included, and differing emphases and interpretations of stories everyone thought should be in his collection. One incident at the tomb that may have occasioned disagreement was something Benedict thought especially wonderful: the relighting of a candle in the days before Pentecost. In Benedict's telling, an unnamed monk sees the candle go out, tells a servant to relight it, and then sees the candle burst into flames again. "Not just one man, I say, saw this glorious vision, but also the people," Benedict then writes defensively, suggesting that there was tension over this incident.[30]

As problematic as "seeing" miracles in the tomb chapel could sometimes be, there does seem to have been at least one, and usually more than one, monk there on watch. But the crypt chapel was not the only place in the cathedral that people experienced miracles. Benedict writes of being responsible for the multitudes of ill people "in the entire church."[31] It seems likely that he and other monks made rounds to keep an eye on the crowds, but he never speaks of the monks "seeing" the course of a miracle anywhere but the tomb chapel. For incidents at the martyrdom site,[32] at the "doors of the church,"[33] on a "marble pavement,"[34] "in the middle of the church,"[35] or simply "in the church,"[36] the monks were sometimes alerted by shouts of joy among the crowds,[37] but most often, it appears, the people involved found a monk to talk to or made their way to the tomb. In one chapter, for instance, Benedict describes how a woman cured at the martyrdom went to the tomb "with witnesses" to tell her story, suggesting that no monk had been watching at the martyrdom.[38] What was especially difficult was when people emerged from the crowds, with no fanfare from others and no ostentatious behavior beforehand, to say that they had just been cured. In his account of the blind boy William of Horsepool, Benedict states William "was wholly unknown to us": "I confess that I saw him seeing when he left, but I did not see him blind when he came."[39] Benedict probably included this story in order to demonstrate to his readers how careful he usually was with such cases: he may well have left similar cases unrecorded.

Worse than trying to fathom the truth of stories like that of William of Horsepool, though, was Benedict's realization that there were miracles in the cathedral that the monks were missing altogether. Even miracles that happened at the tomb itself were not necessarily being spotted by the monks, as Benedict knew from the case of a young shepherd who felt himself cured after he kissed the tomb repeatedly, but went home without mentioning his healing to anyone. The monks only found out about this cure because when the shepherd's master "heard that the boy had left us secretly," he personally "led the healed boy back to us."[40] In the miracle windows, the boy's miracle is portrayed exactly as Benedict describes it, with the boy kissing the tomb and a monk on duty busily mixing up the water and not noticing a thing (Figure 12). Benedict was convinced that there were many more people leaving secretly and gripes repeatedly about this problem in his collection. At the end of a chapter in his second book Benedict complains that "up to ten people on the same day recovered from various illnesses, but we rejected those lacking a witness and we are not able to call back those who slipped away."[41] In his third book, Benedict twice brings up the problem of "the simple and the ignorant who received the benefit of health and departed secretly without our knowledge."[42] "It seems to happen as in the gospel," he grumbles: "'Were not ten cleansed? Where are the nine? He is not to be found, who returns and gives glory to the Lord.'"[43]

Someone like the young shepherd may not have realized that the monks expected him to tell them if he felt better: it was, after all, still a new thing for monks to be trying to record the experiences of the likes of shepherds en masse. Others of the "simple" may have known that the monks wanted to hear their stories, but slipped away to avoid their questioning. Benedict was not content just to record what the monks "saw." Even the people whose miracles the monks saw most directly—the lame man Benedict helped away from the tomb, the blind man pulling his head out of the tomb and shouting "I see," the violent woman becoming sane—had questions to answer. The basics Benedict wanted to know were a name (for women, the name of the husband or father could suffice), where the person came from, length and nature of illness (or the course of a nonhealing miracle), and, for children, an approximate age.[44] Benedict clearly felt that this information was essential if he was to include someone's story in his collection. The few times he does not include such details, he explains that he forgot,[45] or that his informant was not clear on the details.[46] Along with the questions could be inspections or tests. In one case, Benedict states that they "commanded" a girl named Avice to "walk back and forth through the churchyard" in order to prove her cure.[47] Benedict was often careful to report in his collection if people were not altogether cured, so he and his brethren must have watched people in the aftermath of miracles for further signs of healing.[48] That might not be the end of it, either. Sometimes Benedict sent messengers to check up on people even after they left the cathedral. After Mary of Rouen went home, "we afterwards sent a messenger to her to make sure of her liberation [from madness]" writes Benedict.[49] In the case of Walter of Lisors, a leprous knight who stayed at Canterbury for awhile and left still ill, Benedict got word that he was healed on his return journey: "When I heard this," he writes, "I sent a messenger to inquire diligently into the truth of the thing; he found [Walter] very ill, but showing no signs of leprosy."[50] In three other chapters, Benedict notes that he could not confirm the full course of a healing because people left the cathedral early: it seems quite possible that he wished people to stay on until he was fully satisfied with their cure.[51]

Many people, no doubt, happily volunteered details about their cures and were pleased with the monks' attention, but visitors who did not have the good fortune of being seen or taken under the wing of a monk could well have their stories of healing mistrusted or ultimately rejected. There are signs in the collection that Benedict was not always the most patient of listeners. He did not care to weigh down his collection with complicated personal histories, not, at least, from the usual kind of person who experienced miracles in the cathedral. The exception that proves the rule is Benedict's description of the cathedral cure of the "scholar" Richard of Northampton.[52] Benedict tells the reader that he is going to describe Richard's cure at length, because "with the cause and the mode of the illness known, the end is also better understood."[53] For once, Benedict gives his readers the full particulars about the course of an illness. He describes how it began with a month-long stomach flux, and how Richard then had a vision in which he was given the choice of suffering for nine years or dying in nine days. He was diagnosed with dysentery, which later turned into lientery. On the story goes; Benedict includes a long, in-depth account of Richard's later experiences in the cathedral: how he drank the water and felt great torments; how he relieved himself sixteen times in one night; how he vomited out the "seeds of illness"; and how, when he went out of his mind for a time, it felt to him at first as if his inflated stomach had been contracted and compressed, and then as if the church itself were too narrow to contain him.[54]

Richard was a scholar. Benedict trusted him to understand his own illness and answer questions clearly, and this story, told by a literate, likely religious man, was not in the same category for Benedict as the cathedral cures experienced by the laity. With them, Benedict does not appear to have listened with anything like the same degree of interest. To take just one example, Benedict describes in a short paragraph how a certain Saxeva woke in the cathedral to find herself healed. Benedict decided to pass on Saxeva's joyful remark that she felt so good that "she said, hyperbolically, that she was able to fly."[55] Someone commenting like this about her cure probably also had a lot to say about what had initially brought her to the cathedral, but here Benedict only tells us the bare essentials, that Saxeva was suffering from pain in parts of her body and that she "wearied of her life."[56] But why? If Saxeva explained further, Benedict either waved her off or, if he did listen, he did not think her history worthy of description in his collection. There are many other cathedral stories in his collection that feel similarly abbreviated.[57]

One of the few extraneous details Benedict *did* want to hear from the laity, however, was if they had gone to confession before coming to the cathedral. After describing how Wedeman of Folkstone confessed his sins and had his daughter with crippled hands confess hers "lest his own sins or those of the girl hinder healing,"[58] Benedict dedicates a whole chapter to explaining how "hardly anyone presumes to approach the saint's sepulcher to ask for anything, or even to enter the doors of the church of Canterbury, unless they have first been rebaptized in the fountain of confession and their tears, promising to change their lives in the future."[59] Not too many decades earlier, Osbern and Eadmer had told stories of Dunstan's miracles that had encouraged the monks of Christ Church to confession and commitment to a purer lifestyle.[60] Now, Benedict sees Becket's miracles as having this effect on the laity: "We can venture without doubt to assert in truthful words that many, involved in evil courses for many years and sickened without the medicine of confession, fled to the light of innocence through the way of confession before they dared to come to his most holy body, renouncing, out of reverence for him, their old life and the darkness of their faults."[61] It seems highly likely that in person as well as in his text, Benedict heaped praise on lay men and women who had made confession—this some forty years before Lateran IV.[62] Benedict's collection represents an early crystallization of notions about lay people needing to tell their stories—both of miracles and of sins—to the proper religious authorities. His desire to see people deposit their "little sack of sins," as he puts it in one chapter, and to be brought to "tears of the heart" and "internal contrition," as he says in another, is especially striking when compared to William, who, though he was part of the same community, cared little about such things.[63]

At the beginning of his second book, Benedict dedicates nearly forty-two chapters in a row to cathedral miracles. He then states, in a particularly intriguing passage, that Becket's enemies were spreading rumors that the miracles at Canterbury were not real, but the results of "devilish arts" by the monks of Canterbury. The monks were supposedly casting spells to make people feel ill, and then, by releasing them from the spells, the people seemed to be cured. But, Benedict says triumphantly, these rumors were cast down because miracles "multiplied through the whole of England," and "so many true witnesses came to us from all corners of England, that our adversaries were not able to resist or contradict all of them."[64] With this, Benedict shifts to a set of chapters concerning miracles that happened outside of the cathedral.[65] For all the energy Benedict lavished on collecting cathedral miracles, he also had to process and weigh the stories told by "ill people already healed"—people who came to the cathedral to give thanks for cures and miracles that had occurred elsewhere.

Hard, Bad and Incredulous:
Benedict's Collection of the Stories of the Cured

When Benedict began his miracle collection in the early summer of 1171, both the ill [*aegrotos* or *infirmos*] and the "cured" [*curatos*], as he terms them, would have been present in the cathedral.[66] Becket's miracles had not started in the cathedral, nor had they ever been confined to it. Once the monks opened the crypt to all visitors in April, people came to give thanks as well as to seek healing. Over the course of his collecting project, it is likely that Benedict saw the numbers of the cured swell, particularly as the "water" distributed by the monks was brought home by many pilgrims and used to effect further miracles. The ill and the cured must have made a striking visual contrast. The cured came to the cathedral cheery, walking, and secure in the

knowledge that Becket had chosen to help them, while the ill arrived pale
and fearful. The kinds of experiences they had to recount could also differ.
In contrast to the gradual recoveries and relit candles that were the staples of
cathedral miracles, the cured often had more spectacular stories to tell, stories
of resurrections from the dead, shipwrecks, accidents, pregnancies, and so on.

William liked collecting these stories the best, but Benedict seems to
have always been wary of the cured. For a collector who stressed the importance of "seeing" miracles, here were people claiming miracles he had not
seen before, people who did not need the monks' help or advice, people who
came and left as strangers: people, in sum, who might be lying and whose
stories were hard to confirm. Even the way he speaks of this category—"the
ill already cured *and their witnesses*"—indicates his resolve to double-check
such stories the best he could. Benedict refers to witnesses, oblations, and
oaths in his stories of the cured far more often than he does with cathedral
miracles. These statements usually come at the close of chapters. At the end
of his story of the miracle of the wife of Ansfrid, who nearly died in childbirth
at home in Sussex, Benedict notes that "we heard the voice of those telling
these things, and we had faith in their witnesses and in their many tears."[67]
In the case of the "venerable matron Sibilla," who found alms for Becket in
her purse, Benedict assures the reader that "we found her prepared and ready
to swear by such oaths, that we do not doubt her simple word is to be
believed."[68] After telling the story of some pilgrims rescued at sea, Benedict
writes, "having made their offerings, they told us these things, we believe,
faithfully."[69] People experiencing miracles in the cathedral must have given
offerings too, but most of Benedict's remarks about oblations are found in
the stories of cured. He seems to have clung to such gifts as visual evidence
that a person had truly experienced and was grateful for a miracle. When he
writes that the healed Richard of Rokesley "gave gifts to God and the martyr
in the sight of all the people in the atrium of the house of the Lord, in the
middle of the Jerusalem of Canterbury," it sounds very much like his description of people coming to rejoice at the sight of a miracle.[70]

Though he mentions witnesses frequently, Benedict hardly ever gives
their names, nor does he provide specific details about the oaths the cured
made or the gifts they gave. Taking note of all this information would have
slowed up his processing of the cured and bulked up his collection considerably. He seems to have thought that his readers would agree with this strategy, trusting that he had examined the witnesses but not needing to know
who they were or what they said. This approach was quite different from that

of first men to conduct canonization inquests in England in the early thirteenth century. Sometimes Benedict mentions the absence rather than the presence of witnesses, but this too was a means of assuring his readers that he was carefully scrutinizing the stories of the cured. For instance, in the case of a pauper who made an offering of a gold coin and then told a story about a boat run aground and recovered, Benedict states that "even though he lacked witnesses, we believed him: his simplicity, and the poor correspondence between his oblation and his clothing, argued for his veracity."[71] Another pauper, Beatrice, who claimed to have been blind, also did not have witnesses, or at least, not the kind Benedict wanted. "I confess my incredulity," Benedict writes at the end of his account of Beatrice's miracle,

> if indeed it is to be called incredulity, as I did not doubt for myself but for others, so that the bar of incredulity might be thrown away from everyone's heart. Doubting in myself over those things that she said had happened to her, who was despicable by clothing and appearance, and with no witness to commend her except a girl, now I demanded more harshly for witnesses, now I presented to her an unmerciful appearance as if I were contradicting her. She answered back with hard and bitter words, as if they came from the action of an angry soul. She called me hard, bad and incredulous, and considered me inconsiderate and unworthy for the obedience of such a martyr, as I seemed to envy his glory, and to detract from his miracles with too much care for the investigation of truth.[72]

Benedict never affixed such a passage to an account of a cathedral miracle. He clearly wrote it expecting that his readers would cheer him for his willingness to be railed at by a beggar woman for the sake of the "investigation of the truth." Later on in the collection, Benedict expresses doubt more gently in a story about a resurrected boy, stating that the boy's parents "truly believed that he had been left dead," but that "I do not know whether I ought to say he was dying or dead."[73] Still, if voices were raised in anger rather than joy when Benedict was discussing a miracle with a layperson, it seems very likely it would have been with one of the cured, and then more likely a woman rather than a man. It is often in his accounts of cured women's miracles that one finds Benedict making comments about doubt and uncertainty, such as this passage at the close of a story about two women healed outside of Canterbury: "Those who did not produce witnesses, or were not dissolved down to pure truth by us, not a few we let go out of our ears as easily as we had allowed them in, not wishing to mix chaff with grain, to insert the doubtful with the certain."[74]

Benedict made visual inspections of the cured. He notes, for instance, that when the Welshman Griffin arrived at the cathedral, "we saw him so improved, that hardly any vestige of the disease remained: new skin had grown over [the tumor on his leg]."[75] The scrofulous swellings on the body of William of Lincoln, a toddler, were so reduced that "hardly any vestige remained" of the illness.[76] Benedict also took pains to examine the objects the cured sometimes brought along with them, the stones, bones, worms, pyxes, and the like, that had been involved in their miracles. When the young Durand of Eu came to the cathedral, he brought along the bloody stone that had gotten stuck inside his ear. "He who wishes to see (the stone)," Benedict concludes his account, "let him come to the martyr, and his desire will be satisfied."[77] The arrival of the cured could itself be spectacular: Gilbert, cured of terrible skin ulcers, ran all the way from London to Canterbury in one day and stood nude before the monks to demonstrate his cure [*se ipsum nobis nudum et perfecte curatum ostendens*].[78]

For the most famous of Becket's miracles, though, Benedict did not feel that questions, inspections, or witnesses were enough. When Eilward of Westoning, a pauper who was blinded and castrated in Bedford and whose pilgrimage to Canterbury was slowed by crowds eager to see him, finally arrived at the cathedral, the monks must have questioned him very carefully (Figure 1). Benedict's account of Eilward's cure is the longest story in his collection. And yet, Benedict assures his readers he had special, additional support for the story: while they had heard the story from many people even before Eilward arrived at the cathedral, Benedict writes, they were satisfied only when they received a letter of confirmation of Eilward's story from the burgesses of Bedford—a letter that Benedict then copies in full into his collection.[79] The second longest story in Benedict's collection concerns the resurrection of a son of the knight Jordan Fitz-Eisulf. Here too, though Jordan and his wife asserted to the truth of the miracle with "many tears," gifts, and witnesses, at the conclusion of the story Benedict tells his readers that he sent a letter of inquiry "secretly" [*occulte*] to Jordan's local priest, who "wrote back saying that the boy was without doubt dead and revived by the water of the martyr."[80]

While Benedict must have been eager to see Eilward arrive at the cathedral and rejoiced in the recovery of Jordan's son, he does not seem to have worried if he missed other stories of the cured. More so than people cured in the cathedral, the cured had to show some initiative to get their stories heard by a monk. Benedict often uses terms like "display" or "exhibit" in his accounts of the cured: Godfrey of Lillingston, Benedict writes, "showed himself among the other cured ones of the martyr," while Wivelina of Littlebourne "exhibited herself healed among the others cured by our father."[81] Benedict also describes two instances in which people would have left the cathedral without saying anything about their miracles if it were not for a chance encounter with a monk.[82] Benedict knew he was not hearing all the stories of the cured who came to the cathedral, but, strikingly, this does not seem to have bothered him. In contrast to his oft-expressed frustration with unreported cathedral miracles, Benedict never complains about the lost stories of the cured.

He was also unimpressed with the distances people traveled to Canterbury to tell their stories. The first "foreign" miracles in Benedict's collection, the cure of Thomas of St. Valery in the cathedral and the stories brought to the cathedral by a Flemish family, appear without any hoopla from Benedict whatsoever.[83] In the fourth book of his collection, Benedict included more miracles from people coming from outside of England, including Scotland, Ireland, and France, but again he does not comment about this nor segregate these stories into a separate category. What interested Benedict more than overseas miracles was what was happening at Newington, a little Kentish village located about twenty miles west of Canterbury on the road to London. Newington is quite unknown now, and must have been equally unfamiliar to many of Benedict's medieval readers, but a cross had been set up there in the aftermath of Becket's murder to commemorate his confirmation of children on that spot. The area around the cross became a place where people on their way to or from Canterbury sometimes experienced miracles.[84]

Benedict dedicates thirteen chapters in a row at the close of his third book to miracles at Newington—he does such a thing for no other site except for the cathedral itself.[85] Newington was part of a manor of the justiciar Richard de Lucy, a former enemy of Becket, and Benedict believed that the miracles there were meant to make de Lucy respect the saint.[86] But the main reason he included so many of these stories in his collection, it appears, was because of the close proximity of Newington to Canterbury. Benedict never says whether he traveled to Newington himself, but it seems very possible. The few times Benedict mentions making trips to investigate miracles, they are to places in Kent. He tells his readers that he went to Sarre, a village located about eight miles from Canterbury, "that I might more diligently examine the truth, and know from the testimony of those who live there, whether the martyr had truly revived [a boy of the village] from the dead."[87] He also seems to have made investigatory trips to Rochester, about thirty miles away (to get there, he would have gone through Newington),[88] and to Ifield, a Kentish village that was part of an estate of Canterbury cathedral.[89]

It is ironic that the first miracle collector concerned with England's only international cult was happiest focusing on miracles close to home, and was so in part because of the broadened audience for his collection, an audience for whom Benedict wanted to create an impeachable text. As he listened to the cured, Benedict looked for signs of sincerity such as marks of illness or healing on bodies, objects involved in a miracle, offerings, tears, and witnesses who could pledge to a story and a person's identity. Some people were subject to "harsh and incredulous" questioning before Benedict was satisfied. In certain cases, Benedict went even further, writing letters or traveling himself to get more information about a miracle outside of the cathedral. But not all the healthy visitors coming to the cathedral with stories of miracles needed to be so tested and tried. Among them were the religious men. Collecting their stories was generally the most easy and congenial part of Benedict's project.

Their Own Eyes: Benedict's Collection of the Stories of Religious Men

When Benedict tells his readers that he derived stories from "the testimony of religious men, who had seen [miracles] with their own eyes," he was saying to his readers that his third source was them, or people like them. Benedict viewed religious men and the secular elite as collaborators, people whose stories and letters provided reliable and labor-free material for his collection. He fashioned close to a third of his collection's chapters from their stories. He heard and recorded stories told by abbots visiting from Jervaulx, Sulby, and Croxton Kerrial.[90] Monks, canons, and chaplains had stories to tell too: Benedict recounted stories told by Ralph, the subprior of St. Augustine's, and Richard, chaplain to the sheriff of Devon, among others.[91] Then there were the many men Benedict designates simply as "clerks," such as Thomas, a "venerable clerk," Walter, a "clerk of Hatcliffe, near Grimsby," and Roger, a "clerk of London."[92] Benedict also collected stories from village priests, though their stories did not carry the same weight. Benedict was reluctant to put names to all of them,[93] and he will sometimes reassure the reader about a priest's religious dedication. He describes the priest Ranulf of Froyle, for instance, as "a man, in our opinion, very devoted to God and the holy martyr."[94] In contrast to the dozens of stories he took from religious men, Benedict includes very few about religious women: one concerns Wlviva, a "religious woman" who ran a hospital in Canterbury, and another Lecarda, a nun who lived "twenty-seven miles from Canterbury."[95] There is also a third story that a noblewoman, Constance, told about her daughter, a nun at Stixwold.[96] Religious women would not have been as free to travel, and of these three women only Wlviva, who lived in Canterbury itself, seems to have told her story in person to the monks.[97] When Benedict writes that he derived stories from the testimony of "religious men," he does mean men.

With their tonsures and habits, or, in the case of noble visitors, expensive garments and trimmings, these special visitors to Canterbury would have been immediately distinguishable in the crowds, if they found themselves mingling much with the crowds at all.[98] It seems to have been rare for religious men to come to Canterbury ill. There are only two stories in Benedict's collection about religious men experiencing cures within the cathedral: one is about William, a priest of London, and the other concerns Richard, the scholar of Northampton whose symptoms Benedict discusses at such length.[99] Prior Robert Cricklade of St. Frideswide's also came to Canterbury hoping for a cure, but seems to have left quickly after prayer at the tomb. He felt his first sensations of healing at Rochester.[100] When religious men had cures of their own to describe to Benedict, they were usually ones that they experienced at home, in their own beds, a more seemly place to suffer. The clerk Philip of Alnwick, for instance, seems to have been at home when, lying in bed with debilitated feet and swollen genitals, he had a vision in which he saw Thomas come out of a shrine, grasp his genitals with two of his fingers, and pierce them with his fingernails.[101]

More than cures, the miracles religious men experienced and Benedict recorded involved things like losing and finding money,[102] seeing mysterious lights,[103] having strange experiences with the water,[104] calming barking dogs (Benedict's own personal miracle),[105] dangerous episodes at sea,[106] or visions.[107] Though these incidents usually occurred outside of the cathedral, Benedict never mentions asking for witnesses or looking for visual evidence or oblations from religious men. Their eyes were like his eyes, as he states in the conclusion of a story told by Henry of Houghton, a man who had been one of Becket's clerks: "Although our eyes did not see these things, we do not waver to add them as if they had, certified by 'our' eyes and mouth of Henry."[108] Considering that Benedict often used the texts of letters in his collection, he might have added "their pens are like our pens."[109] On occasion, Benedict asked religious men to compose their own stories themselves. At the conclusion of a very long account of the healing of Prior Robert Cricklade, Benedict remarks that "the prior, having been asked by us, wrote these things about himself."[110]

There is only one case in the collection where one can see Benedict asking for more evidence from a religious man. Master Edmund, the archdeacon of Coventry, told the monks about a leper from his region named Humphrey who had been cured in Canterbury cathedral. "Since, however, this archdeacon only knew this from the hearing of it," Benedict writes, "although we had faith in his words, we did not want to commend it to writing, unless the leper were sent back to us with letters from his dean."[111] The obstacle for Benedict seems to have been this was supposedly a cathedral cure, and yet he had no knowledge of it—here again was the problem of people leaving without telling the monks about their miracles. The elusive Humphrey did return to Canterbury with a letter from his dean, Saffrid, who had strong words about Humphrey's failure to speak when he was cured at Canterbury. Saffrid wrote, "[Humphrey] neglected to give thanks to God and the martyr . . . I send him back to you, that he might make good to the saint what he had poorly done."[112] Both Dean Saffrid and Master Edmund, then, acted as Benedict's partners in rooting out the truth of Humphrey's cure.

A remarkably high percentage (two-thirds) of the stories Benedict heard from his religious informants were not about the speakers themselves. Religious men told stories about members of their own communities, wandering preachers, priests, and monks or canons at other houses.[113] Mostly, though, they told stories about the laity. They described the miracles of their parishioners and of their servants.[114] One religious man told a story about his father's pious death.[115] Another told about a miracle involving his nephew.[116] A clerk told about the healing of his son and a woman in his "familia," and a priest told about the healing of a daughter.[117] The religious also felt free to tell stories about laypeople that had tenuous or no ties to them at all, such as master Richard, a monk of Ely, who told Benedict a story about a woman who put some of the water into her beer mash to make it ferment.[118] Other religious men took it upon themselves to send letters along with pilgrims heading to Canterbury. When William of Gloucester arrived at Canterbury to tell about his miracle, he carried along a letter written by Geoffrey, the dean of Gloucester: "Let it be known," Geoffrey writes, "that the bearer of this letter, William, was buried in a small pit."[119]

If lay men or women wanted to tell him a story about anyone but themselves, Benedict seems to have shooed them off. He hardly ever included secondhand or hearsay stories from the laity in his collection.[120] But he was willing to accept hearsay stories from the religious and the secular elite on a regular basis. Countess Berta, widow of Giffard of Ely, told Benedict a story about Hedewic, a laywoman; another countess told a story about Stephen, a canon of St. Paul's, Bedford; and earl Simon of Northampton told a story about his baker—Benedict put all of these stories into his collection.[121] In contrast with his interrogation of the cured and his investigation of cathedral miracles, Benedict conveys very little anxiety about the truth of the stories of the religious. Once, he did write about something that made him angry. Rochester monks were saying that a blind man who had been to Canterbury and had the blood rubbed on his eyes was cured by Ithamar, not Becket, because the man regained his sight in Rochester. There is no mistaking the rancor in Benedict's comment: "Although we believe the miracle [*virtute*] to have happened at our sanctuary, yet the aforementioned servants of God ascribe it to the blessed Ithamar, and we do not contradict them; however, we know of a similar miracle that unquestionably happened in the middle of the public street, which no-one might presume to steal away or extort from the glory of our martyr."[122] Given Benedict's interest in miracles occurring close to Canterbury, it is possible he would not have been so irritated if this incident had not concerned Rochester.

Benedict shows a different kind of discomfort with an incident in Canterbury cathedral that happened to a man he knew well. Benedict had a special interest in miracles concerning Becket's blood and the water mixture made from it. In every book of his collection, he devotes series of chapters to stories about the water disappearing or appearing, pyxes breaking when they came in contact with the water, visions about the blood, and so on.[123] In a pair of chapters in his third book, Benedict describes first how one of his old schoolfellows (whom he leaves unnamed) had received some of the water at the tomb, but every time he tried to walk away, the water would boil up in his pyx. A Christ Church monk at the tomb (also unnamed), said "it seems it does not want to be taken by you," and laughed at Benedict's unfortunate friend.[124] In the next chapter, Benedict describes how this same monk was himself made a laughingstock. The monk was hanging up a number of pyxes that had burst or cracked when they came in contact with the water, when he came across a less damaged one and greedily decided to keep it for himself. It was promptly struck out of his hand. "We asked," Benedict writes, what he had done and why this had happened to him, "as if he were one of the people" [*quasi unus de populo*]. The monk promptly confessed his intentions "lest he be suspected of something worse," and the miracle, Benedict writes, was seen as much of a joke as a wonder.[125]

Benedict's sense that only "one of the people" would or should be punished by Becket for greediness is a far cry from earlier sensibilities. Eadmer had told numerous stories of Christ Church monks receiving mysterious blows for showing disrespect to the saints.[126] For Benedict, though, such things were meant for the people. The role of the monks, and religious men more generally, was to watch, weigh, and rejoice. Religious men were Benedict's allies in his collecting enterprise, people whose stories could be trusted, whose letters could be copied, and who could help him with long-distance investigations. Most of the encounters between Benedict and the religious who came to tell stories to the Christ Church monks seem to have been comfortably obliging. When Richard, abbot of Sulby at Welford, arrived at the cathedral to say that he had met some Welsh pilgrims on the road who had just experienced miracles, but who were too poor to afford a return trip to Canterbury, perhaps Benedict was pleased. He could talk to the abbot instead of facing yet another group of the cured.[127]

In the fourth book of his collection, Benedict complains that his hands cannot possibly write fast enough to keep up with Becket's miracles.[128] He refuses to expand on a certain miracle because "the way before me is great."[129] He worries that "the continual repetition of the same miracle may create disgust," and so, though more lepers were being healed by Becket than any saint had healed before, he will only tell a few of their stories.[130] He explains that while there were many more stories of sea rescues to tell, "the one and the same kind of food cannot be taken without disgust," and he will move on.[131] Such jaded remarks (there are more of them)[132] are not the only signs that Benedict's enthusiasm for miracle collecting was waning. Toward the close of the fourth book, he copies in letters more frequently than he ever had before.[133] Instead of putting together pairs of miracles, he writes sets of four, five, or even six miracles.[134] Series of very brief chapters become more common, and careful rhetorical linkages between chapters less so.[135] The impression is of someone burning through his notes. In his last addition to the collection, Benedict writes of expecting something new, sighing for new things, and the tedium of familiarities.[136] Like many large-scale miracle collectors, Benedict did not give his text any formal conclusion. Later copyists, if they wanted one, would have to make one up themselves.[137] He had had enough. He had written the largest miracle collection attempted up to that point in England, a text Prior Odo later praised as "tried and examined, such that there is nothing mixed in [the miracles] that may appear false."[138] If he wrote any narrative compositions after 1173, they do not survive; he probably never attempted anything so ambitious again. He put down his burden and pursued his administrative career.

Benedict must have handed over a stack of used and unused notes and letters to his younger colleague William at some point, as William would use some of the same materials in his collection. William's collection, "the second work," would show him to be exuberant where Benedict was sober, nonchalant where Benedict was cautious, judgmental where Benedict was forgiving, and excessive where Benedict was restrained. Though it was Benedict's collection that would be read and recopied and circulated widely, in many ways William was the more natural miracle collector. William's maxim was "choose what you will," and with it, he created an even longer and very different kind of collection of the miracles of Thomas Becket.

CHAPTER TEN

Choose What You Will:
William of Canterbury
and the Heavenly Doctor

In the introduction of his *vita* for Becket, William of Canterbury provides an evocative glimpse into his work as "the martyr's scribe."[1] He describes how he had a vision after he had been asked by his brothers to take up "incorrect and imperfect notes" and write a miracle collection.[2] In the vision, the saint said to him, "'Choose what you will'": "hearing this, he felt in himself the mercy of the martyr. . . . Rejoicing and freed from care, he awaited his choices to be turned into the best ones, his vision into truth, and work into rest . . . [knowing that] according to the lord's admonition, he need seek out only those that deserved to be heard."[3] William had this vision sometime after mid-1172, at a point when Benedict had written a large part of his collection. If visiting religious men were not already congratulating Benedict and clamoring for copies of his text, they soon would be. We know that Benedict passed on notes to William, likely including ones he had found too tedious or "imperfect" to write up.[4] It was a recipe for writer's block. William may well have dithered and sorted and resorted his notes until it came to him: choose what you will.

William compiled the first six books of his collection from mid-1172 through 1175. After a halt c.1175, he made a long addition c.1176–77. By the time he finished, he had found more than four hundred stories he thought "deserved to be heard" and made a collection 40 percent longer than Benedict's. Benedict had proclaimed his intention to "doubt every one." William's goal was quite different: he wanted to lay out a feast of stories for his readers, to "show the sumptuous food he has to the reclining guests."[5] He saw what he took to be miracles in Canterbury cathedral,[6] but he did not invest these stories with the same emotional resonance that Benedict had. Nor did he tell as many. Fewer than 8 percent of his collection's chapters concern cathedral miracles.[7] William focused instead on what he termed "the people coming for prayer."[8] He delighted in the sensational stories they had to tell: he recounts the miracles of a woman who was given a ring by Becket in a vision, a man who put Becket relics near a lavatory, a woman tempted to have sex with a handsome knight, a boy kicked in the head by a horse, a boy gored by a bull, a boy run over by an iron cart, a young man struck by lightening, a jester slipping on a wet floor, a man hung on the gallows, a woman just missed by a falling tree, and many other stories about visions, drownings, sea rescues, and accidents.[9]

Benedict worried about stories like these. Before he accepted them, he wanted to hear from witnesses and to see other signs that the lay teller was being truthful. William felt that there was little need for so much suspicion and more than once expresses his frustration with the distrusting attitude of his brothers. For instance, after describing how the son of a woman named Agnes was caught under a mill-wheel and survived through Becket's aid, he appended this coda:

> She indicated the day and hour of the accident and spoke of the circumstances of the fall. The devotion of the woman, the cause of her journey, and the long way she had traveled in humble style and great suffering were able to make faith. But the brothers, not giving heed to a plain yes, yes or no, no, demanded witnesses from nearby who were knowledgeable of the thing; she was not able to satisfy them with her plain words. For they were mistrustful on account of the evil times and the stealthy introduction of false brethren, who strove to obfuscate the truth by the mixture of evil, lying in wait after the holy action, and challenging the victor after the victory.[10]

William explains nothing more about who these "false brethren" [*fratres falsos*] are supposed to be, nor how exactly they would have influenced Agnes's story.[11] In this manner, though, he managed to include Agnes's story into his collection despite the objections of his witness-demanding brethren (one in particular leaps to mind). On the rare occasions William presents himself as a doubter—mostly in the later addition to the collection—his portrayal is done tongue-in-cheek and needs to be read in the same playful spirit in which it was written.[12] Benedict had given over nearly a third of his collection to stories from religious men, most of them second-hand accounts of lay miracles, because he thought these stories were particularly trustworthy. William did not give the stories of the religious such preferential treatment. He rarely told more than one story in a row by the same teller (compare Appendices 2 and 3).[13] He was instead on the hunt for good stories—stories told by monks and priests, certainly, but also by knights, women, the leprous, the resurrected, and so on.[14]

Freed from the strictures Benedict had placed on himself both by the expansion of Becket's cult and by his own temperament, William created a collection emblematic of the exuberant spirit of the late twelfth century. I conclude this chapter with a brief look at William's overall rhetorical strategies, but I will focus the bulk of it on William's approach to stories of healing. William's collection is a touchstone case of what has been termed the "medicalization" of miracle collections in the late twelfth century.[15] He uses far more medical terminology in his descriptions of illness and disease than Benedict—indeed, more than any other English collector of the period—and must have made some study of medical texts.[16] Monica Green has shown that England was "precocious" in its possession of medical manuscripts. In the twelfth century, she writes, "few other places in western Europe [outside of southern Italy] had . . . so large a presence of Latin medical literature in their monastic houses, cathedrals and (perhaps) courts as did England."[17] No catalogue of the library of Christ Church survives from the twelfth century, so it is not possible to know exactly which texts William would have had available to him as he collected Becket's miracles.[18] However, William likely had done his reading and acquired most of his medical learning before he started the text: there was only a year and a half between his entry into the community and the commencement of his miracle collection.

Though we have no surviving reference to him as a *medicus*, it is possible that William considered himself to be a doctor. In his study of Anglo-Norman physicians, Edward Kealey has found that some 13 percent of them were monks.[19] Walter Daniel, the Cistercian who wrote a *vita* for Aelred of Rievaulx, is a pertinent example of a contemporary who was a physician, a monk, and a hagiographer.[20] The twelfth-century conciliar decrees that the religious must not make financial profit from their medical learning or study medicine outside the cloister also suggests the large number of monk-physicians and the appeal of medical study.[21] The foundation and support of hospitals by the monks in the twelfth century is another indication of the close intersection of religion and medicine in this period.[22] At the time William was writing his collection, many new pilgrim hospitals were being established in Kent.[23] William's close acquaintance with doctors is evident both in his *vita* for Becket and his miracle collection. Of all the Becket *vita*-writers, William is the only one to describe an episode involving Becket's doctor, a man also named William.[24] In his miracle collection, William describes the visions of Master Feramin, the doctor in charge of the Christ Church infirmary; he speaks of a certain Peter as a well-known doctor [*non ignoti nominus medicus, vocabulo Petrus*]; and he seems to have discussed the healing of an Englishman ill at Perigueux with a doctor named Walter.[25]

There is an element of pure showmanship in William's deployment of medical terms and information in his descriptions of Becket's miracles. John of Salisbury's complaint in his *Metalogicon* about students returning from Salerno or Montpellier could equally apply to William: "they quote Hippocrates and Galen, pronounce mysterious words, and have aphorisms ready to apply to all cases. Their strange terms serve as thunderbolts which stun the minds of their fellow men."[26] But William did not employ his medical learning just to impress his listeners with his own learning, but also because he wanted his readers to fully appreciate Becket's healing powers. He portrays Becket as acting as a good doctor of the time should, able to cure diseases known to be incurable, and especially to be admired because he treated the "causes" of diseases. From the point of view of a visitor to Canterbury, William would have been the one to tell a story of healing: there was probably no sharper difference between the two collectors than William's intense interest in the course of a disease.

You Are Healed, Remove Your Cataplasm: Becket's Cures and William's Medical Learning

William begins his collection with stories of early visions, a set of miraculous punishments suffered by doubters of Becket's miracles, a section of chapters concerning the famous miracle of Eilward of Westoning, and then a chapter about the miracles experienced by the family of Jordan Fitz-Eisulf.[27] After these preliminaries, he could start on his own path. At the beginning of the next chapter, what is in many ways the real commencement of the collection, he writes:

Epilepsy is one of the long-lasting diseases. It attacks once a year, once a month, once a week, once a day, or more, and holds the entire person captive. Three streams [of this disease] pour out in the earth, like the rivers of Babylon. The first is epilepsy, which has its origin from the brain, seizing the sufferer suddenly and leaving froth when it ceases to attack. The second is catalepsy, which draws its origin from the hands, arms, and legs, and is felt before it comes. The third flows from the stomach, which they call analepsy. These three are found far and wide, as if the whole face of the earth is irrigated by streams. One drop of the blood of the martyr remedies all three of them, the one halts the three, like calm to a storm. That which was poured from the head [i.e., Becket's blood] calms the agitation of the brain, brings light to the darkness and mist of the eyes, restores memory, and frees the blocked-up stomach of bloody humors. Whatever strikes is repelled by a contrary force of heavenly power, as the multitude of people and the health of the cleansed demonstrate.[28]

Only after this does William introduce the person who provoked this deluge of information: the epileptic nun Petronella of Polesworth, whose story is the first of a set of five on epilepsy and coughing.

There is a pent-up quality to William's medical discourses here and elsewhere in the collection. William had heard Benedict's collection read aloud in the chapterhouse before he started his own, and it seems likely that he had found Benedict's discussion of illnesses feeble.[29] Benedict could identify the basics: lameness, blindness, paralysis, dropsy, leprosy. William saw these problems too, but he also saw before him, in his words, the "nephritic," those suffering from kidney stones,[30] the "splenetic," those with problems with the spleen,[31] and the "syntectic" or "phthisic," those suffering from consumption.[32] He recognized sufferers of semitertian fevers [*hemitritaeus*][33] and colic [*iliaca passione*].[34] He saw those who had endured or were still plagued by apoplexy [*apoplexia*], diarrhea [*diarria*], gout [*podager*], dysentery [*dysenteria*], piles [*ficum*], and other problems he carefully described by Greek terms, such as a headache he terms a *cephalica* and a problem of the throat he terms *arteriata*.[35]

William also had a much keener eye and broader vocabulary for anatomical features. He describes the effects of diseases not just on the nose, but on the nostrils, not just on the eye, but on the eyebrows, eyelids, pupils, and even the corners of the eye, using the exceedingly unusual word *hyrquos*.[36] He wrote not just of arms and hands, but the armpit [*acella*] and the space between the joints of the hand [*internodiis manus*].[37] He deployed specialized vocabulary to describe how the membranes of the brain [*cerebrum miringis*] of a boy were injured in a blow and how Thomas, in a vision, stroked the injury away, moving his hands from the occipital to the sincipital region [*ab occipite et sincipite*].[38] William described illnesses or accidents affecting the thorax, the lung, the liver, the hips, the ribs, the vertebra of the spine, and cartilage.[39] He discusses veins, arteries, the pulse, and the heart.[40] In stories about ulcerous sores, kidney stones, piles and pregnancies, he refers to the anus, the urinary tract, the testicles, the penis, the breast, the uterus, and the vulva.[41] He had a wide vocabulary for the swellings, ulcers, fissures, openings, pustules, and pimples that appeared on the bodies of diseased or wounded individuals. He uses the rare word *anthraces* to describe virulent ulcers,[42] for example, and *glandulous* to describe the swellings on a leprous man.[43]

The parallel miracles, stories that both collectors told, display a great deal of medical one-upmanship on William's part. When describing the leprosy of a foundling at Abingdon abbey, Benedict had written, "A foul leprosy enveloped his whole body . . . protuberances grew more and more on his face, and his whole body decayed more and more."[44] William, talking about the same boy, writes: "He was struck by the disease of elephantiasis . . . with his face full of protuberances, eyes weeping, eyebrows thin. Wide ulcers on his arms and leg reached to the bones . . . his rough voice could barely be heard by those standing beside him, and his bandages needed to be changed every day or every other day because of the effusion of diseased blood."[45] When describing the vengeance Becket took on the knight Thomas of Etton, Benedict says that the knight was nearly choked by "a dangerous sickness of quinsy, as it is thought" [*periculoso, ut putabatur, squinantiae morbo percussus*].[46] In William's account, there is no question about the diagnosis: Thomas of Etton was "struck with an intemperate quinsy" [*percussus igitur incontinenti synanchia*], and he uses the Greek term *synanchia* rather than Benedict's pedestrian *squinantia*.[47] William uses the occasion of the healing of the leper Hugh of Ebblinghem to enthuse about Becket's ability to cure "all types of leprosy, not only *tyria* and *leonina*, but also *elephantia* and *alopecia*," and to speculate on the reasons Becket was curing so many lepers.[48] William begins Hugh's story, moreover, by quoting a passage from Galen, in which Galen writes that he never saw a cure of leprosy except from drinking wine fouled by a snake. "But we," William exults, "have seen two cleansed without any sign of leprosy remaining, having received no other medicine than the blood and water of the martyr."[49] Benedict just says Hugh was "struck by a sudden leprosy" and had a lot of swellings.[50] Galen and tricky Greek terminology never come into it, with Hugh's cure or with anyone else in Benedict's collection.

William never presents himself as providing medical advice to pilgrims telling him their stories or suffering at the tomb, but he certainly uses his collection as a platform to dispense medical information to his brethren and other readers. He discusses the four types of dropsy, two of them curable and two of them not.[51] He explains that "quinsy, as physicians say, when it is acute and strikes suddenly, restrains the breath and closes the throat, and the first or second or third day it kills."[52] "The disease of diabetes arises from heat and from the defect of the power of containment, as the kidneys that have wetness are not able to retain it," he writes, before telling about the healing of a priest.[53] A few chapters later, he tells the reader that "vertigo is a corruption of sight; it appears to those who suffer from this disease that everything is flying, cloudy or dark, and it is thought that it seems to them as if everything moves falsely."[54] Before discussing the miracle of a man with a kidney stone, William writes informatively, "Stones are produced in the kidneys by viscous and dense humors burned up by too much heat, just as we see the vases of potters harden by the dry fire, so that water is not able to dissolve them." He even adds a bit of preventive advice: "So, take care lest you generate fat or viscous material in your kidneys. It is better to avoid the wound than to seek its remedy."[55]

Whether or not William told pilgrims at the tomb about such things, he must have encouraged them to tell him their stories at length. He took note of and devoted long passages to descriptions of the desperate measures people took to cure themselves, making for some of the most toe-curling reading of any English miracle collection. Baldric of Northumbria, William tells us, injured his testicles getting off a horse. He suffered an enormous swelling, making it impossible for him to urinate. He inserted an iron into his urinary tract, hoping to open it up: "What did this accomplish?" William writes, "The superfluity [of urine] was ejected, but the means of ejecting failed."[56] A certain Peter, suffering from a cancer on his foot, was told that he must cut off a diseased toe. He did so, but the pain and problem only grew worse, and he was advised to cut off another.[57] Ralph, a clerk and man of letters, suffered from hemorrhoids and constipation. After a month of this, he swelled up. "His private parts were filled with the downward-flowing and corrupt humors," and it all began to putrefy, the flesh and skin dissolving together. A woman—William does not say who—felt the area, holding a handkerchief to her nose as she immersed her fingers "up to the ribs or a solid point," finding "corrupted flesh and a great deal of sanies" (sanies is a bloody discharge frequently referred to by William). The sick man "took a knife and cut the hanging ulcer" and removed the skin from his testicles, but even this did not stop the disease: "a cancer broke out on the head of the penis, piles on his rear, fistula on his buttocks. An opening underneath the penis trickled continually."[58]

As this story of poor Ralph indicates, William wanted to know specific details about material expelled from the body. Urine inspection was a trademark of the medieval doctor, as one can see in one of the few depictions of a doctor in the Canterbury cathedral miracle windows (Figure 13). William includes so much detail about urine, excrement, vomit, blood, and expelled objects in his collection that he must have asked about such things if visitors did not supply the information themselves. He tells us that when the earl of Albemarle was suffering from stones, "his excrement looked like coal and his urine like blood." When the kidney stone was finally expelled it was "in the size and form of an almond, the color of a chestnut, wider in the middle, narrower at the head."[59] A remarkable number of bones or bone fragments emerge or even burst out of wounds in William's collection—this is always a good thing for the person involved.[60] Benedict would speak of people vomiting, but William wanted information about the vomit itself: after drinking poison, Henry vomited out what William terms a "multicolored sanies,"[61] while the ill Heiliff vomited and voided what William describes as "a dense and sanies-like blood, in the form of a viscous and liverish liquid" for five days and nights.[62] William of Oxford, with a stomach disorder, was close to death when the blood coming from his body was "the kind that usually comes from a vein."[63] William was also interested in change in a discharge: when Gerard vowed himself to a pilgrimage, William, writes, the sanies from his wound, formerly red, became white and lessened.[64]

William also wanted to know what people had been eating or drinking, another key part of the medieval diagnosis of illness.[65] He notes that a young boy named Simon, newly resurrected from the dead, refused to eat anything but strawberries and mulberries until he arrived with his family at Canterbury, at which point he got his full appetite back.[66] He describes how a doctor foolishly allowed Roger of Middleton, who had recently recovered from an illness, to eat codfish. A bad case of dropsy was the result, and Roger, William writes, thought of eating the wrong kind of food again in order to

Figure 13. Doctors examine a leprous monk. Canterbury Cathedral, Trinity Chapel Ambulatory Window s.VII (36). Author's photograph used with the kind permission of the Dean and Chapter of Canterbury Cathedral.

find an end to his torment.[67] In two other chapters, William tells how a priest with a rupture unwisely drank new beer, which made everything much worse, and how John of Pontefract, in the first year of his novitiate, ate salmon and went weak and blind.[68] Godfrey of Binbrooke combined both dangerous foodstuffs, eating a "noxious fish" and drinking new beer: when he woke the next morning, he was paralyzed. William writes that Godfrey did not take warning "of what the people say, 'Not everything tasty in the mouth is good for the stomach.'"[69] William introduces Godfrey's story with a long discourse about how paralysis is often caused by too much food or drink or because of too little, and how it is cured either by taking away the excess or augmenting the lack: "We say what our eyes have seen, many gluttons [have been] struck by paralysis."[70]

The message William wants his readers to take away from Godfrey's story is clear; less evident is whether Godfrey himself had blamed his paralysis on the fish and beer he had consumed. Did Godfrey come to William with a tale about a foolish diet followed by paralysis, or did William, hearing that Godfrey's problem had been paralysis, ask him what he had been eating and drinking and then draw his own conclusions? Many stories in the collection raise similar questions, such as that of Margaret of Hamilton's pregnancy and stillbirth. William writes that Margaret had a bad nosebleed as she neared the end of her pregnancy, and that this nosebleed drained the menstrual blood that the mother reserves from the time of conception to sustain the fetus [*exhaustaque sunt menstrua per inanitionem quae mater a conceptione foetui nutriendo reservaret*].[71] Sometime later, Margaret no longer felt the fetus move or kick, and when it came time to give birth, she labored for three days with no result, nearly dying before finally delivering a baby with "putrid nostrils and ears." Was the nosebleed a part of Margaret's story from the start? Did she always attribute the death of her fetus to it, or did William, after hearing her story, ask questions and put two and two together?

Thinking that greedy eating could cause paralysis or worrying about the impact of a heavy nosebleed late in a pregnancy does not seem impossible for an uneducated person like Godfrey or Margaret. In some stories, though, William's differing diagnosis is plain. Early in his second book, William describes how Augustine, the infant son of the priest Ralph of Somershall, became so thin that "he had less of fleshiness in his whole body than someone healthy would have in one of their fingers." He writes, "The substance of his body had been consumed by a severe disease, produced by an ulcer on the lung, or by the clamor of crying or by other causes a physician might assign: no-one of sound mind believes the fabulous nonsense of the people, that, as it is thought, children are substituted or transformed."[72] Ralph and his wife must have thought their baby was a changeling! William goes on to describe, in considerable detail, how the baby was so wasted that he no longer looked human to his parents. Regretting their clerical marriage, the parents made a vow to the martyr, and "that night in which the vow was made, vigor agitated the dried-up limbs, bones and viscera nourished each other in mutual union" and the child took on human appearance again. William concludes the story by stating that he heard the story from Augustine's parents and "we saw him wholly restored." What, though, did he say to Ralph and his wife? Did he propose his alternate diagnoses—an ulcer on the lung, the effects of too much crying—to parents rejoicing that Becket had brought back their real son?[73]

In the case of Hingram's interpretation of the cause of his epilepsy, William does not appear to have been circumspect. Hingram, an older Italian man who suffered epileptic fits once a week, "attributed his falling to the stars." "But [the fits] occurred in this manner whether the moon was waxing or waning," William writes, "it was not the fault of the constellation." William explains how, yes, the waxing moon causes "wetness" to increase and this could have an effect on an epileptic, but the moon is not the origin of epilepsy: "not here does the noxious thing take hold; let no one slip into error, thinking that the making of good things or the causes of the bad are held in the heavens." Driving his point home, he continues: "Therefore let not the lunatic ascribe his vexation to the provocation of the moon, but rather let him accuse the authors of the spirit of seduction, those who observe the times of the moon . . . and incite people into error, such that they believe that bodily distress comes upon them from the moon."[74]

William was also irritated that Hubert, a monk, would resort to "idolatrous remedies and secrets" to cure his blindness. Hubert seems to have consulted a wise-woman (William terms her a *muliercula*); Hubert "went and returned, returned and went": "Why, miserable and blind of mind man, did you seek out incantations [*carmina*]? Why seek out the funeral rites of secret magic? Is there not a God in Israel?"[75] A few chapters later, William describes the visit of William, a military commander, to a similar woman in hopes of curing his son's blindness. Even though the woman, after examining the boy, told the commander that she could not help him because "incantations cannot cure such a difficult thing," William has no kind words for her, referring to her as a *mulier malefica*.[76] In another chapter, William describes how the mother of a crippled and contracted boy named Henry made many attempts to cure him until finally "the notion of a vulgar and old woman settled in her soul, that she should put him in a bath of warm water." She hoped that this would soften her son's rigid limbs enough so that she could straighten them out herself—a strategy that nearly killed him.[77]

It is not clear in Henry's case whether the "old and vulgar woman" who had the warm bath idea was the mother herself, or whether she too had consulted some wise-woman of the neighborhood. But although visitors might get a tongue-lashing if they were foolish enough to confess to William that they had appealed to "bad" women for healing or thought that the stars had made them sick, in general William seems to have been eager to hear what kinds of things people or their doctors had done in pursuit of a cure. He tells how a constipated boy was given sea water in hopes of it having a laxative effect; how a doctor smeared an ointment of "noxious excrement" on the pustules of a boy's feet—this soothed the pain, but also made the disease spread; and how turpentine was put on the ulcers on the breast and chest of the daughter of William, priest of Burton, causing her torment.[78] William unleashed his full stock of vocabulary to tell how Robert of Bromton hoped to cure his dropsy by the use of "many draughts, pills, decoctions, plasters and ointments" [*multis potionibus, pillulis, et apozematibus, emplastris et unguentis usus*].[79] He also explains how the *tyriaca* (misspelled for *theriaca*, a Greek term meaning antidote) forced through the lips of the deathly ill Simon, a canon of Beverley, failed to have any effect.[80]

It seems very unlikely that Simon used anything like the word *tyriaca* when he talked to William about his recovery. When William writes that a castrated deacon heard Becket say in a vision, "You are healed, remove your cataplasm" [*Sanus es, solve cataplasma*],[81] one has to suspect editorial embellishment, as one does with most of the other technical medical vocabulary found in the collection. In the case of William's description of the cancerous Cecilia of Plumstock, it is quite clear that William was reworking her story and substituting more technical vocabulary. For their accounts of Cecilia's miracle, both Benedict and William were lifting words and phrases from the same textual source, likely a letter from the local priest. Both Benedict and William describe the stench of Cecilia's disease, but while Benedict simply says that there were bad smells [*foetores*], William uses the much more fancy term *mephitis*, almost certainly not found in the original source.[82] William's frequent references to humors were also likely his own reading. "Humors" came out of ulcers in Odo of Aldrington's jaw every day until he put his head into one of the windows in Becket's tomb.[83] When Adelicia of Turvin drank the water, the ulcer in her chest broke, and "whatever of the injurious humor the unbalance of the body had produced erupted out."[84] In the course of the cure of the blind Agnes of Happisburgh, "the hurtful humor flowed out and the sanies was drained, and what had impeded her vision was struck out."[85] Alan of Lindsey and Roger of Middleton both sweated out humors through their skin in the course of their cures, and so on.[86]

William's medical learning provided him with fancy terms for what he was seeing and hearing at the tomb and primed him to the nuances of the many hundreds of stories of illness that he would hear in his years as Becket's miracle collector. As eager as William was to diagnose people's problems, however, it was not always possible: once he tells the reader that the son of a noble had "either dysentery or lientery, for we cannot be fully certain of the type of disease from the description of illiterates."[87] Still, throughout his collection William shows his desire to take the "descriptions of illiterates" and try to figure out what had happened to their bodies—what had been wrong, what the symptoms were, where the problems had been, how the illness progressed—from the perspective of his understanding of medicine. But what most impressed him was how Becket, the "heavenly doctor," could cure what was wrong.

"What Advice, Galen?": Becket the "Heavenly Doctor"

In his description of the healing of Petronella of Polesworth, the epileptic nun whose story is preceded by William's lengthy exposition on the types of epilepsy, William writes that her sisters, "not knowing what they might give to her as a remedy, chose that which was the most powerful to act, not seeking the work of mercenaries or those who are not doctors, who see one growing strong and send forth one faint and languishing, but sending to the shepherd of the sheep the diseased sheep to be healed." After praying to Becket at Canterbury, Petronella leaves, not knowing if she is healed, but she is never struck by the problem again, and she never needs to use any other medicines, "no purgations, calefactions, or laxatives." Petronella was safe with "the good and faithful doctor" [*bonus et fidelis medicus*].[88] In the chapter immediately following, William writes that one of the monks of Canterbury was suffering from a cough and prayed to Becket, "Have mercy, martyr, have mercy, heal my superfluity of humors by heavenly medicine." The martyr does, saying to the monk in a vision, "Behold, am I not a good doctor?" [*Heus, nonne bonus medicus sum?*]."[89]

The phrase "Thomas is the best doctor of the worthy sick" [*optimvs egrorvm medicus fit toma bonorom*] has been found inscribed on pilgrims' badges of the late twelfth and early thirteenth century,[90] and William must have heard pilgrims referring to Becket as their "doctor" quite frequently. One can occasionally find similar rhetoric in Benedict's collection: for instance, Benedict describes how the broken leg of a girl was bound up with cloth and a coin; after the leg was found whole, the girl "gave the medicine by which she had been cured by her doctor [*medicus*] as a gift."[91] But William did more than just term Becket a doctor here and there: he sought out and frequently presents stories in which Becket acts as a doctor of the day. For instance, he describes how the dropsical Roger of Middleton was told in a vision that "there are two doctors in the house . . . they will be able to give you health." They turned out to be St. Edmund of Bury and St. Thomas. An extraordinary consulting scene follows, with Roger complaining about his illness, Becket telling him "you are burdening your nature with draughts and medications," and Edmund piping in, "beyond what is necessary." Becket eventually pronounces that Roger should renounce all medications and pray: "Pray to the Lord for these things, and we will pray for you as well." Roger does, and eventually he is restored to health "by an easy and unusual manner of cure": he urinated so much that he filled and refilled the chamber pot, and his legs and lower regions sweated so much that "the kindling of the corruption was wholly boiled out and the intercutaneous humor was exuded."[92]

In Roger's story, Becket is the head doctor; in the story of the healing of Peter, a doctor of Perigord, he is a consulting surgeon. Peter, "as he cared for the ill, grew ill himself," contracting one of the incurable types of dropsy. He too has a vision; in his, he sees the Virgin, Becket, and two others, St. Cosmas (probably meaning the martyr and doctor famed for refusing to take payment for cures) and "the physician Alexander," another martyr-doctor. When Becket sees the ill Peter, he says "take him from the bed and stretch him out." Then Becket orders that an incision be made in the stomach and the liver taken out and washed. "Then, with the liver washed, the saint ordered that it be returned to its place and the stomach stitched up." When Peter woke, he found "the scar of the incision and the remains of humors which testified to a true cure."[93] In other visions, Becket appears alone, often touching his patients and displaying a superb bedside manner. When Richolda swelled up so badly with disease it appeared that she was pregnant, she saw the martyr coming to her saying "your priest ought to bring [the water] to you," and then adding, "In which part do you feel the most trouble? Place my hand [on it]." With his hand having been placed, he said "This pains you, but you will not die." "At the touch of the hand of power," she felt the pain and swelling subside.[94] When the daughter of William was deaf in one ear, her parents chose "the doctor Thomas among the heavenly doctors; he was asked to place his hand on the virgin" [*inter medicos coelestes medicus Thomas eligeretur qui rogaretur virgini manum suum imponere*].[95] Adelicia is blessed because "she merited to be cured and even sanctified not by a human hand, but by the most courteous hand of heavenly doctors."[96]

William frequently describes how people were warned or decided not to look to human doctors for treatment of their ills. The blind Adelicia of Faversham, in a vision, is told that "Unless you seek the cure of doctors, you will receive your sight,"[97] while Avicia, with a broken arm, is advised by her husband to seek heavenly medicines and to "disregard the human," which she does: "I will not seek any other doctor."[98] Hugh de Prac, a knight, becomes very ill, but he would not allow his urine or pulse to be inspected: "he fixed all his hope on the martyr."[99] Robert of St. Jacques, suffering with the stone, would use only the blood, seeking no other medications, while William Kellet, a carpenter who cut his leg, declared that he would not seek the help of mortals: "I commit my whole cure to the lord and martyr Thomas."[100] Still, William did not think of human doctoring and heavenly doctoring as mutually exclusive. While William does criticize doctors, his complaints are usually mild. William sometimes indirectly criticizes doctors for their fees: he pointed out, for instance, that a young man wounded in the arm spent a lot of money on doctors, but did not find a remedy.[101] On the other hand, the doctor attending to Ralph the clerk despairs of curing him and returns his money, "What I received from you, I return. I go. Provide for your soul."[102] In another chapter, a doctor refuses to take on a case of a girl wounded in the head because he thought her brain had been injured and feared she could not be cured.[103] When the knight Robert went to his doctor, the doctor sent him to another after he "inspected his urine, and with vainglorious knowledge distinguished between the four types of dropsy" (a dangerous criticism, one would think, for William to make).[104] But the main censure William has about human doctors is that they do not always discover or cure the cause of an illness. When the clerk Robert of Marton submitted himself for bloodletting, the vein would not close: "Those came who professed to be doctors, powerful of words and expert in knowledge, but ignorant in operation. They, seeing the blood pouring forth, did not find a cure, because they did not seize upon the cause of the flow."[105] Doctors examining a girl with a broken abscess behind her ear, "found the cause but not the cure; they conducted their business by word and not by deed."[106] When Matthew of Walcourt's hand did not heal up after a wound, surgeons inspected the wound, "but the seed-plot of the pain was not found."[107]

Becket, though, *does* find the cause, as William states in many stories: this is why the reader should understand him to be a remarkable healer. The coughing monk at the beginning of the collection "believed that the doctor is faithful who cures diseases and the causes of diseases."[108] A man with an injured arm, Richard of Villedieu, came into the "presence of the powerful doctor," and "by a hidden power he expelled the cause of the pain": Richard reached into the wound and pulled out a bone nearly the length of a finger "in the sight of those who resided at the tomb."[109] After the castrated deacon "removed his cataplasm" and drank the water, "the cause of the pain with a great deal of sanies and coagulated blood" was expelled.[110] When the leper Peter of Poitiers seemed to have been cured, he became ill again, "by the hidden industry of the heavenly doctor": "Lest the material of the disease later sprout forth in him who had received his cure," Becket "brought out the harmful humors."[111] The cure of blind Agnes of Happisburgh also impressed William. After the blood was placed on her eyes, her eyes began to painfully discharge: "but this was not harmful, but the way to sight." What was happening was that "the harmful humor and sanies were drained, and what had impeded her vision was struck out": in this way, "the skilled doctor had ordered a new way of healing: those things which usually blind the seeing brought sight to the blind."[112]

In his account of the story of the earl of Albemarle, who was in the dangerous and extremely painful position of having a kidney stone half-in and half-out of his penis, William writes, "What advice would you give, Galen? What remedy, Quintilian?" He explains how using their remedies— hanging the man upside down to return the stone to the kidney, or using a silver awl to try to extract it—would only kill him. It was a prayer and the Lord's doing that cured the earl: "the stone was thrust out by a divine force."[113] Becket bore up under the blasphemy of Gerard of Lille: after all, as William writes, a doctor knows that a delirious patient doesn't mean what he says, and so too Thomas "understood that he spoke the damnable words not from his heart but from his torment," and cured him.[114] In another case, Becket kindly healed the leper Odelina: "the redness of her face diminished, the hair of the eyebrows sprouted out, the roughness of the voice cleared up, and the rest of the accidents of this illness were destroyed" all except for one thing, the "binding of the nostrils" [strictura narium]. In this way, Becket "left to the cure of men what man is able to do himself: he took away what exceeds human powers and only heavenly power can do."[115]

What especially impressed William was how quickly Becket could cure. When a boy with a kidney stone was vowed to a pilgrimage, "the remedies of the heavenly doctor were prompt . . . the stone was crushed. The ill boy did not put an ointment on himself, he did not take any diuretic food or drink; he obtained the remedy for his health only from a vow."[116] In the case of a man with a rupture, William writes that it was "a marvelous thing: as the vow parted his lips, the swelling of the genitals was broken open, and with the sanies emitted the viscera which had flowed out returned to their place."[117] The girl with a broken abscess behind her ear found that at the same time a drop of Becket's blood entered her ear, health arrived.[118] In the case of Hugh de Perae, who may or may not have died, William addresses himself to his brothers, declaring that even if he were not dead, "nonetheless the miracle is stupendous, in the sudden bringing of strength to the dying, and in the routing of four types of illness in a moment."[119]

William was entranced by instant cures and powerful heavenly forces manipulated by the "heavenly doctor." Even as his descriptions of illness and diseases are far longer and more detailed than Benedict had ever attempted, his descriptions of the healings themselves are usually quite short. William concludes his lengthy diatribe in his account of Hingram, the Italian epileptic who thought his disease was caused by the stars, with a brisk wrap-up: "he drank the water brought from the sepulcher of the martyr and reddened with blood, and he became well" [convaluit].[120] The woman who had turpentine applied to her ulcerous breast and chest "wholly obtained her health on her third pilgrimage."[121] Peter, who had cut off a toe and was advised to cut off another, "went to the new divine doctor. Experiencing the true medicine, he reckoned his ignorance who had believed the ignorant."[122] Ralph, the clerk who cut off an ulcer and skinned his testicles to little effect, found that when a candle with his measurements arrived at the tomb, he expelled viscous humors and "the split members came back together, the wounds of cutting contracted, the piles and ulcers dried up: he showed the scars to our eyes."[123] End of story. In the rare cases in which William does admit a relapse or a delay in cure, he will provide explanations. In terms of Alan of Lindsey's relapse into illness (which was cured again, William is careful to note), William concludes his story by noting "what caused this, I only know this: the Lord knows."[124] In another story, he suggests that perhaps Robert, a priest, was not cured of paralysis until he got home so that the people there would believe too.[125]

Speaking of a knight, Simon, who was struck with a paralysis, William writes that the paralysis was "not without cause, for there is nothing without cause. . . . Suppose the cause of the illness to be the coldness of age from the abundance of phlegm, or youthful heat from the flowing of blood; suppose it to be the hot fever of wine; suppose it the cold indigestion of food, or labor, or something else that is able to make something spring up in wretched bodies: you will assert more truly that the righteous anger of God makes these injuries in him."[126] William points to no specific sin committed by Simon, just noting that "the Lord wishes salvation for all people" and that his paralysis made Simon realize that he should go to Canterbury. Yet for

William, it was not the ultimate cause of illness (i.e., God) that interested him the most or provoked much comment in his collection. He was far more enthralled by the workings of "the abundance of phlegm," "the flowing of the blood," "the cold indigestion of food," and all the other things that could "make something spring up in wretched bodies"—and then how the heavenly doctor could make these things right.

William's interest in precise medical descriptions would be a feature of later canonization dossiers.[127] Doctors were often involved in late medieval canonization processes—and indeed, they still are. But these medical men did not usually write up accounts of miracles themselves. William's overall miracle collecting style—choosing what he would and playing with the rhetorical possibilities of the collection—would not be imitated or appreciated by later generations.

"Write, Hand!": Rhetoric and William's Construction of His Collection

William tended to work harder on the composition of individual chapters and stories than Benedict had. He labored to give each story what he considered to be its due—and not just the stories of healing. He used abstruse vocabulary and inserted references to classical authors whereever he could. The most striking rhetorical feature of William's collection is his use of direct or reported speech. Benedict had used direct speech a few times in his collection,[128] but William was to take this rhetorical device to remarkable heights. He begins writing chapters in direct speech in his first book: in the first such chapter, he has William, a clerk from Lincoln who had suffered from a fistula, describe the healing of a neighbor: "There is a woman by us, who, if certainty of the thing requires and the truth of it seems more clear in this way, we are able to designate her by name and by descent. She is called Adelicia, the daughter of a certain Hugo by us, and joined to me by a first-order level of descent. She had suffered from the same disease as me, but in a more pernicious place . . ." After telling about Adelicia's cure, the clerk concludes that she could not come to Canterbury, and so he was "asked by her to take pains to announce to your ears what is known by trustworthy eyes."[129]

William writes twenty-nine chapters in a similar manner, most of them in his sixth book and in the addition to the collection. Many provide charming little vignettes of people standing at the tomb presenting their oblations and telling their stories.[130] In one, a husband tells the story of his wife, as they both stand before the brothers;[131] in others, parents tell of the healing of their children,[132] and, especially toward the end of the collection, people tell stories about themselves, such as Robert, a knight, who "showed us his hand," and then begins to speak.[133] In a couple of cases, William was not even present at the scene he reimagines for the reader. In one chapter, he has Ralph FitzBernard and Bernard FitzReginald talk to the subprior of Christ Church about their miracles and oblations; one of the noblemen says to the subprior, "I wish you to tell your brothers what I tell you."[134] In another chapter, William describes a conversation between two clerics as they traveled together to Canterbury—it is the same imaginary scenario of the Canterbury Tales, some three hundred years before Chaucer would imagine it.[135] William himself appears as a character in these chapters too. One chapter begins simply, "You seek, brother William, who I am, why and whence I come," with the name of the speaker being revealed in the ensuing speech.[136]

Brother William allowed all his puckish impulses full play in the addition to his collection. In it, he tells many animal stories. One concerns an ill falcon owned by Henry II (an honored guest by this time). The king's falconer had a vision about the pustules on the bird that eventually led to the bird's cure: "These things being told to the king," William lightly concludes, "he gave thanks for the preservation of his delights and sports."[137] William also tells a couple of animal stories that have the ring of folktales, including the story of a skinned and dead cow, and another, "told by the Bretons," about a starling squawking out Thomas's name as it was captured in the talons of a kite.[138]

But perhaps the most interesting chapters in the addition are those in which William conducts debates—with pilgrims, with himself, with the reader—about the truth or falsity of the stories he was hearing. He starts one chapter by writing, "Azelicia suffered in childbirth for fifteen days," and then immediately interrupts himself: "What, reader, do you counsel? Should I speak, or be silent? Should I say what the truth of the thing is, or suppress the truth? If I am silent, less will be known of her of whom I speak; if I speak, I fear lest it be judged of little consequence." William decides to go on, because "who, having begun speech, is able to end it?"[139] Not much farther on, William dedicates a series of stories to the same issue. He begins a chapter by stating that he does not like discounting or doubting people's stories—if people appear to be of good life and report, their stories should also be accepted. "Speak, therefore," William writes, "Elfwin, who lives eight miles across the Thames, and give glory to God." Elfwin dutifully speaks out, "My daughter fell into a well . . ."[140] When

Elfwin finishes his story, William writes, "You, Robert of Flanders, speak," and then Robert tells his story. The same conceit continues through the next two chapters. In the last of them, William writes, "You say, Eadwin, that your son . . . was revived through the martyr's water. . . . You noted his name, age, and place of birth. But beware . . . lest you tell a lie, and according to your name make lies." Eadwin tells William that despite his name (apparently a common name for a blockhead), those who are ignorant of letters still know that falsity is wrong.[141]

In another chapter in the addition, William argues with his own hand about whether or not to write a miracle: "'Write, hand, that the first son of the noble English lady Mabel was placed, dead, on the ashes, but from the water of the martyr he received life.' 'It is not for me,' says the hand, 'to write of anything of which the truth is not certain.' 'We heard the lady' says the scribe, 'and examined her as it was proper of a noblewoman, and we are able to presume the truth of her story from her pilgrimage and in reference to her devotion. For although faith is rare, as many say much, yet as beggars are liars, so we conjecture little about nobles who conciliate divine favor by pilgrimage.'"[142] The point of this chapter is less to criticize beggars than to lightly mock the standards of truthfulness and falsity adopted by Benedict and likely others of the Christ Church brothers. By the end of the collection, names, places, times, and status no longer mattered to William. The story was what counted. In one of the very last chapters of the collection, William writes, "there came before us a certain not-ignoble man from Northamptonshire and his son, whose name we did not ask for, being contented to know the miracle" [*cujus nomen non interrogavimus, miraculum scire contenti*].[143]

William's addition to his collection was hardly ever read in the medieval period. Only one copy of it is known to survive, and that one copy may be missing something at the end. William's style in this addition was well removed from the more sober approach of Benedict and other collectors of the period; it is not a great surprise that it went unread. However, it probably would have been a surprise to the Christ Church monks to learn that this addition, compiled around 1176–77, would be the last miracle collection worthy of the name to be written by a Christ Church monk. The children resurrected, the sailors rescued, the lepers healed, all the people cured by Canterbury saints: only the tiniest handful of these stories would be noted down by Christ Church monks in the years to come. In the conclusion to the book, I will explore why this would be so.

The End of Miracle Collecting

The endings of long miracle collections are often ragged. Most collections begin with a substantial, carefully composed and rhetorically sophisticated prologue, but few were granted anything similar at their conclusion. Many lengthy miracle collections simply stop, without explanation, their endings as frayed and unsatisfying as that of the Bayeux Tapestry.

Miracle collecting as a whole came to a similarly tattered conclusion in England. In the first two decades of the thirteenth century, miracle collecting continued at a fairly brisk pace. Substantial collections were composed in the course of the canonization bids for Gilbert of Sempringham (canonized 1202), Wulfstan of Worcester (canonized 1203), and Hugh of Lincoln (canonized 1220).[1] In these early decades, collections were composed for Abbot Waltheof of Melrose and for Archbishop Remigius of Lincoln, and an anonymous author made another addition to the collection of John of Beverley.[2] One of the biggest events in English miracle collecting came in 1220, the year of Thomas Becket's translation out of the crypt to his new shrine in the upper cathedral. By this year, the marvelous "miracle windows" surrounding Becket's new shrine were completed and open to view. These windows pictured dozens of miracle narratives drawn from Benedict's and William's collections compiled in the 1170s. The set of Becket's miracles put on show in the Trinity Chapel is the sole miracle collection created in high medieval England for the consumption of the ordinary pilgrim.[3]

Ironically, the unveiling of the Canterbury miracle windows came just at the point when the enthusiasm for miracle collecting that had gripped English monks and canons since the late eleventh century was evaporating. Past the year 1220, few new collections were written.[4] Between the early thirteenth century and the dissolution of English monasteries in the early sixteenth century, some major miracle collections were compiled—those for Simon de Montfort, Thomas Cantilupe, and Henry VI are particularly well known.[5] Taken in total, though, these three centuries produced far fewer miracle collectors than did the late twelfth century.[6] The hundreds of surviving pilgrims' badges and the many thousands of pennies tallied in shrine accounts make it clear that pilgrimages to established English shrines continued apace through the late medieval period.[7] Brand new cultic centers also frequently appeared in these centuries, as we know from chronicles and other documents.[8] With few exceptions, though, new miracle collections were not being made.

Even at Canterbury, a center for miracle collecting since the late eleventh century, miracle collecting all but ceased. The only miracle stories that can be confidently attributed to Christ Church authorship from the thirteenth to the sixteenth century are four narratives appended to Benedict's collection for Thomas Becket around 1200 and one lonely story about Becket composed in 1445.[9] This lack of interest in miracle collecting at Canterbury is remarkable when one considers not just the unending stream of pilgrims to Becket's shrine but also that two more archbishops of Canterbury, Edmund of Abingdon (d. 1240 and buried at Pontigny) and Robert Winchelsey (d. 1313 and buried in Canterbury cathedral), were celebrated as miracle-working saints. Christ Church monks were closely involved in the attempts to canonize these two men, but in neither case did a monk compile a collection like those of his predecessors.[10]

Why would English monks and canons abandon a pursuit they had once taken up so eagerly? One reason may have been that so many collections now existed for English saints. What had once seemed so fluid and open to the original collectors struggling to choose and compose narratives rapidly took on a solidified and closed character to their readers. Year by year, the collections created in the long twelfth century appear to have taken on more, not less, authoritative weight. The last collector of Becket miracles at Christ Church, a monk who did no more than add four stories to the end of a manuscript of Benedict of Peterborough's collection, may well have been intimidated by the work of his predecessors. This author describes how prior Geoffrey (1191–1206) had asked him to "commit to the memory of letters" the story of a Becket relic that Geoffrey had lost in France but had found again, amazingly, in Canterbury cathedral.[11] However, the monk postponed the job, even after he had been asked by Geoffrey to get to work a second time. Then he discovered that his own personal Becket reliquary had gone missing. Thinking that this was a just judgment from God, he vowed that he would hasten to write if he could find it again. And he did, in a place he had searched before, no less. Giving thanks, and hoping for Thomas's mercy, he finally got to work.[12] In the late eleventh century, when Bernard of Angers was urged to add a new book to his own miracle collection for St. Foy, he too demurred: "not only was it the case that more powerful miracles than those I had already written could not be found, but, further, there were none even equal to those."[13] How much more might a potential collector of Thomas Becket miracles feel that no matter which stories he had heard, or how long he labored, his work could never vie with the mass of wonders told by the first generation? In his little addition to Benedict's collection, the anonymous monk aimed for colorful quality rather than bulky quantity. And once he finished his short stint ca. 1200, that was it. No monk at Canterbury attempted even such a tiny collection ever again.[14]

At the point when the last Christ Church collector laid down his pen, schoolmen were beginning to grapple with the definition, concept, and significance of the miracle. During the eleventh and twelfth centuries, when miracle collecting reached its apogee, there was hardly any speculative activity concerning miracles. Benedicta Ward has noted that "very little direct discussion of miracles took place from the time of Augustine to that of Thomas Aquinas."[15] Thirteenth-century thinkers, in contrast, created and wrote highly structured arguments about miracles. They separated marvels and miracles into distinct categories, defined the miracle as something beyond nature, and fiercely debated issues of cause and significance.[16] Strikingly, though, these speculations left untouched the rich well of personal stories preserved by hundreds of earlier writers, as well as all the stories currently circulating in the oral world, and even those miracles that might have been claimed by the scholar himself. Often, the schoolmen did not discuss any specific miracles at all, and if they did, they almost always focused on biblical and unquestionably authoritative stories such as that of Jesus turning water into wine. It is remarkable, in fact, the extent to which the schoolmen avoided contemporary miracle stories. The instability of the oral, the complications of the personal, the unpredictability of the divine, and the emotional ramifications of such stories made them difficult subjects for formal academic analysis.

As the schools began absorbing much of the intellectual energy of the medieval elite and providing more comfortable and controlled arenas in which to think about miracles than ever before, new types of miracle collections, ones not focused on contemporary personal stories, were being assiduously compiled and distributed. The "Miracles of the Virgin," the loose collection of legendary tales about Mary's miraculous intervention first developed in twelfth-century England, became immensely popular in the late medieval period.[17] Instead of strings of stories along the lines of "he came to the tomb and was healed," the Miracles of the Virgin included only particularly captivating stories, like those of the pregnant abbess or the inebriated monk, and these stories were captivatingly told. As a text that blurred the boundaries between devotion and delight, the Miracles offered more solid entertainment value in exchange for a reader's time than a shrine collection ever could. Moreover, these stories provided ideal subject matter for sophisticated writers to display their rhetorical abilities: it was considerably easier to try one's hand at retelling the story of Theophilus than to sift through dozens of oral stories for good subjects. The last full-length miracle collection known to have been compiled by a Christ Church monk was, tellingly, a Latin versification of the Miracles of the Virgin. The author, Nigel (d. after 1206), was a devotee of Thomas Becket and a fierce defender of the rights of Christ Church, but rather than versifying some of Becket's miracles, he chose to work on the legends of Mary, as did so many other late medieval authors.[18]

If late medieval readers wanted not entertainment but material for preaching and moral crusade, there was a new kind of collection for them too. Collections of *exempla*, little didactic tales or "examples" designed for preachers, were an invention of the thirteenth century.[19] Like the stories in shrine collections, *exempla* sometimes revolve around a miraculous incident.[20] Quite unlike the stories in shrine collections, though, these stories are never just about one saint's (or even any saint's) intervention. *Exempla* rarely name the individuals involved or set the story in any specific time or place. They all, in addition, have a point, such as that of a story from a collection by Jacques de Vitry about a corrupt bishop who gave an appointment of an archdeanery to his young nephew, so young that the boy defecated in his stall.[21] Such stories filled the new demand for preaching material in the thirteenth century as shrine miracle collections never could—indeed, were never designed to do. It must have been quite satisfying, furthermore, to compile an *exempla* collection. *Exempla* were easy to manipulate and stack into neat categories: stories good for preaching to bishops, to Benedictine nuns, to crusaders, to craftsmen, to the grieving, to the greedy. Collections of *exempla* were clearly made in the confident expectation that they would do many people good.

The thirteenth century was also, of course, the period in which canonization procedures were developed and solidified.[22] The formal inquest of a
saint's miracles was intended to answer one question alone: was a saint
performing miracles? Yes or no? This was such an obvious and elementary
question for the miracle collectors of the old school that few bothered much
with it, but now the pope and his commissioners made it seem as if this
were the only point that mattered. If the high medieval collectors were like
amateur hobbyists fascinated by the many contours presented by miracle
stories, the papal professionals were like lab techs pulverizing them to extract a strand of DNA. What was wanted was not a lovingly executed collection, but a notary's account of the inquisition of witnesses. The less
emotionally involved the notary was in the proceedings, moreover, the better. One particularly interesting stage in the transition from amateur to
professional miracle collecting is seen in the canonization of Edmund of
Abingdon, archbishop of Canterbury from 1234 to 1240. In his lifetime,
Edmund had been a hardened foe of the Christ Church community, but
there was one Christ Church monk, Eustace of Faversham, who accompanied Edmund into exile as his chaplain and revered him as a saint after his
death.[23] Eustace, along with the archdeacon of Canterbury Simon Langton,
were charged with the task of uncovering evidence of Edmund's miracles in
the summer of 1246.[24] This effort was necessary because Pope Innocent IV
was unhappy with the investigations of his commissioners, and John of
Toledo, an English cardinal, hoped to salvage the canonization process by
means of a renewed effort to find satisfying stories.[25] Strikingly, though,
neither Eustace nor Simon wrote a collection for the pope. Their mission
was not to collect and present stories, but to collect and present *people*. In
a letter to John of Toledo, Simon described how he and Eustace had found
many people eager to affirm Edmund's posthumous miracles.[26] The hard
part was convincing some of them to go with Eustace to the papal curia so
they could be questioned to the pope's full satisfaction: they became angry
when it was clear what they wanted [*contra clericos et praelatos in scandala et
contumelias prorumperunt*]. In the end, the archdeacon and the chaplain did
persuade a few to make the trip, and their efforts were rewarded. After the
new witnesses arrived and had been interrogated by a series of cardinals and
then by the pope himself, Innocent finally coughed up what Simon and
Eustace had wanted: a bull of canonization.[27]

The idea of collecting people instead of stories did not last for long.[28]
Still, the image of Eustace shepherding a small herd of reluctant witnesses to

the curia aptly illustrates the papal desire to take final decisions about saint-hood out of the hands of the local elite. Simon and Eustace were delegated only to collect the (very) raw material for such judgments, not to process it themselves in any way. Eustace had written a *vita* for Edmund, a text appar-ently designed to move the process forward more quickly, but he never seems to have made a miracle collection, not even of the stories of the people he and Simon sought out and with whom he had traveled so far.[29] As popes and their commissioners developed formularies for questioning witnesses in a canonization inquest, they increasingly dictated how miracle stories were to be told. Rather than speaking at their own pace and in their own way, wit-nesses were often to speak only in response to questions, as if they were at a trial. Telling a miracle story was becoming more like a fearful oral exam than a walk on the beach, and all for a purpose and process that probably meant far less to the dragooned witnesses than to Simon and Eustace. Reading the canonization inquests for Edmund and others, one gets the sense that the men in charge wanted to feel that they were collecting evidence, not stories. Notaries were to write fast to keep up as the investigators threshed out the data: names, places, professions, dates, types of illness, lengths of illness, na-ture of healings, and then, compulsively and insistently, witnesses to all those names, places, professions, dates, types of illness, lengths of illness, and nature of healings. The more proper procedures were followed, the more they could convince themselves that they were extracting crystals out of the coal bed of personal stories, even as all these procedures and factoids did not help much in the ultimate evaluation of the truth of individual miracles. Further layers of bureaucracy were eventually built in to process the results of the process: minions at the curia read the inquest records and summarized the material into headings, cardinals summarized the summaries to give to the pope, and this all before the real deliberations began.[30]

Such developments were probably quite satisfying to canon lawyers like Innocent IV. Many historians have found the raw data-like feel of these inquests equally appealing. Yet these procedures did much to ring the death knell of personal miracle collecting in the old style. One must now bid fare-well to the prologues, personal reflections, and rhetorical flourishes of the earlier collections, and greet the coming of crisp notarial legalese: item, so-and-so did such and such; item, so-and-so swears to the above, and so on. The goal was a clean monotony. Miracle collectors with the rhetorical sensi-bilities of a William of Canterbury were being removed and removing them-selves from the miracle collecting process altogether.

By the early fourteenth century, after Archbishop Winchelsey died and some began to push for his canonization, Christ Church monks appear to have been very much distanced from the miracle collecting process, rather startlingly so, in fact. In the spring of 1319, Prior Henry Eastry (1285–1331), probably the most impressive of all the Christ Church priors, formally presided over a canonization inquest held for Winchelsey in Canterbury.[31] As one would expect, it was a notary, not Prior Henry, who wrote up the proceedings. Less expected is the fact that the impetus for the inquest came not from the prior or any of his monks, but from a layman, the earl Thomas Lancaster. Lancaster twice asked for written material on Winchelsey's miracles from Prior Henry and twice, it appears, was disappointed. Finally he sent his own clerk to Canterbury to get an inquest underway.[32] Even more telling evidence of the monks' lack of engagement with Winchelsey's miracles is in the inquest itself. In the document, Christ Church monks can be heard testifying at length to their knowledge of Winchelsey's saintly life. They describe Winchelsey's harsh and ascetic lifestyle—how he hardly ever slept and how he gloried in the mortification of his flesh. They describe how Winchelsey was a generous almsgiver and how he wept so much while celebrating mass that the altar cloths became soaked. None of the monks, though, can be heard telling a story about any of Winchelsey's posthumous activities—others, lay men and women, did that.[33]

The last miracle story known to have been written down by a Christ Church monk, a 1445 letter about a crippled man, Alexander from Aberdeen, does little to dispel this image of general indifference toward stories of personal miracles. The text, consisting of just the single story, is an open letter addressed "to all those sons of the church to whom this present letter comes." It survives in two forms: what looks to be an original letter, the text written on a narrow strip of parchment, and a somewhat abbreviated version of the text copied into one of the great fifteenth-century registers of Christ Church.[34] Signed by John Salisbury (prior of Christ Church, 1438–46), and the chapter of Christ Church, the letter concludes with a precise dating clause—"given at Canterbury in our chapter on the twenty-seventh day of July, 1445"—and once again gestures to the fact that this letter was about to travel to recipients unknown: "we therefore beseech all to whom this letter shall come to praise God worthily in his saints." It looks as if this letter was something Alexander was going to carry away with him. Indeed, it seems very likely that it was written up at Alexander's request and for his own purposes, not for the monks'. Over two hundred years earlier, Christ Church monks had copied incoming letters like this into their miracle collections; now, they copied this single outward bound text into a collection even more bulky but quite different in spirit: a register of incoming and outgoing deeds, confirmations, charters, and other correspondence.

More than anything else, the end of miracle collecting was brought about by the attitude apparent here: that contemporary miracles were something most of interest and significance for a person like Alexander of Aberdeen, not for a Christ Church monk. This attitude had been building for a long time. It is evident already in the late twelfth century in Benedict's and William's collections, particularly in Benedict's question to a brother who suffered a miraculous punishment: "why did this happen, as if you were one of the people?"[35] The rise of the schools and the making of new kinds of miracle collections separated the religious elite from the complications of oral and contemporary miracle stories, while the application of canonization procedures drove in the same wedge even further, removing the care of miracle stories from the hands of the local religious and strongly suggesting that the life of a saint, not his or her miracles, was what was truly worthy of their attention and reflection.

Miracle stories, at least the new ones, no longer felt like they were "theirs" anymore. A sense of possession, or at least a strong desire to possess, is the first and most important requirement for any collecting effort. Monks and canons in charge of saints' relics had become interested in possessing and collecting other things. There had always been a faddishness about high medieval miracle collecting, and now, in a different world, the fads were turning in other directions. What fifteenth-century Benedictine monks especially liked to collect, as is clear in the fascinating "chronicle" (really more of a memorandum book) of the Christ Church monk John Stone, were facts about themselves.[36] Stone's chronicle is focused on two things: the visits of dignitaries to Canterbury, and, most especially, the deaths of Christ Church monks. Stone memorialized each monk who died between 1415 and 1471 in a paragraph in his book. He recorded and remembered details about their origins, offices, length of tenure as a monk, date of death, and often specific information about how they died and where they were buried. Though deaths and visits, not miracles, are Stone's focus, the chronicle has the same rather obsessive feel, personal character, and underlying drive to preserve the memory of precious and of passing things that typifies the high medieval miracle collections.[37]

Miracles, however, are not wholly absent from Stone's chronicle. Under the year 1467, Stone copied in a poem written by the otherwise unknown "Gilbert Banystre."[38] The poem, written in Middle English, celebrates "a mervelys thyng / Which was done the vijth day of July" by Thomas Becket. In five stanzas, Banystre describes how Thomas prevented the devil from drowning pilgrims on their way to Canterbury, something that happened, he proclaims, "not longe ago." All we know about Banystre is that he was not a Christ Church monk. His poem, like the open letter written for Alexander, the account books recording donations to Becket's shrine, and numerous other references to Becket's cult in the fourteenth and fifteenth centuries, is one more indication of the continuing appeal and life of Thomas Becket's cult in the late medieval centuries.[39]

"Thomas thunders forth with new miracles" [*nouis fulget Thomas miraculis*] Banystre declares happily at the end of every stanza—and yet the best a Christ Church monk could do at the time was to copy someone else's work into his datebook. In scholarly treatments of late medieval Canterbury and other similar cultic sites, it is often implied that no new miracle collections were made because there were no miracles to collect. But I would suggest this, at least in the case of Canterbury, is comfortable fiction of our own, allowing us to envision a miracle-free environment and also letting the Christ Church monks off the hook completely.[40] The truth is, we do not have many late medieval English miracle collections because John Stone, his brethren, and most other literati did not care to collect miracle stories, no matter how easy or difficult that task might have been. They wanted to do other things. The flow of new miracle stories throughout the medieval period is probably best envisioned as a river that could rise and fall, jump its banks, dry up in some years and flood in others. It was a river that most late medieval religious men, more interested in theology, in their finances and rights, in hosting dignitaries, and in the lives and deaths of their brethren, were content to let flow by as it would.

The Christ Church monks did continue, though, to read the stories collected by Benedict and William. As late as 1524, just a few years before Henry VIII would bring the community to a permanent end, the monks at Canterbury College in Oxford had a copy of a *Vita et Miracula S. Thome* in their library.[41] How often these young scholars read the miracle portion of this text is of course impossible to say, but it is nice to imagine them pulling down this manuscript after a day of disputation and reveling in the centuries-old stories of the meeting of the personal and the divine. And if these readers had known of the world-shattering disaster that was about to befall them and their Thomas, perhaps they would have set aside their studies to make more copies of this text, or even to collect a few new stories of their own, writing, as Osbern had for Dunstan so many years earlier, in the anxious hope that "in future times all English people might know what honor and reverence they owe to the name of such a man."[42]

Manuscripts of the Christ Church Miracle Collections for Thomas Becket

A. Surviving Manuscripts Containing Full or Partial Copies of Benedict of Peterborough's *Miracula S. Thomae*

Late twelfth century

Brussels, Bibl. royale, MS IV.600 (*prov: Aulne*)
Douai, Bibl. de la Ville, MS 860
Lisbon, Bibl. nacional cod. Alcobaça CCXC/143 (*prov: San Mames de Lorvão*)
◇ London, British Library, Egerton MS 2818 (*prov: Pontigny*)
‡Montpellier, Bibliothèque interuniversitaire section médicine MS 2 (*prov: Clairvaux*)
*Oxford, Bodleian Bodley MS 509
**Rome, Vatican MS 6933
‡**Stuttgart, Württembergische Landesbibliothek, Cod. Theol. et phil. 4 654 (*prov: Weissenau*)

Twelfth/thirteenth century

Cambrai, Bibl. de la Ville, MS 488
Lisbon, Bibl. nacional, cod. Alcobaça CCLXXXIX/172
*Heiligenkreuz, Stiftsbibliothek Cod. Sancrucensis 209 (*prov: Heiligenkreuz*)
*Heiligenkreuz, Stiftsbibliothek Cod. Sancrucensis 213 (*prov: Heiligenkreuz*)
Paris, Bibl. Nationale, MS lat. 5320
**Rome, Vallicelliana MS Tomus III

Early thirteenth century

Cambridge, Trinity College, MS B.14.37 (*prov: St Augustine's, Canterbury*)
Charleville, Bibl. de la Ville, MS 222 (*prov: Signy*)

Heidelberg, Universitäts-Bibliotheck, cod. Salem IX.30 (*prov: Salem*)
*Oxford, Bodleian Lyell MS 5
◊ Rome, Vallicelliana MS B 60
**Tuy, Archivo de la Catedral de Tuy, MS 1

Thirteenth century

Brussels, Bibl. royale, MS 3190
Évreux, Bibl. de la Ville MS lat. 10 (*prov: Lyre*)
**Lilienfeld, Stiftsbibliothek Cod. Campililiensis 134
London, Lambeth Palace MS 135
Porto, Bibl. Públ. Mun. MS 349 (*prov: Santa Cruz de Coimbra*)
◊ Rome, Casanatense MS 463

Fourteenth century

—none known—

Fifteenth century

‡*Cambridge, Corpus Christi College MS 464
*Paris, Bibl. Nationale MS lat. 5615
*Rome, Vatican MS lat. 1221
*Paderborn, Erzbischöfliche Akademische Bibliothek Theodoriana Ba 2
(*prov: Böddeken*)

B. Surviving Manuscripts Containing Full or Partial copies of William of Canterbury's *Miracula S. Thome*

Late twelfth century

‡Montpellier, Bibliothèque interuniversitaire section médicine MS 2 (*prov: Clairvaux*)
‡**Stuttgart, Württembergische Landesbibliothek, Cod. Theol. et phil. 4 654
(*prov: Weissenau*)

Twelfth/thirteenth century

Winchester, Winchester College MS 4

Thirteenth century

Évreux, Bibl. de la Ville, MS lat. 77 (*prov: Lyre*)

Fourteenth century

—none known—

Fifteenth century

‡*Cambridge, Corpus Christi College MS 464

‡ manuscript contains material from both collections

* manuscript contains lengthy selections, at least 25 narratives

** manuscript contains short selections, under 25 narratives

◇ manuscript is damaged but likely once contained a complete copy

The Construction of Benedict
of Peterborough's *Miracula S. Thomae*

Appendices 2 and 3 are designed to illustrate two things: first, how Benedict and William linked stories together as they constructed their collections for Thomas Becket (linked chapters are marked); and second, the strong contrasts between the collections. Benedict preferred connecting two or three stories together, whereas William tended to create longer sets of miracles. Bold type on Appendix 2 indicates an important transitional chapter in Benedict's collection. Darker boxes indicate later additions to the collections.

Book 1 of Benedict of Peterborough's *Miracula S. Thomae*

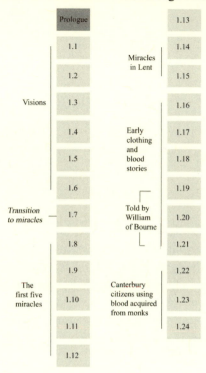

Prologue

Visions — 1.1, 1.2, 1.3, 1.4, 1.5, 1.6

Transition to miracles — 1.7

The first five miracles — 1.8, 1.9, 1.10, 1.11, 1.12

Miracles in Lent — 1.13, 1.14, 1.15

Early clothing and blood stories — 1.16, 1.17, 1.18, 1.19

Told by William of Bourne — 1.19, 1.20, 1.21

Canterbury citizens using blood acquired from monks — 1.22, 1.23, 1.24

Book 2 of Benedict of Peterborough's *Miracula S. Thomae*

	2.1			
	2.2	2.23	Accusations of incantations — 2.43	2.63
Easter stories	2.3	2.24	2.44	2.64
	2.4	2.25	2.45	2.65
	2.5	Becket's relics hidden — 2.26	2.46	Good deaths — 2.66
Crypt opened — 2.6		2.27	2.47	Told by Thomas, clerk — 2.67
Lame women	2.7	2.28	Fistula cures — 2.48	2.68
	2.8	Marble tomb built — 2.29	2.49	Sea stories — 2.69
Vomiting stories	2.9	Openings in the tomb — 2.30	2.50	2.70
	2.10	2.31	Told by Robert of Cricklade — 2.51	Men with arm complaints — 2.71
	2.11	2.32	2.52	2.72
	2.12	Invention of the Cross — 2.33	Same ailment — Same family — 2.53	Pilgrims from same region — 2.73
Neighbors cured	2.13	2.34	2.54	2.74
	2.14	2.35	Religious men curing many others — 2.55	Blindness cures — 2.75
	2.15	Washing miracles — 2.36	2.56	2.76
Boys denied healing	2.16	2.37	Becket clothing cures — 2.57	2.77
	2.17	2.38	2.58	
	2.18	2.39	2.59	
Water disappearing	2.19	Crippled boys cured — 2.40	2.60	
	2.20	2.41	2.61	
	2.21	2.42	2.62	
	2.22			

Book 3 of Benedict of Peterborough's *Miracula S. Thomae*

	3.1		
Pentecost candle miracles	3.2		
	3.3		
	3.4		
Miracles at martyrdom	3.5		
	3.6		
Marble pavement	3.7		
Lame men cured at tomb	3.8		
	3.9		
	3.10		
Confession of sins	3.11		
	3.12		
Blindness	3.13		
	3.14		
	3.15		
	3.16		
	3.17		

Blood miracles	3.18		
	3.19		
	3.20		
	3.21		
End of pyx breaking miracles	3.22		
	3.23		
Blood miracles	3.24		
	3.25		
	3.26		
Cathedral cures	3.27		
	3.28		
Carts leaving empty	3.29		
Variety in places of cures	3.30		
	3.31		
	3.32		
Cathedral cures	3.33		
	3.34		
	3.35		
Cure of wife & daughter of Henry	3.36		
	3.37		

Menstrual problems	3.38		
	3.39		
Wales and Welsh pilgrims	3.40		
	3.41		
Told by Abbot of Welford	3.42		
	3.43		
	3.44		
Blindness	3.45		
	3.46		
	3.47		
Cured women	3.48		
	3.49		
Told by Edric, priest of Ramsholt	3.50		
	3.51		
	3.52		
	3.53		
	3.54		
Coin/money miracles	3.55		
	3.56		
	3.57		

Daughter & sister-in-law of Constance	3.58		
	3.59		
	3.60		
Told by Abbot of Jorvaux	3.61		
	3.62		
Told by Henry of Houghton	3.63		
	3.64		
	3.65		
	3.66		
	3.67		
	3.68		
Newington miracles	3.69		
	3.70		
	3.71		
	3.72		
	3.73		
	3.74		
	3.75		
	3.76		
Similar places	3.77		

Book 4 of Benedict of Peterborough's *Miracula S. Thomae*

Too many miracles —	4.1		4.21		4.41	Fistula	4.60
Eilward of Westoning	4.2		4.22		4.42		4.61
Leprosy	4.3		4.23	Sea stories	4.43	Drownings	4.62
	4.4		4.24		4.44		4.63
	4.5	Philip of Alnwick and family	4.25		4.45	Sons of Jordan Fitz-Eisulf	4.64
Fires	4.6		4.26		4.46	Resurrections, letters	4.65
	4.7		4.27		4.47		4.66
	4.8	Leprosy	4.28		4.48		4.67
Two from Essex cured	4.9		4.29	Cures at Croxton (letter?)	4.49		4.68
	4.10		4.30		4.50		4.69
	4.11	Blindness	4.31		4.51		4.70
Blood miracles	4.12		4.32		4.52		4.71
Told by priest Ranulf	4.13	Blindness as punishment	4.33		4.53		4.72
	4.14		4.34	Women with dropsy	4.54	Leprosy	4.73
	4.15		4.35		4.55		4.74
	4.16		4.36		4.56		4.75
	4.17		4.37		4.57		4.76
Told by Tetion	4.18	Coin/money miracles	4.38	Commands	4.58	*cont.*	
	4.19		4.39		4.59		
	4.20		4.40				

Book 4, cont., and Additions to Benedict of Peterborough's *Miracula S. Thomae*

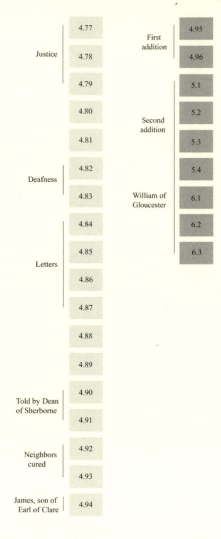

The Construction of William of Canterbury's *Miracula S. Thomae*

Books 1, 2 and 3 of William of Canterbury's *Miracula S. Thomae*

BOOK ONE

Letter to Henry II

Visions — Visions

| Prol. | 1.1 | 1.2 | 1.3 | 1.4 | 1.5 | 1.6 | 1.7 | 1.8 | 1.9 | 1.10 | 1.11 |

Punishments — Transition to miracles — Eilward/neighbor — Fitz-Eisulf — Epilepsy/coughing

| 1.12 | 1.13 | 1.14 | 1.15 (R 2.1) | 1.16 (R 2.2) | 1.17 (R 2.3) | 1.18 (R 2.4) | 1.19 (R 2.5) | 1.20 (R 2.6) | 1.21 (R 2.7) | 1.22 (R 2.8) | 1.23 (R 2.9) | 1.24 (R 2.10) |

Fistula

| 1.25 (R 2.11) | 1.26 (R 2.12) | 1.27 (R 2.13) | 1.28 (R 2.14) | 1.29 (R 2.15) | 1.30 (R 2.16) | 1.31 (R 2.17) | 1.32 (R 2.18) | 1.33 (R 2.19) | 1.34 (R 2.20) | 1.35 (R 2.21) | 1.36 (R 2.22) | 1.37 (R 2.23) | 1.38 (R 2.24) |

Irish war/knights — Dropsy — Paralysis

| 1.39 (R 2.25) | 1.40 (R 2.26) | 1.41 (R 2.27) | 1.42 (R 2.28) | 1.43 (R 2.29) | 1.44 (R 2.30) | 1.45 (R 2.31) | 1.46 (R 2.32) | 1.47 (R 2.33) | 1.48 (R 2.34) | 1.49 (R 2.35) | 1.50 (R 2.36) | 1.51 (R 2.37) | 1.52 (R 2.38) |

BOOK TWO

Resurrected children — Resurrections

| 2.1 (R 2.39) | 2.2 (R 2.40) | 2.3 (R 2.41) | 2.4 (R 2.42) | 2.5 (R 2.43) | 2.6 (R 2.44) | 2.7 (R 2.45) | 2.8 (R 2.46) | 2.9 (R 2.47) | 2.10 (R 2.48) | 2.11 (R 2.49) | 2.12 (R 2.50) | 2.13 (R 2.51) |

Leprosy — Stone

| 2.14 (R 2.52) | 2.15 (R 2.53) | 2.16 (R 2.54) | 2.17 (R 2.55) | 2.18 (R 2.56) | 2.19 (R 2.57) | 2.20 (R 2.58) | 2.21 (R 2.59) | 2.22 (R 2.60) | 2.23 (R 2.61) | 2.24 (R 2.62) | 2.25 (R 2.63) | 2.26 (R 2.64) | 2.27 (R 2.65) |

Pregnancy — Resurrections — Paralysis — Blind women

| 2.28 (R 2.66) | 2.29 (R 2.67) | 2.30 (R 2.68) | 2.31 (R 2.69) | 2.32 (R 2.70) | 2.33 (R 2.71) | 2.34 (R 2.72) | 2.35 (R 2.73) | 2.36 (R 2.74) | 2.37 (R 2.75) | 2.38 (R 2.76) | 2.39 (R 2.77) | 2.40 (R 2.78) | 2.41 (R 2.79) |

Priests and religious

| 2.42 (R 2.80) | 2.43 (R 2.81) | 2.44 (R 2.82) | 2.45 (R 2.83) | 2.46 (R 2.84) | 2.47 (R 2.85) | 2.48 (R 2.86) | 2.49 (R 2.87) | 2.50 (R 2.88) | 2.51 (R 2.89) | 2.52 (R 2.90) | 2.53 (R 2.91) |

BOOK THREE

Falls/burials — Women

| 3.1 | 3.2 | 3.3 | 3.4 | 3.5 | 3.6 | 3.7 | 3.8 | 3.9 | 3.10 | 3.11 | 3.12 | 3.13 | 3.14 |

Stories relating to Henry II — Knights/Irish war/sons of knights

| 3.15 | 3.16 | 3.17 | 3.18 | 3.19 | 3.20 | 3.21 | 3.22 | 3.23 | 3.24 | 3.25 | 3.26 |

Lost and found items — Feet — Abbot of Welford

| 3.27 | 3.28 | 3.29 | 3.30 | 3.31 | 3.32 | 3.33 | 3.34 | 3.35 | 3.36 | 3.37 | 3.38 | 3.39 | 3.40 |

Sea stories — Madness

| 3.41 | 3.42 | 3.43 | 3.44 | 3.45 | 3.46 | 3.47 | 3.48 | 3.49 | 3.50 | 3.51 | 3.52 | 3.53 | 3.54 |

Women — Candles

| 3.55 | 3.56 | 3.57 | 3.58 | 3.59 |

Books 4, 5 and 6 of William of Canterbury's *Miracula S. Thomae*

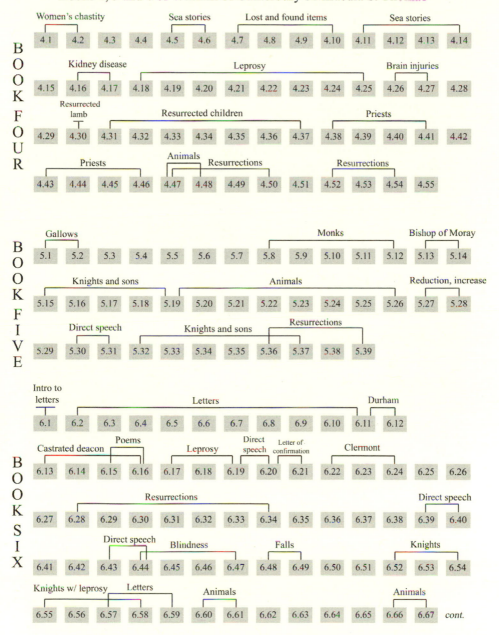

Book 6, cont., and Additions to William of Canterbury's *Miracula S. Thomae*

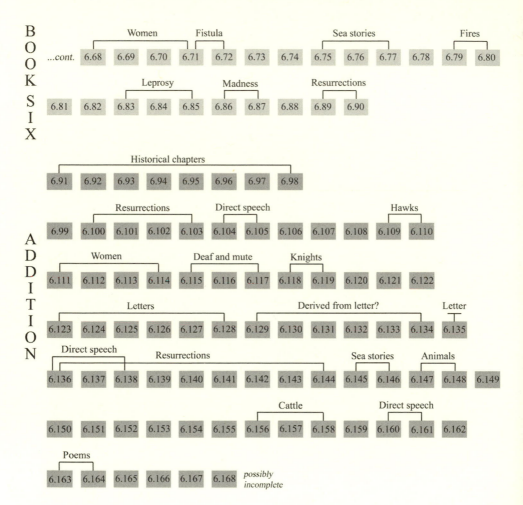

ABBREVIATIONS

AASS	*Acta Sanctorum*. Ed. J. Bollandus et al. Antwerp, Brussels, etc., 1643-.
AB	*Analecta Bollandiana*.
BL	British Library.
BP, *MT*	Benedict of Peterborough, *Miracula S. Thomae Cantuariensis*. Ed. J. C. Robertson in *MTB*, II: 21–281.
BP, *Passio*	Benedict of Peterborough, *Passio S. Thomae Cantuariensis*. Ed. J. C. Robertson in *MTB*, II: 1–19.
EETS	Early English Text Society.
EC, *Anselm*	Eadmer of Canterbury, *The Life of St. Anselm, Archbishop of Canterbury*. Ed. and trans. R. W. Southern. Reprinted OMT. Oxford, 1972.
Gervase	Gervase of Canterbury, *Opera Historica*. Ed. W. Stubbs, *The Historical Works of Gervase of Canterbury*. 2 vols. RS 73. London, 1879–80.
Godric	*Libellus de uita et miraculis S. Godrici, heremitae de Finchale*. Ed. J. Stevenson. SS 20. Durham, 1845.
Lantfred	Lantfred of Winchester, *Translatio et miracula S. Swithuni*. Ed. and trans. Michael Lapidge, *CSS*, 252–333.
Lapidge, *CSS*	Michael Lapidge, *The Cult of St. Swithun*. Winchester Studies 4.2. Oxford, 2003.
LE	*Liber Eliensis*. Ed. E. O. Blake. Royal Historical Society, Camden 3rd ser. 92. London, 1962.
LMODO	*Eadmer of Canterbury, Lives and Miracles of Saints Oda, Dunstan, and Oswald*. Ed. Andrew J. Turner and Bernard J. Muir. OMT. Oxford, 2006.
HCY	*Historians of the Church of York and its Archbishops*. Ed. J. Raine. 3 vols. RS 71. London, 1879–94.
MTB	*Materials for the History of Thomas Becket, Archbishop of*

	Canterbury. Ed. J. C. Robertson and J. B. Sheppard. 7 vols. RS 67. London, 1875–85.
MDun	*Memorials of St. Dunstan, Archbishop of Canterbury*. Ed. William Stubbs. RS 63. London, 1874.
MEdm	*Memorials of St. Edmund's Abbey*. Ed. T. Arnold. RS 96. 3 vols. London, 1890–96.
OC, *MD*	Osbern of Canterbury, *Miracula S. Dunstani*. Ed. in *MDun*, 129–61.
OC, *Vita*	Osbern of Canterbury, *Vita S. Dunstani*. Ed. in *MDun*, 69–128.
OMT	Oxford Medieval Texts.
PL	*Patrologiae cursus completus: series latina*. Ed. J.-P. Migne. 221 vols. Paris, 1841–64.
QM	"Quaedam miracula gloriosi martyris Thomae archiepiscopi Cantuariae," *AB* 20 (1901): 427–29.
RS	Rolls Series: *Rerum Britttanicarum Medii Aevi Scriptores, Chronicles and Memorials of Great Britain and Ireland During the Middle Ages*, 99 vols. 1858–96.
SS	Surtees Society.
TM, *MW*	Thomas of Monmouth, *The Life and Miracles of St. William of Norwich*. Ed. and trans. Augustus Jessopp and Montague Rhodes James. Cambridge, 1896.
WC, *MT*	William of Canterbury, *Miracula S. Thomae Cantuariensis*. Ed. J. C. Robertson in *MTB*, I: 137–546.
WC, *Vita*	William of Canterbury, *Vita S. Thomae Cantuariensis*. Ed. J. C. Robertson in *MTB*, I: 1–136.
WFS	William FitzStephen, *Vita S. Thomae*. Ed. J. C. Robertson in *MTB*, III: 1–154.
WM, *GP*	William of Malmesbury, *Gesta Pontificum Anglorum: The History of the English Bishops*. Ed. and trans. M. Winterbottom with the assistance of R. M. Thomson. OMT, Oxford, 2007.
WM, *GR*	William of Malmesbury, *Gesta Regum Anglorum: The History of the English Kings*. Ed. and trans. R. A. B. Mynors, completed by R. M. Thomson and Michael Winterbottom. OMT, Oxford, 1998.

Note to citation WC, *MT*: J. C. Robertson based his edition of William of Canterbury's *Miracula S. Thomae* on a manuscript that did not mark a division between the collection's first and second books. Robertson decided to place this division just fourteen chapters into the text, creating a very short first book. An early manuscript of William's collection, Montpellier, Bibliothèque interuniversitaire section médicine MS 2, does mark a division between the first and second books—at what is now book 2, chapter 39, in Robertson's edition. Since Robertson's division has led to mistaken assumptions about William's collection, I have renumbered the relevant chapters in the first and second books using the Montpellier division (see also Appendix 3). When I cite these chapters, I will use the Montpellier numbering first and then Robertson's numbering in parentheses to aid reference to his edition.

NOTES

INTRODUCTION

1. A good sense of the range of medieval miracle collecting can be gained from the seminal studies by Sigal, *L'homme et le miracle*, and Ward, *Miracles and the Medieval Mind*. For an intensive effort to pull together research on medieval hagiographic texts and quantify hagiographic production, see the remarkable series of volumes edited by Guy Philippart, *Hagiographies*.

2. Southern, "The Place of England," 171–74; see, however, Thomson, "England and the Twelfth-Century Renaissance," 11, where he considers that the extensive literature of wonders "sits oddly" with the other achievements of the age.

3. See, for example, Bolton, "Signs, Wonders, Miracles," 157.

4. This is a conservative estimate based on the editions of miracle collections that presently exist. See Figures 2, 3, and 5 for a visual representation of the density of miracle collecting in England in this period. In this count, I include a collection created in Wales for Wenefred at Holywell and another created in Scotland for Æbbe of Coldingham because these texts appear to have been compiled by English monks (from Shrewsbury and Durham respectively).

5. The chronicles have, of course, received far more attention than the collections. The best surveys are to be found in Southern, "Aspects," and Gransden, *Historical Writing*. For recent work, see especially Otter, *Inventiones*, and Watkins, *History and the Supernatural*. A particularly good study is Partner, *Serious Entertainments*.

6. See the approach of Yarrow, *Saints and Their Communities*; Bull, *Miracles of Our Lady*; Head, *Hagiography and the Cult of the Saints*; and others.

7. Most work on English miracle collections has been published as introductions to editions, introductions to translations, or in article form. These studies will be cited in the relevant chapters below. The two monographs devoted to English miracle collections are Finucane, *Miracles and Pilgrims*, a foundational study taking a social history approach, and Yarrow, *Saints and Their Communities*, a study of six English collections that concentrates on local monastic politics. Ward, *Miracles and the Medieval Mind*, devotes two chapters to English material; Webb, *Pilgrimage in Medieval England*, draws extensively on miracle collections; and Ridyard also discusses some miracle collections in her study, *The Royal Saints of Anglo-Saxon England*. For a discussion of recent trends in the study of

medieval miracle stories more generally, see the introduction to the essays in *Mirakel im Mittelalter: Konzeptionen, Ersheinungsformen, Deutungen*, ed. Martin Heinzelmann, Klaus Herbers, and Dieter R. Bauer (Stuttgart, 2002), 9–22, and Patrick J. Geary, "Saints, Scholars and Society: The Elusive Goal," in *Living with the Dead in the Middle Ages* (Ithaca, N.Y.: 1994), 9–29.

8. For other regional studies of miracle collections, see Annegret Wenz-Habfleisch, *Miracula Post Mortem: Studien zum Quellenwert Hochmittelalterlicher Mirakelsammlungen Vornehmlich des Ostfränkisch-Deutschen Reiches* (Siegburg, 1998); Krötzl, *Pilger, Mirakel und Alltag*; and Sigal, *L'homme et le miracle*.

9. Constable, *The Reformation of the Twelfth Century*, 4.

10. The best discussion of canonization dossiers and their development is to be found in Vauchez, *Sainthood in the Later Middle Ages*, 33–58; for the canonizations of the late twelfth century, see also Kemp, "Pope Alexander III and the Canonization of the Saints."

11. Susan Stewart, *On Longing: Narratives of the Miniature, the Gigantic, the Souvenir, the Collection* (Baltimore, 1984), xii. I am grateful to Katherine O'Brien O'Keeffe for bringing Stewart's work to my attention.

12. Yarrow, *Saints and Their Communities*, 214.

CHAPTER 1. NARRATING THE SAINT'S WORKS:
CONVERSATIONS, PERSONAL STORIES, AND THE MAKING OF CULTS

1. BP, *MT* 4.2, 179.

2. On this panel, see Caviness, *The Windows of Christ Church*, 190, figs. 279, 279a, 283. The inscription that goes with this panel is now in n. III (14).

3. BP, *MT* 4.2, 180: "plurimorum praecurrisset testimonium."

4. McNamara, "Problems in Contextualizing Oral Circulation," 33.

5. Yarrow, *Saints and Communities*, 20. For similar comments, see Morison, "The Miraculous and French Society," 77–83; Sigal, "Le travail des hagiographes," 152–55; Head, *Hagiography and the Cult of the Saints*, 77, etc.

6. Geoffrey of Burton, *Life and Miracles*, c. 48, 203–5.

7. *MEdm*, vol. 1, c. 2, 162.

8. *Alia Miracula I*, c. 2; trans. in Wilson, *After-Life of St. John*, 182.

9. *Alia Miracula I*, c. 6; trans. in Wilson, *After-Life of St. John*, 187.

10. See Southern, *Saint Anselm and His Biographer*, 278. Southern was not impressed with such talk: "this chatter was accorded the status of an intimate spiritual revelation, and it does an injustice to Eadmer's sense of seriousness in reporting it to overlook the reverence with which such talk was commonly received." See also Southern's comments in *St. Anselm: Portrait in a Landscape*, 313.

11. Cubitt, "Folklore and Historiography," 188. Cubitt is talking about the Anglo-Saxon context, but these foci are evident in medievalists' work in other fields as well. See Marco Mostert, "A Bibliography of Works on Medieval Communication," in *New*

Approaches to Medieval Communication, ed. Marco Mostert, intro. Michael Clanchy (Turnhout, 1999), 193–297.

12. See Cubitt, "Folklore and Historiography," 197–98. Smith, "Oral and Written," is largely focused on such stories as well. For a particularly good recent study of such stories, see Alexander, *Saints and Animals*.

13. McGuire, "Friends and Tales": see especially his chart accompanying the article.

14. See McGuire, "Friends and Tales," 244: see also McGuire's study of these written sources in "Written Sources and Cistercian Inspiration," an article that was published a year before his longer study of the oral sources.

15. In the Christ Church collections, 42 letters appear in the 709 total chapters (two letters are repeated between the two collections). See appendices 2 and 3 for the location of most of these chapters within Benedict of Peterborough's and William of Canterbury's collections. There are a few more chapters that appear to have been pulled (sometimes silently) from letters or other formally written texts, discussed below. The Christ Church collectors often include their own account of a miracle—from an oral source—in addition to the letter's account.

16. See the *Life and Miracles of St. Modwenna*, xxviii–xxix, for the editor's discussion of the overlap in wording between a charter and a chapter in the miracle collection. Geoffrey of Burton wrote this charter himself, so it should be taken as a form of self-plagiarism rather than the utilization of a written source.

17. For a review of recent work, see Jane Elliott's textbook, *Using Narrative in Social Research: Qualitative and Quantitative Approaches* (London, 2005). I have found the following particularly helpful in my conceptualization of the oral world behind medieval miracle collections: Stahl, *Literary Folkloristics*; Slater, *Trail of Miracles*; Ochs and Capps, *Living Narratives*; Hagan, *Migration Miracle*; and Gubrium and Holstein, *Analyzing Narrative Reality*.

18. Osbern of Canterbury, *Vita et Translatio S. Elphegi*, 141.

19. On the "flowering staff" motif, see Love, *Three Eleventh-Century Anglo-Latin Saints' Lives*, 59, n. 7. How such stories could develop in the hands of different authors is well evoked by Richard and Fiona Gameson's description of the elaboration of the story of St. Augustine of Canterbury and the fishtails: see Gameson and Gameson, "From Augustine to Parker," 33.

20. *Miracula S. Swithuni*, c. 42, 676–79.

21. WC, *MT* 6.148, 529–30.

22. *Miracula S. Swithuni*, c. 54, 688–91; c. 52, 685–87.

23. Bull, *Miracles of Our Lady*, 34. For related observations on the differences between miracles of living saints and posthumous miracles, see Moore, "Between Sanctity and Superstition," 55–70.

24. BP, *MT* 4.50, 218.

25. The seminal and still useful article defining the personal story vs. the "fabulate" is William Labov and Joshua Waletzky, "Narrative Analysis: Oral Versions of Personal Experience," in June Helm, ed., *Essays on the Verbal and Visual Arts* (Seattle, 1967), 12–44.

See also the important article by Dégh and Vázsonyi, "The Memorate and the Proto-Memorate."

26. See the discussion of Dégh and Vázsonyi, "The Memorate and the Proto-Memorate," 228.

27. "The Miracles of the Hand," c. 25, 17.

28. *Book of the Foundation*, bk. 2, c. 27.

29. *Alia Miracula I*, c. 5; trans. in Wilson, *After-Life of St. John*, 186.

30. See the comments of Bull, *Miracles of Our Lady*, 39. The assumption is usually that the collectors wrote down all the stories they knew: see Ward, *Miracles and the Medieval Mind*, 30: "The miracles of a particular saint and a particular shrine existed, and the writers used everything that could be gathered under such a title."

31. Ochs and Capps, *Living Narrative*, 3.

32. Charles Keil, "The Concept of 'the Folk'," *Journal of the Folklore Institute* 16 (1979): 209.

33. See Slater, *City Steeple, City Streets*, 9, n. 16. Even in her tight focus on stories from saints' lives—the folkloric kind of story—Slater still felt overwhelmed by the number of tellers and stories available to her: see *Trail of Miracles*, 18, 20–21. See also the very interesting work of Jacqueline Maria Hagan, a sociologist who studies the role of religion in the lives of undocumented migrants attempting to enter the United States from Mexico or Central America. Many of these migrants tell stories of *milagros*, "a divine intervention that allowed them to escape apprehension, assault, or even death": *Migration Miracle*, 14.

34. Morison, "The Miraculous and French Society," 27. Hedwig Röckelein also notes that "the authors of translation and miracle narratives hesitate simply to borrow from other stories and thus to make their own work more complete. This is an amazing fact considering that hagiographers 'invented' saints' Lives without caring whether their accounts were realistic or not": "Miracle Collections of Carolingian Saxony," 274.

35. Collectors would sometimes closely imitate stories in the New Testament—see, for instance, Carol Rawcliffe's discussion of how one of Thomas of Monmouth's accounts of William of Norwich's miracles "replicates in every detail one of Christ's most celebrated miracles" in Mark 6:25–34: "Curing Bodies," 113. But Thomas of Monmouth (and other collectors who imitated gospel miracles) do not seem to be trying to bulk up their collections by such borrowing. The point was rather to draw parallels between a saint's powers and those of Christ. Thomas of Monmouth complained about the fresh appearance of miracle stories that forced him to write more and reenter "the labyrinth of labor": TM, *MW* bk. 7, prologue, 262. For a very unusual example of a miracle collector lifting material verbatim from another collection, see Sharpe, "Some Medieval *Miracula* from Llandegley," 166–76.

36. McGuire, "Oral Sources," 224–25. For more examples of such high status conversations, see Yarrow, "Narrative, Audience," 74–75.

37. For the dating, see the editors' introduction, Alexander of Canterbury, *Dicta Anselmi et Quaedam Miracula*, 19–30. The text exists in two quite different recensions.

38. Alexander, *Dicta Anselmi et Quaedam Miracula*, c. 41, 238–39 (Baldwin); c. 21, 196–200 (Hugh); c. 46, 249–53 (Anselm); c. 51, 264–65 (Tytso); c. 43, 242–44 (archbishop of Lyons).

39. Alexander, *Dicta Anselmi et Quaedam Miracula*, 19.

40. Cubitt, "Folklore and Historiography," 202.

41. For examples from the Christ Church collections for Thomas Becket, see WC, *MT* 4.42, 352 (neighbors); for priests of their parishioners, BP, *MT* 1.19–21; for husbands and wives, WC, *MT* 3.6, 264–65; for chance acquaintances, BP, *MT* 3.46, 150–51; and an innkeeper and his customer, BP, *MT* 2.1, 58.

42. BP, *MT* 3.51, 153–55; 3.45, 149–50.

43. *Liber Eliensis*, bk. 3, c. 43.

44. The burgesses of Bedford sent the Christ Church monks a letter about Eilward's miracle. Benedict describes in his account of the miracle how the bishop of Durham, then in London, held Eilward there while he waited for confirmation of his story: see BP, *MT* 4.2.

45. Slater, *Trail of Miracles*, 85.

46. On the reappearance of this story, see Brown, "The Development of the Legend," 179.

47. On Osbern's life and career, see Rubenstein, "The Life and Writings of Osbern of Canterbury."

48. OC, *MD*, c. 24, 156–58.

49. See, e.g., the collection of essays in *Fama: The Politics of Talk and Reputation in Medieval Europe*, ed. Thelma Fenster and Daniel Lord Smail (Ithaca, N.Y., 2003).

50. See especially Stahl, *Literary Folkloristics*, 119: "All of the tools of folkloristics— the type and motif indexes, the ballad catalogues, the riddle and proverb dictionaries, the compendiums of folk belief, children's rhymes, dances, games, and customs, the taxonomies of house types, farming tools, quilt patterns, even the bibliographies, libraries, and archives—all serve this one basic objective, to aid in the identification of *tradition* in that whole range of artistic, social, communicative activities usually called folkloric." Very little of that helps when it comes to personal narratives.

51. Rom Harré, "'He Lived to Tell the Tale,'" *Journal of Narrative and Life History* 7 (1997): 331–34, at 332.

52. On what one researcher thinks necessary for an accurate reading of a personal narrative, see Stahl, *Literary Folkloristics*, chaps. 4 and 5, and also Stahl's complex diagram of the "folk-group" contexts of personal narratives (35), a diagram that Stahl notes is itself only partial. See also Gubrium and Holstein, *Analyzing Narrative Reality*, 23: "Concern with the production and reception of stories in society requires that we step outside of narrative texts and consider questions such as who produces particular kinds of stories, where are they likely to be encountered, what are their purposes and consequences, who are the listeners, under what circumstances are particular narratives more or less accountable, how do they gain acceptance, and how are they challenged?"

53. Janet Holmes notes that in the study of personal narratives, "unpacking the

underlying message is often only possible with extensive ethnographic research to supply necessary contextual detail": "Struggling Beyond Labov and Waletzky," *Journal of Narrative and Life History* 7 (1997): 91–96, at 94.

54. Stahl, *Literary Folkloristics*, 44.

55. Gubrium and Holstein warn their readers not simply to study transcripts of stories: see *Analyzing Narrative Reality*, xv: "The accent on the transcribed texts of stories tends to strip narratives of their social organization and interactional dynamics." As Stahl notes, "in every case, it seems, the printed page inevitably fails to do what the collector-transcriber hopes it could do. No text, not even one weighted with intricately coded analytical information, can demonstrate even the relatively well understood relationship between the specific text and the context of a conventional performance ethnography" (*Literary Folkloristics*, 3).

56. Paul Ricoeur reminds us that "whatever ultimately may be the nature of the so-called religious experience, it comes to language, it is articulated in a language, and the most appropriate place to interpret it on its own terms is to inquire into its linguistic expression": "Philosophy and Religious Language," 35. The most productive historical approach to miracles is to conceptualize them as stories rather than as events.

57. Religious personal narratives are not often the subject of scholarly research: see Gillian Bennett, " 'Belief Stories': The Forgotten Genre," *Western Folklore* 48 (1989): 289–311.

58. The use of this word in the Vulgate demonstrates its potency as a metaphor. It appears in Exodus 40:33 to describe the majesty of God shining forth from the tabernacle (*maiestate Domini coruscante*), when even Moses could not approach. It also appears in Luke 17:24: *Nam sicut fulgur coruscans de sub caelo in ea quae sub caelo sunt fulget ita erit Filius hominis in die sua.*

59. For an interesting attempt to outline the "typical components of a saint's cult in the medieval period," see Riches, "Hagiography in Context," 45–46.

60. See, for instance, Goodich, *Violence and Miracle*, 151.

61. Smith, "Oral and Written," 315. In his overview of oral tradition in the medieval period, W. F. H. Nicolaisen writes, "it is probably true to say that most of the manifestations of oral tradition never enter any literate or literary culture at all while continuing to function effectively in their own cultural register": see Nicolaisen, "Introduction," 2.

62. An aristocrat-centered view of cultic activity was propounded by Peter Brown in his seminal work *The Cult of the Saints*. For an insightful critique of Brown, though still retaining the focus on the elite, see Hayward, "Demystifying the Role of Sanctity," 115–42.

CHAPTER 2. TO EXPERIENCE WHAT I HAVE HEARD:
PLOTLINES AND PATTERNING OF ORAL MIRACLE STORIES

1. *The Life and Miracles of St. William*, ed. Jessopp and James, xv.

2. See Sumption, *Pilgrimage: An Image*, 151; Goodich, "Filiation and Form," 305; Ashley and Sheingorn, *Writing Faith*, 24; Yarrow, *Saints and Their Communities*, 16.

3. For a good sense of the general range of narrative categories in a typical posthumous miracle collection, see the "Index of Miracles" in Bull, *Miracles of Our Lady*, 223. For one of the most extraordinary attempts to typecast miracle stories, see E. Cobham Brewer, *A Dictionary of Miracles: Imitative, Realistic, and Dogmatic* (Philadelphia, 1895). For a recent study of "vengeance scripts" in miracle collections, see White, "Garsinde v. Sainte Foy."

4. Röckelein, "Miracle Collections of Carolingian Saxony," 267. Röckelein goes on to argue that the miracle collections by Sulpicius Severus and Gregory of Tours "had a standardizing effect and became authoritative for the genre." This article was originally published in the 1950s and was echoing ideas articulated still earlier by Hippolyte Delehaye.

5. Bull, *Miracles of Our Lady*, 13-14. Jonathan Sumption writes, "The extraordinary repetitiveness and lack of originality which characterize almost every medieval miracle collection, is in a large measure due to the fact that their authors were modeling themselves on Sulpicius Severus": *Pilgrimage: An Image*, 151. For similar arguments, see also Ashley and Sheingorn, *Writing Faith*, 156 n. 28, and Slocum, *Liturgies*, 83.

6. Head, "I Vow Myself to Be Your Servant," 230. For similar arguments, see Gurevich, "Oral and Written Culture," 62-63, Yarrow, *Saints and Communities*, 214-15, and Alexander, *Saints and Animals*, 159.

7. Signori, "The Miracle Kitchen," 280, 291. "Raw" is a word commonly used to describe oral miracle stories: see, e.g., Cownie, "The Cult of St. Edmund," 190.

8. OC, *MD*, c. 18, 143-44, and c. 25, 158-59.

9. Rubenstein, "Liturgy Against History," 287.

10. Rubenstein, "Liturgy Against History," 289.

11. For a translation of the knight of Thanet's story, see the chapter above. Jaber Gubrium and James Holstein urge researchers in the social sciences to be attentive to "intertextuality": "'Their own stories,' as we continue to argue, are shaped by other stories and circumstances" (*Analyzing Narrative Reality*, 186). In their chapter on intertextuality, Gubrium and Holstein write that "decisions and accounts made in one setting typically consider prior decisions, accounts, and actions from other settings . . . and anticipate the impact of current decisions and accounts on anticipated actions and settings" (187). This is the basic dynamic I see behind the creation of personal miracle stories.

12. For a marvelous study of the power of a narrative in the medieval context, see Rubin, *Gentile Tales*. For a study of oral narrative patterning in a modern context, see especially Showalter, *Hystories: Hysterical Epidemics*. Robin Tomlin Lakoff, *Talking Power: The Politics of Language in Our Lives* (New York, 1990) also formed my thinking.

13. For some of the other attempts to read the narrative architecture behind miracle stories, see Goodich, "Filiation and Form," 305-22; Moore, "Between Sanctity and Superstition," 57-58; and Yarrow, *Saints and Communities*, 18-19.

14. Sally Crumplin finds the "same characteristics" in a miracle story from 1998 and the stories in a late twelfth-century miracle collection: see Crumplin, "Modernizing St. Cuthbert," 186-87.

15. Situations in which one person's story suggests a course of action to someone else are frequently recounted in miracle collections. See, for example, a chapter in Aelred of Rievaulx's rendering of Osbert of Clare's miracle collection for Edward the Confessor in which Osbert's preaching about his healing from quartan fever inspires a knight in the crowd to ask Edward for healing for his own quartan fever: Aelred of Rievaulx, *Vita S. Edwardi*, c. 37.

16. For the seminal account of the formation of this meta-narrative, see Brown, *The Cult of the Saints*.

17. Measuring for candle-making was a widespread invocation practice: see the interesting comments by Edmund Craster, "The Miracles of St. Cuthbert," 7–8. Coin-bending was termed an English custom by those writing the canonization proceedings for Thomas Cantiuple in the early fourteenth-century: see Finucane, *Miracles and Pilgrims*, 94–95.

18. I discuss the beginnings of Becket's cult and the use of the "water" at more length in Chapters eight and nine. See also Sigal, "Naissance et premier développement," 35–44.

19. See Rawcliffe, "Curing Bodies," 121: "The high Middle Ages witnessed an almost insatiable demand for water in which the relics of saints or other sanctified objects had been diluted, powdered or immersed, since it could be more widely deployed for prophylactic or healing purposes." To take just one example of this, most of the miracle stories concerning the hand of St. James at Reading in the late twelfth century involve the use of the "water of St. James," that is, water that had come into contact with the hand reliquary kept at Reading: see "The Miracles of the Hand," 1–19.

20. BP, *MT* 1.23, 55: "Cujus medicaminis efficaciam licet multi jam experti fuissent, non tamen absque timore dabatur petentibus; nec mirum—inusitatum exstiterat homines humano cruore potari."

21. BP, *MT* 1.22, 54.

22. WFS, 150.

23. BP, *MT* 1.22, 54.

24. BP, *MT* 1.12, 43.

25. BP, *MT* 1.23.

26. BP, *MT* 2.18, 68.

27. WC, *MT* 2.53, 252 (Robertson 2.91).

28. WC, *MT* 6.2, 407–9, at 408.

29. BP, *MT* 2.56, 103–4.

30. BP, *MT* 2.56, 104.

31. On the medieval devotion to the Eucharist, see Miri Rubin, *Corpus Christi: The Eucharist in Late Medieval Culture* (Cambridge, 1991). For a blood relic that did *not*, interestingly, inspire a popular cult, see Vincent, *The Holy Blood*, 79–81.

32. BP, *MT* 4.89, 253–54.

33. For example, in his analysis of Scandinavian miracle collections, Christian Krötzl found that 30 percent of the stories concerned blindness and 22 percent paralysis: see

Pilger, Mirakel und Alltag, 188. See also the statistical charts in Sigal, *L'homme et le miracle*, 256, 297–301, and Theilmann, "English Peasants and Medieval Miracle Lists," 292.

34. On potential causes of blindness in the period, see Rawcliffe, "Curing Bodies," 132–33.

35. Benedict describes how a man faking blindness (to acquire relics) was later punished with a true blindness: see BP, *MT* 4.32.

36. Showalter, *Hystories: Hysterical Epidemics*, 6.

37. I think Marcus Bull has it right when he writes, "underlying the spread of information about which pilgrimage sites were 'in' was a more fundamental flow of ideas about what could be hoped for from invocation of saintly patronage—in crude terms, what saints might actually be expected to do. Present experiences would then be slotted into explanatory frameworks constructed from the lessons of past stories, and the miraculous as an interpretative mode would thus reproduce itself, in the process generating new material for future generations in turn to recall": *Miracles of Our Lady*, 35.

38. David Wilkinson, *The Prayer of Jabez: Breaking Through to the Blessed Life* (Sisters, Ore., 2000). For very interesting work on one aspect of the "prosperity gospel," see Milmon Harrison, *Righteous Riches: The Word of Faith Movement in Contemporary African-American Religion* (New York, 2005).

39. For Curbaran's story, see BP, *MT* 3.53, 156.

40. See, e.g., the two stories following that of Curbaran: BP, *MT* 3.54–55.

41. For these stories, see BP, *MT* 6.1 and WC, *MT* 3.1; WC, *MT* 4.28; and BP, *MT* 4.2 and WC, *MT* 1.16 (Robertson, 2.2).

42. See Marcus Bull's comments about "inaudita" miracles: "the very value attached to 'unheard-of' miracles demonstrates that stories that were in fact *audita*—in the sense of resembling earlier instances of the same sort of thing happening—were the common currency" (*Miracles of Our Lady*, 15).

43. The picture painted by Ronald Finucane is representative: "An uncouth peasant gesticulates wildly as he tries to explain his miraculous cure to the monk in charge of the tomb; he knows no Latin, no French, and his English dialect is scarcely comprehensible to the guardian-monk. The recorder of the miracles, perhaps a monk named William of Canterbury, scribbles briefly on a scrap of parchment and waves away the pilgrim, who shrugs and shuffles from the crypt and goes up into the Kentish sunshine" (*Miracles and Pilgrims*, 9–10).

44. See Sigal, *L'homme et le miracle*, 297–301.

45. See, for instance, the charts and discussion in Finucane, *Miracles and Pilgrims*, 143–51. In the set of late medieval collections of interest to Leigh Ann Craig, 70.1 percent of women's miracles are healings versus 47.2 percent of men's: see Craig, *Wandering Women*, fig. 8, 274.

46. WC, *MT* 3.5, 263.

47. WC, *MT* 1.52, 198–99 (Robertson 2.38).

48. See WC, *MT* 1.52, 199 (Robertson 2.38), where William notes that the ring that Godelief claimed to have received from Becket looked to be of human manufacture:

"Haec cum dixisset, de superaltari tulit argenteum annulum, operis, ut videbatur, humani."

49. BP, *MT* 2.73, 107–8; see also BP, *MT* 2.12, for a similar story about the dreams of Robert, a smith.

50. OC, *MD*, c. 4, 131–32.

51. OC, *MD*, c. 20.

52. For a sense of the complexities of the relationships between gender, status, and conversational stories in a contemporary context, see Susan A. Speer, *Gender Talk: Feminism, Discourse, and Conversation Analysis* (London, 2005), and Gubrium and Holstein's chapter on status in *Analyzing Narrative Reality*, 149–60.

53. BP, *MT* 6.3, 266–67.

54. For an interesting study of such changes with a miracle of Thomas Cantiuple, see Finucane, "The Toddler in the Ditch," esp. 143: "Knowing how miracles are supposed to be described, they created their own interpretation of events: they emphasize the hardness of the rock; the more elaborate signing by Syward; the cure happening 'in the blink of an eye,' a topos in descriptions of miracles attributed to countless other saints; the lack of wounds; and Roger's immediate recovery and return to health. No witness of 1307 made such claims; even the vicar, a part to the letter of 1303, did not claim instantaneity of cure in 1307."

CHAPTER 3. A DROP FROM THE OCEAN'S WATERS: LANTFRED OF FLEURY AND THE CULT OF SWITHUN AT WINCHESTER

1. Love, *Goscelin of Saint-Bertin*, xxxiii.

2. For a survey of late Anglo-Saxon Latin hagiography with an extensive bibliography, see Lapidge and Love, "Latin Hagiography," 216–23. Old English hagiography is discussed with similar thoroughness in Whatley, "Late Old English Hagiography, ca. 950–1150." The "handlist" of John Blair is an indispensible aid for any study involving Anglo-Saxon saints: see Blair, "A Handlist," 495–565.

3. On this late Saxon interest in saints' cults generally, see Rollason, *Saints and Relics*, 167–95. Blair, "A Saint for Every Minster?" is also essential reading. There is not yet a comprehensive study devoted to saints' cults in the context of the Benedictine reform movement. Some of the best work on this subject has been done by Alan Thacker: see his articles "Æthelwold and Abingdon," "Cults at Canterbury," and "Saint-Making and Relic Collecting."

4. See Gransden, "The Composition and Authorship," 26. The two stories of possible eleventh-century derivation concern the invasion of the Danes and a story of sanctuary.

5. See Love, *Goscelin of Saint-Bertin*, lxi–lxxi, and her edition and translation of the early twelfth-century text in the same volume, 95–131. Versions of the same stories—likely closer to Ælfhelm's original—were integrated into the *LE*, bk. 1, cc. 41–49. For discussion of these stories, which mainly concern a wicked archpriest who questioned Æthelthryth's

sanctity, see Keynes, "Ely Abbey 672–1109," 16–17. See also Ridyard's discussion of Ely's saints in *Royal Saints*, 51–56, 181–96.

6. For an edition and discussion of this text, see *The Anglo-Saxon Chronicle*, vol. 17, lxxii–cxxiv, 109–42.

7. See Wulfstan of Winchester, *Life of St. Æthelwold*, cvi–cvii, 65–69; and Byrhtferth of Ramsey, *Lives of St. Oswald and St. Ecgwine*, 281–303.

8. For the text and discussion, see *Historia de Sancto Cuthberto*, esp. 1–14, 32–36. I find the arguments for an early eleventh century date the most convincing.

9. For an edition, see "An Old English Vision of Leofric," 180–87, and for discussion, Jackson, "Osbert of Clare and the *Vision of Leofric*," 285–86.

10. See Goscelin of St.-Bertin, *Vita et Translatio S. Edithe*, c. 16, 285–92. See also the discussion of the Edith legend by Ridyard, *Royal Saints*, 40 and 148–54.

11. See OC, *Vita*, 70.

12. For an edition and discussion of this text, see Lapidge, "The Cult of St. Indract," 419–52. See also Ridyard, *Royal Saints*, 30, for a possible lost text of Edburga's miracles at Pershore in Old English.

13. On these parchment sheets, see Blair, "A Saint for Every Minster?" 479, n. 69.

14. I use Lapidge's translation for the citations and quotations from Lantfred's *Translation and Miracles* in this chapter.

15. Lapidge, *CSS*, 66–67.

16. For discussion of Swithun's early cult and Lantfred's career and writings, see Lapidge, *CSS*, 3–22, 217–38.

17. The title "Translation and Miracles" is not medieval. In a manuscript of the text copied at Winchester c.1000, the text is entitled simply "Of the Miracles of Swithun," a much more appropriate title: see Lapidge, *CSS*, 217, n. 2.

18. Lantfred, c. 4, 287.

19. Lantfred, prefatory letter, 253.

20. Webb, *Pilgrimage in Medieval England*, 31.

21. Webb, *Pilgrimage in Medieval England*, 21.

22. These texts are all edited and translated in Lapidge's monumental volume: see Wulfstan of Winchester, *Narratio Metrica de S. Swithuno*, 335–552; *Epitome Translationis et Miraculorum S. Swithuni*, 564–74; and Ælfric of Winchester, *Life of St. Swithun*, 590–610.

23. Wulfstan, *Narratio Metrica*, ll.1072–74, 465; Ælfric, *Life of St. Swithun*, 607.

24. For the new stories in Wulfstan's versification, see *Narratio Metrica*, 455–65. Chapters 19 and 26 of Ælfric's *Life of St. Swithun* have no source in Lantfred or the epitome. One concerns a joker who pretended to be Swithun and was struck ill, the other a man with a binding around his head that broke: see Lapidge, *CSS*, 601–2, 607.

25. For discussion of what he terms "the great Anglo-Norman rebuild," see Crook, *The Architectural Setting*, 182–241.

26. Lantfred, prefatory letter, 253.

27. Lapidge, *CSS*, 66–67.

28. Lantfred, preface, 259.

29. Lanfred, prefatory letter, 253.

30. Lapidge, *CSS*, 232–33, points out that Lantfred's *inventio* has similarities to that of Lucian's *Epistola* concerning St. Stephen.

31. He will sometimes use phrases such as "in those days," "at the same time," "in the same year," or "not long afterward" to introduce a new chapter and miracle, but these vague phrases function as transitional markers rather than serious attempts to put the stories in a chronological framework. Once Lantfred states that a set of miracles happened on a specific day—the Assumption of the Virgin—but he provides no sense of which year this was in: see Lantfred, *Translatio et Miracula* c. 14, 299.

32. Lantfred, c. 5, 289.

33. Lantfred, cc. 16, 29.

34. Lantfred, cc. 5, 8, 9, 11, 13, 15, 16, 17, 21, 28, 30, 33, 37 concern healings of four people or less at the tomb at Winchester. Chapters 10, 12, 14, 25, 19, 22, and 23 describe larger numbers of healings at the tomb. Lantfred discusses healings happening outside of Winchester in cc. 7, 18, 29, 31, 32, 35, 36.

35. For bound slaves, see Lantfred, cc. 6, 20, 38, and 39; for judicial punishment and healing and freeing of prisoners, cc. 24–27 and 34. For analysis of these stories, see O'Keeffe, "Body and Law in Anglo-Saxon England," 218–32.

36. Lantfred, c. 39, 333.

37. Lantfred, c. 40, 333.

38. Lantfred, preface, 259.

39. Lantfred, cc. 14, 12, 23.

40. For stories about Winchester citizens—nearly all of them, interestingly, liberation miracles rather than healings—see Lantfred cc. 1, 3, 6, 16 (about a Winchester citizen in Rome when he heard about Swithun's miracles), 20, 25, 38, and 39. There are a number of chapters in which the origin of the person is unclear—see cc. 9, 15, 26, 31.

41. Lantfred, preface, 257. See also the mass-set that Lantfred likely composed for Swithun. One line reads, "O blessed race of the English, to whom the Lord of things granted so great a patron saint, that he might duly be worshipped as one of the apostles by the peoples of the aforesaid race": Lapidge, *CSS*, 79.

42. Lantfred, c. 31, 319.

43. Lantfred, c. 8, 291 and c. 7, 291.

44. Lantfred, c. 32, 321–23.

45. Lantfred, c. 32, 323—this phrase is from the poem carved in the candle.

46. Lantfred, c. 4, 287.

47. Lapidge, *CSS*, 229.

48. Lapidge, *CSS*, 223–24.

49. Lapidge, *CSS*, 222.

50. *Regularis concordia anglicae nationis monachorum sanctimonialiumque*, ed. and trans. Thomas Symons (New York, 1953), 3.

51. Osgar is mentioned in the letter Lantfred sent to Archbishop Dunstan; for the story told by Æthelwold, see Lantfred, c. 35, 329.

52. Lantfred states that "the sun is now unrolling the tenth year" since the translation of 971 in the third chapter of the collection (c. 3, 287). Lapidge believes that a scribe probably amended Lantfred's text here to reflect the date of his own manuscript copy, and that Lantfred's text would have originally read "second," "third," or "fourth" (see *CSS*, 286, n. 161). Lapidge also writes that "all the miracles recorded by Lantfred arguably took place during the year 971/2," and that Lantfred was writing "probably during the years 972 x 974, and in any case not later than c.975": Lapidge, *CSS*, 236–37. I agree that Lantfred could have completed the writing of the collection within a timeframe of a year or two, but I do not share Lapidge's confidence that Lantfred recorded miracles in a roughly chronological sequence, nor that there were "no significant time intervals" between the miracles—for instance, Lantfred must have made a trip to France after he became interested in Swithun's cult but before he finished the collection. I am more comfortable with a date range that places the composition of the text sometime between late 971 and the early 980s.

53. Lapidge, *CSS*, 77–80. Lapidge also tentatively identifies Lantfred as the author of a poem that concludes with praise of Æthelwold: see *CSS*, 223, and Lapidge, "Three Latin Poems from Æthelwold's School at Winchester," *Anglo-Saxon England* 1 (1972): 85–137.

54. Lapidge edits and translates the letter in *CSS*, 220–22.

55. Lapidge, *CSS*, 219.

56. Lapidge, *CSS*, 8; see also 12.

57. Gretsch, *Aelfric and the Cult of Saints*, 193.

58. Robert Deshman, "Swithun in Art," in *CSS*, Winchester Studies 4.2 (Oxford, 2003), 182. In her discussion of Ælfric's translation of Lantfred's collection, Elaine Treharne too insists that the text "foregrounds above all else the concerns of the Benedictine reform": see Treharne, "Ælfric's Account of St. Swithun," 178.

59. Lantfred did read some miracles in his day as relating to monastic reform—but not those of Swithun. He writes in the collection for Swithun as an aside that the miracles of Ælfgifu, the mother of King Edgar, were "partly as a result of her own, partly as a result of her son's merits. During his reign nearly all the monasteries which formerly had been left in ruin by previous kings have been successfully restored through his sympathy" (c. 36, 329). Swithun, the long dead bishop, does not seem to have been connected in his mind with reform in a similar way.

60. Lapidge, *CSS*, 285, n. 160.

61. The first phrase is something Swithun says in a vision (Lantfred, c. 10, 295); the second phrase is taken from a line Lantfred carved on a candle in hopes of a healing (Lantfred, c. 32, 321–23). For similar sentiments, see also the mass-set that Lantfred probably composed for Swithun: Lapidge, *CSS*, 78–79.

62. Lantfred, c. 40, 333.

63. Lantfred's account of the *inventio* of Swithun's cult contains internal contradictions and its chronology should be treated very warily. Wulfstan's account of miracles at Swithun's gravesite before the translation is much richer than that of Lantfred: see *Narra-*

tio, bk. 1, ll. 799–986. Scholars have become increasingly aware that outdoor monuments and sites often served as focal points for Anglo-Saxon cultic activity: see Blair, "A Saint for Every Minster?" 486. For the importance of graveyards in Celtic cults—with striking parallels to what appears to have been happening around Swithun's grave at Winchester—see Edwards, "Celtic Saints and Early Medieval Archaeology," 227–43.

64. For a reading of Æthelwold's translations of relics as a means to "bring the past under control," see Blair, *The Church in Anglo-Saxon Society*, 353. There is not yet a monograph devoted to Æthelwold: for work on his life and reforming efforts, see the articles in *Bishop Æthelwold: His Career and Influence*, ed. Barbara Yorke (Woodbridge, 1988).

65. Wulfstan, *Life of Æthelwold*, c. 26.

66. Lantfred, c. 35, 329.

67. Wulfstan of Winchester describes this explusion in his *Life of Æthelwold*, c. 18, 33; see also the introduction to the *Life*, xlv–li and Thacker, "Æthelwold and Abingdon," 43–64. Wulfstan mentions Eadsige in his *Narratio*, where he describes him as "a devout man . . . one to be respected for the total honesty of his behavior," who gave "attentive care" to Swithun's relics (*Narratio*, bk. 2, ll. 135–50).

68. Sacrists often appear in later English miracle collections as informants: see, e.g., *MEdm*, vol. 1, 160–62, 164–68, and 192–93 for stories from Tolinus the sacrist at Bury; *Alia Miracula I*, c. 4, for Alfred, the sacrist at Beverley; the *Waltham Chronicle*, c. 20, 45–51, for Turkill, the sacrist at Waltham; and "The Miracles of the Hand of St. James," c. 8, 9, for the sacrist at Reading. It is often possible to determine a single, particularly important informant for a miracle collector: see, e.g., Brian Patrick McGuire's study of Caesarius of Heisterbach's *Dialogus Miraculorum* and the importance of the stories of Abbot Herman of Marienstatt: McGuire, "Friends and Tales," 171–85.

69. Lantfred, c. 1, 265.

70. Ibid.

71. Lantfred, cc. 20, 37, 5.

72. The disruption caused by Swithun's miracles is also noted by Wulfstan in the *Narratio*. He describes having to "abandon the delights of the table," and missing lessons because of Swithun's miracles: "while we young oblates were together in class learning either some chant or some particular text, it so happened that we were able to learn virtually nothing in the space of that day because of the burgeoning miracles": bk. 2, ll. 232–65.

73. Lantfred, c. 10, 297.

74. Lantfred, cc. 14 and 22.

75. Lantfred, c. 1, 265.

76. Lantfred, cc. 35, 27, 19.

77. Lantfred, prefatory letter, 253.

78. Lapidge, *CSS*, 217. See also Lapidge, *CSS*, 66, 217, and 253, n. 8. Gretsch writes "Lantfred dedicated his work to the monks of the Old Minster, and it therefore was probably composed at Bishop Æthelwold's instigation" (*Aelfric and the Cult of Saints*, 175).

79. Printed in Alexandre Vidier, *L'historiographie a Saint-Benoit-sur-Loire et les miracles de Saint Benoit* (Paris, 1965); for discussion of Adrevald's collection and the later additions by other authors, see Head, *Hagiography and the Cult of the Saints*, and Rollason, "The Miracles of St. Benedict," 73–90.

80. Lapidge, *CSS*, 233–34.

81. Lapidge, *CSS*, 224: see Lapidge's full analysis of Lantfred's prose style, 224–32.

82. See Lapidge's discussion of these manuscripts, *CSS*, 238–42.

83. For discussion of the Benedictional image, see Deshman, "Swithun in Art," 179–90, and also Deshman, *The Benedictional of Æthelwold*. Lapidge discusses, edits, and translates the set of benedictions in *CSS*, 86–88. For the rebuilding of the Old Minster, see Biddle, "*Felix Urbs Winthonia*," 123–40. The full excavation reports and analysis are forthcoming in Winchester Studies 4.1.

84. Lapidge, *CSS*, 217.

85. See Blanton, *Signs of Devotion*, 100–101 for an interesting chart ranking saints based on Anglo-Saxon litanies. Swithun is in a tie for third with Dunstan and Guthlac in this ranking, with Cuthbert and Æthelthryth coming in first and second. On this period in English monastic history generally, see the excellent discussion in Gransden, "Traditionalism and Continuity," esp. 53–70.

CHAPTER 4. FRUITFUL IN THE HOUSE OF THE LORD:
THE EARLY MIRACLE COLLECTIONS OF GOSCELIN OF ST.-BERTIN

1. WM, *GR*, vol. 1, bk. 4, c. 342, 593. The most extensive treatment of Goscelin's life and works remains the dissertation by Hamilton, "Goscelin of Canterbury." On the historical significance of Goscelin's works, see Gransden, *Historical Writing*, 107–11, and van Houts, "The Flemish Contribution," 111–27.

2. Love, "The Life of St. Wulfsige," 101.

3. For listings of Goscelin's corpus, see Lapidge and Love, "Latin Hagiography," 225–33; Sharpe, *A Handlist of the Latin Writers*, 152–53; and *The Life of King Edward*, Appendix C, 146–49. On the Ely materials and Wærburh, see the new edition and discussion in Love, *Goscelin of St.-Bertin*.

4. None of these works is yet in a modern edition. For parts of Goscelin's miracle collection for Ivo, see W. D. Macray, *Chronicon Abbatiae Rameseiensis*, RS 83 (London, 1886), lix–lxxiv, and for Augustine, *AASS* Maii VI (1688), 373–443, and *PL* 150, 743–64.

5. See *The Life of King Edward*, 81; *Vita S. Rumwoldi*, 114–15; and *Vita S. Erkenwaldi*, 97.

6. Folcard of St. Bertin, *Vita S. Iohannis*, c. 13, 260; translation from Wilson, *Life and After-Life*, 156.

7. For analysis and an English translation of Goscelin's *Life of Wulfsige* (*Vita S. Wulsini*), see Love, "The Life of St. Wulfsige," 98–123. Quotations of the *Life of Wulfsige* in this chapter are taken from Love's translation. For an English translation and discussion of Goscelin's *Life and Translation of Edith* (*Vita et Translatio S. Edithae*), see Wright and

Loncar, "Goscelin's Legend of Edith," 21–93 (*Vita*, 21–68, *Translatio*, 69–93). Quotations from these texts in this chapter are taken from Wright and Loncar's translations. For the *Life and Miracles of Kenelm* (*Vita et Miracula S. Kenelmi*) see Love, *Three Eleventh-Century Anglo-Latin Saints' Lives*, discussion lxxxix–cxxxix, edition and translation, 49–89. Love believes the text probably, but not certainly, was composed by Goscelin. Michael Lapidge argues convincingly for Goscelin's composition of this text based on stylistic similarities to his other works: see Lapidge, *CSS*, 618–20.

8. Lapidge and Love, "Latin Hagiography," 225.

9. The conventional dating for Herman's assumption of the bishopric at Sherborne is 1058. For the c. 1062 dating see Simon Keynes, "Regenbald the Chancellor," *Anglo-Norman Studies* 10 (1988): 185–222, at 202–3. For an overview of Goscelin's career, see Lapidge and Love, "Latin Hagiography," 225–33.

10. For Goscelin's use of the term *adolescentulus* and discussion of his age more generally, see O'Keeffe, "Goscelin and the Consecration of Eve," esp. 253, n. 22. For the 1107 date, see Lapidge and Love, "Latin Hagiography," 233–34.

11. See Love's discussion of this text in *Goscelin of St. Bertin*, lxxvii–lxxviii. For an interesting discussion of this and other works of Goscelin, see Alexander, *Saints and Animals*, 54–55, 85–112. On the tradition of writing hagiography at St.-Bertin, see Ugé, *Creating the Monastic Past*, esp. 50–96.

12. Goscelin makes these comments in book four of his *Liber Confortatorius*. In this chapter, I quote from Otter's English translation of the text, *Goscelin of St. Bertin: The Book of Encouragement and Consolation* (for the comments on his lodging, see 127).

13. Tom Licence has recently argued that a set of lections on St. Eadwold of Cerne should be attributed to Goscelin, which, if correct, would make the lections some of the earliest writings of his career: Licence, "Goscelin of St. Bertin and the Life of St. Eadwold," 182–207.

14. Goscelin, *Life of Wulfsige*, 102–3.

15. Goscelin, *Translation of Edith*, c. 22, 90.

16. See, for instance, Goscelin, *Translation of Edith*, c. 20, in which Goscelin describes how Ælfgifu, abbess of Wilton, "long before her death . . . declared [her vision] with many tears to her only sister, who was a nun, and to her only successor in piety as much as in office, who is now abbess of this church."

17. Goscelin, *Life and Miracles of Kenelm*, 51–53; see also *The Life of King Edward*, 139 n. 59.

18. On the degree of difference in their ages, and for these pet terms, see O'Keeffe, "Goscelin and the Consecration of Eve," esp. 253.

19. For analysis and bibliography on the *Liber confortatorius*, see the essays in *Writing the Wilton Women*, ed. Hollis et al., 1–11, 341–415, and Otter, *Goscelin of St. Bertin: The Book of Encouragement*, 1–16, 168–73.

20. For discussion of this relationship, see O'Keeffe, "Goscelin and the Consecration of Eve," Stroud, "Eve of Wilton," 204–12, and the essays in *Writing the Wilton Women*.

21. Goscelin, *Life of Wulfsige*, 103, and c. 21, 115.

22. *Book of Consolation*, 26.

23. Love places the date of composition for this text to 1066–75: *Three Eleventh-Century Lives*, xc–xci; Paul Antony Hayward, however, argues for a later date: see Hayward, "Translation-Narratives," 73.

24. Goscelin, *Life of Edith*, prologue 23.

25. See the discussion of Wulfsige's cult in Love, "The Life of St. Wulfsige," 98–103, and Goscelin's reference to this early translation, *Life of Wulfsige*, c. 13.

26. On Edith and her cult, see Ridyard, *Royal Saints*, 140–54 and Hollis, "St. Edith and the Wilton Community," 244–80.

27. See Love's discussion of Kenelm's cult, *Three Eleventh-Century Lives*, cx–cxvii.

28. Goscelin, *Life of Wulfsige*, c. 21, 115.

29. Goscelin, *Life of Wulfsige*, cc. 21–23.

30. For Goscelin's accounts of Edith's recent miracles, see *Translation of Edith*, cc. 15, 18, 21, 22.

31. Goscelin finds three very short chapters to be sufficient for describing the miracles of Kenelm from "last year": *Life and Miracles of Kenelm*, cc. 28–30. The final chapter of the collection in Love's edition (c. 31) is not in all manuscripts and was likely a later addition by another author.

32. Goscelin, *Translation of Edith*, c. 18, 87.

33. Love notes in her discussion of the *Life and Miracles of Kenelm* that "it seems fairly certain that the *Vita* and most of the *Miracula* were conceived as a single unit. . . . The narrative style and Latinity of the *Vita* and the *Miracula* are uniform": *Three Eleventh-Century Lives*, xci.

34. The final chapter of the collection appears to have been a later addition: see Goscelin, *Translation of Edith*, c. 22 (where Goscelin brings the text to a firm conclusion) and c. 23, where a new miracle starts in a style quite unlike that of Goscelin.

35. Goscelin, *Life of Wulfsige*, c. 4, 106.

36. Goscelin, *Life of Wulfsige*, c. 24, 116.

37. Goscelin, *Translation of Edith*, c. 16, 82–85: "This things were publicly described in the presence of the Abbess Brihtgifu . . . and committed to writing in the vernacular."

38. Goscelin, *Life and Miracles of Kenelm*, 51–53. Goscelin states that there was a copy of a *passio* of Kenelm at Paris, but does not seem to have had that *passio* in hand himself.

39. Goscelin, *Life of Wulfsige*, 102.

40. Goscelin, *Life of Edith*, prologue 24.

41. Goscelin, *Life and Miracles of Kenelm*, c. 24, 81.

42. Goscelin, *Life of Wulfsige*, 102–3.

43. Goscelin, *Life of Edith*, prologue 24.

44. Goscelin, *Translation of Edith*, cc. 10, 17.

45. Goscelin, *Life and Miracles of Kenelm*, 52, n. 1. Barlow notes that Herman had been Queen Edith's priest: Barlow, *The English Church, 1000–1066*, 114.

46. Goscelin, *Translation of Edith*, c. 22, 90.

47. Goscelin, *Life and Miracles of Kenelm*, c. 26.

48. Goscelin, *Translation of Edith*, cc. 15 and 18; *Life of Wulfsige*, c. 23.

49. For this story, see Goscelin, *Life of Wulfsige*, c. 15.

50. Goscelin, *Translation of Edith*, c. 19; Goscelin, *Life of Wulfsige*, c. 17; Goscelin, *Life and Miracles of Kenelm*, cc. 28–30.

51. Goscelin, *Translation of Edith*, c. 1, 69.

52. Goscelin, *Life and Miracles of Kenelm*, c. 18.

53. Goscelin, *Life of Wulfsige*, c. 10.

54. Love, "The Life of St. Wulfsige," 121 n. 63; see also notes 55, 56, 58, 59, 67 in the same edition.

55. William of Malmesbury ran into similar problems when he attempted to compile histories of dioceses: Barlow notes that William was "often defeated by the lack of records, especially Lives of their saints and abbatial lists": *The English Church, 1000–1066*, 314.

56. Goscelin, *Life and Miracles of Kenelm*, c. 17, 73.

57. Goscelin, *Life of Wulfsige*, c. 15, 112.

58. Goscelin, *Translation of Edith*, cc. 12–14.

59. Goscelin, *Life and Miracles of Kenelm*, cc. 18–26.

60. Goscelin, *Translation of Edith*, cc. 16–18. Most of the Wulfthryth miracles also appear to have been from the 1040s/50s (see cc. 8–11).

61. Goscelin, *Life of Wulfsige*, cc. 16–19, 24.

62. Goscelin, *Life and Miracles of Kenelm*, c. 27, 85.

63. Goscelin, *Translation of Edith*, c. 22.

64. Stories of translations permeate these texts: see Goscelin, *Life and Miracles of Kenelm*, cc. 9–17; *Translation of Edith*, cc. 1 and 2 (for Edith's translation), c. 6 (for Wulfthryth's translation of the relics of Ywi), and *Life of Wulfsige* cc. 12, 13, 17, 18, 21.

65. For the distaff and spindle, see Goscelin, *Life of Wulfsige*, c. 15; for the psalter, *Life and Miracles of Kenelm*, c. 16; for the pallium, *Life of Edith*, c. 27; for the chains, *Translation of Edith*, c. 18; for the staff, *Life of Wulfsige*, c. 11; for the ring, *Translation of Edith*, c. 11; for the gifts and gold to the shrines (from Cnut), *Translation of Edith*, c. 13, and *Life of Wulfsige*, c. 14.

66. Goscelin, *Life of Wulfsige*, c. 15, 112.

67. Goscelin, *Life of Wulfsige*, c. 25, 117.

68. See Lantfred, c. 3, 279, for passing mention of Iudoc's healing miracles.

69. Goscelin, *Translation of Edith*, c. 3, 72.

70. Goscelin, *Life of Wulfsige*, c. 21, 115.

71. Goscelin, *Life of Wulfsige*, c. 25, 117. It is interesting to note, however, that Goscelin does not tell any miracle stories concerning a statue of St. Swithun that had apparently been in the church of Sherborne since the time of bishop Ælfwold (after 1045 to 1062). Some decades later, an anonymous author would include four chapters concerning this statue in an expanded miracle collection for Swithun: see Lapidge, *CSS*, 641–97, cc. 44–46 and 53.

72. Goscelin, *Translation of Edith*, c. 12, 78.

73. Goscelin, *Translation of Edith*, c. 14 and 15.

74. Goscelin, *Translation of Edith*, c. 20, 88.

75. Goscelin, *Translation of Edith*, c. 22, 90–91.

76. Hayward, "Translation-Narratives," 77, 79.

77. Hayward, "Translation-Narratives," 89, 93.

78. Hollis, "St. Edith and the Wilton Community," 276; see also her similar arguments in "Goscelin's Writings," 234.

79. Ridyard, *Royal Saints*, 175.

80. Love, "The Life of St. Wulfsige," 99.

81. For discussion of these manuscripts, see Hollis, "Goscelin's Writings," 236–44.

82. On these manuscripts, see the detailed discussion in Love, *Three Eleventh-Century Lives*, cxxii–cxxxix.

83. Love, *Three Eleventh-Century Lives*, cx.

84. See also WM, *GP*, vol. 1, bk. 5, c. 269, 641–42, for a story of Bishop Osmund seeking out the arm bone of St. Aldhelm, creating a silver casket for it, and using it to cure the illness of his archdeacon named Everard.

85. On Lanfranc's attitude toward English saints, see Cowdrey, *Lanfranc*, 175–84, and Chapter 5.

86. Goscelin, *Life of Edith*, prologue 23.

87. Ibid.

88. Goscelin, *Life of Wulfsige*, 103.

89. Goscelin, *Life of Edith*, prologue 24.

90. Goscelin, *Book of Consolation*, 32–33.

91. Goscelin, *Book of Consolation*, 33.

92. Goscelin, *Life of Wulfsige*, 103; *Life of Edith*, prologue, 24.

93. Reginald's comments on Goscelin are cited and translated by Barlow in his edition of *The Life of King Edward*, 141–42.

94. Goscelin, *Libellus contra inanes*, c. 10, 77–78.

95. WM, *GR*, vol. 1, bk. 4, c. 342, 593.

96. Goscelin, *Life of Edith*, 23.

CHAPTER 5. THEY OUGHT TO BE WRITTEN: OSBERN OF CANTERBURY
AND THE FIRST ENGLISH MIRACLE COLLECTORS

1. OC, *MD*, 129.

2. *LE*, bk. 2, c. 133.

3. On Goscelin's works, see Chapter 4 above. Goscelin wrote so much about St. Augustine that David Townsend terms his work "something of an overkill"; see Townsend, "Omissions, Emissions," 291.

4. Bertrann's *De miraculis sancti Eadmundi* was edited under the name "Hermann the Archdeacon" in *MEdm*, vol. 1, 26–92. For the attribution of the text to Bertrann, see

Gransden, "Composition and Authorship" 39–44; for variants from other manuscripts, see the same article, 45–52. For discussion of the collection, see Cownie, "The Cult of St. Edmund," 178–82, and Yarrow, *Saints and Their Communities*, 24–62.

5. For the posthumous miracles in Faricius's *Vita S. Aldhelmi*, see cc. 14–30. For Winterbottom's recent discovery of a longer manuscript of the *Vita* and further discussion of the text and its author, see Winterbottom, "Faricius of Arezzo's Life of St. Aldhelm," 109–31.

6. This little collection has been edited with its early twelfth-century additions as the *Capitula de Miraculis et Translationibus Sancti Cuthberti*: for the growth of the text, see Rollason, *Symeon of Durham*, lxxv–lxxvi; Aird, "The Making," 1–24; Colgrave, "The Post-Bedan Miracles," 305–32; and Abou-El-Haj, "St. Cuthbert: Post-Conquest Appropriation," 178–79, 194–200.

7. For the miracle stories, see *Passio S. Eadwardi regis et martyris*, 13–16. Fell, the editor, believes the work may have been written by Goscelin, but this attribution is not generally accepted. Michael Lapidge has demonstrated that this text does not share stylistic parallels with Goscelin's early corpus: see Lapidge, *CSS*, 620–21, n.53. Paul Antony Hayward reads the text as a composition of a nun of Shaftesbury that "abounds with structural parallels" with Goscelin's works: Hayward, "Translation-Narratives," 85–86.

8. See Eadmer, *Vita S. Wilfridi*, cc. 149–50. For the dating of the text, see pp. xxix–xxx in Muir and Turner's edition and also Turner and Muir's more recent assessment in *Eadmer of Canterbury: Lives and Miracles*, xxii.

9. The dating of the work is based on a passage in which Osbern states that no one like Lanfranc could be found after his death: see OC, *MD*, c. 20, 151, and the discussion by Rubenstein, "Life and Writings," at 38. See also Budny and Graham, "Dunstan as Hagiographical Subject or Osbern as Author?," at 83–84, where they point out that Osbern refers to an Albert who became a cardinal. Budny and Graham identify this Albert as "the cardinal priest of Santa Sabina in Rome who was cardinal perhaps by the spring of 1091 and certainly by March 1095."

10. One was written in the late tenth century by an Anglo-Saxon in exile in Liège, the other was composed by a monk from Ghent in the early eleventh century: for discussion of these *vitae*, see Thacker, "Cults at Canterbury," 223–24, and Lapidge, "B. and the *Vita S. Dunstani*," 247–59.

11. On the possible Old English *Life*, see Winterbottom and Thomson, *William of Malmesbury: Saints' Lives*, xviii–xxii, xxix.

12. See, for instance, Hayward, "Translation-Narratives," 89–93; Winterbottom and Thomson, *William of Malmesbury: Saint's Lives*, xxxi; Webb, *Pilgrimage in Medieval England*, 16; etc.

13. Rubenstein, "Life and Writings," 28.

14. Love, *Three Eleventh-Century Saints' Lives*, xxxiii–xlviii. On the "cultural assimilation" point, see the wide-ranging discussion of Townsend, "Anglo-Latin Hagiography," 385–433.

15. WM, *GR*, bk. 4, c. 342, 593.

16. OC, *Vita*, c. 2, 70; he repeats this again at *Vita*, c. 46, 128.

17. Gransden, *Historical Writing*, 128.

18. For the letters to Lanfranc, see *S. Anselmi Opera Omnia*, ed. Schmitt, vol. 3, nos. 39 and 66; the letters to prior Henry are nos. 58 and 67. The letters are translated by Walter Fröhlich in *The Letters of Saint Anselm*. Citations and quotations are taken from Fröhlich's translation.

19. *Letters of Saint Anselm*, no. 58, 170; no. 67, 189.

20. Lapidge and Love, "Latin Hagiography," 238: see also Southern, *St. Anselm: A Portrait*, 315, where he speaks of Osbern as a "chief trouble-maker."

21. Rubenstein, "Life and Writings," 30; see OC, *MD*, c. 19, 144–51.

22. *Letters of Saint Anselm* no. 39, 140–41; no. 66, 188.

23. For the date, see Rubenstein, "Life and Writings," 31.

24. Goscelin, *Life of Edith*, prologue, 23; see Chapter 4.

25. See the discussion in Morris and Rumble, "Osbern's account of the translation," 283–315, and Paul Antony Hayward, "Translation-Narratives," 70–73.

26. EC, *Anselm*, c. 30, 53–55. For Lanfranc's treatment of the liturgical calendar at Canterbury, see the contrasting views of Pfaff, "Lanfranc's Supposed Purge," and Heslop, "The Canterbury Calendars."

27. Osbern, *Vita et Translatio S. Elphegi*, 122; translation from Shaw, *Life of Alfege*, 26.

28. Eadmer, *De reliquiis sancti Audoeni*, 367–69.

29. On this dispute, see Sharpe, "Goscelin's St. Augustine and St. Mildreth," 502–16, Sharpe, "Setting of St. Augustine's Translation," 4–5 and Cowdrey, *Lanfranc*, 169–71.

30. Sharpe, "Setting of St. Augustine's Translation," 5.

31. For discussion and editions of these works, see Sharpe, "Goscelin's St. Augustine and St. Mildreth," Rollason, *The Mildrith Legend*, Rollason, "Goscelin of Canterbury's Account of St. Mildrith," and Goscelin, *Libellus contra inanes*.

32. See Sharpe, "Setting of St. Augustine's Translation," 1–13.

33. WM, *GR*, bk. 4, c. 342, 593.

34. On Goscelin's writings for Augustine, see Emms, "The Historical Traditions," 159–68, and R. Gameson and F. Gameson, "From Augustine to Parker," 13–38.

35. OC, *MD*, c. 1, 129.

36. OC, *MD*, c. 1, 129. William of Malmesbury makes a similar pitch for his readers' forbearance before describing present-day miracles of Aldhelm: "the reader . . . will do well to believe no less than he would want to be believed if he spoke or wrote an account of some wonder of his own days": *GP*, bk. 5, c. 273, 653.

37. OC, *MD*, c. 1, 129.

38. OC, *MD*, c. 1, 130.

39. See *Corpus Benedictionum Pontificalium*, Corpus Christianorum, Series Latina, clxii (1971–79), no. 994. See also the discussion in Thacker, "Cults at Canterbury," 235–45, and Ramsay and Sparks, "Cult of St. Dunstan," 311–13. They do not mention Wulfstan of Winchester's comment about hearing about many miracles at Dunstan's tomb: see

Wulfstan of Winchester, *The Life of St. Æthelwold*, c. 14, 26. In Abingdon, writing about the same time (between 992 and 1002), Ælfric celebrated "the miracles which God performs through [Dunstan and Æthelwold]": see Ælfric of Winchester, *Life of St. Swithun*, c. 28, 607. An anonymous early eleventh-century prayer also praises Dunstan as a miracle worker: see *MDun*, 440. Dunstan receives as many mentions in the litanies of the late Anglo-Saxon period as Swithun: see the chart in Blanton, *Signs of Devotion*, 100–101.

40. OC, *Vita*, 128.

41. OC, *MD*, c. 9, 135.

42. OC, *MD*, c. 10, 135.

43. OC, *MD*, c. 11, 136–38.

44. OC, *MD*, c. 12, 138–39.

45. See Chapter 4 for a discussion of Goscelin's collecting methods.

46. Eadmer moved Osbern's story about the cripple cured at Easter to a later point in his collection, so that it would come after the story of the 1067 fire rather than before. Compare Eadmer, *Miracula S Dunstani* c. 15, 177, and OC, *MD*, c. 13, 139–40.

47. OC, *MD*, c. 15.

48. OC, *MD*, c. 16, 142.

49. Turner and Muir write that this "infant son" possibly refers to a son of Harold I rather than of Harold Godwinson (*Eadmer of Canterbury: Lives and Miracles*, 173 n. 16), but I believe the use of the adjective "pagan" to describe the infant probably refers to its lack of baptism.

50. Bertrann, writing c.1100, and William Kellet, writing not much later about the miracles of John of Beverley, would both write about the "greed" of the Normans, but that is as far as their criticism goes: see Bertrann, *De miraculis* c. 24, 58; Kellet, *Miracula Johannis*, c. 2. Later generations, writing at a safe distance, would be more critical about the Norman takeover, but equally circumspect in their telling of contemporary stories. Eadmer of Canterbury's rewriting of the *Miracles of Dunstan* and William of Malmesbury's rewriting of the *Life of Aldhelm* are particularly good examples of this: both insert more tension between Normans and English into their retelling of older stories, and both refuse to get entangled in the telling of many new stories.

51. OC, *MD*, c. 17, 142.

52. Cowdrey, *Lanfranc*, 179; Ridyard, "'Condigna Veneratio,'" 179–206.

53. See especially Rubenstein, "Liturgy Against History," 295, where he terms Lanfranc as being "anti-saint." R. W. Southern portrayed the Christ Church monks as "a lot of old gossips chattering about wonders and miracles and gifts of relics . . . no doubt it was very vexatious to Lanfranc, especially since he doubted whether their so-called saints deserved this title at all": Southern, *St. Anselm: A Portrait*, 313.

54. Thomas, *English and the Normans*, 292–93.

55. This miracle was much talked about: see *The Letters of Lanfranc*, no. 16, 91–92; *Vita Lanfranci*, ed. in *PL* 150, c. 14, cols. 54–55, and the *Vita Gundulfi*, c. 11. For a similar story about a young monk gone mad, see *LE*, bk. 2, c. 129.

56. WM, *GP*, bk. 5, c. 265, 631.

57. WM, *GP*, bk. 5, c. 266, 633.

58. WM, *GP*, bk. 5, c. 267, 633–35.

59. Thomas, *English and the Normans*, 219, 200.

60. On Abbot Walter, see Ridyard, "'Condigna Veneratio,'" 204–5, and the "Acta proborum virorum," in *Chronicon abbatiae de Evesham*, ed. W. D. Macray, RS 29 (London, 1863) 323–25. Dominic's account of Abbot Walter in his *Miracula Ecgwini* is very tame: see c. 88, 102–5. See also the interesting comparative material in Head, "The Genesis of the Ordeal of Relics by Fire."

61. The situation with minor saints was different: for discussion of oral stories and minor saints, see Chapter 6 below.

62. Gransden, "Composition and Authorship," 34.

63. OC, *MD*, c. 20, 152.

64. OC, *MD*, c. 21, 153.

65. OC, *MD*, c. 19, 145.

66. OC, *MD*, c. 19, 147.

67. OC, *MD*, c. 20, 151.

68. OC, *MD*, c. 23.

69. OC, *MD*, c. 24. For a translation of this chapter and discussion, see Chapter 1.

70. For other cases of such prayers and speeches, see OC, *MD*, c. 12, 138–39; c. 15, 140–42; c. 19, 144–51; etc.

71. OC, *MD*, c. 8, 135; c. 9, 135; c. 25, 159.

72. OC, *MD*, c. 26, 160.

73. On the lack of writers at Christ Church in the tenth and eleventh centuries, see Brooks, *The Early History*, 209.

74. For Bertrann's use of written sources, see Gransden, "Composition and Authorship," 22–33.

75. For these manuscripts, see *MDun*, xlii–xlvii.

76. Sharpe, "Setting of St. Augustine's Translation," 4.

77. See Gransden, "Composition and Authorship," 43–44.

78. On Eadmer and Faricius, see *LMODO*, xxiv. Hayward reads one of Eadmer's texts as directly responding to Goscelin: see Hayward, "An Absent Father," 201–18.

CHAPTER 6. OBVIOUS MATERIAL FOR WRITING:
EADMER OF CANTERBURY AND THE MIRACLE COLLECTING BOOM

1. Eadmer, *Vita S. Dunstani*, prologue, 47. The citations and translations of Eadmer's works for Dunstan are taken from Turner and Muir's edition; citations and translations from Eadmer's works for Anselm from Southern's edition; translations of Eadmer's writings on Ouen and Bregwine are my own.

2. See especially the changes Eadmer made to the story of Lanfranc's chaplain's healing: compare OC, *MD*, c. 21, 153, with Eadmer, *Miracula S. Dunstani*, c. 22, 195.

3. Compare OC, *MD*, c. II, 136–38, and Eadmer, *Miracula S. Dunstani*, c. II, 168–69.

4. OC, *MD*, cc. 22, 24, 25.

5. Eadmer, *Miracula S. Dunstani*, c. 19, 189. Osbern was the best musician of his age.

6. For Eadmer's life and career, see Turner and Muir, *LMODO*, xii–xxxv; Southern, *Saint Anselm and His Biographer*, 274–313; and Southern, *Portrait in a Landscape*, 404–36. For recent work, on Eadmer, see Rubenstein, "Liturgy Against History," Hayward, "An Absent Father," 201–18.

7. For these dates, see *LMODO*, xxxv–xxxvi, lxvii–lxix.

8. For a listing of Eadmer's oeuvre, see Sharpe, *Handlist of Latin Writers*, 104–5.

9. Eadmer, *Miracula S. Anselmi*, 170.

10. See Eadmer's prominent place in Gransden's survey of "Anglo-Norman Sacred Biography and Local History" in *Historical Writing in England c.550–c.1307*, 105–35.

11. Whatley, *The Saint of London*, ix.

12. For a survey of the literary production of the period, see Rigg, *A History of Anglo-Latin Literature 1066–1422*, 9–64.

13. Eadmer, *Vita S. Dunstani*, 47–49.

14. On the growing wealth and size of established English monasteries in this period, see Cownie, *Religious Patronage*.

15. Gameson, *Manuscripts of Early Norman England*, 5. For the growth of libraries after the Norman Conquest, see also Rodney Thomson's useful essay, "The Norman Conquest and English Libraries," 27–40.

16. See Gameson, *Manuscripts of Early Norman England*, esp. 20–39; for this work specifically at Canterbury, see Webber, "Script and Manuscript Production," 145–58.

17. This interesting collection is printed in full for the first time in the monumental volume by Michael Lapidge: see *CSS*, 641–97. The same anonymous author also wrote the first *vita* for Swithun, also edited by Lapidge in the same volume, 611–40.

18. This revision and addition is found in a beautifully illuminated manuscript, New York, Pierpont Morgan Library MS 736, dated to before 1124. The text has not been edited. It was later reworked as part of a compilation of Edmund's miracles made by a monk of Bury in the late twelfth century: this later revision, *Opus de miraculis S Edmundi*, is edited under the name "Samson of Bury," in *MEdm*, vol. 1, 107–208. For discussion of the Pierpont text and manuscript, see Thomson, "Two Versions," 383–408; Gransden, *A History of the Abbey of Bury*, 123–24; and Hahn, "*Peregrinatio et natio*: The Illustrated Life of Edmund," 119–39. For illuminated hagiographic manuscripts in this period, with some discussion of the Pierpont manuscript, see Abou-El-Haj, *The Medieval Cult of Saints*.

19. On these additions, edited as part of the *Capitula de Miraculis et Translationibus Sancti Cuthberti*, see Rollason, *Symeon of Durham*, lxxv–lxxvi; Aird, "The Making," and Abou-El-Haj, "St. Cuthbert: The Post-Conquest Appropriation," 177–206.

20. *Miracula S. Ætheldrethe*, 99.

21. See Love, *Goscelin of St.-Bertin*, lxi–lxxi.

22. See the discussion in Thompson and Stevens, "Gregory of Ely's Verse Life," 333–90.

23. Jennifer Paxton has noted that a set of ten miracle narratives (*LE*, bk. 2, cc. 27–36) from the time of bishop Hervey (1108–31) "has the look of an independent work that has been incorporated into the text": Paxton, "The Purpose of the *Liber Eliensis*," 22. Other miracle narratives that may date to a similar time period are found in bk. 2, cc. 143–48, bk. 3, cc. 42–43, and also possibly bk. 3, cc. 57–61. For discussion of the texts from Ely in this period, see the introductory materials in Love, *Goscelin of St.-Bertin*, and the excellent overall discussion by Keynes, "Ely Abbey," 3–58.

24. William of Malmesbury's reworking of Faricius's text is found in his *Gesta Pontificum Anglorum*, bk. 5, cc. 187–278, 498–663.

25. WM, *GP*, bk. 5, prologue, 499–501. William interweaves stories from Faricius's *Vita Aldhelmi* with numerous documents and a few stories he himself knew. Like Eadmer, William cut out the most personal of Faricius's stories: the story of Faricius's own vision of Aldhelm, for example, is nowhere to be found in his text.

26. Interestingly, none of Goscelin of St.-Bertin's many collections were ever significantly revised or expanded. Monks of St. Augustine's, for instance, would not address Augustine's history themselves until the late thirteenth and early fourteenth centuries, at which point English Benedictine monks as a body no longer felt it necessary to rewrite *vitae* or collect miracle stories: see Richard and Fiona Gameson, "From Augustine to Parker," 28.

27. For the date of Eadmer's *Miracula S. Oswaldi*, see *LMODO*, cvi–cvii.

28. Eadmer, *Miracula S. Oswaldi*, c. 9, 319.

29. Thomas of Marlborough copied Dominic of Evesham's *Miracula S. Ecgwini* wholesale into his thirteenth-century chronicle. Dominic's "first book" (the *vita*) is edited by Michael Lapidge, "Vita S. Ecgwini episcopi et confessoris" in *AB* 96 (1978): 65–104. These texts have received very little study.

30. Dominic, *Miracula S. Ecgwini*, prologue 77.

31. For the dating of the text, see the discussion in Wilson, *Life and After-life*, 9–10. The citation is taken from Wilson's translation of Kellet's *Miracula S. Johannis*, 157.

32. See Geoffrey of Burton, *Life and Miracles*, c. 43, 181; for the dating of the text, see Bartlett's edition, xi, n. 1.

33. Southern, "The Place of England," 172. Scholars who do not share Southern's arguments about Norman skepticism still think that writings were required for cults to function properly: see, for example, Susan Ridyard's conclusion to her ground-breaking article, "*Condigna Veneratio*," 205–6: "the inspiration for post-Conquest hagiography lay . . . with Norman churchmen who perceived the usefulness of the English saints and who realised that those saints could be successfully utilised only if their history was fully documented and their function effectively publicised." For similar statements, see Lapidge and Love, "Latin Hagiography," 225 and Webb, *Pilgrimage in Medieval England*, 16. Monika Otter writes that "the need for such texts was greatly stimulated by the need to reassert rights and privileges, and generally to reestablish historical continuity, after the disruption

caused by the Norman Conquest," but goes on to say that "there was also a more general desire to fill in the historiographical gaps, to consolidate in writing what was previously oral or sparsely documented local traditions": *Inventiones*, 22.

34. Clanchy, *From Memory to Written Record*, 146–49. See also van Houts, *Memory and Gender*, 144: "Descriptions of ways in which knowledge about the past were preserved should be considered as genuine attempts to salvage what was thought to be necessary information for posterity."

35. *MEdm*, vol. 1, c. 10, 181.

36. For a discussion of the frustration of twelfth-century historians and hagiographers with their predecessors, see Campbell, "Some Twelfth-Century Views of the Anglo-Saxon Past," 209–28, and Gransden, "Traditionalism and Continuity," 74–79. It is especially with this desire to preserve stories for posterity that the work of historians and hagiographers merged in this period. For discussion of the blending of medieval hagiographical and historical aims, see Lifshitz, "Beyond Positivism and Genre."

37. Gransden, *History of the Abbey*, 126. For Osbert's text, see the *Opus de Miraculis S. Edmundi*, a late twelfth-century compilation edited in *MEdm*, vol. 1, 107–208. The section derived from Osbert's collection is cc. 8–20, 178–207. On Osbert himself, see Robinson, "A Sketch of Osbert's Career."

38. See *MEdm*, vol. 1, c. 8, 179, c. 15, 192.

39. Bloch's edition of Osbert's *Vita S. Edwardi* is based on a manuscript that includes just the first six chapters devoted to posthumous miracles and events (edited as cc. 25–30, 112–23). Aelred of Rievaulx later rewrote Osbert's text and included the five additional stories: see Aelred of Rievaulx, *Vita S. Edwardi regis*, *PL* 195, cols. 737–90. We are much in need of fresh research into the works of Osbert. For an interesting article on Osbert's use of an Old English source, see Peter Jackson, "Osbert of Clare and the *Vision of Leofric*."

40. For the story of this bid, see Scholtz, "The Canonization," 41–49, and Bozoky, "The Sanctity and Canonisation."

41. Cited in Scholtz, "The Canonization," 47.

42. On letter writing in this period, see Van Engen, "Letters, Schools and Written Culture," 97–132, and Giles Constable, *Letters and Letter-Collections*, Typologie des Sources du Moyen Age Occidental 17 (Turnhout, 1976).

43. On this text and cult, see Watkins, "The Cult of Earl Waltheof," 95–11. See also Lapidge and Love, "Latin Hagiography," 248–49, where they note that a thirteenth-century abbot referred to a *Libellus conscriptus de miraculis eius* about Waltheof at Crowland.

44. For discussion of this text, see Winterbottom and Thomson, *William of Malmesbury: Saints' Lives*, xiii–xvii. For an overview of the development of Wulfstan's cult, see Mason, *St. Wulfstan*, 254–85.

45. See William of Malmesbury, *Vita Wulfstani*, esp. bk. 3, c. 29, 153–54.

46. The text of this letter is edited in *MDun*, 412–23, and is translated by Sharpe, "Eadmer's Letter." The citation here is taken from Sharpe, 214. On the Glastonbury

claims to Dunstan, see Sharpe's introduction to his translation and Gransden, "Growth of the Glastonbury Traditions."

47. See Winterbottom and Thomson, *William of Malmesbury: Saints' Lives*, xxii.

48. See William of Malmesbury, *Vita Dunstani*, bk. 2, c. 34, 299, and the editors' note, xxiii: "he never wrote that book, of which no trace has been found."

49. In the early twelfth century, an anonymous author wrote a short *passio* for Indract at Glastonbury: this text does include some miracle stories. See Lapidge, "The Cult of St. Indract," 426.

50. Hayward, "Sanctity and Lordship."

51. Lapidge and Love, "Latin Hagiography," 233. Osbert's early twelfth-century *vita* concerning yet another Edburga—the one at Nunnaminster—may also reflect some ongoing controversy between the monks of Pershore and the nuns at Winchester: see the discussion by Ridyard, *Royal Saints*, 36–37, where she terms the text, by Osbert of Clare, "a delicate diplomatic exercise." See also the five entries on Eadburh in Blair, "Handlist of Anglo-Saxon Saints," 525–27.

52. See Love's discussion of the text in *Goscelin of St.-Bertin*, xcix–c. A collection of miracles concerning Wenefred's well at Holywell would be compiled later in the century: see Chapter 7 below.

53. For this text, see William D. Macray, ed., *Chronicon Abbatiae de Evesham*, RS 29 (London, 1863), Appendix I, 313–20. See also the discussion by Lapidge and Love, "Latin Hagiography," 242–43: Dominic's authorship is likely, but not certain.

54. Sharpe, "Eadmer's Letter," 210–11. For interpretations of this passage, see van Houts, "The Flemish Contribution," 117; Hayward, "An Absent Father," 217; and Rubenstein, "Liturgy Against History," at 300.

55. For this collection and a discussion of the identity of its author, see "The *Miracula Inventionis Beate Mylburge Virginis*," ed. Hayward.

56. The first tour was described by Guibert of Nogent soon after 1112, and the second by Hermann of Tournai in the 1140s: see the discussion of these texts in Yarrow, *Saints and Communities*, 63–99.

57. On Anselm of Bury, see Southern, "English Origins," 199–200. Eadmer knew and liked this Anselm: see Thomas, *The English and the Normans*, 217.

58. Southern, "English Origins," 204. For further discussion of Dominic's contribution to the *Miracles*, see Jennings, "The Origins," and Canal, "El libro"; for William of Malmesbury's contribution, see Carter, "The Historical Content," 127–65.

59. For the dating of this text, see the editors' introduction, 19–30. The text exists in two quite different recensions.

60. See especially book ix, "The Miracles of the English," in Henry of Huntingdon, *Historia Anglorum*, 622–97. Henry, worried that his accounts would not be considered truthful, derived most of his material from Bede's *Ecclesiastical History*. For marvels in twelfth-century chronicles, see the discussion of Watkins, *History and the Supernatural*.

61. On Eadmer's personal manuscript, see Southern, *Saint Anselm and His Biographer*, Appendix III, 367–74; Muir and Turner, *Life of Wilfrid by Edmer*, lxiii–lxv; T. Webber, "Script and Manuscript Production," 148–50.

62. See Eadmer, *Vita Bregowini*, c. 14, 146–47.

63. Eadmer, *Vita Bregowini*, c. 5, 141.

64. Eadmer, *Vita Bregowini*, cc. 12 and 13.

65. Eadmer, *Vita Bregowini*, c. 13, 145: "Et quidem ut multi affirmant, hunc inter se morem Saxones praestantius habent, ut maiores suos dignius honorent, et irreuerentiae subditorum non pareant ne insolescant. Morem igitur suae gentis et mundo exemptus filiis suis studiit bonus pater exhibere, ut eos moneret quae reuerentia se debeant erga maiores suos habere."

66. In a different context, Nicholas Brooks notes that Eadmer's perspective on the Anglo-Saxon community needs to be treated with caution: see Brooks, *The Early History*, 261.

67. Eadmer, *Vita Bregowini*, c. 11, 144–45.

68. Eadmer, *Vita Bregowini*, c. 15, 147.

69. The text is edited by A. Wilmart in *Revue des sciences religieuses* 15 (1935): 190–91.

70. Pfaff, "Lanfranc's Supposed Purge," 102–3.

71. Rubenstein, "Liturgy Against History," 307.

72. WM, *GP*, bk. 5, c. 265, 631.

73. See Ridyard's discussion of Abbot Paul in "'Condigna Veneratio,'" 189–90.

74. William of Malmesbury was clearly very unhappy with Abbot Warin's "impudence" at Malmesbury, but, as Ridyard notes, "the indignation of contemporaries was perhaps less than the indignation of William": Ridyard, "'Condigna Veneratio,'" 194.

75. For Eadmer's mention of Dunstan's "daily" miracles, see his *Vita S. Dunstani*, c. 67, 159, and *Miracula S. Dunstani*, c. 29, 209–10.

76. See Eadmer's *Vita S. Wilfridi* and *Vita S. Odonis*.

77. EC, *Anselm*, c. 30, 50–54.

78. In his account of Lanfranc's translation of Dunstan's relics, Osbern does not bother to mention that Lanfranc translated Ælfheah too: see OC, *MD*, c. 17, 142–43. In his rewriting of the text Eadmer makes sure his readers know that "the most precious bodies of the bishops of Christ, Dunstan *and Ælfheah*, were elevated" (my emphasis). See Eadmer, *Miracula S. Dunstani*, 16, 177–79.

79. EC, *Anselm*, c. 30, 50 and 52. Eadmer's report of this conversation should be treated very cautiously. We do not know if Eadmer was present for it. Even if he were, he wrote this passage at a distance of some twenty-five years from the conversation.

80. See Eadmer of Canterbury, *De reliquiis sancti Audoeni*. Richard Sharpe notes that "fragments of *Miracula* [concerning Ouen] printed by A. Wilmart in *AB* 51 (1933): 288–92 and N. R. Ker, *AB* 64 (1946): 51–53, appear not to be by Eadmer": *A Handlist of the Latin Writers*, 104.

81. Eadmer, *De reliquiis sancti Audoeni*, 369.

82. Eadmer, *De reliquiis sancti Audoeni*, 362.

83. See Gervase, vol. 1, 294.

84. EC, *Anselm*, c. 67, 145.

85. For these stages of composition, see Eadmer, *Anselm*, ix–xxiii.

86. Eadmer, *Miracula S. Anselmi*, prologue, 152.

87. Eadmer, *Miracula S. Anselmi*, 154: the incipit of the work is "Incipit Quaedam Parva Descriptio Miraculorum Gloriosi Patris Anselmi Cantuariensis." I refer to the text as "Miracula S. Anselmi" for convenience.

88. Eadmer, *Miracula S. Anselmi*, 163–65.

89. Eadmer, *Miracula S. Anselmi*, 154–56, 158–60, 163–65.

90. Eadmer, *Miracula S. Anselmi*, 158–60.

91. Eadmer, *Miracula S. Anselmi*, 165.

92. See Eadmer, *Miracula S. Dunstani*, c. 29, 209–10. A passage in Eadmer's *Miracula S. Oswaldi* suggests that Eadmer thought the populace should not have easy access to relics: see c. 4, 301: "[Ealdwulf] recognized that there was easy access to [Oswald]—more than was just" and so determined "to raise up the limbs of this preeminent father from the earth and to set them down in a place free of the bustle of secular persons and removed from access by the irreverent."

93. Eadmer, *Miracula S. Anselmi*, 170.

94. Eadmer, *Miracula S. Anselmi*, 171.

95. For the manuscripts of Osbern's *vita* and miracles, see *MDun*, xlii–xlvii; for the manuscripts of Eadmer's miracle collection for Anselm, which is found in only three manuscripts aside from CCCC 371, see Southern, *Life of St. Anselm*, xxii–xxiv; for his miracles of Dunstan, see *LMODO*, lxxvii–lxxxvii.

96. See John of Salisbury, *Vita S. Anselmi*, and the discussion in Chapter 7.

97. Of the ten manuscripts preserving the *Vita S. Swithuni* written by an anonymous monk c.1100, only five include the same author's *Miracula S. Swithuni*: see Lapidge, *CSS*, 643. Geoffrey of Burton's *Life and Miracles of St. Modwenna* survives in two manuscripts. One copyist included the posthumous miracle stories composed by Geoffrey, whereas the other skipped nearly all of them: see Bartlett's discussion in his edition, xl–xlii. The same is true for Faricius of Arezzo's *Vita S. Aldhelmi*: see Winterbottom, "Faricius of Arezzo's Life of St. Aldhelm," 109–31. Such examples could be multiplied.

CHAPTER 7. WHAT THE PEOPLE BRING: MIRACLE COLLECTING IN THE MID- TO LATE TWELFTH CENTURY

1. WC, *MT* 5.30, 395.

2. Sally Crumplin discusses the "modernization" of Cuthbert's miracles, noting that "by the later twelfth century, a formal, legally tinged pattern for the proclamation and depiction of saints was developing": "Modernizing St. Cuthbert," 184.

3. Watkins, *History and the Supernatural*, discusses the new interest in explaining causes and interpreting *signa* in later twelfth-century English chronicles: see esp. 25–38 and 47–55. Benedict of Peterborough's interest in the "causes" of mysteriously breaking pyxes and appearing and disappearing blood especially bears comparison to Watkins's discussion of the sensibility of these chroniclers: see BP, *MT* 1.20, 2.19, 3.22.

4. For the proliferation of new foundations and the increasing complexity of the

English monastic landscape in the later twelfth century, see Burton, *Monastic and Religious Orders*, esp. 63–84.

5. Social historians have found these texts especially interesting: see Finucane, *Miracles and Pilgrims*, Gordon, "Child Health," and Theilmann, "English Peasants." The growing number of healing miracles in later twelfth century collections has been noted by many historians. Benedicta Ward, for instance, has argued for a comprehensive change in the twelfth century as "acts of power for protection and vengeance . . . were replaced by miracles of mercy and cures": *Miracles and the Medieval Mind*, 215. See also the comments of Murray, "Confession Before 1215," 62: "In dark age culture a shift, broadly dateable to the eleventh century, has been noticed from supernatural to natural means for guarding public order. Miracles worked by relics, for instance, hitherto frequently designed to defend monastic property, come to leave such 'dirty work' to secular courts, freeing themselves for a humanitarian function." In my view, what underlies these changes is the collectors' shift away from their own stories to those of the laity.

6. For recent work on lay-religious associations in this period, see Brian Noell, "Expectation and Unrest Among Cistercian Lay Brothers," *Journal of Medieval History* 32 (2006): 253–74; Clark, "Monastic Confraternity"; Jochen G. Schenk, "Forms of Lay Association with the Order of the Temple," *Journal of Medieval History* 32 (2008): 79–103; Postles, "Religious Houses and the Laity," Vincent, "Some Pardoners' Tales," and Payer, *Sex and the New Medieval Literature of Confession*.

7. See Constable, *Reformation*, esp. 296–328. Julie Kerr notes that in the twelfth century, English Benedictine "communities certainly felt that they were now more greatly burdened by guests than their predecessors": Kerr, *Monastic Hospitality*, 5. On the building of parish churches in England, see Blair, "Introduction," and the other essays in *Minsters and Parish Churches: The Local Church in Transition, 950–1200*. Some stories in the collections of the period suggest that people were being more insistent about access to saints' relics: see, e.g., Arcoid, *Miracula S. Erkenwaldi*, c. 14, and BP, *MT* 2.6. For a provocative study of these twelfth-century changes, see Brown, "Society and the Supernatural."

8. For the dating and authorship of this text, see Whatley's edition, *The Saint of London*, 36–40.

9. WM, *GP*, bk. 2, c. 73, 228.

10. Arcoid, *Miracula S. Erkenwaldi*, prologue, 103.

11. Arcoid, *Miracula S. Erkenwaldi*, c. 12, 151. The prologue to the collection is also addressed to Arcoid's "most dear brothers" [*fratres karissimi*]. Only one of the stories of recent vintage is directly related to the personal experience of a canon of St. Paul's, and that story, about a feverish canon being healed, is tacked on to a longer translation account: see c. 14.

12. Arcoid, *Miracula S. Erkenwaldi*, c. 6, 135.

13. Arcoid, *Miracula Erkenwaldi*, c. 2, 113. The speaker is later punished, but Arcoid gives him two paragraphs of such complaints.

14. Duffy, "St. Erkenwald," 151–52. Duffy's sense that Arcoid's collection is "unmatched" for its number of vengeance stories is mistaken, though Arcoid certainly was

alert to such stories. A good point of comparison is Geoffrey of Burton's collection for Modwenna, written just a decade or two earlier. Geoffrey was also fascinated with miracles of "anger": see *Life and Miracles*, c. 47, 198, and c. 50, 208. The compiler of the *Liber Eliensis* was also very attentive to punishments: see the remarkable listing of punishments suffered by people the compiler knew, *LE*, bk. 3, c. 138.

15. For these stories, see Arcoid, *Miracula Erkenwaldi*, cc. 2, 6, 10, 12, 17.

16. For a recent study of the "vengeance scripts" of eleventh-century monastic stories, see White, "Garsinde v. Sainte Foy," 169–81. A contrast is sometimes drawn between the "vengeful" saints of early medieval collections and the "merciful" saints of the later ones, but vengeance miracles of some sort are found in almost every medieval miracle collection, early or late. What changes over time is the typical proportion of vengeance to healing stories, and, most interestingly, the subjects and sources of the vengeance stories. For punishment stories involving Jews, a new feature of these later twelfth-century collections, see Philip of Oxford, *Miracula S. Frideswidae*, c. 39, and BP, *MT* 2.20.

17. For the dating of this text and further analysis, see "Miracles of St. Ithamar," and Yarrow, *Saints and Communities*, 100–121.

18. "Miracles of St. Ithamar," cc. 10, 15, and 16.

19. "Miracles of St. Ithamar," c. 11, 434–35.

20. For analysis of such stories, see Alexander, *Saints and Animals*.

21. "Miracles of St. Ithamar," c. 11, 434.

22. For these stories, see TM, *MW*, bk. 3, cc. 20–21, bk. 3, c. 29, and bk. 6, c. 19; *Alia Miracula II*, c. 9; *Book of the Foundation*, bk. 2, cc. 5, 6, 25; WC, *MT* 3.24, 3.58, 4.30, 4.47–49, 5.19–26, 6.60–61, 6.66–67, 6.109–10, 6.147–48, and 6.156–58; and *Godric*, cc. 589–90.

23. Briony Aitchison discusses some twelfth-century texts along with later medieval examples in "The Miraculous Cures of Animals in Late Medieval England." For discussion of the animal miracles in the Farne collection, which have a rather different tenor, see Alexander, *Saints and Animals*, 132–68.

24. On these texts, see Wilson, *Life and After-Life*, 72–81, 177–201. For the animal miracle, see *Alia Miracula II*, c. 9.

25. Wilson, *Life and After-Life*, 12.

26. Even Goscelin's *Translation of Edith*, despite being based on stories told by the nuns at Wilton, has as many stories about men as about women.

27. For examples of such extremely short accounts of women's miracles, see *Godric*, cc. 415–13; Philip of Oxford, *Miracula S. Frideswidae*, cc. 52–55; *Miracles of Saint Æbbe*, cc. 15–16 and c. 33.

28. On the proportions of male to female stories in the collections for Godric and Frideswide, see Finucane, *Miracles and Pilgrims*, 126–29; for Æbbe, see *Miracles of Saint Æbbe*, xxiii–iv. The twelfth century saw a spike in foundations of nunneries in England and closer relationships between monks and canons and religious women: of the growing literature on this topic, see especially Thompson, *Women Religious*, Elkins, *Holy Women*, Bruce L. Venarde, *Women's Monasticism and Medieval Society: Nunneries in France and*

England, 890–1215 (Ithaca, N.Y., 1997), 76–88, and the essays in Samuel Fanous and Henrietta Leyser, eds., *Christina of Markyate: A Twelfth-Century Holy Woman* (New York, 2005).

29. William Kellet, for example, told a long story about a lecherous schoolmaster: see *Miracula S. Johannis*, c. 8.

30. See WC, *MT* 3.9; Philip of Oxford, *Miracula S. Frideswidae*, c. 46. Henry Mayr-Harting treats some of these kind of stories, though not this one, in his article about Frideswide: "Functions of a Twelfth-Century Shrine," esp. 198–205. For lengthy stories about women's visions of a type not seen in earlier collections, see *LE*, bk. 3, c. 60; *Book of the Foundation*, bk. 2, c. 12; "Miracles of the Hand of St. James," c. 8; *Miracles of Saint Æbbe*, c. 7; and WC, *MT* 1.50 (Robertson, 2.36).

31. For pregnancy stories in Philip of Oxford's *Miracula S. Frideswidae*, for instance, see cc. 36, 38, and 41.

32. For discussion and an edition of this text, see "The Lives of St. Wenefred."

33. Ed. in *AASS*, Nov. 1, 691–708. For discussion of this text, see Winward's discussion in "Lives of St. Wenefred," 114–18, and Catherine Hamaker's essay in *Two Mediaeval Lives of Saint Winefride*, trans. by Ronald Pepin and Hugh Feiss (Toronto, 2000), 117–26.

34. *Vita S. Wenefrede*, trans. Ronald Pepin and Hugh Feiss, in *Two Mediaeval Lives of Saint Winefride*, "The Second Life," c. 25, 110–11.

35. "The Second Life," c. 27, 112.

36. See BP, *MT* 4.64 and 4.94, among many other examples. Philip of Oxford also concludes his collection with the story of a resurrection: see *Miracula S. Frideswidae*, c. 110. On resurrection stories in general, see Finucane, *Miracles and Pilgrims*, 73–76 (he notes that "those revived were often infants or children"); and his study *The Rescue of the Innocents*.

37. See, for example, WC, *MT* 4.49, 360–62.

38. "The Second Life," c. 27, 112.

39. In an influential article, Gavin Langmuir argued that Thomas of Monmouth was the inventor of the libelous ritual murder narrative that would recur for centuries and cause untold misery: see his "Thomas of Monmouth: Detector of Ritual Murder." John M. McCulloh, however, has recently demonstrated that "[Thomas of Monmouth's] text remained virtually unknown outside of Norwich, and it is better seen as a manifestation of the ritual murder libel than as the source of the tradition": McCulloch, "Jewish Ritual Murder," 740.

40. For the dating of the collection, see McCulloh, "Jewish Ritual Murder," 706–9. The whole of the seventh book is sometimes dated to the 1170s because its last chapter is dated to 1172, but the last two chapters are clearly later additions to a text that was completed in the 1150s.

41. The miracles are discussed by Ward, *Miracles and the Medieval Mind*, 68–76, and Yarrow, *Saints and Their Communities*, 122–68. Yarrow provides a map of the Norwich cathedral estates and the origin of the pilgrims at 168.

42. TM, *MW* bk. 4, c. 9, 175.

43. See Finucane, *Miracles and Pilgrims*, 118–21.

44. TM, *MW*, bk. 2, c. 1, 58.

45. TM, *MW*, bk. 2, c. 2, 65.

46. The manuscript is Cambridge, Trinity College Add. MS 3037: see McCulloch, "Jewish Ritual Murder," 709–17, for his conclusion that Thomas's work was little known.

47. TM, *MW*, bk. 2, c. 2, 65. See also his declaration not to allow William's miracles to "pass away in oblivion": prologue, 3. For similar laments that earlier miracles were not preserved, see *Alia Miracula I*, prologue 177; Philip of Oxford, *Miracula S. Frideswidae*, c. 4; *Book of the Foundation*, prologue; "Miracles of the Hand of St. James," prologue, 6; *The Waltham Chronicle*, c. 24, 65; and Reginald of Durham, *Libellus*, c. 2, 4.

48. Another text that was written in this region in the 1150s is an anonymous *Translation and Miracles of Guthlac*, a text that remains unpublished in part. The author focused on telling the story of Guthlac's translation in 1136 and its accompanying miracles. The text is partially edited in *AASS*, April 2, 54–60: see the discussion by Lapidge and Love, "Latin Hagiography," 249.

49. TM, *MW*, bk. 7, prologue, 262.

50. See BP, *MT* 4.1; WC, *MT* 6.1; *LE*, bk. 3, c. 58; Philip of Oxford, *Miracula S. Frideswidae* c. 99, 586; and *Book of the Foundation*, bk. 2, c. 27.

51. See Clanchy, *From Memory to Written Record*, 60, 102.

52. See Duggan, ed., *The Correspondence of Thomas Becket*, lxviii.

53. Reginald's *Libellus* for Cuthbert is discussed by briefly by Ward, *Miracles and the Medieval Mind*, 62–66. The most extensive studies of the text are by Tudor, "The Cult of St. Cuthbert," and Crumplin, "Modernizing St. Cuthbert."

54. Reginald, *Libellus*, c. 2, 4.

55. For discussion of these stages, see Tudor, "Cult of St. Cuthbert," 448–49. For Crumplin's suggestion for a different split between the first and second stages, "Modernizing St. Cuthbert," 180, n. 6. For an interesting analysis of Reginald's organization of his collection by location, see Crumplin, "Cuthbert the Cross-Border Saint," 119–29.

56. Lapidge and Love, "Latin Hagiography," 262.

57. Crumplin, "Modernizing St. Cuthbert," 191. See also the discussion of Marner, *St. Cuthbert*, 31–33.

58. For these manuscripts, see Sally Crumplin, "Rewriting History in the Cult of St Cuthbert from the Ninth to the Twelfth Centuries" (Ph.D. dissertation, University of St. Andrews, 2004), 184.

59. See Tudor, "Cult of St. Cuthbert," 448, n. 8, and 449: "The component of the *Libellus* dervied from literary sources is virtually non-existent."

60. E. O. Blake, the editor of the *Liber Eliensis*, gave the text an extremely wide date range (1131–1174). For the dating of the *Liber*'s composition to the late 1160s and early 1170s, see Keynes, "Ely Abbey," 7–8, and Paxton, "Monks and Bishops," 18.

61. For the miracle narratives, see *LE*, bk. 1, cc. 22–23, 29–31, and 41–49; bk. 2, cc. 129–33, and 143–48; and bk. 3, cc. 27–36, 42–43, 57–61, 93, 116–22, 130–32, 137–38.

62. For Blake's work on the sources, see *LE*, xxxi–xlii. There is much room here for further research.

63. *LE*, bk. 3, cc. 137–38.

64. See *De sanctis ecclesiae Hagustaldensis* and the English translation of Freeland and Dutton, "The Saints of the Church of Hexham and Their Miracles." Aelred's most interesting quasi-hagiographical work is a lengthy letter sent to an unidentified recipient concerning "A Certain Wonderful Miracle." The letter, composed around 1160, tells the story of a Gilbertine nun who became pregnant by a laybrother and then was forced to castrate him by her infuriated fellow nuns. The letter is edited in *PL* 195, cols. 789–96, trans. in *Lives of the Northern Saints*, 109–22, and discussed in depth by Constable, "Aelred of Rievaulx and Nun of Watton," 205–26.

65. The only edition of this text is in *PL* 195, cols. 737–90. For a translation, see Fr. Jerome Bertram, *The Life of Saint Edward*.

66. For this narrative of Edward's canonization, see Scholtz, "The Canonization," and Kemp, "Pope Alexander III," 13–28.

67. See Scholz, "The Canonization," 49–57. It appears that the "book of miracles" Alexander inspected was Osbert's text from the late 1130s: see Scholtz, 49–51.

68. See the discussion of Yohe, "Aelred's Recrafting," and Bequette, "Ælred of Rievaulx's Life of Saint Edward."

69. There has been some misunderstanding on this point because Bloch's edition of Osbert's text was based on a manuscript that did not include the last five chapters.

70. On this canonization attempt, see *The Correspondence of Thomas Becket*, no. 10, and Duggan's entry and references on Anselm in Appendix 1 of the same volume. See also Kemp, *Canonization and Authority*, 83, and Urry, "Saint Anselm and His Cult at Canterbury," 571–93.

71. On this point, see Somerville, *Pope Alexander III and the Council of Tours*, 59–60.

72. *Correspondence*, no. 10, 27–28.

73. In *Sainthood in the Later Middle Ages*, Vauchez terms the twelfth century a period of transition and treats the papal canonization process as originating in the first third of the thirteenth century. For a description of the later canonization process in England, see also Daly, "The Process of Canonization," 125–35.

74. The text is edited in *PL* 199, cols. 1009–40 (posthumous miracles 1035–40); for discussion and an English translation, see Pepin, *Anselm and Becket*, 7–12, 17–72. The text is also discussed by Nadeuz, "Notes on the Significance." On John of Salisbury's relationship with Becket, see Duggan, "John of Salisbury and Thomas Becket."

75. John eliminated two of Eadmer's stories, one concerning the sweet fragrance emanating from Anselm's tomb (Eadmer, *Miracula S. Anselmi*, 168) and the other about man at the point of death who was cured when Anselm died (Eadmer, *Miracula S. Anselmi*, 156–57). He did most of his rearranging of the stories that Eadmer included at the close of the *vita* and beginning of the miracle collection. He inserted the new miracle concerning Elphege near the close of the text between a story of a cure performed by Anselm's belt (Eadmer, *Miracula S. Anselmi*, 165–67) and the fire at Bury St. Edmunds (Eadmer, *Miracula S. Anselmi*, 168–70).

76. Bartlett, "The Hagiography of Angevin England," 40.

77. For new work on the *vitae*, see Staunton, *Thomas Becket and His Biographers*; for liturgies, Slocum, *Liturgies*, and Reames, "Reconstructing and Interpreting a Thirteeth-Century Office." The letter collection is edited by Anne Duggan, *Correspondence*. A. G. Rigg notes that "there are literally hundreds of hymns" concerning Becket, most of them unpublished: see Rigg, *A History of Anglo-Latin Literature*, 82. The best overall survey of the huge mass of literature devoted to Becket over the course of the late medieval period remains Paul Alonzo Brown's 1930 dissertation "The Development of the Legend of Thomas Becket."

78. On these stories, see Webb, *Pilgrimage in Medieval England*, 53–58; Ward, *Miracles and the Medieval Mind*, 105–9; Bartlett, "Hagiography of Angevin England," 40–41; *The Miracles of Saint Aebbe*, 36–37, 66–67; and Hayward, "Sanctity and Lordship." 140. The Canterbury pilgrimage is also mentioned in the miracle collection for Bega's bracelet at St. Bee's in Cumbria: *Register of the Priory of St. Bees*, 518. For a reference to a miracle mentioning Becket in an early thirteenth-century collection compiled at Chartres, see Hayes, *Body and Sacred Place*, 84.

79. See the original miracle stories at the end of the anonymous *vita* edited in *MTB*, vol. 2, 286–88 and at the close of another anonymous *passio* edited in *MTB*, vol. 4, 196–200. A thirteenth-century manuscript now in Vienna presents a short but wholly original account of what the writer terms Becket's "first six" miracles: see Vienna, Österreichische Nationalbibliothek Codex Vindobonensis Palatinus 984, ff. 79b–80a.

80. The "Quaedam miracula" writer relates some of stories found in the first two books of Benedict of Peterborough's collection, but the text is clearly not sourced from Benedict. Compare QM, c. 1, the mute priest from London, with BP, *MT* 1.12; QM, c. 3, germinating fruit stones, with BP, *MT* 2.10; QM, c. 4, the mute man cured on Easter, with BP, *MT* 2.1; QM, c. 5, the son of the servant of Canterbury, with BP, *MT* 2.2; and QM, c. 11, a story about a madman, with BP, *MT* 2.13. The anonymous author also tells stories that are not found in Benedict's collection at all: he states that he saw a blind man in Canterbury cured by a piece of cloth stained with Becket's blood, and focuses especially on the healing of a knight with leprosy named Walter Enicurt.

81. The edition of QM in the *Analecta Bollandiana* was made from from Douai, Bibl. de la Ville MS 315, ff. 193r–193v. The same text or extracts from it are also to be found in London, British Library Add. MS 10,050, f.115v; Paris, Bibl. Nationale MS lat. 12607; Dijon, Bibl. Mun. MS 646 (386), ff. 272–74; Paris, Bibl. Nationale MS lat. 3088, f. 126v; and Olmütz, Vědecká knihovna, MS II 159, 180r–182r. This text was also used as a part of breviaries from Reims and Lisieux: see Meaux, Bibl. mun MS 5; Soissons, Bibl. mun. MS 105–6 and Caen, Bibl. mun. MS In 4019. I am very grateful to Sherry Reames for these breviary references and to Daniel Hobbins for bringing my attention to the Olmütz manuscript.

82. Benedict copied part of Peter of Celle's letter into his collection, so such a text was circulating before he completed his text: see BP, *MT* 4.87, 252, and *Letters of Peter of Celle*, no. 142, 522–25.

83. For a listing of these stories, see Orme, "A Reconstruction of Robert," 397–98.

The saga—likely composed in the thirteenth century, though the first surviving manuscript is from the fourteenth—is edited as *Thómas Saga Erkibyskups*. On this text, see Antonsson, "Two Twelfth-Century Martyrs," 41–44.

84. The antiquarian Thomas Stapleton selected seventeen stories out of the sixty-seven in the collection and printed them in an appendix to his *Tres Thomae*; Charles Du Canda published a summary (in French) of all the stories. Unfortunately, the manuscript they used has now disappeared. Stapleton's selections were reprinted and are most easily accesible in *Anecdota Bedae*, 137–64; for the summary, see Charles Du Canda, *La vie de S. Thomas Archevesque de Cantorbie* (St. Omer, 1615), 223–76. On Stapleton's *Tres Thomae*, with brief discussion of the importance of Becket's miracles to Stapleton, see Sheils, "Polemic as Piety," 79–80. The fullest discussion of the Dommartin collection is by Corblet, *Hagiographie*, vol. 4, 628–38.

85. I examine the dating of Benedict's and William's collections and the chronology of Becket's canonization and in detail in Chapter 8.

86. BP, *MT* 1.9, 39–40.

87. BP, *MT* 3.11, 126.

88. WFS, 151.

89. WFS, 151: "Sed de miraculis ejus in Anglia, sacerdotum et bonorum virorum testimonio declaratis, et in capitulo Cantuariensis ecclesiae publice recitatis, magnus codex conscriptus exstat, praeter alia quae longe lateque in Gallia, in Hibernia, et ubique terrarum operatus est sanctus Thomas, quibus memoriae commendandis defuit qui scribere." This passage has been taken as evidence that ordinary pilgrims heard readings from Benedict's collection before touring the rest of Canterbury cathedral: Caviness, citing E. Walberg, mentions such readings "to pilgrims" briefly (*Early Stained Glass*, 143–44); the idea is especially taken up by Harris, "Pilgrimage, Performance." However, FitzStephen certainly does not suggest that groups of pilgrims were being ushered into the monks' chapterhouse, nor does any other medieval writer. This interpretation overlooks the problem of the collections existing only in the Latin in which they were composed.

90. See WC, *MT*, prologue, 138.

91. In the *Liber Eliensis*, a knight healed by Æthelthryth arrived at Ely, and then "was led, after his prayers, into chapter, and in the presence of us all related the sequence of events, received membership of the brotherhood, and went away rejoicing": *LE*, bk. 3, c. 42 (translation from Fairweather, *Liber Eliensis*, 342). At Reading, a sheriff "went into the chapter house and told how he had been healed, and his request that he might be received into confraternity with the convent was granted": "The Miracles of the Hand of St. James," c. 1, 7. A reference to a layman telling his miracle in the chapterhouse is found in the *Book of the Foundation*, bk. 2, c. 16, and Osbert of Clare also refers to a cleric telling a miracle to the senior Bury monks "in chapter": *MEdm*, vol. 1, 195–96. Monks and canons generally reserved their chapterhouses for themselves, as is clear from Thomas of Monmouth's description of why the relics of William were eventually moved out of the Norwich chapterhouse into the church proper: "the monks who abode in the cloister could no longer put up with the daily pressure of so great a multitude. For how could

their peace help being disturbed when every day a large number of men and women passed before them?": TM, *WT*, bk. 5, c. 1, 186.

92. See *The Miracles of Saint James*, xxxiv, and Díaz y Díaz, Piñero and Trigo, *El Códice Calixtino*, 77, 134–35.

93. On these manuscripts, see Duggan, "Lorvão," 57–58, 60, and "Santa Cruz," 36–37.

94. J. C. Robertson edited and printed this letter using the text from Brussels, Bibl. Royale, MS IV.600: see *MTB*, vol. 2, xlix. The other manuscript with Odo's letter is Charleville, Bibl. de la Ville, MS 222. The "better book" that was lost is often thought to have been a copy of William's collection. Robertson believed this to be so, and he has been followed by Ward, *Miracles and the Medieval Mind*, 93 and Bull, "Criticism of Henry II's Expedition to Ireland," 113. However, Odo clearly meant a more carefully written, larger, or otherwise more impressive copy of Benedict's collection: see Duggan, "Aspects," 7–9 and "Lorvão," 57 n. 41.

95. See Duggan, "Lorvão," 57–58.

96. Duggan's work on the Portuguese manuscripts of Benedict's collection also illuminates the ways in which one copy could be circulated and recopied in a region: see Duggan's latest assessment in "Santa Cruz," 44–46.

97. The Lansdowne Anonymous, 146.

98. For Duggan's discussion and listing of the complete copies of Benedict's collection, see Duggan, "Lorvão," 60–62, and her updated list in "Santa Cruz," 30–38. I have not included two short fragments on Appendix 1 (Rome, Vatican MS lat. 1196, a single folio with material from Benedict's collection, and Carpentras, Bibl. municipale, MS 116, with seven folios with material from William's collection).

99. The longest of these is Winchester College MS 4, the basis for Robertson's edition. For a description of this manuscript see N. R. Ker and A. J. Piper, *Medieval Manuscripts in British Libraries* vol 4, Paisley-York (Oxford, 1992), 605. The selections from William's collection in the Corpus Christi College manuscript are not mentioned in M. R. James's catalogue; see *A Descriptive Catalogue of the Manuscripts in the Library of Corpus Christi College Cambridge* (Cambridge, 1912), vol. 2, 395–96. From ff. 125v–f. 145r of this manuscript, the copyist included slightly abbreviated copies of WC, *MT* 6.27–29; 6.32–33; 6.36; 6.38; 6.41–42; 6.45; 6.48–50; 6.60; 2.17 (not verbatim, and probably not derived from William's collection); 6.61; 6.63–67; 6.69; 6.73–74; 6.79; 6.88–89.

100. A new manuscript with selections from Benedict's *Miracula* at Tuy cathedral has recently come to light: see González, "Un *Libellus.*" Two manuscripts with Becket miracles that I have recently located and not yet been able to examine are a fourteenth-century collection of saints' lives with thirty-two folios dedicated to a "Vie et miracles de saint Thomas Becket" (Bibliothèque Mazarine MS 1731, ff. 26r–58v), and St. Gall MS 580, a lengthy copy of Becket miracles that Gustav Scherrer says does not conform to Benedict's text: see Scherrer, *Verzeichniss der Handschriften der Stiftsbibliothek von St. Gallen* (New York, 1975), 188.

101. For the manuscript circulation of St. Foy's collection, see Luca Robertini, ed.,

Liber Miraculorum Sancte Fidis (Spoleto, 1994), 3–12. For the Codex Calixtus, see Díaz y Díaz, Piñeiro, and Tirgó, *El Códice Calixtino*, esp. 327–33.

102. The inscription has been printed and the entire manuscript carefully analyzed by Duggan, "Lorvão."

103. Waclaw Uruszczak notes that a manuscript of Becket miracles, probably Benedict's collection, was in Krakow in the late twelfth or early thirteenth century: see Uruszczak, "Les répercussions,"116.

104. It is likely that Henry VIII's proclamation against Thomas Becket meant the loss of more of these manuscripts in England than elsewhere. On the Reformation and the Becket cult, see Roberts, "Politics, Drama."

105. The references for Rochester, Ramsey, Reading, Reading-Leominster, Glastonbury, Thorney are found in *English Benedictine Libraries: The Shorter Catalogues*, ed. by R. Sharpe, J. P. Carley, R. M. Thomson, and A. G. Watson, in *Corpus of British Medieval Library Catalogues* [CBMLC], vol. 4, (London, 1996): B79.145, B68.231, B71.126b, B75.77, B39.89c, B100.39. For Peterborough, see CBMLC vol. 8 (London, 2001), BP3.48. For Titchfield, Bradsole, and Meaux, see CBMLC vol. 3 (London, 1992), P6.61b, P2.60, and Z14.72. For St. Augustine's, CBMLC vol. 13 (London, 2008), BA1.1543.17. For the Canterbury texts, see James, *Ancient Libraries*, nos. 357, 974, 1061, 1082, 1179, and 1577 for the six Christ Church copies; and no. 120 for the Canterbury College, Oxford reference. There are numerous references to copies of "*Vita Thome*" in British library catalogues. As cataloguers tended to note only first items in manuscripts, it is possible that some of these manuscripts included some or all of Benedict's collection. I have mapped only two of these *vita* references on Figure 7. The first, a late twelfth-century reference from Whitby [CBMLC, vol. 4, no. B110.2], reads *Benedictus abbas de Burgo aliquid scriptsit de uita S Thomae* and seems very likely to have contained miracles. The second, a reference from Llanthony Secunda [CBMLC vol. 6, no. A16.282 and A16.283], reads "Vita sancti Thome. magnum volumen" and "Vita sancti Edmundi archiepiscopi." The editors of the CBMLC volume believe that this entry is to be identified with Lambeth Palace Library MS 135, a handsome volume that features Benedict's miracle collection. The copy at Exeter College, Oxford, is known from an inscription in Douai, Bibl. de la Ville, MS 860, a late twelfth-century manuscript. The inscription states that the manuscript was given to Exeter College by William Reed, the bishop of Chichester (d. 1385), who had acquired it from John Tryllek, the bishop of Rochester (d. 1372). On this manuscript, see Duggan, "Lorvão," 61.

106. We do not have such catalogs from many English monastic libraries, including celebrated and large libraries of like that of St. Albans. Even the catalogs that do exist generally do not list all the volumes in a monastery's library, all the items in individual manuscripts (an especially difficult problem for locating *miracula*), or books kept outside the library.

107. Alban Butler mentions an English translation of Benedict's collection in *The Lives of the Fathers, Martyrs, and other Principal Saints* (Dublin, 1833), vol. 2, 1102, but he was referring to a translation made by an early seventeenth-century antiquarian found in Oxford, Bodleian MS Engl. hist. c. 322. For a description of this interesting manuscript

and the tentative identification of the translator as William St. George, see Mary Clapinson and T. D. Rogers, *Summary Catalogue of Post-Medieval Western Manuscripts in the Bodleian Library, Oxford* (Oxford, 1991), vol. 1, 231–32.

108. See Guernes, *La vie de Saint Thomas le Martyr*, l. 6158. For discussion of Guernes's work, see Staunton, *Thomas Becket and His Biographers*, 32–35, and Ruth A. Dean and Maureen B. M. Boulton, *Anglo-Norman Literature: A Guide to Texts and Manuscripts* (London, 1999), 282.

109. The story is the vision of Master Feramin, which Guernes said he heard Feramin relate himself: see Guernes, *La vie* ll. 6091–6120. William also tells this story in his collection (WC, *MT* 1.4), but his version is different, and is in a part of the collection that he probably composed *after* Guernes had finished his text.

110. For discussion of this text, see Short, "The Patronage of Beneit's *Vie De Thomas Becket*," 239–56, and Orme, "A Reconstruction of Robert," xx.

111. On the manuscripts, see Dean and Boulton, *Anglo-Norman Literature*, nos. 508–9, 282–84.

112. OC, *MD*, cc. 22 and 24; *MEdm*, vol. 1, c. 10, 181 (the section from Osbert's booklet); and Aelred of Rievaulx, *Vita S. Edwardi regis*, c. 37 (this story was derived from Osbert's text).

113. "The Miracles of St. Ithamar," c. 10, 434.

114. The only source I have located referring to the use of written stories for preaching is in Henry of Huntingdon's *Historia Anglorum*, bk. 9, c. 1, 623, where he writes of religious men wrongly preaching miracles for hope of material gain: "if they [religious men looking for money] discover any anonymous record, they are so bold as to teach and proclaim it [*legere et predicare*] in the revered presence of God . . . However, if miracles are narrated to me in this way I do not openly contract them unless they are obviously frivolous, nor give them constant affirmation unless I observe them to be fully corroborated by well-known proofs and trustworthy persons."

115. On this point, see Wenzel, "Preaching the Saints in Chaucer's England," 67: "beyond retelling an occasional miracle and referring to the saint's intercessory power, the sermons I have read cannot be said to advertise their subjects as aids in specific needs. . . . monks or canons who tended a major shrine in medieval England may have advertised its miraculous and healing powers . . . but if they did so, their advertisement has left no traces in the sermons I have read and analyzed."

116. See BP, *MT* 1.4, and Roberts, *Thomas Becket: An Inventory of Sermons*, no. 151. I am most grateful to Phyllis Roberts for her help with these sermons, in particular for her generosity in sending me her notes and photocopies of the manuscripts of sermons of interest.

117. See Slocum, *Liturgies in Honour of Thomas Becket*. Benedict's composition is edited as *Historia de S. Thoma Cantuariensi*, in *Analecta Hymnica Medii Aevi* 13 (1892): 238–41. When an office was composed in honor of Becket's translation in 1220, a new little collection of four miracles was compiled for the occasion: see Reames, "The Remaking of a Saint," and "Reconstructing and Interpreting a Thirteenth-Century Office."

118. For a description of this manuscript, see Albertus Poncelet, *Catalogus Codicum Hagiographicorum Latinorum Bibliothecarum Romanarum* (Brussels, 1909), 303–4. The folios of interest are ff. 169–174v.

119. There are manuscripts in which Becket *vitae* are divided into lections but the miracles are not: this is the case for Lisbon, Bibl. nacional cod. Alcobaça CCXC/143; London, British Library, Egerton MS 2818; and Rome, Vatican MS 6933.

120. See Grim, *Vita*, 440–41, and *MTB*, vol. 4, 431–41, miracles 439–41. Robertson derived his edition of this *passio* from a friend's copy of "a manuscript from the monastery of Subiaco": the same anonymous passio and miracle stories are found in Vienna, Cod. Vind. Pal. 571, ff. 23–28v.

121. Thomas von Froidmont, *Die Vita des Heiligen Thomas Becket Erzbischof von Canterbury*, ed. by Paul Gerhard Schmidt (Stuttgart, 1991). Thomas of Froidmont wrote at the behest of abbot Aegidius of Aulne; it is possible that he utilized the copy of Benedict's collection that we know to have been at Aulne.

122. On Grandisson's *vita*, see Lapidge and Love, "Latin Hagiography," 292.

123. Bull has come to a similar conclusion with his analysis of a miracle collection compiled in the late twelfth century: "it is unlikely that the collection's primary purpose was to provide teaching material for use in the instruction of lay people" (*The Miracles of Our Lady*, 92).

124. The windows are catalogued and discussed in Caviness, *The Windows of Christ Church Cathedral Canterbury*, 180–214. See also Harris, "Pilgrimage, Performance," and Paul Binski's study of the Trinity Chapel in *Becket's Crown*, 3–27.

125. See Yarrow, *Saints and Communities*, 8: "These [Becket] collections stimulated a revival of interest in posthumous miracles, whose influence can be gauged from the contexts of miracle collections newly commissioned in their wake."

126. See TM, *MW*, bk. 7, c. 19, and *LE*, bk 3, c. 143.

127. The massive collection for Godric is found in a single late twelfth-century manuscript, Oxford, Bodleian MS Laud E 47 (413), which also contains the sole copy of Reginald of Durham's life of Godric. The collection is discussed by Finucane, *Miracles and Pilgrims*, 126–27 (see also the diagram and map 167–68), and Ward, *Miracles and the Medieval Mind*, 76–82.

128. The monk of Selby who wrote the *Historia Selebiensis monasterii* dedicated the first half of the text to the story of a wandering monk who brought the finger of St. Germanus of Auxerre to Selby and the subsequent foundation of a Benedictine monastery there c.1070. The second half of the text is a miracle collection with over thirty chapters: Richard Barrie Dobson writes that the author "dwells at inordinate length on the many somewhat conventionalised miracles wrought by the agency of St. Germanus": "The First Norman Abbey," 31. The author dates his work to 1174. This text awaits a modern edition: a seventeenth-century transcription of the sole manuscript (now in the Bibliothèque Nationale) was reprinted in *AASS* July 7, 301–15, and was reprinted again in *The Coucher Book of Selby*, 1–54.

129. *The Book of the Foundation of St. Bartholomew's Church* survives in a single

manuscript dated c.1400. This manuscript contains both the Latin text of the *Book*, compiled sometime between 1174 and 1189 by an Augustinian canon of the house, and a Middle English translation that likely dates to the late fourteenth century. The text is divided into two books: the first, which describes the life of the founder of St. Bartholomew's, Rahere, includes eighteen chapters devoted to miracle stories; the second book of twenty-seven chapters is entirely devoted to miracles. The Latin text is unedited. The Middle English is edited by Norman Moore, *The Book of the Foundation of St. Bartholomew's Church in London: The Church Belonging to the Priory of the Same in West Smithfield, Edited from the Original Manuscript in the British Museum, Cotton Vespasian B ix*. EETS 163 (London, 1923). The miracles are discussed by Webb, *The Records of St. Bartholomew's Priory*, 64–70. A modern English translation of the Latin text of the *Book* was made for Webb in the 1920s by Humphrey H. King and William Barnard: this translation was located by Tina Bird and is now reproduced with permission of the Webb family on her website, www.raheresgarden.com.

130. The collection survives only as a seventeenth-century copy of a fourteenth- or fifteenth-century copy made on a set of wooden tables (now lost): for the text, see *HCY*, vol. 3, 531–43. As we know it now, the collection consists of thirty-three miracles, all supposedly occurring in the week of Pentecost in 1177 among pilgrims to William's tomb in York Minster. The collection may have been compiled by a priest and doctor living in York named Paulinus. For analysis of this intriguing collection, see Norton, *St. William of York*, 150–64.

131. This text, edited as *The Waltham Chronicle*, is not usually considered to be a miracle collection. The original title of the work, however, was *De inventione sancte crucis*, a more accurate description of its contents. The text consists of some thirty chapters, most of them concerning the legendary discovery of a black stone cross that was thought to work miracles. While the text was certainly written after 1177, it includes no stories that appear to date past 1144: the text may be incomplete as it stands. For the date, see *Waltham Chronicle*, xxxiii–xxxviii.

132. This large collection, written by Prior Philip, survives in a single manuscript (Oxford, Bodleian MS Digby 177) and is edited in *AASS*, Oct. 8 (1853), 568–89. For analysis, see Finucane, *Miracles and Pilgrims*, 127–29; Ward, *Miracles and the Medieval Mind*, 82–88; Yarrow, *Saints and Their Communities*, 169–89; and Mayr-Harting, "Functions of a Twelfth-Century Shrine," 193–206.

133. On William de Vere's *vita* and miracle collection for Osith, which was based on an earlier twelfth-century text, see Bethell, "The Lives of St. Osyth of Essex and St. Osyth of Aylesbury," 75–127, and Barrow, "A Twelfth-Century Bishop," 177–78.

134. Jocelin mentions this miracle collection in his *Chronicle*, 16: "At this time [1181] the holy boy Robert suffered martyrdom and was buried in our church, and many signs and wonders were performed among the common folk, as I have set down elsewhere."

135. Dating miracle collections is often difficult, and more research is needed to determine whether collections for John of Beverley and Wenefred discussed above should also be dated to this post-Becket period.

136. Tudor, "Cult of St. Cuthbert," 455.

137. Reginald's *Life of Godric* is the focus of Licence, "The Benedictines, the Cistercians," 315–29, and Ridyard, "Functions of a Twelfth-Century Recluse Revisited," 236–50.

138. Ward, *Miracles and the Medieval Mind*, 81. This collection of 263 chapters is about one-third the length of Reginald's collection of Cuthbert miracles with its 141 chapters.

139. Philip of Oxford, *Miracula S. Frideswidae*, c. 106, 587.

140. On this collection, see Hayward, "Sanctity and Lordship," 105–44.

141. See *The Miracles of Saint Aebbe*, xvii–xx.

142. For discussion of this collection, unfortunately as yet no more precisely dated, see Bartlett, "Cults of Irish, Scottish and Welsh saints," 70–72. The text is edited in *The Register of the Priory of St. Bees*, 497–520.

143. The text is edited by Edmund Craster as "The Miracles of St. Cuthbert at Farne," and discussed by Alexander, *Saints and Animals*, 132–51.

144. On these comings and goings, see Yarrow, *Saints and Their Communities*, 190–95.

145. The miracle collection, found in Gloucester MS 1, an early thirteenth-century manuscript, has not been edited: an English translation has been published by Kemp, "The Miracles of the Hand of St. James," and the collection is analyzed by Yarrow, *Saints and Their Communities*, 190–213.

146. The text is edited in *MEdm*, vol. 1, 107–208, from a section of BL MS Cotton Titus A VIII dated to c.1200. Arnold edited this compilation under Abbot Samson of Bury's name, but Antonia Gransden thinks this attribution is unlikely: see her fresh discussion of this text in *A History of the Abbey of Bury St. Edmunds*, 121–35. On this compilation, see also Thomson, "Two Versions of a Saint's Life," 383–408.

147. On the *Vie Seint Edmund*, see Gransden, *History of the Abbey of Bury St. Edmunds*, 131–33, and Rothwell, "The Life and Miracles of St. Edmund," 135–80.

148. See Wogan-Browne, "*Clerc u lai, muïne u dame*: Women and Anglo-Norman Hagiography," Bethell, "The Lives of St. Osyth of Essex," Zatta, "The *Vie Seinte Osith*," and Wogan-Browne, "The Life of St. Osith," 339–444. Wogan-Browne's article includes Zatta's translation of the *Vie* (posthumously revised by Wogan-Browne) and an edition of the Anglo-Norman text by D. W. Russell.

149. For discussion, see Wogan-Browne, *Saint's Lives*, 251–55, and MacBain, "Anglo-Norman Women Hagiographers."

150. For a translation of the text, see *A Life of Saint Audrey*, ed. McCash and Barban. The text is also discussed in Blanton, *Signs of Devotion*, 173–201, and Wogan-Browne, *Saint's Lives*, 207–12.

151. For a fifteenth-century translation of Arcoid's account of the miracles of Erkenwald: see Whatley, "A 'Symple Wrecche' at Work," 333–43. On hagiography in Middle English prose, see the review essay by Oliver Pickering, "Saints' Lives," in *A Companion of Middle English Prose*, ed. A. S. G. Edwards (Woodbridge, 2004), 249–70.

152. *The Book of St. Gilbert*, lxiii. For a recent study of Gilbert's miracles, see Ruud, "Reading Miracles at Sempringham."

153. *The Book of St. Gilbert*, 169–79.

154. *The Book of St. Gilbert*, 171–72.

155. *The Book of St. Gilbert*, 173.

156. *The Book of St. Gilbert*, 179.

157. See the discussion of the editors of *The Book of St. Gilbert*, xc–cviii; Vauchez, *Sainthood in the Later Middle Ages*, 33–57; and Kemp, *Canonization and Authority*, 104–6. For a useful summary of Innocent III's canonization of English saints, see Cheney, *Pope Innocent III and England*, 51–59.

158. See *The Book of St. Gilbert*, 264–303.

159. *The Book of St. Gilbert*, 305–35.

160. BP, *MT*, prologue, 21–22.

CHAPTER 8. MOST BLESSED MARTYR: THOMAS BECKET'S MURDER AND THE CHRIST CHURCH COLLECTIONS

1. Scholars still rely on an article published by Emmanuel Walberg in 1920 ("Date de la composition") for the dating of the collections. Walberg came to dubious conclusions that I will attempt to correct below. Robertson did not base his editions of the collections on a wide knowledge of the manuscripts. This has caused problems especially in terms of where he put in breaks between the books of the collections. While I will make citations to chapters in the "fifth" and "sixth" books of Benedict's collection in Robertson's edition for easy reference, most medieval readers knew the collection as having four books. Only a few manuscripts have a fifth book demarcated, and it consists of just a few chapters: see Duggan, "Lorvão," 60–62, and "Santa Cruz," 27–55. The "Liber Sextus" demarcation in London, Lambeth Palace MS 135 that Robertson relies on heavily (see his edition, 261, n. 1), is in postmedieval handwriting. No medieval reader would have thought of this collection as having six books. Robertson's placement of the break between the first and second books of William's collection is not supported by any manuscript and has led to mistaken assumptions about the text. I have renumbered the affected chapters according to the book division in the Montpellier manuscript (see Appendix 3). When I cite these chapters, I first use the Montpellier numbering, then Robertson's in parentheses. The most comprehensive treatment of the texts to date is the 1898 study of Abbott, *St. Thomas*, vol. 1, 223–333, and all of vol. 2. Statistical analyses of the collections were published in the 1970s: see Finucane, *Miracles and Pilgrims*, esp. 121–26, and Foreville, "Les Miracula S. Thomae Cantuariensis" (the tables in Foreville's article contain numerous inaccuracies). Ward dedicated a chapter to the Christ Church collections in her pioneering book *Miracles and the Medieval Mind*, 89–109. The most recent analyses are articles focused largely on aspects of William's collection: see Lett, "Deux hagiographes," Langenbahn, "Die wiederentdeckten Himmeroder," and Bull, "Criticism of Henry II's Expedition." See also Bull's discussion of the Christ Church collections in *Miracles of Our Lady*, 51–54.

2. One of the most damaging misconceptions has been that the two Christ Church

collections can be read as a single community production. R. W. Southern referred to the two collections in the singular, as "the greatest collection of miracle stories connected with any single shrine in our period—or indeed in the whole Middle Ages" (*Making of the Middle Ages*, 255). Scholars often refer to the collections' "700 miracles" and cite from the two collections indiscriminately.

3. WC, *Vita*, 133–34.

4. For analysis of the differing accounts of the martyrdom, see Staunton, *Thomas Becket and His Biographers*, 184–215.

5. BP, *Passio*, 15. Gervase, Herbert of Bosham, William FitzStephen, and Anonymous I all also state or imply that Canterbury citizens had access to Thomas's body immediately after his death: see Gervase, vol. 1, 228; Herbert of Bosham, *Vita*, 518–19; Anonymous I, *Vita* 78; and WFS, 150.

6. WFS, 150.

7. The fullest discussion of the development of the "Canterbury Water" is that by Sigal, "Naissance et premier développement," 35–44.

8. This assumption is central to the arguments of Hearn, "Canterbury Cathedral and the Cult of Becket," 19–52, and Kidson, "Gervase, Becket, and William of Sens," 969–91. See also Gibson, "Normans and Angevins," 62. The best study of the monks' relationship with the living Becket is in the pamphlet by Southern, *The Monks of Canterbury*, esp. 7–13.

9. Duggan, *Thomas Becket*, 214.

10. Gervase, William FitzStephen, Herbert of Bosham, Anonymous I and John of Salisbury all mention the placement of Becket's body before the high altar: see Gervase, vol. 1, 228; WFS, 150; Herbert of Bosham, *Vita*, 519; Anonymous I, *Vita*, 78; and *The Letters of John of Salisbury*, no. 305, 737.

11. BP, *Passio*, 16–17.

12. Benedict wrote movingly of the wretchedness of that moment, as did Gervase of Canterbury. See BP, *Passio*, 17, and Gervase, vol. 1, 229.

13. The sources disagree markedly on the question of when the remainder of the blood was collected. Anonymous I states that the monks expelled the townspeople, closed the doors, and then immediately gathered up the rest of the blood: *Vita*, 78. William FitzStephen, on the other hand, says that it was only after the monks had discovered that Becket had been wearing a hair shirt that one of them, Ernold the Goldworker, decided to collect the remaining blood: WFS 148. Edward Grim places the blood cleanup even later, after Becket's burial: Grim, *Vita*, 442. Benedict and Gervase both discuss the collection of the blood immediately after speaking of the townspeople's use of it, but neither of them is forthcoming about when this collection occurred or whose idea it was. Benedict, for instance, states that the remaining blood was collected in a "most comely vessel" and then held in the church, but in the next breath he describes how some of Becket's undergarments were given away to the poor, something that could not have happened before the monks had undressed the body: BP, *Passio*, 15; see also Gervase, vol. 1, 228. This reticence may mean that the monks did not collect the remainder of the blood immediately.

14. William FitzStephen's account of the burial is one of the fullest: see WFS, 149.

15. Walberg, "Date de la composition," 261.

16. Foreville, "Les 'Miracula,'" 444.

17. See, for instance, Barlow, *Thomas Becket*, 265–67. For other assertions of the "chronological order" of the miracles in the first books of Benedict's collection, see Finucane, *Miracles and Pilgrims*, 125; Ward, *Miracles and the Medieval Mind*, 89; Lett, "Deux hagiographes," 207; and Slocum, *Liturgies*, 82.

18. BP, *MT* 1.8, 38.

19. BP, *MT* 1.14, 47.

20. BP, *MT* 1.15, 47–48.

21. BP, *MT* 1.15, 48: "villae nomen barbarum memoriae meae tenaciter non adhaesit."

22. For yet another early miracle and delayed pilgrimage, see BP, *MT*, 1.13. Even the chapters concerning visions that Benedict could potentially have heard and written down immediately after the murder were clearly composed later. After describing a Christ Church monk's very early vision, for instance, Benedict tells the reader how it predicted events that occurred around Easter: see BP, *MT*, 1.6, 34–36.

23. Benedict's decision to choose and present the Sussex woman's story as the "first" miracle, for example, was not accidental. Benedict wants his readers to note the similarity of a "first" miracle happening three days after Becket's murder to Christ's resurrection three days after his death. It is probable that the earliest miracles of Becket were claimed by Canterbury citizens using the blood taken from the cathedral, as FitzStephen would have it. Benedict instead says that the Sussex miracle was the "first," and presents the earliest blood-related miracle as happening later, inside the cathedral, and firmly under the monks' control (see BP, *MT* 1.12), a history that a Christ Church monk would prefer for obvious reasons. Benedict's occasional chronological references were meant to point out what he saw as stages in the development of Becket's cult and resonances between Becket's miracles and the life of Christ (rebirth at Easter, fire at Pentecost, etc.). They need to be treated with great caution.

24. For this terminology, see BP, *MT* 3.18, 130; 3.20, 133; and 3.64, 164. See also 4.72, 242, where Benedict refers to the period "when the martyr first began to shine with miracles."

25. WC, *MT* 1.9, 148.

26. Gervase, vol. 1, 230: "In primis tamen beatus martyr, quasi quaedam pracludia praemittens, minimis quibusdam coepit coruscare miraculis."

27. FitzStephen, *Vita*, 151; *Letters of John of Salisbury*, no. 305, 735; The Lansdowne Anonymous, *MTB*, vol. 4, 145–85, at 160–61; BP, *MT*, 1.12, 43.

28. See Duggan, "Diplomacy, Status, and Conscience" 269–72.

29. On Henry II and Avranches, see the important articles by Duggan, "Diplomacy, Status, and Conscience," and "The Official Record." She notes that "if the king had been truly repentant at this time [i.e., at Avranches], one would have expected to find at least a *pro forma* allusion to his regret in *Sciatis quod*. But there is not a syllable of remorse in the letter": "Diplomacy, Status and Conscience," 278.

30. The monks' longing for news is suggested by Benedict's account of the servant William Patrick's miracle, BP, *MT* 1.14, 46–47. In this story, Benedict says that the monks rejoiced to hear the news of papal censures of Becket's murderers as revealed by the young man's vision. When he tells his story, Benedict comments, "a cordibus nostris, ad quos eventus hujus fama praecurrerat, ambiguitatis strumam amputavit."

31. See BP, *MT* 1.1, 27: "'Si vere surrexisti, et inter martyres computandus es, ut credimus, quare teipsum non manifestas mundo?'"

32. For Benedict's account of the opening of the crypt, see BP, *MT* 2.6.

33. For a secret visitor to the crypt, see Benedict's account of William of London's miracle: *MT*, 1.12. William of London's miracle is found in other, independent accounts of Becket's miracles: see, e.g., QM, c. 1, 427: "Is ad sepulchrum sancti martyris admissus sequenti nocte loquendi recepit facultatem." Gervase presents William of London's miracle as the beginning of the monks' distribution of the blood: see vol. 1, 229: "Divulgatum est ilico verbum hoc in populo, et jam petentibus plurimis aquae limpidae mixtus et sic aegrotantibus ad potandum porrectus est, ne videlicet sacer sanguis citius effunderetur, vel indignis daretur uberius."

34. BP, *MT* 2.6, 60–61.

35. BP, *MT* 1.6, 35.

36. See BP, *MT* 2.26–27, and The Lansdowne Anonymous, 161: "Sed ut dicunt (utinam nec diceretur nec verum esset), in corpus sancti martyris vel in ecclesiam Cantuariensem vindicari minatus est; usque adeo enim iniqui susurratores et serpentini instigatores eum exasperaverant."

37. BP, *MT* 2.29.

38. BP, *MT*, prologue, 26.

39. BP, *MT* 1.15. This passage should be read along with the conclusion to the previous chapter in the collection.

40. On John of Salisbury's *vita*, see Staunton, *Thomas Becket and His Biographers*, 26. For the dating of the initial letter, see Duggan, *Thomas Becket*, 228.

41. For the fullest account of Benedict's career, see King, "Benedict of Peterborough."

42. The letter is edited by Stanley Chodorow and Charles Duggan, *Decretales Ineditae Saeculi XII*, vol. 4, no. 36, 36–37.

43. This is Anne Duggan's dating: see her discussion of the delegation in Duggan, *Thomas Becket*, 217–18.

44. *Decretales Ineditae Saeculi XII*, vol. 4, no. 36, 36–37.

45. Anonymous II also states that a first petition for Becket's canonization was rejected: see *MTB*, vol. 4, 143.

46. See BP, *MT*, prologue, 26, and the story of Eilward of Westoning: *MT* 4.2.

47. The letter is edited in *MTB*, vol. 7, no. 788, 551–52.

48. For these letters, see *MTB*, vol. 7, nos. 783–85.

49. William, *Vita*, 2; WC, *MT* 6.90, 484. In another chapter, William describes a couple of pilgrims anxious for their story to be inscribed in the "roll" or "list" [*matricula*]

so that they could begin their long journey home: WC, *MT* 5.30, 396. Unfortunately, none of these preliminary notes, tablets, or listings have survived.

50. For these pairings and sets, see Appendix 2. Benedict approached his compositional task as if it were a kind of miracle mah-jongg. He did not link up every story in the collection, but every time he sat down to write, he was clearly on the hunt for matches, harmonies, and resonances. He was more keen to pair stories together than to think about or record dates, and found loose parallelisms more satisfying than the temporal or causal connections modern readers expect and demand from their own compositions.

51. In her wonderful study of twelfth-century English history-writing, Nancy Partner has observed that "medieval Latin history shares with the great mass of medieval fictional narrative the appearance of a 'string of juxtaposed, mutually independent episodes,' which is called, in French, the *roman à tiroirs*, 'a phrase that makes us think of a chest of drawers which are explored one after the other'": Partner, *Serious Entertainments*, 201. This neatly describes the literary nature of Benedict's composition as well.

52. For these apologies, see BP, *MT* 2.18, 3.18, and 4.72. Brian Patrick McGuire sees Caesarius of Heisterbach working through his *Dialogus Miraculorum* in the same way: "the *Dialogus Miraculorum* was written between 1219 and 1223, and it seems more than likely that its chapters were inserted more or less in the order that we have them": "Friends and Tales in the Cloister: Oral Sources," 198.

53. BP, *MT* 4.38, 209. William once refers to his collection as a "series": see WC, *MT* 5.22, 389.

54. For discussion of the chapterhouse readings, see Chapter 7.

55. WC, *Vita*, 2. For discussion of William's *vita* (usually dated to before 1174), see Staunton, *Thomas Becket and His Biographers*, 49–55, esp. 52–55.

56. On these Williams, see Joan Greatrex, *Biographical Register of the English Cathedral Priories of the Province of Canterbury, c. 1066–1540* (Oxford, 1997), 109 and 320.

57. See WC, *MT*, prologue, 137–39.

58. WC, *MT*, prologue, 138: "tandem fratri qui circa haec operam dederat a principio cooperator et coadjutor accessit. Cum enim vires ejus res incepta videretur excedere, et emergentia miracula frater ille solus audire non sufficeret et scribere."

59. WC, *MT*, prologue, 138: "Mane vero, congregatis fratribus et conquerentibus quod minus sollicita diligentia miraculis audiendis adhiberetur, quae in ecclesia Cantuariensis coruscabant, et quae populi frequentia venientis ad orationem referebat, ex decreto communi injunctum est et huic partes suas interponere."

60. BP, *MT* 4.1, 173.

61. For translations and discussion of these eighteen stories, see Abbott, *St Thomas*, vol. 2, 76–273. On Figure 10, I have mapped seventeen of the eighteen stories. I eliminated one, the story of the leper Elias of Reading (BP, *MT* 4.72; WC, *MT* 6.8), because William's account is a copy of a letter written by a monk of Reading that appears to have arrived at Canterbury long after Benedict had completed his collection.

62. See Winchester College MS 4, 105, and Montpellier, Bibliothèque interuniversitaire section médicine MS. 2, f. 62r. In the Montpellier manuscript, Benedict's collection is introduced as "the first work," *primum opus*, at f. 6r.

63. The letters were from the burgesses of Bedford and from the dean of Gloucester. The texts are the same in both collections: compare BP, *MT* 4.2, 181, and WC, *MT* 1.16, 155–56 (Robertson 2.2) and BP, *MT* 6.1, 262–63, and WC, *MT* 3.1, 256.

64. Compare BP, *MT* 4.65, 237, and WC, *MT* 1.49, 192–93 (Robertson 2.35). The eyeskip and missing passage in Robertson's edition of Benedict's text of the bishop's letter should be ignored. Anne Duggan has identified manuscripts of Benedict's collection that include complete copies of the letter.

65. Compare BP, *MT* 4.86, and WC, *MT* 2.14 (Robertson 2.52).

66. Compare BP, *MT* 4.42–45, and WC, *MT* 3.45–46 and 3.44.

67. For Cecilia of Plumstock, see BP, *MT* 4.65, and WC, *MT* 1.49 (Robertson 2.35); for Hugh Scot, BP, *MT* 4.66, and William, *MT* 2.2 (Robertson 2.40).

68. Benedict mentions the letter from the priest in Hugh Scot's case at the close of his account: see BP, *MT* 4.66. Abbott suggests that these accounts were taken from letters: *St Thomas*, vol. 2, 161 and 169.

69. See WC, *MT* 1.49 (Robertson 2.35), 190: "Memini me dixisse de quodam Jordane, cujus filium vidimus revocatum a mortuis." I suspect that William wrote his account of Jordan Fitz-Eisulf's miracle (found very early in his collection, *MT* 1.19 (Robertson 2.5)) before he received the set of notes with Jordan Fitz-Eisulf's, Cecilia's, and Hugh's miracles. There is no relationship between Benedict and William's accounts of the Fitz-Eisulf miracle.

70. WC, *Vita*, 2: "Nam cum miracula ejus, quae in schedulis occultabat incorrecta et imperfecta, rogaretur a fratribus exponere transcribenda, ait ei in visu noctis, 'Elige tibi quod vis.'"

71. For the exchange of notes between the writers of the miracle collection of St. Foy, see Sheingorn, *The Book of Sainte Foy*, 25: "It appears that the monk-author of Book Three had Bernard's notes in hand and used them to write up some of the stories Bernard had collected."

72. Even with the stories of Cecilia and Hugh Scot, it is clear the collectors had to have been paraphrasing common sources rather than the text of the other's collection because Benedict includes details that William skips and William includes details that Benedict skips. For instance, William, unlike Benedict, includes specific details about a vision of a certain Agnes in his account of Cecilia's miracle, whereas Benedict includes details about how Cecilia had to lean on her knees and elbows rather than sit or kneel, something William does not mention (compare BP, *MT* 4.65 and WC, *MT* 1.49 (Robertson 2.35)).

73. Other notes may well lie behind other stories in the beginning books of William's collection. For instance, William includes an account of the vision of Abbot Richard of Sulby at Welford that the abbot "wrote with his own hands" [*propriis manibus exaravit*] at the very beginning of his collection: see WC, *MT* 1.10, 148–50. This same Abbot Richard appears in Benedict's collection in two successive chapters: see BP, *MT* 3.42 and 3.43. It is possible that Benedict had asked Abbot Richard to write up the story of his own vision and that William inherited the result. Abbot Richard, who does not

seem to have been able to stay away from Canterbury, appears yet again later on in William's collection: see WC, *MT* 3.34 and 3.35.

74. This is especially the case for the three stories Benedict trumpeted the most in his collection, those of Eilward of Westoning, the sons of Jordan Fitz-Eisulf, and James, son of the earl of Clare. Compare the story of Eilward of Westoning in BP, *MT* 4.2, and WC, *MT* 1.16 (Robertson 2.2); the story of the sons of Jordan Fitz-Eisulf in BP, *MT* 4.64, and WC, *MT* 1.19 (Robertson 2.5); and James, son of the earl of Clare in BP, *MT* 4.94, and WC, *MT* 2.30 (Robertson 2.68).

75. William's attitude toward this bishop, who had opposed Becket during his lifetime, is less harsh than Benedict's, again suggesting a later time period for composition. Compare BP, *MT* 4.75, and WC, *MT* 2.14 (Robertson 2.52).

76. See WC, *MT* 1.17, 158 (Robertson 2.3): "dies multos mansit apud nos, de martyris substantia stipem habens."

77. Compare BP, *MT* 6.2, and WC, *MT* 3.3.

78. WC, *MT* 3.1, 254—compare with BP, *MT* 6.1.

79. See Walberg, "Date de la composition," 261–64. Michael Staunton, among others, follows Walberg exactly: see *Thomas Becket and His Biographers*, 50. Scholars sometimes change the end date from 1179 to 1177: see, e.g., Ward, *Miracles and the Medieval Mind*, 90, and Lett, "Deux hagiographes," 203.

80. See Walberg, "Date de la composition," 264–74. Only Marcus Bull questions (by silence) the idea that the whole of William's sixth book was a later addition; see Bull, "Criticism of Henry II's Expedition," 116.

81. Bull has shown, for example, that the large collection (over 125 chapters) of the miracles of our Lady of Rocamadour, thought to have been composed over some 25 years, was actually the product of just a year or two: see *Miracles of Our Lady*, 56–63. John M. McCulloh has dated Thomas of Monmouth's composition of his life and miracles of William of Norwich—a work of seven books—to the period 1154–56: see McCulloh, "Jewish Ritual Murder," 740.

82. For the manuscript recensions of Benedict's collection, see Duggan, "Santa Cruz," 30–39. Walberg stated categorically that the prologue of Benedict's fourth book "was without any doubt added much later" ("Date de la composition," 261), but the rhetoric and the ideas Benedict expresses at the beginning of the fourth book are in fact so closely coupled with the conclusion of the third book that in one manuscript the copyist ran them together as one chapter (see Robertson's note at BP, *MT* 4.1, 173 n. 3). Perhaps Walberg thought that Benedict's classical citations or expression of frustration at the beginning of the fourth book represented something quite different, but Benedict had already utilized lines from Ovid and Horace in his second and third books and had started to make complaints about the difficulty of hearing all the stories in the middle of the third book as well. See BP, *MT* 2.35, 2.61, and 3.20. There is nothing here that suggests a rhetorical or temporal break.

83. See BP, *MT* 4.6, 186–87: the story concerns a youth in Rochester waving a Becket ampulla at a fire and so turning it away. Robertson, uncharacteristically, suggested

a date for this chapter in a marginal note in his edition of Benedict's collection. Usually Robertson did this only when Benedict himself had mentioned a date, but in this case Robertson independently found a reference to a fire occurring in Rochester on April 3, 1177, and decided to insert this date in the margin. To his credit, he put a question mark after the date. Magnússon dispensed with the question mark and dated Benedict's fourth book to 1177: see Magnússon, ed. and trans., *Thómas Saga Erkibyskups*, vol. 2, lxxii. Walberg followed suit, though he argued that Robertson read his reference wrong and that the correct date of Benedict's fire in Rochester was actually 1179. Fires frequently afflicted towns in the twelfth century—Benedict himself pairs the story of the fire in Rochester with the story of a fire in Yarmouth (BP, *MT* 4.7, 187). There is nothing in Benedict's account that suggests his story should be connected with the notice of the 1177 fire.

84. The most important internal dating evidence in Benedict's fourth book is a copy of a letter that can be given a firm date range. The letter, not mentioned by Walberg, was written by bishop of Norwich William Turbe: see BP, *MT* 4.65, 236–37. Turbe died in January 1174, so he must have written his letter between 1171 and 1173. Benedict, who does not give any indication that Turbe was dead at the time he was writing, likely copied this letter into his collection in 1172 or 1173. Other stories in Benedict's fourth book, including those surrounding the story of the Rochester fire, also appear to have been composed in a similar timeframe, in 1172/73 rather than 1177 or 1179. Eilward of Westoning's miracle, the story with which Benedict begins his fourth book, had to have occurred before the canonization of Becket in early 1173: the priest in Eilward of Westoning's story wonders whether he can praise Becket as a saint because he is not yet canonized: see BP, *MT* 4.2, 180. Since William uses this story to launch his own collection (see WC, *MT* 1.16), it was probably known to the Christ Church monks before mid-1172. At the beginning of the fourth book, Benedict also describes how a knight, Odo of Falaise, was cured in the summer following the death of Thomas Becket (summer 1171), and that the monks later saw Odo arrive with votive gifts at the tomb. Benedict does not say when Odo arrived, but a timeframe in late 1171 or early 1172 again seems likely: see BP, *MT* 4.5. In another early chapter of the fourth book, Benedict describes how Ralph Langton stayed with the Christ Church monks "from Pentecost to Advent," then left, and then came back again. Benedict does not say which year that was, but it is highly likely that he meant Pentecost to Advent 1171: see BP, *MT* 4.4. In contrast, William's collection contains numerous chapters that were clearly composed later than 1173—his copies of letters addressed to Prior Benedict are just one example of this.

85. Unless Benedict waited until after he knew of Eilward of Westoning's miracle to start writing his collection, which seems unlikely, he did not start his composition with this prologue. He mentions Eilward's miracle at BP, *MT*, prologue, 26.

86. BP, *MT*, prologue, 25: "Quisquis igitur martyri nostro in sede Cantuariensi successerit . . ."

87. BP, *MT*, prologue, 24–25.

88. WC, *MT* 4.10, 321–23: "Progrediens inde clericus, cum Plasentiam venisset, propter pericula locorum deposita numerata pecunia sua apud fidelem matronam . . .

Romam profectus est, de celebranda solennitate martyris nomine fratrum Cantuariensium dominum papam petiturus; quem jam ipsis ignorantibus catalogo martyrum ascripserat."

89. See *MTB*, vol. 7, no. 784, 545–46, at 546: "et de miraculis ejus non solum communi et celebri fama, sed etiam dilectorum filiorum nostrorum Alberti titulo Sancti Laurentii in Lucina, et Theodwini, titulo Sancti Vitalis, presbyterorum cardinalium, et sedis apostolicae legatorum, et aliarum plurium personarum testimonio certitudinem plenam habentes."

90. The earliest external reference to Benedict's collection is a passage in an addition Edward Grim made to his *vita* for Becket, dated to late 1175, in which he refers to Benedict as both the new prior of Christ Church and the author of *Passio* and *Miracula*: see Grim, *Vita*, 448, and the discussion of Duggan, *Thomas Becket: A Textual History*, 193.

91. On the attribution of the *historia* to Benedict, see Duggan, "A Becket Office," 164–65. The text is edited as "Historia de S. Thoma Cantuariensi" in *Analecta Hymnica Medii Aevi* 13 (1892): 238–41. Benedict recycled some of the material in his miracle collection for this short text: compare "Membris donat / castratos masculis, / Orant visu / privatos oculis" with BP, *MT* 4.2 and "Ad Thomae memoriam / quarter lux descendit / Et in sancti gloriam / cereos accendit" with BP, *MT* 3.1–4.

92. Benedict's *passio* was not widely read: it is known only from Quadrilogus II. Benedict directly refers to his *passio* in the fourth book of his collection (see BP, *MT* 4.37). He also speaks of the state of Becket's dead face in both the passio (*Passio*, 15) and in his collection (*MT* 4.52).

93. For these recensions, see Duggan, "Lorvão," 51–68, and "Santa Cruz," 27–55. Robertson's edition of Benedict's collection includes, rather confusingly, four chapters not of Benedict's composition (ed. by Robertson as book 6, chapters 4–7, 267–81). These last four stories were written by an anonymous Christ Church monk during the priorate of Geoffrey (1191–1206), at which point Benedict was long gone from the community and at the end of his life, if not already deceased. These four stories are found in only one manuscript—Cambridge, Trinity College MS B.14.37, ff. 171v–181r—a manuscript that appears to have been a copy of another.

94. See King, "Benedict of Peterborough."

95. Four letters addressed to prior Benedict are found toward the end of William's collection: see WC, *MT* 6.124–25 and 6.127–28.

96. See Appendix 3.

97. WC, *MT* 1.1, 138. This passage is from the prefatory letter to Henry II, a letter William probably wrote. William certainly penned the similar sentiments to be found at the beginning of his account of Eilward of Westoning's miracle, 1.17, 156 (Robertson 2.3): "Ordinem rei non ab re esse putamus ad confirmationem posteritatis in fide dilucidare."

98. WC, *MT* 1.8.

99. WC, *MT* 2.6 [Robertson 2.44].

100. WC, *MT* 4.10.

101. WC, *MT* 5.18.

102. WC, *MT* 6.10.

103. WC, *MT* 6.36.

104. WC, *MT* 6.53.

105. WC, *MT* 6.90, 484.

106. See J. C. Robertson's partial collation of the Montpellier manuscript in *MTB*, vol. 4, xxiv–xxvi and 442–53; Duggan, "Lorvão," 61–62; and "Catalogus codicum hagiographicorum latinorum scholae medicinae Montepessulanensis" *AB* 34–5 (1915–16), 228–39. The copy of William's collection in Évreux, Bibl. de la Ville, MS lat. 77 begins at William's 1.6 and ends at 6.90: on this manuscript, see Duggan, "Lorvão," 56, and Henri Omont, *Catalogue Général des Manuscrits des Bibliothèques Publiques de France: Départements*, vol. 2 (Paris 1888), 442. The copyist of Cambridge, Corpus Christi College MS 464, included the following chapters from William's collection: WC, *MT* 6.27–29; 6.32–33; 6.36; 6.38; 6.41–42; 6.45; 6.48–50; 6.60; 2.17 (not verbatim, and probably not derived from William's collection); 6.61; 6.63–67; 6.69; 6.73–74; 6.79; and 6.88–89.

107. The Montpellier manuscript includes the prefatory letter to Henry II as a prologue, then starts with 1.6 of Robertson's edition. The Évreux manuscript does not have the prefatory letter.

108. These historical chapters appear in the Montpellier manuscript *before* the copies of Benedict's and William's collection: see Duggan, "Lorvão," 61–62. The impressive fifteenth-century lectionary from Paderborn, Erzbischöfliche Akademische Bibliothek Theodoriana Ba 2, includes the chapters known from Robertson's edition as 6.91, 6.93–95, and 6.97 from ff. 159r–160r. William's collection is not otherwise found in the Paderborn manuscript. William may have copied this material into his collection, or it is possible that the Winchester copyist—or an earlier one—introduced this material into his text.

109. See Langenbahn, "Die wiederentdeckten Himmeroder," 149–52.

110. For these letters, see WC, *MT* 6.123–25, 6.127.

111. The text of Winchester College MS 4 ends abruptly at the bottom of the verso of a folio. Ker and Piper note that this manuscript "perhaps ends imperfectly": see N. R. Ker and A. J. Piper, *Medieval Manuscripts in British Libraries* vol. 4, Paisley-York (Oxford, 1992), vol. 4, 605.

112. Gervase, vol. 1, 5.

113. The chronicler was Robert Swaffam, a monk of Peterborough: see J. Sparke, *Historiae Anglicanae Scriptores Varii* (London, 1723), 97–103, at 101.

114. Surveys of these later events can be found in Duggan, *Thomas Becket*, 217–36, and Barlow, *Thomas Becket*, 251–75. See Keefe, "Shrine Time," 115–22, for Henry II's pilgrimages; for the vitae-writing, see Staunton, *Thomas Becket and His Biographers*; and for Alan of Tewkesbury's collection, see Duggan, *Correspondence*, esp. lxxx–lxxxi and lxxxiii.

115. The expense of the rebuilding of the cathedral is briefly mentioned in WC, *MT* 6.97, 493, one of the "historical" chapters. A gift for the new shrine is mentioned in WC, *MT* 6.89, 482.

116. See, for example, BP, *MT* 3.25, 3.45, and 3.64.

117. WC, *MT* 1.51 (Robertson 2.37).

118. WC, *MT* 2.53 (Robertson 2.91). Compare with BP, *MT* 3.45, a miracle concerning a kinsman of Foliot.

119. WC, *MT* 3.18.

120. William mentions the Irish expedition in *MT* 1.39 (Robertson 2.25); 1.41 (Robertson 2.27); 2.6 (Robertson 2.44); 3.17; 3.19; 4.53; 5.7; 6.55; 6.116; and 6.168. For analysis of these stories, see Bull, "Criticism of Henry II's Expedition," 123–29.

121. WC, *MT* 4.20, 332.

122. WC, *MT* 6.28, 440. William does not say which of Henry II's pilgrimages this was, but it was likely the one in 1175.

123. WC, *MT* prologue, 138: Marcus Bull suggests that the reference to William's collection as "libellus" means that only a portion of William's collection was given to the king (Bull, "Criticism of Henry II's Expedition," 114) but Reginald of Durham's massive collection for Cuthbert was also entitled a "libellus." From the manuscript tradition, it is likely that Henry II received a text including at least 1.6 to 6.90, and possibly the first five chapters of book 1 as well.

124. WC, *MT* 1.4, 143. Didier Lett argues that William composed his collection in an attempt to "rehabilitate the king" (see "Deux hagiographes," 203 and 211–16), but he fails to see the progression in William's attitudes or consider that the prefatory letter must have been composed after William had completed the majority of his collection.

125. WC, *MT* 6.147, 529.

126. See, e.g., WC, *MT* 5.13–14 and 6.25.

127. WC, *MT* 2.26 (Robertson 2.64) and 3.5.

128. William includes direct copies of thirty-seven letters in his collection (not counting the prefatory letter): the longest set of letters is found at the beginning of his sixth book, cc. 2–11.

129. See WC, *MT* 3.21 and 6.72. Richard, the abbot of Sulby in Welford, does not seem to have been able to keep away from Canterbury. He appears in Benedict's collection (*MT* 3.42–43), then twice more in William's collection: *MT* 1.10, 3.34–35.

130. WC, *MT* 6.11, 422; see also 6.19.

131. See Benedict, *MT* 3.64–76.

132. William mentions Newington in *MT* 1.46 (Robertson 2.32) and also in 3.57.

133. WC, *MT* 3.30, 287.

134. For the chapels, see WC, *MT* 6.150 (near Devizes), 6.129 (in Germany), and 6.80 (in Ireland). On the chapel in Germany, see Langenbahn's discussion in "Die wiederentdeckten Himmeroder," 121–64. For the hospital, see WC, *MT* 6.149.

135. WC, *MT* 1.46 (Robertson 2.32).

136. WC, *MT* 4.6.

137. WC, *MT* 4.15, 327. Accounts of the oblations at Becket's tomb were not kept until 1198. For these later accounts, see Nilson, *Cathedral Shrines*, 147–54, 211–15.

CHAPTER 9. I TAKE UP THE BURDEN: BENEDICT OF PETERBOROUGH'S EXAMINATION OF BECKET'S MIRACLES

1. BP, *MT*, prologue, 26.

2. BP, *MT* 1.6.

3. BP, *MT* 1.6, 36. The Becket cult can be profitably read in the context of the "revivals" discussed by Gary Dickson in his articles "Revivalism as a Medieval Religious Genre," and "Encounters in Medieval Revivalism: Monks, Friars and Popular Enthusiasts."

4. *The Letters of Peter of Celle*, no. 142, 522–25, at 522.

5. BP, *MT* 1.9, 39–40.

6. There has been remarkably little examination of Benedict's collection except in these terms (e.g., Finucane, *Miracles and Pilgrims* and Foreville, "Les *Miracula*"). Didier Lett writes of Benedict's collection as "conformist" before moving on to William's collection, a text that interests him more: see Lett, "Deux hagiographes," 205–9.

7. BP, *MT* 1.7.

8. By my count, the exact percentages are 29 percent cathedral miracles, 44 percent the cured, and 27 percent religious men, with different proportions in different books. Someone else's count might well result in slightly higher or lower numbers. It is usually but not always clear to which category a chapter should belong.

9. For these runs of cathedral miracles, see BP, *MT* 2.1–2.17, 2.23–2.40, and 3.1–14.

10. BP, *MT* 3.2.

11. BP, *MT*, prologue, 25–26; see also 1.7 and 1.4, 33: "et ecclesiae, diutini squalore moeroris afflictae, per miraculorum coruscationem redderetur laetitia."

12. Gervase, later, would refer to the collection as "the miracles which Benedict saw and wrote": [*miracula quae vidit et conscripsit Benedictus*]: Gervase, vol. 2, 391.

13. BP, *MT* 3.5: "residentibus nobis ibidem."

14. BP, *MT* 2.31, 82–83.

15. BP, *MT* 2.32, 83.

16. BP, *MT* 4.37, 208–9.

17. BP, *MT* 3.19, 131.

18. BP, *MT* 2.38.

19. BP, *MT* 4.59, 225.

20. BP, *MT* 3.8.

21. BP, *MT* 2.76, 116. Extreme pain, vomiting, or flow of bloody matter often seemed to him to announce the approach of a cure, especially if that pain or purging occurred after a drink of the water or contact with Becket's blood—see 2.60 and 2.64. On three different occasions, Benedict describes people saying they felt as if a bolt of lightening had exploded in their heads: see 2.12, 2.35, 3.16.

22. BP, *MT* 2.53, 101; see also 2.27, 2.28.

23. BP, *MT* 2.16.

24. BP, *MT* 2.17. For more "urging," see 2.5.

25. BP, *MT* 3.42, 90: "Mirati sumus, qui affuimus, praesumptuosum orationis principium; mirati nihilominus devotioni ejus condigno fidei pretio tam subito esse responsum." Compare with Benedict's account of the healing of a blind woman, 1.8, 32: "Mirum fidei florem mirabilior fidei fructus secutus est." For the story of the dead knight, see 2.65.

26. BP, *MT* 4.3, 182.

27. BP, *MT* 4.3, 182–83.

28. BP, *MT* 4.3, 183.

29. For "we who were there," see BP, *MT* 2.32, 83; 2.40, 90; 3.9, 125.

30. BP, *MT* 3.1, 119.

31. BP, *MT* 1.15.

32. See, e.g., BP, *MT* 2.33 and 2.40.

33. See BP, *MT* 2.1, 2.38, 3.3, 3.33.

34. BP, *MT* 3.7. Benedict may have been referring to a marble pavement before the high altar: on this pavement, see Tatton-Brown, "Canterbury and the Architecture," at 91.

35. BP, *MT* 3.10.

36. See, for instance, BP, *MT* 2.53, 4.83.

37. BP, *MT* 2.33.

38. BP, *MT* 3.5. William would later mention monks stationed at the martyrdom: see WC, *MT* 3.54, 308.

39. BP, *MT* 4.56, 224.

40. BP, *MT* 4.76, 245–47.

41. BP, *MT* 2.34.

42. BP, *MT* 3.29.

43. BP, *MT* 3.46. In three other chapters, Benedict notes that the monks were not certain of the course of a cathedral cure because the person had left early, without the monks' knowledge: see BP, *MT* 4.23, 4.33, and 4.35. See also Prior Philip's very similar complaint of people not telling anyone about the miracles they had experienced at Frideswide's shrine: Philip of Oxford, *Miracula S. Frideswidae*, c. 79, 584.

44. This information appears in almost all Benedict's accounts. Exact ages often appear in accounts of children's cures: Benedict tells us that Henry, son of Eilmer and Edilda of Beche, was nine years old when he was healed (2.40), the daughter of Wedeman of Folkestone, seven years old (3.10), Geoffrey, the son of Liviva of Chalgrave, fourteen years old (2.76), etc.

45. BP, *MT* 3.28.

46. BP, *MT* 3.23.

47. BP, *MT* 3.15. See also 2.31 and 3.12.

48. See, e.g., BP, *MT* 2.5, 2.7, and 3.16.

49. BP, *MT* 4.21.

50. BP, *MT* 4.27.

51. BP, *MT* 4.23, 4.33, 4.35.

52. BP, *MT* 2.25.

53. BP, *MT* 2.25, 74: "ut cognita causa modoque infirmitatis, finis quoque melius innotescat."

54. BP, *MT* 2.25, 74–77. This chapter, it should be noted, is so similar to William's work that it is possible he wrote it up for Benedict.

55. BP, *MT* 2.24, 74: "ut volare se valere hyperbolice diceret."

56. Ibid: "taedebat animam suam vitae suae."

57. One example is the story of the "mad" Mary of Rouen: see BP, *MT* 4.21.

58. BP, *MT* 3.10, 126.

59. BP, *MT* 3.11, 126.

60. See OC, *MD*, c. 19, 151, and Eadmer, *Miracula S. Dunstani*, c. 19, 189.

61. BP, *MT* 3.11, 126.

62. For other miracle stories involving confession, see BP, *MT* 2.30, 2.45, 2.50, 2.64, 2.72, 3.10, 3.18, 3.25, 3.59, 4.2, 4.32, 4.89, etc. Alexander Murray discusses the appearance of stories concerning confession in miracle collections (though not Benedict's) in "Confession Before 1215." See also Brian Patrick McGuire's discussion of Caesarius of Heisterbach's interest in the pastoral needs of the laity: McGuire, "Friends and Tales in the Cloister: Oral Sources," 230–35.

63. See BP, *MT* 2.72, 115, and 2.44, 92. Benedict also describes feats of constancy and faithfulness among the laity—see BP, *MT* 1.8, 1.11, 3.48, 4.2, 4.64, etc.—and was willing to tell stories about people being rewarded with a miracle despite doing wrong things. What counted for Benedict was right devotion, not right action: see, e.g., 3.53 and 4.47. William made far fewer references to lay confession and faithfulness. For William's lack of interest in such topics, compare Benedict's account of Hugh of Ebblingham's miracle, BP, *MT* 5.4, 259–60, with WC, *MT* 4.20, 332–34.

64. BP, *MT* 2.43, 91.

65. Benedict interlaced a few cathedral miracles into this section of the book: see BP, *MT* 2.49 (paired with 2.48), 2.53 (paired with 2.52), 2.65 (paired with 2.66), and then the run of cathedral miracles from 2.74–77.

66. For this terminology, see BP, *MT* 2.73, 3.30, 3.47, and 4.32.

67. BP, *MT* 4.16.

68. BP, *MT* 4.38. For more oath-taking, see 4.43.

69. BP, *MT* 2.68, 113.

70. BP, *MT* 2.61, 106. For more oblations, see BP, *MT* 2.46, 3.48, 4.5, 4.14, 4.64.

71. BP, *MT* 4.42.

72. BP, *MT* 3.31, 140.

73. BP, *MT* 4.8, 188.

74. BP, *MT* 3.77, 171.

75. BP, *MT* 3.41, 147.

76. BP, *MT* 2.41, 89.

77. BP, *MT* 4.22, 201. See especially the fruit stones in BP, *MT* 2.10.

78. BP, *MT* 2.48, 95.

79. BP, *MT* 4.2, 180–81.

80. BP, *MT* 4.64, 233.

81. BP, *MT* 3.30, 139, and 3.47, 151.

82. BP, *MT* 1.15 and 4.42.

83. BP, *MT* 3.32 and 3.55–56.

84. Benedict himself explains this in the first of the stories of the sequence: see BP, *MT* 3.64, 164–65.

85. For these stories, see BP, *MT* 3.64–76. Sally Crumplin discusses Reginald of Durham's accounts of Cuthbert's miracles at different locales in "Cuthbert the Cross-Border Saint."

86. BP, *MT* 3.64: "ut memorati æmuli sui menti diletionem sui sanctus insereret."

87. BP, *MT* 4.63, 228.

88. See BP, *MT* 4.34, and also 2.1.

89. BP, *MT* 6.2. For Bertrann's travels to investigate the miracles of St. Edmund, see Gransden, "Composition and Authorship," 34.

90. BP, *MT* 3.60–62; 3.42–43; 4.49. These abbots are known from other sources: see the relevant entries in *The Heads of Religious Houses, England and Wales I, 940–1216*, ed. David Knowles, C. N. L. Brooke, and Vera C. M. London (Cambridge, 2001).

91. BP, *MT* 4.40 and 4.39.

92. BP, *MT* 2.66–67, 4.57, 2.56.

93. For unnamed priests as informants, see BP, *MT* 4.52, 4.64, 4.66.

94. BP, *MT* 4.12, 191.

95. BP, *MT* 1.17 and 4.10.

96. BP, *MT* 3.58.

97. Lecarda seems to have sent physical evidence of the miracle (an offering to Becket that did not get wet in the rain) rather than coming herself: see BP, *MT* 4.10.

98. Julie Kerr discusses the different hospitality arrangements at Benedictine monasteries for elite and ordinary guests; see *Monastic Hospitality*, 43, and esp. 103: "The grading of guests in this way might seem rather incongruous to the monastic spirit . . . however, this was acceptable for the time and did not mean that lesser guests should be neglected, but that those of note should be suitably honored."

99. BP, *MT* 1.12 and 2.25.

100. BP, *MT* 2.52.

101. BP, *MT* 4.24. For a chaplain's story of healing at home, see BP, *MT* 2.64, and for a religious man's trouble with constipation, see 2.67.

102. BP, *MT* 4.39–40.

103. BP, *MT* 3.78.

104. BP, *MT* 3.43.

105. BP, *MT* 4.58.

106. BP, *MT* 4.46.

107. See BP, *MT* 1.1, 1.5, 1.6, 1.12.

108. BP, *MT* 3.63.

109. For silent plagiarism, see Chapter 8 and BP, *MT* 4.65, 4.66, and 4.86.

110. BP, *MT* 2.52. One wonders what Benedict thought when he found out that Robert Cricklade decided to compose his own collection of miracles for Thomas Becket. For an account likely written by Ranulf of Froyle, see BP, *MT* 4.14, 195. William of Canterbury includes an account of a vision that Abbot Richard "wrote with his own hands": WC, *MT* 1.10, 148–50.

111. BP, *MT* 4.4, 183.

112. BP, *MT* 4.4, 184.

113. See BP, *MT* 3.60, 4.49, 1.20, 3.64, 3.61, and 4.87.

114. See BP, *MT* 3.51, 4.13, 1.12, and 4.84.

115. BP, *MT* 2.66. Benedict paired this story with the pious death of a knight in the cathedral (2.65).

116. BP, *MT* 4.90.

117. BP, *MT* 4.25–26 and 3.50. These stories did not elicit any negative comment from Benedict.

118. BP, *MT* 4.89.

119. BP, *MT* 6.1, 262.

120. Benedict included just four hearsay stories from the laity in his collection. All four, strikingly, have to do with the "water" acting strangely. For such stories, Benedict was willing to bend his usual rules: see BP, *MT* 2.22, 3.23, 4.6, and 4.47.

121. BP, *MT* 3.71, 4.51, and 4.29.

122. BP, *MT* 3.44, 149.

123. See Appendix 2.

124. BP, *MT* 3.20.

125. BP, *MT* 3.21. See also WM, *GP*, bk. 5, c. 7, 647: "This is [Aldhelm's] practice, familiar to us all: he will tolerate being wronged for a long time, but once he decides to put up with it no longer, he makes a spectacle before the whole world of him who wronged him. In many cases we have laughed when this has happened; in many we look forward hopefully to it happening one day."

126. See, e.g., Eadmer, *Vita Bregowini*, cc. 12 and 13.

127. BP, *MT* 3.42.

128. BP, *MT* 4.1.

129. BP, *MT* 4.12.

130. BP, *MT* 4.4.

131. BP, *MT* 4.46.

132. See also BP, *MT* 4.52, 4.62, 4.64, and 4.79. Benedict's first statement about the "tedium" that might be felt by the reader is found in 3.22.

133. See BP, *MT* 4.64–66 and 4.84–87. Though Benedict gives no indication that 4.86 was based on a letter, we know it was because William copied this letter verbatim into his collection: see WC, *MT* 2.50.

134. In Benedict's fourth book, one finds five stories of blindness (4.30–35), six sea stories (4.41–46), five resurrection stories (4.62–66), five leprosy stories (4.72–76), four justice stories (4.77–80), and four stories in a row derived from letters (4.84–87).

135. For very brief chapters, see BP, *MT* 4.90–93 and 5.1–3.

136. See BP, *MT* 5.4: "ne ergo usque ad taedium trita teramus, novi aliquid exspectemus"; the following chapter, 6.1, begins, "nova suspiravimus."

137. The early-thirteenth copyist of Oxford, Bodleian Lyell MS 5 added his own explicit: see Albinia De La Mare, *Catalogue of the Collection of Medieval Manuscripts Bequeathed to the Bodleian Library Oxford by James P. R. Lyell* (Oxford, 1971), 8–13. The

fifteenth-century copyist of Paderborn, Erzbischöfliche Akademische Bibliothek Theodoriana Ba 2 made up his own explicit out of passages from BP, *MT* 4.4.

138. *MTB* vol. 2, xlix.

CHAPTER IO. CHOOSE WHAT YOU WILL:
WILLIAM OF CANTERBURY AND THE HEAVENLY DOCTOR

1. For William's description of himself as "scriptorem suum," see WC, *Vita*, 2, and WC, *MT*, prologue, 139.

2. WC, *Vita*, 2: "miracula ejus, quae in schedulis occultabat incorrecta et imperfecta, rogaretur a fratribus exponere transcribenda."

3. WC, *Vita*, 2–3.

4. For these notes and the dating of William's collection, see Chapter 8.

5. WC, *MT*, prologue, 139: "epulas quas habet recumbentibus exhibet."

6. See especially WC, *MT* 3.11, 3.16, and 5.18.

7. By my count, 32 of the 425 chapters in William's collection concern cathedral miracles. They are found here and there in all the books of the collection rather than in the long series that characterize Benedict's second and third books.

8. See WC, *MT*, prologue, 138, "quae populi frequentia venientis ad orationem referebat."

9. For these stories, see WC, *MT* 1.52 (Robertson 2.38); 2.81; 3.9; 2.6 (Robertson 2.44); 3.37; 4.29; 5.38; 2.9 (Robertson 2.47); 5.1; and 6.41.

10. WC, *MT* 4.34, 346–47.

11. For a very similar story included despite the teller's lack of witnesses, see WC, *MT* 2.19 (Robertson 2.57). William talks about "false and decoying brothers" in this story as well.

12. It appears to have been these stories that led scholars to state that William was *more* doubtful than Benedict (see, e.g., Lapidge and Love, "Latin Hagiography," 287).

13. For the few times William does include more than one story told by the same person, see WC, *MT* 3.34–35; 5.13–14; 6.22–24; 1.1–3; 1.4–5. William also does not separate out stories from "the testimony of religious men" as Benedict had. He seems to have seen just two major categories of miracles: those that "flashed out" in Canterbury cathedral, and "the many told by the people coming for prayer." See WC, *MT*, prologue, 138.

14. See Appendix 3 for William's grouping of stories by teller and by type of story. Most commentators on William's collection have noted the large number of stories about knights in his collection (see 1.39–42; 2.19–26; 5.32–37, etc.). It is not correct, however, that William "approached his task with greater prejudice against the 'lower orders' of society [than Benedict]," or that he had a "contempt for the underprivileged": Finucane, *Miracles and Pilgrims*, 126; Lett, "Deux hagiographes," 207. These assessments depend too heavily on passages from stories in the final addition to the collection in which William is amusing himself with debates over questions of truth and falsity. William thought that Becket had a soft spot for knights, but emphasized too that they were not the only benefi-

ciaries of Becket's aid: "he confines this mercy to no class of person, no place, no time, but he extends it without choice of person, and here and there, and everyday, which we see with eyes and hear with ears": WC, *MT* 2.10 (Robertson 2.48).

15. For "medicalization," see Crumplin, "Modernizing St. Cuthbert," 185, n. 25. Research has only just begun on this topic.

16. The difference in medical terminology is one of the few distinctions between the Christ Church collections that is regularly noted by scholars: see, e.g., Finucane, *Miracles and Pilgrims*, 126, and Ward, *Miracles and the Medieval Mind*, 96.

17. See Monica Green, "Salerno on the Thames: The Genesis of Anglo-Norman Medical Literature," in *Language and Culture in Medieval Britain: The French of England, c. 1100–c.1500*, ed. Jocelyn Wogan-Browne, with Carolyn Collette, Maryanne Kowaleski, Linne Mooney, Ad Putter, and David Trotter (York, 2009), 221. I am very grateful to Monica Green for allowing me to see this forthcoming article and for the other articles and references she generously shared with me.

18. On this point, see Rawcliffe, *Leprosy in Medieval England*, 173.

19. See Kealey, *Medieval Medicus*, 39–40.

20. Kealey, *Medieval Medicus*, 149.

21. On these decrees, see Rawcliffe, "Curing Bodies," 116.

22. See Sweetingburgh, "Supporting the Canterbury Hospitals," Kealey, *Medieval Medicus*, 85, and Sweetinburgh, *Role of the Hospital*, esp. 36. Ziegler writes that in the medieval period, "overlap, sometimes even ambiguity, now seems more appropriate to describe the relationship between medicine and theology, between the carers for bodies and for souls, between medical and spiritual approaches to disease": "Religion and Medicine," 4.

23. On hospitals in Kent, see Sweetinburgh, *Role of the Hospital*, 68–126, esp. 80, 88–89.

24. WC, *Vita*, 114–15. Duggan rejects Barlow's suggestion that this doctor was William the collector: see Duggan, *Thomas Becket*, 203–4. For a Master William *medicus* who witnessed two charters dated 1148 x 1154 with Thomas Becket, see Kealey, *Medieval Medicus*, 150.

25. William tells two of Master Feramin's visions in *MT* 1.4–5 and describes him as "vir honestae conversationis, fratrum infirmorum res administrat" (1.4, 143). On doctor Peter, see WC, *MT* 3.4, 261. William discusses the involvement of the "medicus Walterus, sancti Salvatoris Ovetensis civitatis canonicus" in 4.54. For another story about a doctor, see 6.101, 496–97.

26. Cited and translated in Kealey, *Medieval Medicus*, 37.

27. See Appendix 3. Benedict had devoted many pages to the story of Jordan Fitz-Eisulf, second only to the story of Eilward of Westoning.

28. WC, *MT* 1.20, 162–63 (Robertson 2.6).

29. Compare William's discussion of the types and causes of epilepsy with Benedict's discussion of "the falling sickness": see BP, *MT* 4.93, 3.37, and 4.26.

30. WC, *MT* 4.16–17.

31. WC, *MT* 1.34 (Robertson 2.20); 3.7.

32. WC, *MT* 2.5 (Robertson 2.43), 6.54.

33. WC, *MT* 2.1 (Robertson 2.39), 4.54, 5.31.

34. WC, *MT* 2.26 (Robertson 2.64), 6.34.

35. WC, *MT* 2.48 (Robertson 2.86) for apoplexy; 2.42 (Robertson 2.80) for diarrhea; 4.38 for gout; 1.39 and 2.46 (Robertson 2.25 and 2.84) for dysentery; 4.46 for piles; 1.31 (Robertson, 2.17) for *cephalica*; and 3.30 for *arteriata*.

36. For *hyrquos*, see WC, *MT* 2.39 (Robertson 2.77).

37. WC, *MT* 4.39 for the armpit [*acella* for *axilla*]; and 3.55 for *internodiis manus*.

38. WC, *MT* 4.27.

39. See WC, *MT* 1.45 (Robertson 2.31), 6.81, 6.83 for the thorax; 4.26 for the lung; 3.4 for the liver; 1.45 (Robertson, 2.31) for the hips; 1.34 (Robertson 2.20) for ribs; 2.5 (Robertson 2.43) for the vertebra of the spine; and 1.32 (Robertson 2.18) for cartilage.

40. See WC, *MT* 3.37 for veins; 2.1 (Robertson 2.39) for arteries; 4.4 for the pulse; and 2.50 (Robertson 2.88) for the heart.

41. See WC, *MT* 4.46 for the anus; 4.17 and 5.5 for the urinary tract; 1.34 (Robertson 2.20) and 5.5 for the testicles; 1.34 (Robertson 2.20) for the penis; 1.38 (Robertson 2.24) for the breast; 2.28 (Robertson, 2.66) for the uterus; 3.6 for the vulva.

42. WC, *MT* 3.32 and 4.7.

43. WC, *MT* 2.16, 216 (Robertson 2.54).

44. BP, *MT* 4.75, 245.

45. WC, *MT* 2.14, 213–14 (Robertson, 2.52).

46. BP, *MT* 2.44, 92: "periculoso, ut putabatur, squinantiae morbo percussus paene praefocatus est."

47. WC, *MT* 1.13, 153.

48. WC, *MT* 4.20, 333. See Rawcliffe, *Leprosy in Medieval England*, 75, for these types of leprosy.

49. WC, *MT* 4.20, 332.

50. BP, *MT* 5.4, 259–60.

51. WC, *MT* 3.4.

52. WC, *MT* 3.51.

53. WC, *MT* 2.45, 245 (Robertson 2.83).

54. WC, *MT* 2.49, 248–49 (Robertson 2.87). He had a sense, too, that vertigo and epilepsy were somehow connected: in the same chapter, William, priest of Coutances, worries that his vertigo would turn into madness or epilepsy if it went on too long, and in an earlier chapter, Emma is cured of her epilepsy except for some vertigo (1.24 (Robertson, 2.10)).

55. WC, *MT* 4.16, 328–29.

56. WC, *MT* 5.5, 376.

57. WC, *MT* 6.73.

58. WC, *MT* 1.34, 176–77 (Robertson 2.20).

59. WC, *MT* 2.26, 222–25 (Robertson 2.64).

60. See WC, *MT* 1.29 and 40 (Robertson, 2.15 and 2.26), 2.4 (Robertson 2.42), 3.16, 6.12, 6.64.

61. WC, *MT* 6.81, 478.

62. WC, *MT* 1.32, 175 (Robertson 2.18).

63. WC, *MT* 3.37, 292.

64. WC, *MT* 3.21.

65. See Nancy Siraisi's discussion of "disease and treatment," in *Medieval and Early Renaissance Medicine*, chap. 5, esp. 123–24.

66. WC, *MT* 2.31 (Robertson 2.69).

67. WC, *MT* 1.45 (Robertson 2.31).

68. WC, *MT* 2.47 (Robertson 2.85) and 5.9.

69. WC, *MT* 4.40, 351.

70. WC, *MT* 4.40, 350.

71. WC, *MT* 2.28, 226–27 (Robertson, 2.66).

72. WC, *MT* 2.5, 204 (Robertson, 2.43).

73. On changelings and this story, see Watkins, *History and the Supernatural*, 62. For discussion of a story that similarly demonstrates a difference in the writer's and the teller's understanding of an illness, see McCleery, "*Multos ex medicinae*," 195–97.

74. WC, *MT* 1.22, 165–66 (Robertson 2.8).

75. WC, *MT* 5.11, 382–83.

76. WC, *MT* 5.15.

77. WC, *MT* 1.47 (Robertson 2.33).

78. See WC, *MT* 1.26 (Robertson 2.12) for seawater; 3.33 for ointment; 6.71 for turpentine.

79. WC, *MT* 1.46, 187 (Robertson 2.32).

80. WC, *MT* 1.33, 175 (Roberston 2.19).

81. WC, *MT* 6.13, 426.

82. Compare BP, *MT* 4.65, 234, and WC, *MT* 1.49, 190 (Robertson 2.35).

83. WC, *MT* 1.36 (Robertson 2.22).

84. WC, *MT* 3.38, 294.

85. WC, *MT* 2.41, 242 (Robertson 2.79).

86. WC, *MT* 1.28 and 1.45 (Robertson 2.14 and 2.31).

87. WC, *MT* 5.36, 403.

88. WC, *MT* 1.20, 162–64 (Robertson 2.6)

89. WC, *MT* 1.21, 164–65 (Robertson 2.7)

90. For discussion and examples of these badges, see Spencer, *Pilgrim Souvenirs*, 45, 47, and 53. See also J. Alexander and P. Binski, eds., *Age of Chivalry: Art in Plantagenet England, 1200–1400* (London, 1987), 218–20.

91. BP, *MT* 3.55, 157.

92. WC, *MT* 1.45, 184–87 (Robertson 2.31).

93. WC, *MT* 3.4, 261–62. At the close of the story, William writes, unusually for him, about how the story came to his hearing: it was told throughout the region of

Perigord, from whence it came to Canterbury, but the bishop of Perigord, lest he be mislead by "the many tales of the multitude" [*vulgari multiloquio*], sought out the doctor himself, heard the story from him, and, William concludes, "we learned what we say from his mouth."

94. WC, *MT* 3.12, 271.

95. WC, *MT* 6.37, 447.

96. WC, *MT* 3.5, 264.

97. WC, *MT* 2.39, 240 (Robertson, 2.77).

98. WC, *MT* 3.14, 273.

99. WC, *MT* 5.32, 398.

100. See WC, *MT* 4.17 and 3.15, 273.

101. WC, *MT* 1.40 (Robertson 2.26). See also 2.47 (Robertson 2.85).

102. WC, *MT* 1.34, 176 (Roberston 2.20).

103. WC, *MT* 6.114.

104. WC, *MT* 1.46, 187 (Robertson 2.32).

105. WC, *MT* 1.31, 174 (Robertson 2.17).

106. WC, *MT* 6.37, 447.

107. WC, *MT* 3.22, 280.

108. WC, *MT* 1.21, 165 (Robertson 2.7).

109. WC, *MT* 3.16, 274–75.

110. WC, *MT* 6.13, 426.

111. WC, *MT* 2.18, 217–19 (Robertson 2.56).

112. WC, *MT* 2.41, 242–43 (Robertson 2.79)

113. WC, *MT* 2.26, 222–25 (Robertson 2.64).

114. WC, *MT* 6.72, 471.

115. WC, *MT* 4.19, 330–332.

116. WC, *MT* 2.27, 225 (Robertson 2.65).

117. WC, *MT* 6.54, 457.

118. WC, *MT* 6.37.

119. WC, *MT* 5.32, 401.

120. WC, *MT* 1.22 (Robertson 2.8).

121. WC, *MT* 6.71, 470.

122. WC, *MT* 6.73, 472.

123. WC, *MT* 1.34 (Robertson 2.20).

124. WC, *MT* 1.28 (Robertson 2.14).

125. WC, *MT* 2.48 (Robertson 2.86).

126. WC, *MT* 2.34, 234–36 (Robertson 2.72).

127. On this point, see especially Joseph Ziegler's article, "Practitioners and Saints."

128. See BP, *MT* 2.54, 3.63, and 4.42.

129. WC, *MT* 1.38, 180 (Robertson 2.24).

130. See WC, *MT* 5.25, 6.44, 6.51, 6.68, and 6.89.

131. WC, *MT* 3.6.

132. WC, *MT* 6.40 and 6.104.

133. WC, *MT* 6.160 and 6.161.

134. WC, *MT* 6.89, 483.

135. WC, *MT* 6.79, 476–77.

136. WC, *MT* 5.31, 397.

137. WC, *MT* 6.147, 529. The idea that Becket protected the king's falcons may have lived on: Edward I gave a wax image of a falcon to the shrine in the late thirteenth century. See Benjamin F. Byerly and Catherine Ridder Byerly, eds., *Records of the Wardrobe and Household, 1285–1286* (London, 1977), no. 368, 2239.

138. WC, *MT* 6.158 and 6.148.

139. WC, *MT* 6.113, 504.

140. WC, *MT* 6.136, 522.

141. WC, *MT* 6.138, 523.

142. WC, *MT* 6.140, 524.

143. WC, *MT* 6.162, 540.

CONCLUSION: THE END OF MIRACLE COLLECTING

1. On Gilbert, see Chapter 7. A large collection of thirteenth-century miracles concerning Wulfstan is edited by Reginald Darlington in *The Vita Wulfstani of William of Malmesbury*, Camden Society 3rd ser. 40 (London, 1928), 115–88. For analysis, see Mason, *St. Wulfstan of Worcester*, 254–85, and Finucane, *Miracles and Pilgrims*, 130–31. For Hugh's miracles, see the edition in David H. Farmer, "The Canonization of St. Hugh of Lincoln," *Lincolnshire Architectural and Archaeological Reports and Papers* 6, 2 (1956): 86–117, and Farmer's discussion in "The Cult and Canonization of St. Hugh," 75–88. See also Hugh's miracles in *Gerald of Wales: The Life of St. Hugh of Avalon, Bishop of Lincoln 1186–1200*, ed. and trans. Richard Morgan Loomis (New York, 1985).

2. For discussion of these texts and hagiography more generally in the early part of the thirteenth century, see Bartlett, "The Hagiography of Angevin England," 37–52. Susan Wilson dates *Alia Miracula III* of John of Beverley, an anonymous collection of nine chapters, to c. 1219: see Wilson, *The Life and After-life*, 13.

3. On these windows, see Caviness, *The Early Stained Glass*, and her catalogue, *The Windows of Christ Church Cathedral Canterbury*. See also Harris, "Pilgrimage, Performance."

4. English collections dating from the mid-thirteenth century are sparse. Lapidge and Love, "Latin Hagiography," 258 n.197 mention "a small collection of miracles of Eadburh at Pershore, still unpublished," and Bartlett has edited a collection of the miracles of Margaret of Scotland that he dates to the middle decades of the thirteenth century: see *The Miracles of Saint Æbbe of Coldingham and Saint Margaret of Scotland*, xxxi–xxxviii.

5. For the collection of Simon de Montfort, see *The Chronicle of William de Rishanger of the Barons' Wars*, ed. James Halliwell, Camden Society 15 (London, 1840), and John Edward St. Lawrence III, "The *Liber miraculorum* of Simon de Montfort: Contested

Sanctity and Contesting Authority in Late Thirteenth-Century England," Ph.D. dissertation, University of Texas at Austin, 2005. The canonization procedure for Thomas Cantilupe dated to 1307 is partially edited in *AASS* October 1, 549–629 and has interested many scholars: see, e.g., Flint, "The Saint and the Operation of the Law," 342–57, and Bartlett, *The Hanged Man*. The miracles of Henry VI are discussed by Hanham, "Henry VI and His Miracles," 638–52. A little-studied canonization dossier for Osmund of Salisbury also survives from the fifteenth century: see A. R. Malden, ed., *The Canonization of St. Osmund*, Wiltshire Record Society (Salisbury, 1901), and Brown, *Popular Piety in Late Medieval England*, 57–66. Finucane, *Miracles and Pilgrims*, used the miracles of Montfort and Cantiuple (see esp. 131–37); see also Theilmann's discussion of the miracles of Montfort, Cantiuple, and Henry VI in "English Peasants and Medieval Miracle Lists," 286–303.

6. More late medieval collections will no doubt be found. James Clark, for instance, has recently discovered a lengthy collection of the miracles of Alban in a manuscript dated between c.1390 and c.1415: see Clark, "The St. Albans Monks," 222. It would take an enormous rash of such discoveries, however, before one could start to equate late medieval collecting with that of the long twelfth century.

7. The best introduction to English pilgrim badges is Spencer, *Pilgrim Souvenirs and Secular Badges*; for shrine accounts, see the excellent study by Nilson, *Cathedral Shrines*.

8. For some of these new cults, see the chapter titled "Unofficial Pilgrimage" in Webb, *Pilgrimage in Medieval England*, 141–79.

9. The four narratives are edited in *MTB*, vol. 2, 267–81, as chapters 6.4–6.7 of Benedict of Peterborough's *Miracula S. Thomae*. In his edition, Robertson reversed the order of the final two chapters, thinking that they read better that way: see his footnote n. 3, 273. This addition is preserved in only one manuscript.

10. On these saints, see Lawrence, *St. Edmund of Abingdon*, 1–47, and his revision and expansion of his ideas in his edition of Matthew Paris's life of St. Edmund of Abingdon; see also Denton, *Robert Winchelsey*, 15–33.

11. *MTB*, vol. 2, bk. 6, c. 4, 268–69.

12. *MTB*, vol. 2, bk. 6, c. 4, 270. See also the author's introduction to the story, 268: "desiderantes scribendo, licet sero scripserimus, ab ipso consequi veniam apud quem de taciturnitate plurimam timemus incurrisse offensam." For a similar story, see the collection of miracles for St. Gangolf edited in *AASS* May 2, 648–55, at 654. The procrastination of this collection's author was so severe that Gangolf nearly had to kill him before he would fulfill his promise to write.

13. *The Book of Sainte Foy*, bk. 2, c. 7, 130. Bernard was eventually convinced to continue.

14. One other little anonymous collection of four stories about Becket, linked to an account of the translation in 1220, was compiled sometime in the thirteenth century, probably closely following on the translation itself. It appears, though, that this little collection was not of Christ Church manufacture. See the discussion by Reames, "The Remaking of a Saint," 31. The text has been edited by J. C. Robertson, *MTB*, vol. 4, 426–30, and is also found in Paderborn, Erzbischöfliche Akademische Bibliothek Theod-

oriana MS Ba 2, f. 170v–171v (this manuscript was not known by Robertson). In describing the Paderborn manuscript, Francis Halkin, "Legendarii Bodecensis Menses Duo in Codice Paderbornensi," *AB* 52 (1934): 321–33, at 327 is incorrect to state that the "last" miracle of this account is missing—the last story in Robertson's edition is here at the beginning of the set of four.

15. Ward, *Miracles and the Medieval Mind*, 1.

16. For an overview of this activity, see Goodich, *Miracles and Wonders*; Bynum, "Miracles and Marvels"; and Bynum, "Metamorphosis."

17. An indication of the volume of these manuscripts is the number housed just in the British Library alone: see the section devoted to the *Miracles of the Virgin* in H. L. D. Ward, *Catalogue of Romances in the Department of Manuscripts of the British Museum*, vol. 2 (London 1893), 586–740. For Middle English versions, see Ruth Wilson Tryon, "Miracles of Our Lady in Middle English Verse," *PMLA* 38 (1923): 308–88. The text continued to be popular in the early modern period: see, for instance, Chavasse, "Piety, Penance, and Popular Reading."

18. On Nigel's career, see the introduction to Jan Ziolkowski's edition of Nigel's *Miracula*, 1–10, and Rigg, *History of Anglo-Latin Literature*, 102–5. Henry of Avranches began a Latin versification of Becket's miracles (presumably drawing on accounts from Benedict's or William's collections) around the time of Becket's 1220 translation, but quit within a week and destroyed what he had written: see Russell and Heironimus, *The Shorter Latin Poems*, 88–93.

19. On these collections, see J. Th. Welter, *L'exemplum dans la littérature religieuse et didactique du moyen âge* (Paris, 1929); Claude Bremond, Jacques Le Goff, and Jean-Claude Schmitt, *L'exemplum*, Typologie des sources du moyen âge occidental 40 (Turnhout, 1982); and the essays in Jacques Berlioz and Marie Anne Polo de Beaulieu, eds., *Les "exempla" médiévaux: nouvelles perspectives* (Paris, 1998).

20. Some *exempla* collections are filled with personal reminiscences, and as such share much of the flavor of miracle collections: see especially Alexander Murray's discussion of Thomas of Chantimpré's *Bonum universale de apibus*, composed between 1256 and 1260: "Confession as a Historical Source," 286–305.

21. This is the first story in the collection edited and translated by Thomas F. Crane, *The Exempla or Illustrative Stories from the Sermones Vulgares of Jacques de Vitry* (London, 1890), 1.

22. See Vauchez, *Sainthood in the Later Middle Ages*, esp. 33–104.

23. Lawrence, *St. Edmund of Abingdon*, 1–47.

24. Langton describes Eustace as "qui plus omnibus in hoc negotio laboravit" in his letter to John of Toledo dated June 6, 1246: the letter is edited by E. Martène and U. Durand in *Thesaurus Novus Anecdotorum* (Paris, 1717), cols. 1914–15.

25. For the story of Edmund's canonization, see Lawrence's description in his edition of Matthew Paris's life, *The Life of St. Edmund*, 90–99. Richard Wich, bishop of Chichester and former chancellor of Edmund Rich, sent a letter to Innocent IV concerning miracles in England in November 1245: see *English Episcopal Acta: Chichester, 1215–1253*, ed. Phillipa M. Hoskin (Oxford, 2001) vol. 22, no. 164, 130–31.

26. "Qui congregati de magnitudine et multitudine miraculorum per merita beati patris Edmundi factorum tantam certitudinem ostendebant": *Thesaurus Novus Anecdotorum*, col. 1915.

27. Matthew Paris's copy of the bull is printed in Lawrence, *The Life of St. Edmund*, 163–66. On Edmund Rich, see also Jordan, "The English Holy Men of Pontigny," 63–75.

28. For a discussion of this short-lived requirement, see Vauchez, *Sainthood in the Later Middle Ages*, 50.

29. For the *vita*, see Lawrence, *St. Edmund of Abingdon*, 30–47, 203–21.

30. Vauchez seems surprised to have found that "many of the objections made by the Holy See to investigations *in partibus* concerned the way in which evidence had been taken and recorded" or that "the cardinals and the colleagues seem to have been primarily interested in irregularities in the recording the statement": *Sainthood in the Later Middle Ages*, 50, 487. He seems to have hoped that the "great minds" would have "questioned the reality of those [miracle stories] submitted to them" wholesale (498), an unrealistic expectation.

31. On the (ultimately unsuccessful) attempts to canonize Winchelsey, see Denton, *Robert Winchelsey*, 15–33.

32. Lancaster is a fascinating figure: he himself was revered as a saint after his own death. See Walker, "Political Saints," 77–106, and Piroyanksy, "Bloody Miracles of a Political Martyr," 228–38.

33. The proceedings are printed in *Concilia Magnae Britanniae et Hiberniae*, ed. D. Wilkins (1737), vol. 2, 486–90.

34. The 1445 letter (Canterbury Cathedral Archives, Cant. Ant. C, 1303), is edited in *MTB* vol. 2, 295–96, and translated by Ward, *Miracles and the Medieval Mind*, 217–18. An abbreviated copy of the letter is in Canterbury Cathedral Archives, Register S, f. 163r. The text from the register is edited, with some errors, by Stanley, *Historical Memorials of Canterbury*, 280–81.

35. BP, *MT* 3.21, 133.

36. Stone's chronicle is edited in *Christ Church Canterbury. I. The Chronicle of John Stone. II. List of the Deans, Priors, and Monks of Christ Church Monastery*, ed. W. G. Searle, Cambridge Antiquarian Society Publications 8th series 34 (Cambridge, 1902) and discussed in Dobson's magisterial survey, "The Monks of Canterbury in the Later Middle Ages," 112–13, 116.

37. For a study of a very similar notebook written by another fifteenth-century Christ Church monk, see Greatrex, "Culture at Canterbury in the Fifteenth Century," 169–76.

38. See Stone, *Chronicle*, 100. For similar late fifteenth-century poems in Middle English that describe miracles, see Duffy, "The Dynamics of Pilgrimage in Late Medieval England," 168–70.

39. For discussion of Thomas's cult in the late medieval period, see Duggan, "The Cult of St. Thomas," 21–44, and Dobson's excellent "Contrasting Cults," 24–43. I come to different conclusions from Dobson on the extent to which miracle stories about Becket circulated in the late medieval period.

40. Martin Heale stresses in a recent article that late medieval monks continued to be very much engaged in saint's cults and popular devotion: see "Training in Superstition?" 417–39.

41. The reference is from an inventory of the books at Canterbury College compiled in 1524: see James, *The Ancient Libraries*, 168.

42. OC, *MD* 129.

SELECTED BIBLIOGRAPHY

PRIMARY SOURCES

Ælfric of Winchester. *Life of St. Swithun*. Ed. and trans. Michael Lapidge. *CSS*, 590–610.

Aelred of Rievaulx. *De sanctis ecclesiae Hagustaldensis*. Ed. J. Raine in *The Priory of Hexham*. SS 44. Durham 1864. I: 173–203. Trans. Jane Patricia Freeland, ed. Marsha L. Dutton, in Aelred of Rievaulx, *Lives of the Northern Saints*. Kalamazoo, Mich., 2006. 65–108.

———. *Vita S. Edwardi regis*. PL 195. 737–90. Trans. Fr. Jerome Bertram, *The Life of Saint Edward King and Confessor by Blessed Aelred Abbot of Rievaulx*. Wiltshire, 1990.

Alexander of Canterbury. *Dicta Anselmi et Quaedam Miracula*. Ed. R. W. Southern and F. S. Schmitt, O.S.B in *Memorials of St. Anselm*. London, 1969. 105–268.

Alia Miracula I–III. Ed. J. Raine in *HCY*, I: 293–347. Trans. in Susan E. Wilson, *The Life and After-Life of St. John of Beverley: The Evolution of the Cult of an Anglo-Saxon Saint*. Aldershot, 2006. 177–28.

Anecdota Bedae Lanfranci et Aliorum: Inedited Tracts, Letters, Poems, Etc. Ed. J. Giles. London, 1851.

The Anglo-Saxon Chronicle. Vol. 17, *The Annals of St. Neots with Vita Prima Sancti Neoti*. Ed. David Dumville and Michael Lapidge. Cambridge, 1985.

Anonymous I. *Vita S. Thomae, Cantuariensis archiepiscopi et martyris*. Ed. J. C. Robertson in *MTB*, IV: 1–79.

Anonymous II. *Vita S. Thomae, Cantuariensis archiepiscopi et martyris*. Ed. J. C. Robertson in *MTB*, IV: 80–144.

Arcoid. *Miracula S. Erkenwaldi*. Ed. and trans. E. Gordon Whatley, *The Saint of London: The Life and Miracles of St. Erkenwald, Text and Translation*. Binghamton, N.Y., 1989. 100–165.

Benedict of Peterborough. *Miracula S. Thomae Cantuariensis*. Ed. J. C. Robertson in *MTB*, II: 21–281.

———. *Passio S. Thomae Cantuariensis*. Ed. J. C. Robertson in *MTB*, II: 1–19.

Bertrann. *De miraculis sancti Eadmundi*. Ed. Thomas Arnold in *MEdm*, I: 26–92.

The Book of Sainte Foy. Trans. Pamela Sheingorn. Philadelphia, 1995.

The Book of St. Gilbert. Ed. and trans. Raymonde Foreville and Gillian Keir. OMT. Oxford, 1987.

The Book of the Foundation of St. Bartholomew's Church in London: The Church Belonging to the Priory of the Same in West Smithfield, Edited from the Original Manuscript in the British Museum, Cotton Vespasian B ix. Ed. Norman Moore. EETS 163. London, 1923.

Byrhtferth of Ramsey. *The Lives of St. Oswald and St. Ecgwine.* Ed. and trans. Michael Lapidge. OMT. Oxford, 2009.

Capitula de Miraculis et Translationibus Sancti Cuthberti. Ed. Thomas Arnold in *Symeonis monachi opera omnia.* RS 75. London, 1882. I: 229–61, II: 333–62.

The Correspondence of Thomas Becket, Archbishop of Canterbury, 1162–1170. Ed. Anne Duggan. OMT. Oxford, 2000.

Decretales Ineditae Saeculi XII. Ed. Stanley Chodorow and Charles Duggan. Monumenta Iuris Canonici Series B: Corpus Collectionum 4. Vatican City, 1982.

Dominic of Evesham. *Miracula S. Ecgwini.* Ed. and trans. Jane Sayers and Leslie Watkiss, "The Second Book of the Miracles by Dominic," in *Thomas of Malborough: History of the Abbey of Evesham.* OMT. Oxford, 2003. 76–126.

Eadmer of Canterbury. *De reliquiis sancti Audoeni et quorundam aliorum sanctorum quae Cantuariae in aecclesia domini salvatoris habentur.* Ed. André Wilmart in "Edmeri Cantuariensis cantoris nova opuscula de sanctorum veneratione et obsecratione." *Revue des Sciences Religieuses* 15 (1935): 362–70.

———. *Miracula S. Anselmi.* Ed. and trans. R. W. Southern, *The Life of St. Anselm, Archbishop of Canterbury.* Reprinted OMT. Oxford, 1972. 154–71.

———. *Miracula S. Dunstani.* Ed. and trans. Andrew J. Turner and Bernard J. Muir in *LMODO,* 160–211.

———. *Miracula S. Oswaldi.* Ed. and trans. Andrew J. Turner and Bernard J. Muir in *LMODO,* 290–323.

———. *Vita Bregowini.* Ed. Bernhard W. Scholz, "Eadmer's Life of Bregwine, Archbishop of Canterbury, 761–764." *Traditio* 22 (1966): 137–48.

———. *Vita S. Anselmi.* Ed. and trans. R. W. Southern, *The Life of St. Anselm, Archbishop of Canterbury.* Reprinted OMT. Oxford, 1972.

———. *Vita S. Dunstani.* Ed. and trans. Andrew J. Turner and Bernard J. Muir in *LMODO,* 41–159.

———. *Vita S. Odonis.* Ed. and trans. Andrew J. Turner and Bernard J. Muir in *LMODO,* 1–40.

———. *Vita S. Wilfridi.* Ed. and trans. Bernard J. Muir and Andrew J. Turner. *The Life of Saint Wilfrid by Edmer: An Edition with Translation, Historical Introduction and Commentary.* Exeter, 1998.

Edward Grim. *Vita S. Thomae archiepiscopi et martyris.* Ed. J. C. Robertson in *MTB,* II: 353–450.

Epitome Translationis et Miraculorum S. Swithuni. Ed. and trans. Michael Lapidge, *CSS.* 564–74.

Faricius. *Vita S. Aldhelmi.* Ed. Michael Winterbottom, "An Edition of Faricius, *Vita S. Aldhelmi.*" *Journal of Medieval Latin* 15 (2005): 93–147.

FitzStephen, William. *Vita S. Thomae.* Ed. J. C. Robertson in *MTB*, III: 1–154.

Folcard of St. Bertin. *Vita S. Iohannis Beverlacensis.* Ed. James Raine in *HCY*, I: 239–60. Trans. in Susan E. Wilson, *The Life and After-Life of St. John of Beverley: The Evolution of the Cult of an Anglo-Saxon Saint.* Aldershot, 2006. 143–56.

Geoffrey of Burton. *Life and Miracles of St. Modwenna.* Ed. Robert Bartlett. OMT. Oxford, 2002.

Gervase of Canterbury. *Opera Historica.* Ed. W. Stubbs, *The Historical Works of Gervase of Canterbury.* RS 73. 2 vols. London, 1879–80.

Goscelin of St. Bertin. *Libellus contra inanes S. Mildrethae usurpatores.* Ed. Marvin L. Colker, "A Hagiographical Polemic." *Mediaeval Studies* 39 (1977): 69–96.

———. *Liber confortatorius.* Ed. C. H. Talbot, "The Liber Confortatorius of Goscelin of Saint Bertin." *Studia Anselminana* 37. *Analecta monastica* 3rd ser. (1995): 2–117. Trans. Monica Otter, *Goscelin of St. Bertin: The Book of Encouragement and Consolation [Liber Confortatorius].* Woodbridge, 2004.

———. *Translatio S. Mildrethe Virginis.* Ed. David W. Rollason, "Goscelin of Canterbury's Account of the Translation and Miracles of St. Mildrith (*BHL* 5961/4): An Edition with Notes." *Mediaeval Studies* 48 (1986): 139–210.

———. *Vita et miracula S. Kenelmi.* Ed. and trans. Rosalind Love, *Three Eleventh-Century Anglo-Latin Saints' Lives.* OMT. Oxford, 1996. 50–89.

———. *Vita et translatio S. Edithe.* Ed. A. Wilmart, "La légende de Ste. Édith en prose et vers par le moine Goscelin." *AB* 56 (1938): 5–101, 265–307. Trans. Michael Wright and Kathleen Loncar, "Goscelin's Legend of Edith," in Stephanie Hollis et al., *Writing the Wilton Women.* Turnhout, 2004. 21–93.

———. *Vita S. Wulsini.* Ed. C. H. Talbot, "The Life of Saint Wulsin of Sherborne by Goscelin." *Revue Bénédictine* 69 (1959): 68–85, with corrections by P. Grosjean, *AB* 70 (1960), 197–206. Trans. Rosalind Love, "The Life of St. Wulfsige of Sherborne by Goscelin of Saint-Bertin: A New Translation with Introduction, Appendix and Notes." In Katherine Barker, David A. Hinton, and Alan Hunt, eds., *St. Wulfsige and Sherborne: Essays to Celebrate the Millennium of the Benedictine Abbey 998–1998.* Oxford, 2005. 98–123.

Gregory of Ely. *Vita et miracula S. Etheldredae metrice.* Ed. P. A. Thompson and E. Stevens, "Gregory of Ely's Verse Life and Miracles of St. Æthelthryth." *AB* 106 (1988): 333–90.

Guernes de Pont-Sainte-Maxence. *La vie de Saint Thomas le Martyr.* Ed. Emmanuel Walberg. Classiques français du moyen âge 77. Paris, 1936. Trans. Janet Shirley, *Garnier's Becket.* Felinfach, 1975.

Henrici VI Angliae Regis Miracula Postuma ex Codice Musei Britannici Regio 13.C.VIIII. Ed. P. Grosjean. Brussels, 1935. Trans. Ronald Arbuthnott Knox and Shane Leslie, *The Miracles of King Henry VI.* Cambridge, 1923.

Henry, Archdeacon of Huntingdon. *Historia Anglorum: The History of the English People.* Ed. and trans. Diana Greenway. OMT. Oxford, 1996.

Herbert of Bosham. *Vita S. Thomae archiepiscopi et martyris.* Ed. J. C. Robertson in *MTB*, III: 155–534.

Historia de Sancto Cuthberto. Ed. and trans. Ted Johnson South. Woodbridge, 2002.

Historia Selebeiensis Monasterii. Ed. J. T. Fowler. In *The Coucher Book of Selby.* Yorkshire Archaeological Society Record Series 10. Durham, 1891.

Hollis, Stephanie, ed., with W. R. Barnes, Rebecca Hayward, Kathleen Loncar, and Michael Wright. *Writing the Wilton Women: Goscelin's "Legend of Edith" and "Liber confortatorius."* Turnhout, 2004.

Jocelin of Brakelond. *Cronica.* Ed. and trans. H. E. Butler, *The Chronicle of Jocelin of Brakelond.* London, 1949.

John of Salisbury, *Vita S. Anselmi.* Ed in *PL* 199, cols. 1009–40. Trans. Ronald E. Pepin in *Anselm and Becket: Two Canterbury Saints' Lives by John of Salisbury.* Toronto, 2009. 17–72.

———. *Vita S. Thomae martyris.* Ed. J. C. Robertson in *MTB,* II: 301–22. Trans. Ronald E. Pepin in *Anselm and Becket: Two Canterbury Saints' Lives by John of Salisbury.* Toronto, 2009. 73–95.

Kellet, William. *Miracula S. Johannis.* Ed. J. Raine in *HCY,* I: 261–91. Trans. in Susan E. Wilson, *The Life and After-Life of St. John of Beverley: The Evolution of the Cult of an Anglo-Saxon Saint.* Aldershot, 2006. 157–76.

The Lansdowne Anonymous. Excerpts from BL MS Lansdowne 398 Concerning Thomas Becket. Ed. J. C. Robertson, *MTB,* IV: 145–85.

The Letters of John of Salisbury: The Later Letters (1163–1180). Ed. W. J. Millor, S. J. and C. N. L. Brooke. Oxford, 1977.

The Letters of Lanfranc, Archbishop of Canterbury. Ed. and trans. Helen Clover and Margaret Gibson. OMT. Oxford, 1979.

The Letters of Osbert of Clare. Ed. E. W. Williamson. London, 1929.

The Letters of Peter of Celle. Ed. and trans. Julian Haseldine. OMT. Oxford, 2001.

The Letters of Saint Anselm of Canterbury. Trans. Walter Fröhlich. Cistercian Studies Series. 2 vols. Kalamazoo, Mich., 1990.

Libellus de vita et miraculis S Godrici, heremitae de Finchale. Ed. Joseph Stevenson. SS 20. Durham, 1845.

Liber Eliensis. Ed. E. O. Blake for the Royal Historical Society. Camden 3rd series vol. 92. London, 1962. Trans. Janet Fairweather, *Liber Eliensis: A History of the Isle of Ely from the Seventh to the Twelfth Century.* Woodbridge, 2005.

The Life of King Edward Who Rests at Westminster. Ed. and trans. Frank Barlow. 2nd ed. OMT. Oxford, 1992.

A Life of Saint Audrey: A Text by Marie de France. Ed. June Hall McCash and Judith Clark Barban. Jefferson, N.C., 2006.

"The Lives of St. Wenefred (BHL 8847–8851)." Ed. Fiona Winward. *AB* 117 (1999): 89–132. Trans. Ronald Pepin and Hugh Feiss with an essay by Catherine Hamaker, *Two Mediæval Lives of Saint Winefride.* Toronto, 2000.

"The Miracles of the Hand of St. James." Trans. Brian Kemp. *Berkshire Archaeological Journal* 65 (1970): 1–19.

The Miracles of Our Lady of Rocamadour: Analysis and Translation. Trans. Marcus Bull. Woodbridge, 1999.

The Miracles of Saint Æbbe of Coldingham and Saint Margaret of Scotland. Ed. and trans. Robert Bartlett. OMT. Oxford, 2003.

"The Miracles of St. Cuthbert at Farne." Ed. Edmund Craster. *AB* 70 (1952): 5–19. Trans. Edmund Craster, "The Miracles of St. Cuthbert at Farne," *Archaeologia Aeliana* 29 (1951): 93–107.

"The Miracles of St. Ithamar." Ed. D. Bethell. *AB* 89 (1971): 421–37.

The Miracles of Saint James: Translations from the Liber Sancti Jacobi. Ed. and trans. Thomas F. Coffey, Linda Kay Davidson, and Maryjane Dunn. New York, 1996.

Miracula Inventionis Beate Mylburge Virginis. Ed. Paul Antony Hayward in "The '*Miracula Inventionis Beate Mylburge Virginis*' attitributed to 'the Lord Ato, Cardinal Bishop of Ostia.'" *English Historical Review* 114 (1999): 543–73.

Miracula Quaedam S. Willelmi. Ed. J. Raine in *HCY*, III: 531–43.

Miracula S. Ætheldrethe. Ed. and trans. Rosalind Love, *Goscelin of Saint-Bertin: The Hagiography of the Female Saints of Ely.* OMT. Oxford, 2004. 95–132.

Miracula S. Swithuni. Ed. and trans. Lapidge, *CSS.* 641–97.

Miracula S. Withburge. Ed. Rosalind Love, *Goscelin of Saint-Bertin: The Hagiography of the Female Saints of Ely.* OMT. Oxford, 2004. Appendix B, 204–17.

Nigel of Canterbury. *Miracula Sancte Dei Genitricis Virginis Marie, Versifice.* Ed. Jan Ziolkowski. Toronto, 1986.

"An Old English Vision of Leofric, Earl of Mercia." Ed. A. S. Napier. *Transactions of the Philological Society* (1907–10): 180–87.

Opus de Miraculis S. Edmundi. Ed. Thomas Arnold in *MEdm*, I: 107–208.

Osbern of Canterbury. *Vita et Miracula S Dunstani.* Ed. W. Stubbs in *Memorials of St. Dunstan, Archbishop of Canterbury*, RS 63 (London, 1874), 69–161.

———. *Vita et Translatio S. Elphegi.* Ed. H. Wharton in *Anglia Sacra.* London, 1691. II: 122–47. Trans. Francis Shaw, *Osbern's Life of Alfege.* London, 1999.

Osbert of Clare. *Vita S. Edwardi.* Ed. Marc Bloch, "La Vie de S. Édouard le Confesseur par Osbert de Clare." *AB* 41 (1923): 5–131.

Paris, Matthew. *The Life of St. Edmund.* Ed. C. H. Lawrence. Trowbridge, 1996.

Passio S. Eadwardi regis et martyris. Ed. Christine Fell in *Edward, King and Martyr.* Leeds, 1971.

Philip of Oxford. *Miracula S. Frideswidae.* Ed. B. Bossue. *AASS*, Oct. 8. 568–89.

"Quaedam miracula gloriosi martyris Thomae archiepiscopi Cantuariae." *AB* 20 (1901): 427–29.

Reginald of Durham. *Libellus de Admirandis Beati Cuthberti Virtutibus quae Novellis Patratae sunt Temporibus.* Ed. J. Raine. SS 1. London, 1835.

The Register of the Priory of St. Bees. Ed. J. Wilson. SS 126. Durham, 1915.

S. Anselmi Cantuariensis Opera Omnia. Ed. F. S. Schmitt. 6 vols. Edinburgh, 1946.

Thomas of Monmouth. *The Life and Miracles of St. William of Norwich.* Ed. and trans. Augustus Jessopp and Montague Rhodes James. Cambridge, 1896.

Thómas Saga Erkibyskups: A Life of Archbishop Thomas Becket in Icelandic. Ed. and trans. Eiríkr Magnússon. RS 65. London, 1883.

Vita Gundulfi. Ed. Rodney Thomson, *The Life of Gundulf, Bishop of Rochester.* Toronto, 1977.

Vita S. Erkenwaldi. Ed. and trans. E. Gordon Whatley, *The Saint of London: The Life and Miracles of St. Erkenwald, Text and Translation.* Binghamton, 1989. 86–97.

Vita S. Rumwoldi. Ed. and trans. Rosalind Love, *Three Eleventh-Century Anglo-Latin Saints' Lives.* OMT. Oxford, 1996. 91–115.

Vita S. Wenefrede. Ed. in *AASS,* Nov. 1, 691–708. Trans. Ronald Pepin and Hugh Feiss with an essay by Catherine Hamaker, "The Second Life of Winefride of Holywell," in *Two Mediaeval Lives of Saint Winefride.* Toronto, 2000. 97–113.

The Waltham Chronicle: An Account of the Discovery of Our Holy Cross at Montacute and Its Conveyance to Waltham. Ed. and trans. Leslie Watkiss and Marjorie Chibnall. OMT. Oxford, 1994.

William of Canterbury, *Miracula S. Thomae Cantuariensis.* Ed. J. C. Robertson in *MTB,* I: 137–546.

———. *Vita S. Thomae Cantuariensis.* Ed. J. C. Robertson in *MTB,* I: 1–136.

William of Malmesbury. *Gesta Pontificum Anglorum: The History of the English Bishops.* Ed. and trans. M. Winterbottom with the assistance of R. M. Thomson. OMT. Oxford, 2007.

———. *Gesta Regum Anglorum: The History of the English Kings.* Ed. and trans. R. A. B. Mynors, completed by R. M. Thomson and M. Winterbottom. OMT. Oxford, 1998.

———. *Vita Dunstani.* Ed. and trans. Michael Winterbottom and R. M. Thomson in *William of Malmesbury: Saints' Lives, Lives of SS. Wulfstan, Dunstan, Patrick, Benignus and Indract.* OMT. Oxford, 2002. 165–303.

———. *Vita Wulfstani.* Ed. and trans. Michael Winterbottom and R. M. Thomson, in *William of Malmesbury: Saints' Lives, Lives of SS. Wulfstan, Dunstan, Patrick, Benignus and Indract.* OMT. Oxford, 2002. 7–155.

Wulfstan of Winchester. *The Life of St. Æthelwold.* Ed. and trans. Michael Lapidge and Michael Winterbottom. OMT. Oxford, 1991.

———. *Narratio Metrica de S. Swithuno.* Ed. and trans. Lapidge, *CSS.* 335–552.

SECONDARY SOURCES

Abbott, Edwin A. *St. Thomas of Canterbury: His Death and Miracles.* 2 vols. London, 1898.

Abou-El-Haj, Barbara. "St. Cuthbert: The Post-Conquest Appropriation of an Anglo-Saxon Cult." In Paul E. Szarmach, ed., *Holy Men and Holy Women: Old English Prose Saints' Lives and Their Contexts.* Albany, N.Y., 1996. 177–206.

———. *The Medieval Cult of Saints: Formations and Transformations.* Cambridge, 1994.

Aird, W. M. "The Making of a Medieval Miracle Collection: The 'Liber de Translationibus et Miraculis Sancti Cuthberti.'" *Northern History* 28 (1992): 1–24.

Aitchison, Briony. "Holy Cow! The Miraculous Cures of Animals in Late Medieval England." *European Review of History/Revue européenne d'histoire* 16 (2009): 875–92.

Alexander, Dominic. *Saints and Animals in the Middle Ages*. Woodbridge, 2008.

Antonsson, Haki. "Two Twelfth-Century Martyrs: St. Thomas of Canterbury and St. Magnús of Orkney." In Gareth Williams and Paul Bibire, eds., *Sagas, Saints and Settlements*. Leiden, 2004. 41–64.

Ashley, Kathleen and Pamela Sheingorn. *Writing Faith: Text, Sign, and History in the Miracles of Sainte Foy*. Chicago, 1999.

Barlow, Frank. *The English Church, 1000–1066: A History of the Later Anglo-Saxon Church*. 2nd ed. London, 1979.

———. *The English Church, 1066–1154: A History of the Anglo-Norman Church*. London, 1979.

———, ed. *The Life of King Edward Who Rests at Westminster*. OMT. 2nd ed. Oxford, 1992.

———. *Thomas Becket*. Berkeley, Calif., 1986.

Barrow, Julia. "A Twelfth-Century Bishop and Literary Patron: William De Vere." *Viator* 18 (1987): 175–89.

Bartlett, Robert. *The Hanged Man: A Story of Miracle, Memory and Colonialism in the Middle Ages*. Princeton, N.J., 2004.

———. *England Under the Norman and Angevin Kings, 1075–1225*. New Oxford History of England. Oxford, 2000.

———. "Cults of Irish, Scottish and Welsh Saints in Twelfth-Century England." In Brendan Smith, ed., *Britain and Ireland, 900–1300: Insular Responses to Medieval European Change*. Cambridge, 1999. 67–86.

———. "The Hagiography of Angevin England." *Thirteenth-Century England* 5 (1995): 37–52.

Bequette, John P. "Ælred of Rievaulx's Life of Saint Edward, King and Confessor: A Saintly King." *Cistercian Studies Quarterly* 43 (2008): 17–40.

Bethell, Denis. "The Lives of St. Osyth of Essex and St. Osyth of Aylesbury." *AB* 88 (1970): 75–127.

Biddle, Martin. "*Felix Urbs Winthonia*: Winchester in the Age of Monastic Reform." In David Parsons, ed., *Tenth-Century Studies: Essays in Commemoration of the Millennium of the Council of Winchester and the* Regularis Concordia. London, 1975. 123–40.

Binski, Paul. *Becket's Crown: Art and Imagination in Gothic England, 1170–1300*. New Haven, Conn., 2004.

Blair, John. *The Church in Anglo-Saxon Society*. Oxford, 2005.

———. "A Handlist of Anglo-Saxon Saints." In Alan Thacker and Richard Sharpe, eds., *Local Saints and Local Churches in the Early Medieval West*. Oxford, 2002. 495–565.

———. "A Saint for Every Minster? Local Cults in Anglo-Saxon England." In Alan Thacker and Richard Sharpe, eds., *Local Saints and Local Churches in the Early Medieval West*. Oxford, 2002. 455–94.

———. "Introduction: From Minster to Parish Church." In John Blair, ed., *Minsters and Parish Churches: The Local Church in Transition, 950–1200*. Oxford University Committee for Archaeology, Monograph 17. Oxford, 1988. 1–20.

————. "St. Frideswide Reconsidered." *Oxoniensia* 52 (1987): 71–127.

Blanton, Virginia. *Signs of Devotion: The Cult of St. Æthelthryth in Medieval England, 695–1615.* University Park, Pa., 2007.

Bolton, Brenda. "Signs, Wonders, Miracles: Supporting the Faith in Medieval Rome." In Cooper and Gregory, eds., *Signs, Wonders, Miracles.* 157–79.

Boyle, Leonard. "The Inter-conciliar Period, 1179–1215, and the Beginnings of Pastoral Manuals." In Filippo Liotta, ed., *Miscellanea Rolando Bandinelli Papa Alessandro III.* Siena, 1986. 45–56.

Bozoky, Edina. "The Sanctity and Canonisation of Edward the Confessor." In Richard Mortimer, ed., *Edward the Confessor: The Man and the Legend.* Woodbridge, 2009. 173–86.

Brooks, Nicholas. *The Early History of the Church of Canterbury.* Leicester, 1984.

Brown, Andrew. *Popular Piety in Late Medieval England: The Diocese of Salisbury, 1250–1550.* Oxford, 1999.

Brown, Paul Alonzo. "The Development of the Legend of Thomas Becket." Ph.D. dissertation, University of Pennsylvania, 1930.

Brown, Peter. *The Cult of the Saints: Its Rise and Function in Latin Christianity.* Chicago, 1981.

————. "Society and the Supernatural: A Medieval Change." *Daedalus* 104 (1975): 133–51.

Budny, Mildred and Timothy Graham. "Dunstan as Hagiographical Subject or Osbern as Author? The Scribal Portrait in an Early Copy of Osbern's 'Vita Sancti Dunstani.'" *Gesta* 32, 2 (1993): 83–96.

Bull, Marcus. "Criticism of Henry II's Expedition to Ireland in William of Canterbury's Miracles of St. Thomas Becket." *Journal of Medieval History* 33 (2007): 107–29.

————. *The Miracles of Our Lady of Rocamadour: Analysis and Translation.* Woodbridge, 1999.

Burton, Janet. *Monastic and Religious Orders in Britain: 1000–1300.* Cambridge, 1994.

Bynum, Caroline Walker. "Miracles and Marvels: The Limits of Alterity." In Franz J. Felten and Nikolas Jaspert, eds., *Vita Religiosa im Mittelalter: Festschrift für Kaspar Elm zum 70. Geburtstag.* Berlin, 1999. 799–818.

————. "Metamorphosis, or Gerald and the Werewolf." *Speculum* 73 (1998): 987–1013.

Campbell, James. "Some Twelfth-Century Views of the Anglo-Saxon Past." In *Essays in Anglo-Saxon History.* London, 1986. 209–28.

Canal, José. "El libro 'De Miraculis Sanctae Mariae' de Domingo de Evesham (m.c.1140)." *Studium Legionenese* 39 (1998): 247–83.

Carter, Peter. "The Historical Content of William of Malmesbury's Miracles of the Virgin Mary." In R. H. C. Davis and J. M. Wallace-Hadrill, eds., *The Writing of History in the Middle Ages: Essays Presented to Richard William Southern.* Oxford, 1981. 127–65.

Caviness, Madeline Harrison. *The Windows of Christ Church Cathedral Canterbury.* Corpus Vitrearum Medii Aevi: Great Britain 2. London, 1981.

————. *The Early Stained Glass of Canterbury Cathedral.* Princeton, N.J., 1977.

Chavasse, Ruth. "Piety, Penance, and Popular Reading in Devotion to the Virgin Mary and Her Miracles: Italian Incunabula and Early Printed Collections." In R. N. Swanson, ed., *The Church and the Book*. Woodbridge, 2004. 153–62.

Cheney, Christopher R. *Pope Innocent III and England*. Stuttgart, 1976.

Clanchy, Michael. *From Memory to Written Record: England 1066–1307*. 2nd ed. Oxford, 1995.

Clark, James G. "Monastic Confraternity in Medieval England: The Evidence from the St. Albans Abbey *Liber Benefactorum*." In Emilia Jamroziak and Janet Burton, eds., *Religious and Laity in Western Europe, 1000–1400: Interaction, Negotiation, and Power*. Turnhout, 2006. 315–32.

———. "The St. Albans Monks and the Cult of St. Alban: The Late Medieval Texts." In Martin Henig and Phillip Lindley, eds., *Alban and St. Albans: Roman and Medieval Architecture, Art and Archaeology*. British Archaeological Association Conference Transactions 24. Leeds, 2001. 218–30.

Colgrave, B. "The Post-Bedan Miracles and Translations of St. Cuthbert." In Cyril Fox and Bruce Dickins, eds., *The Early Cultures of North-West Europe*. Cambridge, 1950. 305–52.

Constable, Giles. *The Reformation of the Twelfth Century*. Cambridge, 1996.

———. "Aelred of Rievaulx and the Nun of Watton." In Derek Baker, ed., *Medieval Women*. Studies in Church History 1. Oxford, 1978. 205–26.

Cooper, Kate and Jeremy Gregory, eds. *Signs, Wonders, Miracles: Representations of Divine Power in the Life of the Church*. Studies in Church History 41. Woodbridge, 2005.

Corblet, L'abbe J. *Hagiographie du diocèse d'Amiens*. Paris, 1874.

Cowdrey, H. E. J. *Lanfranc: Scholar, Monk, and Archbishop*. Oxford, 2003.

Cownie, Emma. "The Cult of St. Edmund in the Eleventh and Twelfth Centuries." *Neuphilologische Mitteilungen* 99 (1998): 177–98.

———. *Religious Patronage in Anglo-Norman England, 1066–1135*. Woodbridge, 1998.

Craig, Leigh Ann. *Wandering Women and Holy Matrons: Women as Pilgrims in the Later Middle Ages*. Leiden, 2009.

Crook, John. *The Architectural Setting of the Cult of Saints in the Early Christian West, c.300–1200*. Oxford, 2000.

Crumplin, Sally. "Cuthbert the Cross-Border Saint in the Twelfth Century." In Steve Boardman, John Reuben Davies, and Eila Williamson, eds., *Saints' Cults in the Celtic World*. Woodbridge, 2009. 119–29.

———. "Modernizing St. Cuthbert: Reginald of Durham's Miracle Collection." In Cooper and Gregory, eds., *Signs, Wonders, Miracle*. 179–91.

Cubitt, Catherine. "Folklore and Historiography: Oral Stories and the Writing of Anglo-Saxon History." In Elizabeth M. Tyler and Ross Balzaretti, eds., *Narrative and History in the Early Medieval West*. Turnhout, 2006. 189–223.

Daly, Patrick H. "The Process of Canonization in the Thirteenth and Early Fourteenth Centuries." In Meryl Jancey, ed., *St. Thomas Cantilupe: Essays in His Honour*. Hereford, 1982. 125–35.

de Hamel, Christopher. "The Dispersal of the Library of Christ Church, Canterbury, from the Fourteenth to the Sixteenth Century." In James P. Carley and Colin G. C. Tite, eds., *Books and Collectors, 1200–1700: Essays Presented to Andrew Watson.* London, 1997. 263–79.

Dégh, Linda and Andre Vázsonyi. "The Memorate and the Proto-Memorate." *Journal of American Folklore* 87 (1974): 225–39.

Denton, Jeffrey H. *Robert Winchelsey and the Crown, 1294–1313.* Cambridge, 1980.

Deshman, Robert. *The Benedictional of Æthelwold.* Princeton, N.J., 1995.

Díaz y Díaz, Manuel, María Araceli Garcia Piñero, and Pilar del Oro Trigo. *El Códice Calixtino de la Catedral de Santiago: Estudio codicológico y de contienido.* Santiago de Compostela, 1988.

Dickson, Gary. "Revivalism as a Medieval Religious Genre." *Journal of Ecclesiastical History* 51 (2000): 473–96.

———. "Encounters in Medieval Revivalism: Monks, Friars and Popular Enthusiasts." *Church History* 68 (1999): 265–93.

Dobson, Richard Barrie. "Contrasting Cults: St. Cuthbert of Durham and St. Thomas of Canterbury in the Fifteenth Century." In Simon Ditchfield, ed., *Christianity and Community in the West: Essays for John Bossy.* Aldershot, 2001. 24–43.

———. "The First Norman Abbey in Northern England: The Origins of Selby." In Dobson, *Church and Society in the Medieval North of England.* London, 1996. 29–46.

———. "The Monks of Canterbury in the Later Middle Ages, 1220–1540." In Patrick Collinson, Nigel Ramsay, and Margaret Sparks, eds., *A History of Canterbury Cathedral.* New York, 1995. 69–153.

Duffy, Eamon. "St. Erkenwald: London's Cathedral Saint and His Legend." In Janet Backhouse, ed., *The Medieval Cathedral: Papers in Honour of Pamela Tudor-Craig.* Donington, 2003. 150–67.

———. "The Dynamics of Pilgrimage in Late Medieval England." In Colin Morris and Peter Roberts, eds., *Pilgrimage: The English Experience from Becket to Bunyon.* Cambridge, 2002. 164–77.

Duggan, Anne J. "A Becket Office at Stavelot: London, British Library, Additional MS 16964," In Anne J. Duggan, Joan Greatrex, and Brenda Bolton, eds., *Omnia Disce: Medieval Studies in Memory of Leonard Boyle, O.P.* Aldershot, 2005. 161–82.

———. *Thomas Becket.* London, 2004.

———. "The Santa Cruz Transcription of Benedict of Peterborough's *Liber Miraculorum Beati Thome*: Porto, BPM, cod. Santa Cruz 60." *Mediaevalia. Textos e estudos* 20 (2001): 27–55.

———, ed. and trans. *The Correspondence of Thomas Becket, Archbishop of Canterbury, 1162–1170.* OMT. Oxford, 2000.

———. "Ne in dubium: The Official Record of Henry II's Reconciliation at Avranches, 21 May 1172." *English Historical Review* 115 (2000): 643–58.

———. "Diplomacy, Status, and Conscience: Henry II's Penance for Becket's Murder." In Karl Borchardt and Enno Bünz, eds., *Forschungen zur Reichs-, Papst- und Landesgeschichte: Peter Herde zum 65. Geburtstag von Freunden, Schülern und Kollegen dargebracht.* Stuttgart, 1998. Vol. 1, 265–90.

————. "Aspects of Anglo-Portuguese Relations in the Twelfth Century: Manuscripts, Relics, Decretals and the Cult of St. Thomas Becket at Lorvão, Alcobaça and Tomar." *Portuguese Studies* 14 (1998): 1–19.

————. "The Lorvão Transcription of Benedict of Peterborough's *Liber Miraculorum Beati Thome*: Lisbon, cod. Alcobaça CCXC/143." *Scriptorium* 51 (1997): 51–68.

————. "John of Salisbury and Thomas Becket." In M. Wilks, ed., *The World of John of Salisbury*. Studies in Church History, vol. 3. Oxford, 1984. 427–38.

————. "The Cult of St. Thomas Becket in the Thirteenth Century." In Meryl Jancey, ed., *St. Thomas Cantilupe: Essays in His Honour*. Hereford, 1982. 21–44.

————. *Thomas Becket: A Textual History of the Letters*. Oxford, 1980.

Edwards, Nancy. "Celtic Saints and Early Medieval Archaeology." In Alan Thacker and Richard Sharpe, eds., *Local Saints and Local Churches in the Early Medieval West*. Oxford, 2002. 227–43.

Elkins, Sharon K. *Holy Women of Twelfth-Century England*. Chapel Hill, N.C., 1988.

Emms, Richard. "The Historical Traditions of St. Augustine's Abbey, Canterbury." In Richard Eales and Richard Sharpe, eds., *Canterbury and the Norman Conquest: Churches, Saints and Scholars, 1066–1109*. London, 1995. 159–68.

Farmer, David H. "The Cult and Canonization of St. Hugh." In Henry Mayr-Harting, ed., *St. Hugh of Lincoln: Lectures Delivered at Oxford and Lincoln to Celebrate the Eighth Centenary of St. Hugh's Consecration as Bishop of Lincoln*. Oxford, 1987. 75–86.

Farmer, Sharon. *Communities of Saint Martin: Legend and Ritual in Medieval Tours*. Ithaca, N.Y., 1991.

Finucane, Ronald C. "The Toddler in the Ditch: A Case of Parental Neglect?" In Michael Goodich, ed., *Voices from the Bench: The Narratives of Lesser Folk in Medieval Trials*. New York, 2006. 127–48.

————. *The Rescue of the Innocents: Endangered Children in Medieval Miracles*. Basingstoke, 2000.

————. *Miracles and Pilgrims: Popular Beliefs in Medieval England*. New York, 1977.

Flint, Valerie I. J. "The Saint and the Operation of the Law: Reflections upon the Miracles of St. Thomas Cantilupe." In Richard Gameson and Henrietta Leyser, eds., *Belief and Culture in the Middle Ages: Studies Presented to Henry Mayr-Harting*. Oxford, 2001. 342–57.

Foreville, Raymonde. "Les 'Miracula S. Thomae Cantuariensis.'" Reprinted in *Thomas Becket dans la tradition historique et hagiographique*. London, 1981. Section VII.

Gameson, Richard. *The Earliest Books of Canterbury Cathedral: Manuscripts and Fragments to c. 1200*. London, 2008.

————. "The Early Imagery of Thomas Becket." In Colin Morris and Peter Roberts, eds., *Pilgrimage: The English Experience from Becket to Bunyon*. Cambridge, 2002. 46–89.

————. *The Manuscripts of Early Norman England (c. 1066–1130)*. Oxford, 1999.

Gameson, Richard and Fiona Gameson. "From Augustine to Parker: The Changing Face of the First Archbishop of Canterbury." In Simon Keynes and Alfred P. Smyth, eds., *Anglo-Saxons: Studies Presented to Cyril Roy Hart*. Dublin, 2006. 13–38.

Gibson, Margaret. "Normans and Angevins." In Patrick Collinson, Nigel Ramsay, and Margaret Sparks, eds., *A History of Canterbury Cathedral*. New York, 1995. 38–68.

Goodich, Michael. *Miracles and Wonders: The Development of the Concept of Miracle, 1150–1350*. Ashgate, 2007.

———. "Filiation and Form in the Late Medieval Miracle Story." *Hagiographica* 3 (1996): 305–22.

———. *Violence and Miracle in the Fourteenth Century: Private Grief and Public Salvation*. Chicago, 1995.

González, Ana Suárez. "Un *Libellus Sancti Thome Cantuariensis Archiepiscopi* (Archivo de la Catedral de Tuy, *Códice 1*, ff. XIXv–XXVIIr)." *Hispania Sacra* 61 (2009): 9–27.

Gordon, Eleanora C. "Child Health in the Middle Ages as Seen in the Miracles of Five English Saints, A.D. 1150–1220." *Bulletin of the History of Medicine* 60 (1986): 502–22.

Gransden, Antonia. *A History of the Abbey of Bury St. Edmunds, 1182–1256: Samson of Tottington to Edmund of Walpole*. Woodbridge, 2007.

———. "The Composition and Authorship of the *De Miraculis Sancti Eadmundi* Attributed to 'Herman the Archdeacon.'" *Journal of Medieval Latin* 5 (1995): 1–52.

———. "Traditionalism and Continuity in Late Anglo-Saxon Monasticism." Reprint of 1989 article in *Legends, Traditions and History in Medieval England*. London, 1992. 31–80.

———. "The Growth of the Glastonbury Traditions and Legends in the Twelfth Century." Reprint of 1974 article in *Legends, Traditions and History in Medieval England*. London, 1992. 153–74.

———. *Historical Writing in England c. 550–c. 1307*. Ithaca, N.Y., 1974.

Greatrex, Joan. "Culture at Canterbury in the Fifteenth Century: Some Indications of the Cultural Environment of a Monk of Christ Church." In James G. Clark, ed., *The Culture of Medieval English Monasticism*. Woodbridge, 2007. 169–76.

Gretsch, Mechthild. *Aelfric and the Cult of Saints in Late Anglo-Saxon England*. Cambridge 2005.

Gubrium, Jaber and James A. Holstein. *Analyzing Narrative Reality*. Los Angeles, 2009.

Gurevich, Aaron. "Oral and Written Culture of the Middle Ages: Two 'Peasant Visions' of the Late Twelfth to the Early Thirteenth Centuries." In Jana Howlett, ed., *Historical Anthropology of the Middle Ages*. Chicago, 1992. 50–64.

Hagan, Jacqueline Maria. *Migration Miracle: Faith, Hope and Meaning on the Undocumented Journey*. Cambridge, Mass., 2008.

Hahn, Cynthia. "*Peregrinatio et Natio*: The Illustrated Life of Edmund, King and Martyr." *Gesta* 30 (1991): 119–39.

Hamilton, Thomas J. "Goscelin of Canterbury: A Critical Study of His Life, Works, and Accomplishments." 2 vols. Ph.D. dissertation, University of Virginia, 1973.

Hanham, Alison. "Henry VI and His Miracles." *The Ricardian: Journal of the Richard III Society* 12 (2000): 638–52.

Harris, Anne. "Pilgrimage, Performance and Stained Glass at Canterbury Cathedral." In Sarah Blick and Rita Tekippe, eds., *Art and Architecture of Late Medieval Pilgrimage*. Leiden, 2004. 243–81.

Hayes, Dawn Marie. *Body and Sacred Place in Medieval Europe, 1100–1389*. New York, 2003.

Hayward, Paul Antony. "Gregory the Great as 'Apostle of the English' in Post-Conquest Canterbury." *Journal of Ecclesiastical History* 55 (2004): 19–57.

———. "An Absent Father: Eadmer, Goscelin and the Cult of St. Peter, the First Abbot of St. Augustine's Abbey, Canterbury." *Journal of Medieval History* 29 (2003): 201–18.

———. "Demystifying the Role of Sanctity in Western Christendom." In James Howard-Johnston and Paul Antony Hayward, eds., *The Cult of Saints in Late Antiquity and the Middle Ages*. Oxford, 1999. 115–42.

———. "Sanctity and Lordship in Twelfth-Century England: Saint Albans, Durham, and the Cult of Saint Oswine, King and Martyr." *Viator* (1999): 105–44.

———. "Translation-Narratives in Post-Conquest Hagiography and English Resistance to the Norman Conquest." *Anglo-Norman Studies* 21 (1999): 73.

Head, Thomas. "The Genesis of the Ordeal of Relics by Fire in Ottonian Germany: An Alternative Form of 'Canonization.'" In Gábor Klaniczay, ed., *Procès de canonisation au moyen âge: aspects juridiques et religieux/Medieval canonization processes: Legal and religious aspects*. Rome, 2004. 19–37.

———. *Hagiography and the Cult of the Saints: The Diocese of Orleans, 800–1200*. Cambridge, 1990.

———. "I Vow Myself to Be Your Servant: An Eleventh-Century Pilgrim, His Chronicler and His Saint." *Historical Reflections/Réflexions Historiques* 11 (1984): 215–51.

Heale, Martin. "Training in Superstition? Monasteries and Popular Religion in Late Medieval and Reformation England." *Journal of Ecclesiastical History* 58 (2007): 417–39.

Hearn, M. F. "Canterbury Cathedral and the Cult of Becket." *Art Bulletin* 76 (1994): 19–52.

Heslop, T. A. "The Canterbury Calendars and the Norman Conquest." In Richard Eales and Richard Sharpe, eds., *Canterbury and the Norman Conquest: Churches, Saints and Scholars, 1066–1109*. London, 1995. 53–85.

Hollis, Stephanie. "Goscelin's Writings and the Wilton Women." In Hollis et al., *Writing the Wilton Women*. 217–24.

———. "St. Edith and the Wilton Community." In Hollis et al., *Writing the Wilton Women*. 244–80.

Hollis, Stephanie, with W. R. Barnes, Rebecca Hayward, Kathleen Loncar, and Michael Wright, eds. *Writing the Wilton Women: Goscelin's "Legend of Edith" and "Liber confortatorius"*. Turnhout, 2004.

Jackson, Peter. "Osbert of Clare and the *Vision of Leofric*: The Transformation of an Old English Narrative." In Katherine O'Brien O'Keeffe and Andy Orchard, eds., *Latin Learning and English Lore: Studies in Anglo-Saxon Literature for Michael Lapidge*. Toronto, 2005. Vol. 2, 275–92.

James, M. R. *The Ancient Libraries of Canterbury and Dover*. Cambridge, 1903.

Jennings, J. C. "The Origins of the 'Elements Series' of the Miracles of the Virgin." *Medieval and Renaissance Studies* 6 (1968): 85–93.

Jordan, William Chester. "The English Holy Men of Pontigny." *Cistercian Studies Quarterly* 43 (2008): 63–75.

Kealey, Edward J. *Medieval Medicus: A Social History of Anglo-Norman Medicine.* Baltimore, 1981.

Keefe, Thomas. "Shrine Time: King Henry II's Visits to Thomas Becket's Tomb." *Haskins Society Journal* 11 (1998): 115–22.

Kemp, Eric. *Canonization and Authority in the Western Church.* Oxford, 1948.

———. "Pope Alexander III and the Canonization of the Saints." *Transactions of the Royal Historical Society* 4th ser. 27 (1945): 13–28.

Kerr, Julie. *Monastic Hospitality: The Benedictines in England, c.1070–1250.* Woodbridge, 2007.

Keynes, Simon. "Ely Abbey 672–1109." In Peter Meadows and Nigel Ramsay, eds., *A History of Ely Cathedral.* Woodbridge, 2003. 3–58.

Kidson, Peter. "Gervase, Becket, and William of Sens." *Speculum* 68 (1993): 969–91.

King, Edmund. "Benedict of Peterborough and the Cult of Thomas Becket." *Northamptonshire Past and Present* 9 (1996): 213–20.

Kleinberg, Aviad. "Canonization Without a Canon." In Gábor Klaniczay, ed., *Procès de canonisation au moyen âge: aspects juridiques et religieux/Medieval canonization processes: Legal and religious aspects.* Rome, 2004. 7–18.

———. *Prophets in Their Own Country: Living Saints and the Making of Sainthood in the Later Middle Ages.* Chicago, 1992.

Krötzl, Christian. *Pilger, Mirakel und Alltag: Formen des Verhaltens im Skandinavischen Mittelalter.* Helsinki, 1994.

Langenbahn, S. K. "Die wiederentdeckten Himmeroder *Miracula S. Thomae Cantuariensis* (1175). Zugänge zur frühesten narrativen Quelle zur Geschichte von St. Thomas/Eifel." *Kurtrierisches Jahrbuch* 41 (2001): 121–64.

Langmuir, Gavin. "Thomas of Monmouth: Detector of Ritual Murder." *Speculum* 59 (1984): 820–46.

Lapidge, Michael. "The Cult of St. Indract at Glastonbury." In Lapidge, *Anglo-Latin Literature, 900–1066.* London, 1993. 419–52.

———. "B. and the *Vita S. Dunstani.*" In Nigel Ramsay, Margaret Sparks, and Tim Tatton-Brown, eds., *St. Dunstan: His Life, Times and Cult.* Woodbridge, 1992. 247–59.

Lapidge, Michael and R. C. Love. "The Latin Hagiography of England and Wales (600–1550)." In Guy Philippart, ed., *Hagiographies: Histoire internationale de la littérature hagiographique latine et vernaculaire en Occident des origines à 1550.* Turnhout, 2001. Vol. 3, 203–25.

Lawrence, C. H. *St. Edmund of Abingdon: A Study in Hagiography and History.* Oxford, 1960.

Lett, Didier. "Deux hagiographes, un saint et un roi: conformisme et créativité dans les deux recueils de *Miracula* de Thomas Becket." In Michel Zimmermann, ed., *Auctor et auctoritas: Invention et conformisme dans l'écriture médiévale, actes du colloque de Saint-Quentin-en-Yvelines (14–16 Juin 1999).* Paris, 2001. 201–16.

Licence, Tom. "Goscelin of St. Bertin and the Life of St. Eadwold of Cerne." *Journal of Medieval Latin* 16 (2006): 182–207.

———. "The Life and Miracles of Godric of Throckenholt." *AB* 124 (2006): 15–42.

———. "The Benedictines, the Cistercians and the Acquisition of a Hermitage in Twelfth-Century Durham." *Journal of Medieval History* 29 (2003): 315–29.

Lifshitz, Felice. "Beyond Positivism and Genre: 'Hagiographical' Texts as Historical Narrative." *Viator* 25 (1994): 95–113.

Love, Rosalind. "The Life of St. Wulfsige of Sherborne by Goscelin of Saint-Bertin: A New Translation with Introduction, Appendix and Notes." In Katherine Barker, David A. Hinton, and Alan Hunt, eds., *St. Wulfsige and Sherborne: Essays to Celebrate the Millennium of the Benedictine Abbey 998–1998*. Oxford, 2005. 98–123.

———. *Goscelin of Saint-Bertin: The Hagiography of the Female Saints of Ely*. OMT. Oxford, 2004.

———. *Three Eleventh-Century Anglo-Latin Saints' Lives: Vita S. Birini, Vita et Miracula S. Kenelmi and Vita S. Rumwoldi*. OMT. Oxford, 1996.

MacBain, William. "Anglo-Norman Women Hagiographers." In Ian Short, ed., *Anglo-Norman Anniversary Essays*. London, 1993. 235–50.

Marner, Dominic. *St. Cuthbert: His Life and Cult in Medieval Durham*. Toronto, 2000.

Mason, Emma. *St. Wulfstan of Worcester, c. 1008–1095*. Cambridge, 1990.

Mayr-Harting, Henry. "Functions of a Twelfth-Century Shrine: The Miracles of St. Frideswide." In Henry Mayr-Harting and R. I. Moore, eds., *Studies in Medieval History Presented to R. H. C. Davis*. London, 1985. 193–206.

McCleery, Iona. "*Multos ex medicinae arte curaverat, multos verbo et oratione*: Curing in Medieval Portuguese Saints' Lives." In Cooper and Gregory, eds., *Signs, Wonders, Miracles*. 192–202.

McCulloh, John M. "Jewish Ritual Murder: William of Norwich, Thomas of Monmouth, and the Early Dissemination of the Myth." *Speculum* 72 (1997): 698–740.

McGuire, Brian Patrick. "Friends and Tales in the Cloister: Oral Sources in Caesarius of Heisterbach's *Dialogus Miraculorum*." *Analecta Cisterciensia* 36 (1980): 167–247.

———. "Written Sources and Cistercian Inspiration in Caesarius of Heisterbach." *Analecta Cisterciensia* 35 (1979): 227–82.

McNamara, John. "Problems in Contextualizing Oral Circulation of Early Medieval Saints' Legends." In Francesca Canadé Sautman, Diana Conchado, and Giuseppe Carlo Di Scipio, eds., *Telling Tales: Medieval Narratives and the Folk Tradition*. New York, 1998. 21–36.

Moore, R. I. "Between Sanctity and Superstition: Saints and Their Miracles in the Age of Revolution." In Miri Rubin, ed., *The Work of Jacques le Goff and the Challenges of Medieval History*. Woodbridge, 1997. 55–70.

Morison, Patricia R. "The Miraculous and French Society, c. 950–1100." Ph.D. dissertation, Oxford University, 1983.

Morris, Rosemary and Alexander R. Rumble. "*Translatio Sancti Ælphegi*, Osbern's Account of the Translation of St. Ælfheah's Relics from London to Canterbury, 8–11

June 1023." In Alexander R. Rumble, ed., *The Reign of Cnut: King of England, Denmark and Norway*. Studies in the Early History of Britain. Leicester, 1994. 283–315.

Murray, Alexander. "Counselling in Medieval Confession." In Peter Biller and A. J. Minnis, eds., *Handling Sin: Confession in the Middle Ages*. York Studies in Medieval Theology. York, 1998. 63–77.

———. "Confession Before 1215." *Transactions of the Royal Historical Society* 6th ser. 3 (1993): 51–81.

———. "Confession as a Historical Source in the Thirteenth Century." In R. H. C. Davis and J. M. Wallace-Hadrill, eds., *The Writing of History in the Middle Ages: Essays Presented to Richard William Southern*. Oxford, 1981. 275–322.

Nadeuz, Alain. "Notes on the Significance of John of Salisbury's *Vita Anselmi*." In Frederick Van Fleteren and Joseph C. Schnaubelt, eds., *Twenty-Five Years (1969–1994) of Anselm Studies: Review and Critique of Recent Scholarly Views*. Texts and Studies in Religion 70. Lewiston, N.Y., 1996. 67–77.

Nicolaisen, W. F. H. "Introduction." In W. F. H. Nicolaisen, ed., *Oral Tradition in the Middle Ages*. Binghamton, N.Y., 1995. 1–6.

Nilson, Ben. *Cathedral Shrines of Medieval England*. Woodbridge, 1998.

Norton, Christopher. *St. William of York*. Woodbridge, 2006.

O'Keeffe, Katherine O'Brien. "Goscelin and the Consecration of Eve." *Anglo-Saxon England* 35 (2007): 251–70.

———. "Body and Law in Anglo-Saxon England." *Anglo-Saxon England* 27 (1998): 209–33.

Ochs, Elinor and Lisa Capps. *Living Narrative: Creating Lives in Everyday Storytelling*. Cambridge, Mass., 2001.

Orme, Margaret. "A Reconstruction of Robert of Cricklade's *Vita et Miracula S. Thomae Cantuariensis*." *AB* 84 (1966): 379–98.

Otter, Monika, trans. *Goscelin of St. Bertin: The Book of Encouragement and Consolation [Liber Confortatorius]*. Woodbridge, 2004.

———. *Inventiones: Fiction and Referentiality in Twelfth-Century English Historical Writing*. Chapel Hill, N.C., 1996.

Partner, Nancy. *Serious Entertainments: The Writing of History in Twelfth-Century England*. Chicago, 1977.

Paxton, Jennifer. "Monks and Bishops: The Purpose of the *Liber Eliensis*." *Haskins Society Journal* 11 (2003 for 1998): 17–30.

Payer, Pierre J. *Sex and the New Medieval Literature of Confession, 1150–1300*. PIMS Studies and Texts 163. Toronto, 2009.

Pfaff, Richard W. "Lanfranc's Supposed Purge of the Anglo-Saxon Calendar." In Timothy Reuter, ed., *Warriors and Churchmen in the High Middle Ages: Essays Presented to Karl Leyser*. London, 1992. 95–108.

Philippart, Guy, ed. *Hagiographies: Histoire internationale de la littérature hagiographique latine et vernaculaire en Occident des origines à 1550*. Turnhout, 1994–2001.

Piroyanksy, Danna. "Bloody Miracles of a Political Martyr: The Case of Thomas Earl of Lancaster." In Cooper and Gregory, eds., *Signs, Wonders, Miracles*. 228–38.

Postles, Dave. "Religious Houses and the Laity in Eleventh- to Thirteenth-Century England: An Overview." *Haskins Society Journal* 12 (2002): 1–13.

Ramsay, Nigel. "The Cathedral Archives and Library." In Patrick Collinson, Nigel Ramsay, and Margaret Sparks, eds., *A History of Canterbury Cathedral*. New York, 1995. 341–407.

Ramsay, N. L. and M. J. Sparks. "The Cult of St. Dunstan at Christ Church, Canterbury." In Nigel Ramsay, Margaret Sparks, and Tim Tatton-Brown, eds., *St. Dunstan: His Life, Times and Cult*. Woodbridge, 1992. 311–23.

Rawcliffe, Carole. *Leprosy in Medieval England*. Woodbridge, 2006.

———. "'On the Threshold of Eternity': Care for the Sick in East Anglian Monasteries." In Christopher Harper-Bill, Carole Rawcliffe, and Richard G. Wilson, eds., *East Anglia's History: Studies in Honour of Norman Scarfe*. Woodbridge, 2002. 41–72.

———. "Curing Bodies and Healing Souls: Pilgrimage and the Sick in Medieval East Anglia." In Colin Morris and Peter Roberts, eds., *Pilgrimage: The English Experience from Becket to Bunyon*. Cambridge, 2002. 108–40.

Reames, Sherry. "Reconstructing and Interpreting a Thirteenth-Century Office for the Translation of Thomas Becket." *Speculum* 80 (2005): 118–70.

———. "The Remaking of a Saint: Stephen Langton and the Liturgical Office for Becket's Translation." *Hagiographica* 7 (2000): 17–33.

Riches, Samantha. "Hagiography in Context: Images, Miracles, Shrines, and Festivals." In Sarah Salih, ed., *A Companion to Middle English Hagiography*. Woodbridge, 2006. 25–46.

Ricoeur, Paul. "Philosophy and Religious Language." In Mark I. Wallace, ed., *Figuring the Sacred: Religion, Narrative, and Imagination*. Trans. David Pellauer. Minneapolis, 1995. 35–47.

Ridyard, Susan J. "Functions of a Twelfth-Century Recluse Revisited: The Case of Godric of Finchale." In Richard Gameson and Henrietta Leyser, eds., *Belief and Culture in the Middle Ages: Studies Presented to Henry Mayr-Harting*. Oxford, 2001. 236–50.

———. *The Royal Saints of Anglo-Saxon England: A Study of West Saxon and East Anglian Cults*. Cambridge, 1988.

———. "'Condigna Veneratio': Post-Conquest Attitudes to the Saints of the Anglo-Saxons." *Anglo-Norman Studies* 9 (1987): 179–206.

Rigg, A. G. *A History of Anglo-Latin Literature 1066–1422*. Cambridge, 1992.

Roberts, Peter. "Politics, Drama, and the Cult of Thomas Becket in the Sixteenth Century." In Colin Morris and Peter Roberts, eds., *Pilgrimage: The English Experience from Becket to Bunyon*. Cambridge, 2002. 199–237.

Roberts, Phyllis B. *Thomas Becket in the Medieval Latin Preaching Tradition: An Inventory of Sermons About St. Thomas Becket, c. 1170-c.1400*. Instrumenta Patristica 25. The Hague, 1992.

Robinson, J. A. "A Sketch of Osbert's Career." In *The Letters of Osbert of Clare*, ed. E. W. Williamson. London, 1929. 1–20.

Röckelein, Hedwig. "Miracle Collections of Carolingian Saxony: Literary Tradition Versus Original Creation." *Hagiographica* 3 (1996): 267–75.

Rollason, David, ed. and trans., *Symeon of Durham: Libellus de Exordio atque Procursu istius hoc est Dunhelmensis Ecclesie*. OMT. Oxford 2000.

———. *Saints and Relics in Anglo-Saxon England*. Oxford, 1989.

———. "Goscelin of Canterbury's Account of the Translation and Miracles of St. Mildrith (*BHL* 5961/4): An Edition with Notes." *Mediaeval Studies* 48 (1986): 139–210.

———. "The Miracles of St. Benedict: A Window on Early Medieval France." In Henry Mayr-Harting and R. I. Moore, eds., *Studies in Medieval History Presented to R. H. C. Davis*. London, 1985. 73–90.

———. *The Mildrith Legend: A Study in Early Medieval Hagiography in England*. Leicester, 1982.

Rothwell, Harry. "The Life and Miracles of St. Edmund: A Recently Discovered Manuscript." *Bulletin of the John Rylands University Library* 60 (1977–78): 135–80.

Rubenstein, Jay. "Liturgy Against History: The Competing Versions of Lanfranc and Eadmer of Canterbury." *Speculum* 74 (1999): 279–309.

———. "The Life and Writings of Osbern of Canterbury." In Richard Eales and Richard Sharpe, eds., *Canterbury and the Norman Conquest: Churches, Saints and Scholars, 1066–1109*. London, 1995. 27–40.

Rubin, Miri. *Gentile Tales: The Narrative Assault on Late Medieval Jews*. New Haven, Conn., 1999.

Russell, Josiah Cox and John Paul Heironimus. *The Shorter Latin Poems of Master Henry of Avranches Relating to England*. Cambridge, Mass., 1935.

Ruud, Marylou. "Reading Miracles at Sempringham: Gilbert's Instructive Cures." *Haskins Society Journal* 13 (1999): 125–35.

Scholtz, B. W. "The Canonization of Edward the Confessor." *Speculum* 36 (1961): 38–60.

Schuh, Barbara. "*Jenseitigkeit in diesseitigen Formen*": Sozial- und mentalitätgeschictliche Aspekte spätmittelalterlicher Mirakelberichte. Graz, 1989.

Sharpe, Richard. *A Handlist of the Latin Writers of Great Britain and Ireland Before 1540*. Publications of the Journal of Medieval Latin. Turnhout, 1997.

———. "The Setting of St. Augustine's Translation, 1091." In Richard Eales and Richard Sharpe, eds., *Canterbury and the Norman Conquest: Churches, Saints and Scholars, 1066–1109*. London, 1995. 1–13.

———. "Eadmer's Letter to the Monks of Glastonbury Concerning St. Dunstan's Disputed Remains." In Lesley Abrams and James P. Carley, eds., *The Archaeology and History of Glastonbury Abbey*. Woodbridge, 1991. 205–15.

———. "Some Medieval *Miracula* from Llandegley (Lambeth Palace Library, MS. 94, fols. 153v–155r)." *Bulletin of the Board of Celtic Studies* 37 (1990): 166–76.

———. "Goscelin's St. Augustine and St. Mildreth: Hagiography and Liturgy in Context." *Journal of Theological Studies* 41 (1990): 502–16.

Sheils, William. "Polemic as Piety: Thomas Stapleton's *Tres Thomae* and Catholic Controversy in the 1580s." *Journal of Ecclesiastical History* 60 (2009): 74–94.

Sheingorn, Pamela, trans. *The Book of Sainte Foy*. Philadelphia, 1994.

Showalter, Elaine. *Hystories: Hysterical Epidemics and Modern Media*. New York, 1997.

Short, Ian. "The Patronage of Beneit's *Vie de Thomas Becket*." *Medieum Aevum* 56 (1987): 239–56.

Sigal, Pierre-André. "Naissance et premier développement d'un vinage exceptionnel: L'eau de saint Thomas." *Cahiers de civilisation médiévale* 44 (2001): 35–44.

———. "Le travail des hagiographes aux XIe et XIIe siècles: sources d'information et méthodes de rédaction," *Francia* 15 (1987): 149–82.

———. *L'homme et le miracle dans la France médiévale, XIe–XIIe siècle*. Paris, 1985.

Signori, Gabriela. "The Miracle Kitchen and Its Ingredients: A Methodical and Critical Approach to Marian Shrine Wonders (10th to 13th century)." *Hagiographica* 3 (1996): 277–303.

Siraisi, Nancy G. *Medieval and Early Renaissance Medicine: An Introduction to Knowledge and Practice*. Chicago, 1990.

Slater, Candace. *City Steeple, City Streets: Saints' Tales from Granada and a Changing Spain*. Berkeley, Calif., 1991.

———. *Trail of Miracles: Stories from a Pilgrimage in Northeast Brazil*. Berkeley, Calif., 1986.

Slocum, Kay Brainerd. *Liturgies in Honour of Thomas Becket*. Toronto, 2004.

Smalley, Beryl. *The Becket Conflict and the Schools: A Study of Intellectuals in Politics in the Twelfth Century*. Totowa, N.J., 1973.

Smith, Julia M. H. "Oral and Written: Saints, Miracles and Relics in Brittany, c. 850–1250." *Speculum* 65 (1990): 309–43.

Somerville, Robert. *Pope Alexander III and the Council of Tours (1163): A Study of Ecclesiastical Politics and Institutions in the Twelfth Century*. Berkeley, Calif., 1977.

Southern, R. W. *St. Anselm: A Portrait in a Landscape*. Cambridge, 1990.

———. *The Monks of Canterbury and the Murder of Archbishop Becket*. Oxford, 1985.

———. "Aspects of the European Tradition of Historical Writing, 4. The Sense of the Past." *Transactions of the Royal Historical Society* 5th ser. 23 (1973): 243–63.

———. "The Place of England in the Twelfth-Century Renaissance." In Southern, *Medieval Humanism and Other Studies*. Oxford, 1970. 158–80.

———. *Saint Anselm and His Biographer: A Study of Monastic Life and Thought*. Cambridge, 1963.

———. "The English Origins of the 'Miracles of the Virgin.'" *Medieval and Renaissance Studies* 4 (1958): 176–216.

———. *The Making of the Middle Ages*. New Haven, Conn., 1953.

Spencer, Brian. *Pilgrim Souvenirs and Secular Badges: Medieval Finds from Excavations in London*. London, 1998.

Stahl, Sandra Dolby. *Literary Folkloristics and the Personal Narrative*. Bloomington, Ind., 1989.

Stanley, Arthur P. *Historical Memorials of Canterbury*. 10th ed. London, 1904.

Staunton, Michael. *Thomas Becket and His Biographers*. Woodbridge, 2006.

Stock, Brian. *The Implications of Literacy: Written Language and Models of Interpretation in the Eleventh and Twelfth Centuries*. Princeton, N.J., 1983.

Stroud, Daphne. "Eve of Wilton and Goscelin of St. Bertin at Old Sarum c. 1070–1078." *Wiltshire Archaeological and Natural History Magazine* 99 (2006): 204–12.

Sumption, Jonathan. *Pilgrimage: An Image of Mediaeval Religion*. Totowa, N.J., 1975.

Swanson, R. N. *The Twelfth-Century Renaissance*. Manchester, 1999.

Sweetinburgh, Sheila. *The Role of the Hospital in Medieval England: Gift-Giving and the Spiritual Economy*. Portland, Ore., 2004.

———— "Supporting the Canterbury Hospitals: Benefaction and the Language of Charity in the Twelfth and Thirteenth Centuries." *Archaeologia Cantiana* 122 (2002): 237–58.

Tatton-Brown, Tim. "Canterbury and the Architecture of Pilgrimage Shrines in England." In Colin Morris and Peter Roberts, eds., *Pilgrimage: The English Experience from Becket to Bunyon*. Cambridge, 2002. 90–107.

————. "Medieval Parishes and Parish Churches in Canterbury." In T. R. Slater and Gervase Rosser, eds., *The Church in the Medieval Town*. Aldershot, 1998. 236–71.

Thacker, Alan. "Saint-Making and Relic Collecting by Oswald and His Communities." In Nicholas Brooks and Catherine Cubitt, eds., *St. Oswald of Worcester: Life and Influence*. London, 1996. 244–68.

————. "Cults at Canterbury: Relics and Reform Under Dunstan and His Successors." In Nigel Ramsay, Margaret Sparks, and Tim Tatton-Brown, eds., *St. Dunstan: His Life, Times and Cult*. Woodbridge, 1992. 221–45.

————. "Æthelwold and Abingdon." In Barbara Yorke, ed., *Bishop Æthelwold: His Career and Influence*. Woodbridge, 1988. 43–64.

Theilmann, John. "English Peasants and Medieval Miracle Lists." *The Historian* 52 (1990): 286–303.

Thomas, Hugh M. *The English and the Normans: Ethnic Hostility, Assimilation and Identity, 1066-c.1220*. Oxford, 2003.

————. "Miracle Stories and the Violence of King Stephen's Reign." *Haskins Society Journal* 13 (1999): 111–24.

Thompson, Sally. *Women Religious: The Founding of English Nunneries After the Norman Conquest*. Oxford, 1991.

Thomson, R. M. "The Norman Conquest and English Libraries." In Peter Ganz, ed., *The Role of the Book in Medieval Culture, Proceedings of the Oxford International Symposium, 26 September-1 October 1982*. Turnhout, 1986. Vol. 2. 27–40.

————. "England and the Twelfth-Century Renaissance." *Past and Present* 101 (1983): 3–21.

————. "Two Versions of a Saint's Life from St. Edmund's Abbey: Changing Currents in XIIth Century Monastic Style." *Revue Bénédictine* 84 (1974): 383–408.

Townsend, David. "Omissions, Emissions, Missionaries, and Master Signifiers in Norman Canterbury." *Exemplaria* 7 (1995): 291–315.

————. "Anglo-Latin Hagiography and the Norman Transition." *Exemplaria* 3 (1991): 385–433.

Treharne, Elaine. "Ælfric's Account of St. Swithun: Literature of Reform and Reward." In Elizabeth M. Tyler and Ross Balzaretti, eds., *Narrative and History in the Early Medieval West*. Turnhout, 2006. 167–88.

Tryon, Ruth Wilson. "Miracles of Our Lady in Middle English Verse." *PMLA* 38 (1923): 308–88.

Tudor, V. M. "The Cult of St. Cuthbert in the Twelfth Century: The Evidence of Reginald of Durham." In Gerald Bonner, David Rollason, and Clare Stancliffe, eds., *St. Cuthbert, His Cult and His Community to AD 1200*. Woodbridge, 1989. 447–68.

Turner, Andrew J. and Bernard J. Muir, eds. and trans. *Eadmer of Canterbury: Lives and Miracles of Saints Oda, Dunstan, and Oswald*. OMT. Oxford, 2006.

Ugé, Karine. *Creating the Monastic Past in Medieval Flanders*. Woodbridge, 2005.

Urry, William. *Canterbury Under the Angevin Kings*. London, 1967.

———. "Saint Anselm and His Cult at Canterbury." *Spicilegium Beccense* 1 (1959): 571–93.

Uruszczak, Waclaw. "Les répercussions de la mort de Thomas Becket en Pologne (xiie-xiiie siècles)." In Raymonde Foreville, ed., *Thomas Becket: Actes du colloque international de Sédières, 19–24 août 1973*. Paris, 1975. 115–25.

Van Engen, John. "Letters, Schools and Written Culture in the Eleventh and Twelfth Centuries." In Johannes Fried, ed., *Dialektik und Rhetorik in früheren und hohen Mittelalter*. Schriften des Historischen Kollegs Kolloquien 27. München, 1997. 97–132.

Van Houts, Elisabeth. "The Flemish Contribution to Biographical Writing in England in the Eleventh Century." In David Bates, Julia Crick, and Sarah Hamilton, eds., *Writing Medieval Biography, 750–1250: Essays in Honour of Professor Frank Barlow*. Woodbridge, 2006. 111–27.

———. *Memory and Gender in Medieval Europe, 900–1200*. Toronto, 1999.

Vauchez, André. *Sainthood in the Later Middle Ages*. Trans. Jean Birrell. Cambridge, 1997.

Vincent, Nicholas. "Some Pardoners' Tales: The Earliest English Indulgences." *Transactions of the Royal Historical Society* 6th ser. 12 (2002): 23–58.

———. "The Pilgrimages of the Angevin Kings of England, 1154–1272." In Colin Morris and Peter Roberts, eds., *Pilgrimage: The English Experience from Becket to Bunyon*. Cambridge, 2002. 12–45.

———. *The Holy Blood: King Henry III and the Westminster Blood Relic*. Cambridge, 2001.

Walberg, Emmanuel. "Date de la composition des recueils de *Miracula Sancti Thomae Cantuariensis*." *Le Moyen Âge* 22 (1920): 259–74. Reprinted in *La tradition hagiographique de saint Thomas Becket avant la fin du 12e siècle: Études critiques*. Paris, 1929; repr. Geneva, 1975.

Walker, Simon. "Political Saints in Later Medieval England." In R. H. Britnell and A. J. Pollard, eds., *The Mcfarlane Legacy: Studies in Late Medieval Politics and Society*. New York, 1995. 77–106.

Ward, Benedicta. *Miracles and the Medieval Mind: Theory, Record and Event, 1000–1215*. Philadelphia, 1982, rev. ed. 1987.

Watkins, C. S. *History and the Supernatural in Medieval England*. Cambridge, 2007.

———. "The Cult of Earl Waltheof at Crowland." *Hagiographica* 3 (1996): 95–11.

Webb, Diana. *Pilgrimage in Medieval England*. London, 2000.

Webb, E. A. *The Records of St. Bartholomew's Priory and of the Church and Parish of St. Bartholomew the Great, West Smithfield*. London, 1921.

Webber, Teresa. "Script and Manuscript Production at Christ Church, Canterbury, After the Norman Conquest." In Richard Eales and Richard Sharpe, eds., *Canterbury and the Norman Conquest: Churches, Saints and Scholars, 1066–1109*. London, 1995. 145–58.

Wenzel, Siegfried. "Preaching the Saints in Chaucer's England." In Susan J. Ridyard, ed., *Earthly Love, Spiritual Love, Love of the Saints*. Sewanee, Tenn., 1999. 69–87.

Whatley, E. Gordon. "Late Old English Hagiography, ca. 950–1150." In Guy Philippart, ed., *Hagiographies: Histoire internationale de la littérature hagiographique latine et vernaculaire en Occident des origines á 1550*. Turnhout, 1996. Vol. 2, 429–99.

———. *The Saint of London: The Life and Miracles of St. Erkenwald, Text and Translation*. Binghamton, N.Y., 1989.

———. "A 'Symple Wrecche' at Work: the Life and Miracles of St. Erkenwald in the *Gilte Legende*, BL Add. 35298." In Brenda Dunn-Lardeau, ed., *Legenda aurea: sept siècles de diffusions*. Actes du colloque international sur la Legenda aurea: texte latin et branches vernacularies, à l'Université du Québec à Montréal 11–12 Mai, 1983. Montreal, 1986. 333–43.

White, Stephen D. "Garsinde v. Sainte Foy: Argument, Threat, and Vengeance in Eleventh-Century Monastic Litigation." In Emilia Jamroziak and Janet Burton, eds., *Religious and Laity in Western Europe, 1000–1400: Interaction, Negotiation, and Power*. Turnhout, 2006. 169–81.

Willis, R. *The Architectural History of Canterbury Cathedral*. London, 1845.

Wilson, Susan E. *The Life and After-Life of St. John of Beverley: The Evolution of the Cult of an Anglo-Saxon Saint*. Aldershot, 2006.

Winterbottom, Michael. "Faricius of Arezzo's Life of St. Aldhelm." In Katherine O'Brien O'Keeffe and Andy Orchard, eds., *Latin Learning and English Lore: Studies in Anglo-Saxon Literature for Michael Lapidge*. Toronto, 2005. Vol. 1, 109–131.

Winterbottom, Michael and R. M. Thomson, eds. and trans., *William of Malmesbury: Saints' Lives, Lives of SS. Wulfstan, Dunstan, Patrick, Benignus and Indract*. OMT. Oxford, 2002.

Wogan-Browne, Jocelyn. "The Life of St. Osith." *Papers on Language and Literature* 41 (2005): 339–444.

———. *Saints' Lives and Women's Literary Culture, c. 1150–1300: Virginity and Its Authorizations*. Oxford, 2001.

———. "*Clerc u lai, muïne u dame*: Women and Anglo-Norman Hagiography in the Twelfth and Thirteenth Centuries." In Carol M. Meale, ed., *Women and Literature in Britain, 1150–1500*. Cambridge, 1993. 61–85.

Yarrow, Simon. *Saints and Their Communities: Miracle Stories in Twelfth-Century England*. Oxford, 2006.

———. "Narrative, Audience and the Negotiation of Community in Twelfth-Century English Miracle Collections." In Kate Cooper and Jeremy Gregory, eds., *Elite and Popular Religion*. Studies in Church History 42. Woodbridge, 2006. 65–78.

Yohe, Katherine. "Aelred's Recrafting of the Life of Edward the Confessor." *Cistercian Studies Quarterly* 38 (2003): 177–89.

Zatta, Jane. "The *Vie Seinte Osith*: Hagiography and Politics in Anglo-Norman England." *Studies in Philology* 96 (1999): 367–93.

Ziegler, Joseph. "Religion and Medicine in the Middle Ages." In Peter Biller and Joseph Ziegler, eds., *Religion and Medicine in the Middle Ages*. York Studies in Medieval Theology. Woodbridge, 2001. 3–14.

———. "Practitioners and Saints: Medical Men in Canonization Processes in the Thirteenth to Fifteenth Centuries." *Social History of Medicine* 12 (1999): 191–225.

INDEX

Page numbers in *italics* indicate illustrations.

ACKNOWLEDGMENTS

As I complete this project on stories of saintly intercessions, I am aware of how much I owe to my human intercessors—those friends and institutions that have done so much to support me and this project. Here is my oblation of gratitude to them.

Thanks go first to John Van Engen and my other mentors at the University of Notre Dame, Northwestern University, and Calvin College, particularly to Katherine O'Brien O'Keeffe, Kathleen Biddick, Thomas F. X. Noble, Barbara Newman, and Dale Van Kley. I am grateful to them for the models they provide of expansive learning, creative thinking, attention to sources, and superb scholarship. John Van Engen's passion for the study of the medieval past always runs hot. I owe much of the spirit as well as the concrete realization of this project to him.

For funding and research support, I am grateful to the Dolores Zohrab Liebmann Foundation, the Hill Monastic Microfilm Library, and the three institutions that have sponsored my scholarship in numerous ways: the Medieval Institute of the University of Notre Dame and the history departments of Arizona State University and York University in Toronto. For conference funding, research trips, microfilm purchases, teaching releases, and the other means by which these institutions have supported my research, I am most grateful. I am especially obliged to the Arizona Center for Medieval and Renaissance Studies for a Faculty Fellow appointment that freed me from a semester of teaching at a crucial point in the development of this project.

The serious research for this book began in the British Library in London. I am pleased to have had the chance to work in the "old" reading rooms and thankful for the curators' patience and guidance. I have also had the great pleasure and privilege of consulting the resources of the University of London, the Institute for Historical Research, the Warburg Institute, Lambeth Palace Library, the Bodleian Library, the University Library of Cambridge, the libraries of Corpus Christi College and Trinity College in Cambridge, and the archives of Canterbury Cathedral, Durham Cathedral, and York Minster. In addition to the help of the custodians of these wonderful collections, Anne Duggan of King's College, London, aided me as I grappled with the manuscripts of the Becket collections. The early coaching I received from Jane Sayers and Diana Greenaway at an NEH Institute on medieval manuscripts at the Newberry Library in Chicago has proved valuable year after year. Madeline Caviness and Tim Ayers gave me much-needed guidance in the study of the Canterbury windows, while Jeanne Nuechterlein provided a last minute loan of a camera. The anonymous readers for the University of Pennsylvania Press provided suggestions and readings that much improved the manuscript. I am very thankful for their help as well as that of Jerry Singerman and Ruth Mazo Karras of the Press.

I conducted most of my research in the specialist libraries of the Medieval Institute of the University of Notre Dame and the Pontifical Institute for Mediaeval Studies in Toronto. Without these two marvelous resources, I could not have written this book. I am grateful for the visiting scholar appointments from the University of Notre Dame that allowed me to use the Medieval Institute's collections summer after summer, and for the warm generosity extended to me by the PIMS librarians, faculty and staff since I have moved to Toronto.

It is a special joy to be able to thank my friends and colleagues for their help with this project. David Mengel, Christine Caldwell Ames, Carolyn Edwards Adler, F. Thomas Luongo, Lezlie Knox, James Mixson, and David Bachrach have provided invaluable advice, readings and camaraderie. Lisa Wolverton generously gave me extra help when I needed it. No one has read more versions of this book than Daniel Hobbins, and I thank him for working through all those drafts. Rosalynn Voaden, Martin Levin, Linda Sargent Wood, Ian Miller, Crate Herbert, Matthew Whitaker, Retha Warnicke, Phil Soergel, Bob Bjork, Cora Fox, Monica Green, Hava Samuelson, and Noel Stowe have helped me greatly in word and in deed. I am especially grateful to Catherine O'Donnell in her various roles as cheerleader, confidant, and "cranky man." At York University, Tom and Libby Cohen, Marlene Shore, Carolyn Podruchny, Nick Rogers, Myra Rutherdale, Anne Rubenstein, and Molly Ladd Taylor have smoothed my path and helped me in innumerable ways. I am obliged in particular to Richard Hoffman for his openhanded and steadfast support. Debbie Fleetham, Kathleen McGarvey, Ann Dillner, Wendy Plotkin, Susan Haskell Khan, and Nora Faires have always cheered me on, as have Ryan Koopmans, my brother, Lori Weavers, my aunt, and Elizabeth Vander Weerdt, my grandmother. Jeanne Petit, who has heard more about medieval miracle stories than any American historian should have to endure, deserves special thanks.

I dedicate this book to my parents, Sherwin and Karen Koopmans. Though they may not have intended to raise intellectuals, they passed on their love of good books and thoughtful conversation to their children. This book is a token of my gratitude to them for that, and for much more.